# Strategy, Systems, and Integration

## A Handbook for Information Managers

# Dedication

For David and Lynn.

# Strategy, Systems, and Integration

## A Handbook for Information Managers

George M. Hall

TAB Professional and Reference Books

Division of TAB BOOKS

Blue Ridge Summit, PA

## Trademarks

| | |
|---|---|
| **Ada®** | U.S. Department of Defense |
| **Cray®** | Cray Research |
| **dBASE III® , dBASE III+® , dBASE IV™** | Ashton Tate, Inc. |
| **Epcot Center®** | Walt Disney Co. |
| **Excelerator®** | Index Technology Corp. |
| **GM®** | General Motors Corp. |
| **IBM®** | International Business Machines Corp. |
| **Intel 80286™, 80386™, and 80486™** | Intel Corp. |
| **Lotus 1-2-3®** | Lotus Development Corp. |
| **Monopoly®** | Parker Brothers, Inc. |
| **QuickBASIC®** | Microsoft Corp. |
| **Ramis®** | On-line Software, Inc. |
| **Tandy®** | Tandy Corp. |
| **3M®** | Minnesota Manufacturing & Mining Co. |
| **Unix®** | AT&T |
| **WordPerfect®** | WordPerfect Corp. |

FIRST EDITION
FIRST PRINTING


TAB BOOKS is a division of McGraw-Hill, Inc.

Permissions

Glidrose Publications, London, Great Britain, for the Ian Fleming quotation, ©Glidrose Productions 1961.

Merriam-Webster, Inc. *From Webster's Ninth New Collegiate Dictionary*, © 1988 by Merriam Webster Inc., publisher of the Merriam-Webster® dictionaries.



**Library of Congress Cataloging-in-Publication Data**

Hall, George M.
Strategy, systems, and integration : a handbook for information managers / by George M. Hall.
p. cm.
Includes bibliographical references and index.
ISBN 0-8306-3614-5
1. Management information systems. I. Title.
T58.6.H334 1990 90-44415
658.4′038—dc20 CIP

TAB BOOKS offers software for sale. For information and a catalog, please contact TAB Software Department, Blue Ridge Summit, PA 17294-0850.

Questions regarding the content of this book should be addressed to:

Reader Inquiry Branch
TAB BOOKS
Blue Ridge Summit, PA 17294-0850

Acquisitions Editor: Gerald T. Papke
Technical Editor: Mark D. LeSuer
Production: Katherine G. Brown
Book Design: Jaclyn J. Boone

# Contents

# Figures and Tables

# Acknowledgments

I wish to acknowledge James E. Kenyon and Nick Simonds of the Chrysler Corporation, John R. Cook, Herb Bludeau, and George McCall of USAA, Ed Mahler of E. I. duPont de Nemours & Co., and Richard E. Lehman of the Internal Revenue Service for providing photographs and material for the vignettes that begin each part of the book. I also wish to thank Jerry Papke, senior editor; Suzanne Cheatle, executive editor, Laura Crist, editorial assistant, and others at TAB/McGraw-Hill for their work in making this book a reality. And, I cheerfully acknowledge my wife, Marlene Anne, whose patience and support during the preparation of the manuscript was a constant source of encouragement.

# Preface

The original focus of this book was systems integration, motivated by the evidence of many unpublicized failures among the fewer but highly touted successes. The extension into the strategy of information systems arose from the recognition of two items. First, the factors that make integrations work well are what make systems work well. Second, the intent of most integrations is to gain strategic advantage. Unwittingly, I had bought the farm.

While working that soil, I ran into four problems. The first was that corporate management and technology were far from being on a happy collision course. If anything, the increasing complexity of information systems has exacerbated the differences between general management and information managers. Thus, any attempt to bridge that gap must address both parties. That proved to be a challenge beyond my abilities to master. I never did figure out how to describe technological wherewithal without making substantial reference to it.

The second problem was the prevalence of abstract terms with loose definitions, including the word *systems* itself. That ubiquitous word appears in at least ten different contexts. Other troublesome expressions include *artificial intelligence, object programming, knowledge-based systems, function,* and for that matter *strategy.* These terms mean different things to different individuals. In some cases, the approach taken was to define the term for the purposes of the book and then stick to it. In other cases, this approach was inappropriate. The divergence of interpretations suggested that a more fundamental concept was operating at root. Here, glossing over the fine points of various definitions seemed appropriate to get a better grip on that root.

The third item was the problem of describing the different models of distributive processing, which is perhaps the most intriguing and unsettled issue in information systems today. The four orientations developed in chapter 10 are so encumbered with caveats as to render them nearly useless. A computer-based decision support system that could assess various models with respect to a company's requirements would be more appropriate. One of the technical notes takes a stab at outlining the program, but time constraints prevented any preliminary work.

The fourth problem was the availability of references—all 495,000 of them. Even when the research is limited to material written in the English language, more than 300 publishers offer one or more titles each year. Also, more than 1200 periodicals are devoted to the field, plus another 800 or so that frequently include significant articles on the subject matter. The only hope lay in writing a draft of the manuscript, followed by several months of total immersion in as much of the printed matter as time allowed, and concluding with a complete rewrite of the draft. No one is more aware of the inadequacies of this approach than I am.

The upshot of all this is that there are no simple solutions with elegant flowcharts and neat implementation schedules. The problems are just too massive for that treatment. A famed explorer once put the case this way: "Heights charm us, the paths that lead to them do not." This book concentrates on describing those paths—strewn as they are with every conceivable obstacle—and what it takes to negotiate them. The description of these paths is written in management terms without short changing the logical and technical aspects of systems. Whether this approach fulfills the intended utility is a matter for the reader to decide.

# Part I

# A Sense of Strategy

Supreme Court Justice Potter Stewart, in rendering a decision on a difficult constitutional issue, wrote that while he could not define *pornography*, he knew it when he saw it. The same could be said for *strategy*. The term is hard to define, but most managers know a good application of strategy when they see it. Unfortunately, in the practical world of business and institutions, a gossamer understanding of a seminal attribute is probably more costly in terms of wasted effort than no understanding at all.

The central idea of strategy is to obtain better results with existing resources, or alternatively, to achieve the same results with fewer resources. System resources include the usual array of hardware, software, and communications; of personnel and skills; of acquired knowledge and experience; and of data. The strategic utilization of these resources simply means the increase of productivity or the improvement of market position. For nonprofit organizations, the productivity goal still holds, but marketing transforms into the twin objectives of ensuring honest payment for services rendered and reducing waste in the distribution of those services. This leads to the central thesis of this book, which comprises seven arguments:

- First, *strategy* means attaining objectives by the efficient use of informational resources.
- Second, efficient use depends on one or more integrations of those resources.
- Third, a successful integration offers the unhindered and rapid ability to exchange and relate data and programming in the support of strategic objectives, or what this book calls "the advantage of interior lines."
- Fourth, the technique of successful integration applies equally to new systems and to the merger or interfacing of existing systems. The only difference is that, in the latter, the capability must be added after the fact.

- Fifth, the available technology is sufficient to develop information systems far surpassing the majority of those now in use, and the potential can only get better and less expensive as time passes.
- Sixth, the greatest obstacle blocking this potential is the marked inability of general management and information systems managers to fully perceive each other's perspective, and a significant part of this discontinuity arises from the inherent gap between the open-ended subjectivity of strategy and the close-ended technology of systems.
- Seventh, the key to bridging this gap is recognizing the pervasiveness of interior lines, which range from the architecture of a central processing unit to the structure of a well-designed database, to the alignment inherent in a successful system or merger of existing systems, to the ability of senior-level personnel in an organization—as the expression goes—to get their act together. At any rate, this approach is better than attempting to provide a dozen different definitions for the word *system*.

This all might seem a little overwhelming, but then complex projects are not child's play, and no amount of wishful thinking will make them so. On the other hand, the history of information systems offers many fine examples of individuals and teams who confronted extraordinary difficulties and prevailed by dint of good judgment, hard work, and an insightful perspective. Accordingly, the introduction to each part of the book includes an example of this caliber of achievement. For this part, the work being done by the Chrysler Corporation seems particularly apt.

Chrysler Corporation's sense of strategy recognizes that systems for business work well when they contribute to goals, improve productivity, and show a solid return on investment. To do this, they must be practical as well as far-reaching, and they only come about when there is a strong and persistent interaction between the users and the developers. This strategy is exemplified by the *Service Bay Diagnostics* (SBD) system.

The increasing complexity of today's cars—some models have as many as 16 computer chips built into them—demands computerized tools equal to the task. Taking that necessity as a starting point, the company turned it into strategic advantage. The goal went beyond automated trouble-shooting to that of getting each job done right the first try at least 90 percent of the time. This results in satisfied owners and contributes to owner loyalty. Owner loyalty means improved sales over the long run.

But SBD doesn't stop there. The data on repairs is collected methodically and used as input for redesign of the parts and assemblies that appear to be anything more than random problems. This redesign can mean anything from a "quick fix" on the assembly line or a major redesign; whatever is necessary. Finally, information on these changes is distributed to all dealers and authorized service facilities worldwide, including the updating of the programming in the SBD system.

Another component is the *Just-in-Time* (JIT) inventory management system. Chrysler buys approximately $18 billion in raw materials, supplies, and subassemblies every year. The inventory costs on that much material—from warehousing to the lost opportunity of investing the funds elsewhere—amounts to between $4 and $5 billion dollars per year. The JIT system minimizes warehousing by scheduling deliveries as close as possible to use dates, leaving just enough slack to accommodate unforeseen problems. Some deliveries are now made on the hour.

*Fig. I-1. The Service Bay Diagnostics system is a key element in the Chrysler strategic plan for information systems. Its success is largely attributable to the teamwork among users, general management, and systems personnel. Shown here are Joe McCormick, Manager for Customer Satisfaction, Service and Parts Operations; Ted Cunningham, Vice President, Service and Parts Operations; Nick Simonds, Executive Director of Management Information Systems; and John Campbell, Manager, Automobile Sales and Parts Systems, MIS.*[1]

[1]As this book went to press, Mr. Simonds accepted a senior position at Honeywell, Inc., Minneapolis, MN.

A third component of Chrysler's strategy is the *Performance Feedback System* (PFS), which operates on the assembly line. Any flaw or problem with production on any unit at any point in the line, triggers a response down the line (literally) without holding up production, yet in time to take action before the item loses ready accessibility.

Many other components are on the drawing board, but perhaps the real significance to this strategy runs deeper than efficiency, profit, and increased market share. Good planners do not think just in terms of points-of-sale. What they aim for is quality, and that requires long-term resiliency. Other corporations might use computer technology more extensively and with more showcase applications than Chrysler, but few have used it so consistently with the rare combination of strategic thinking, practical goals, sound management, and good judgment.

Keeping this in mind, then, the next four chapters attempt to generalize this sense of strategy. The first chapter addresses the environment in which information managers must operate, and includes a discussion of external factors, management dichotomies, interior lines, integrations, the power curve phenomenon, and trade-off considerations. The second chapter then anchors the concept of strategy for information systems in terms of six explicit principles, and includes a review of operating factors, levels of consideration, necessity, functionality, and the technology vs. requirements issue.

The third chapter descends from the lofty perch of strategy and focuses on the more mundane aspects of systems planning—magnitudes, configurations, and priorities. The argument is that if the planning analysis is first rate, managers can attain an accurate picture of what is needed to implement a system, whether it is a new system, to a system implemented under external constraints, a replacement system, or an integration of systems. The fourth chapter provides an even sharper focus on a crucial aspect of systems, namely return on investment. Although life cycle costs are an important part of systems planning, estimates that run beyond a few years are subject to many uncertainties and errors. It is more practical to concentrate on estimating development costs and accurately projecting the return on investment for the first three to five years.

# 1

# The Meaning of Strategy and Integration

*He had decided that fast and accurate communication lay,*
*in a contracting world, at the very heart of power.*
*Knowledge of the truth before the next man, in peace or war,*
*lay he thought behind every correct decision in history*
*and was the source of all great reputations.*

— Ian Fleming
*Thunderball*

Until recent times, the term *strategy* was used almost exclusively in geopolitics and defense matters. *Webster's Ninth New Collegiate Dictionary* offers as its definition, "the science and art of employing the political, economic, psychological, and military forces of a nation or group of nations to afford maximum support to adopted policies in peace or war." That is a heady definition, and one must ask just what it has to do with information systems.

Ian Fleming offered one answer based on his experience in military intelligence during World War II. That experience included the breaking of the German *Enigma* code using one of the earliest computers—code-named *Colossus*. From the information gleaned, the Allied forces foreshortened the war and kept the casualties from becoming even higher than they were.

Years afterward, Fleming might have been anxious to tell the story, although it remained shrouded in secrecy. If so, he hinted at it indirectly in one of his James Bond novels, from which the chapter opening quotation is taken. Perhaps it is an overstatement, yet the underlying idea seems correct. Though knowledge isn't exactly power, accurate information can hone the competitive edge wielded by any individual or organization. To extend the argument, an information system should give its owners a leg up on the competition, or if non-profit, a head start against the problems and challenges with which it must deal.

After fifty years of awesome technological progress, that competitive edge should have become razor sharp. For transaction-based routine processing, that is perhaps true, but for strategic information systems, it is generally not. Why? Because although the strategic use of computers might rely on much the same data as routine transaction processing, the logic is infinitely more complex and often requires a much more resilient communications network.

## 1.1 THE MEANING OF STRATEGY FOR INFORMATION SYSTEMS

If competition is considered analogous to war and information is considered a resource, the dictionary definition of strategy can be translated into terms meaningful to information managers. A little parsing of the original definition leads to the following translation:

- The phrase *science and art* remains valid, providing *science* is understood to mean the correct use of resources and techniques, while *art* is held to mean configurations, timing, and scheduling.
- The words *political* [and other] forces readily translates to information system resources or those that can be used for that purpose.
- The phrase *a nation or group of nations* easily becomes an organization (or group of organizations).
- The expression *to afford maximum support to adopted policies* becomes *to produce advantageous conditions in the pursuit of business or provision of services*.
- This leaves *in peace or war*, which is extraneous for all but defense-oriented information systems and perhaps some police investigative units.

Combining these restated phrases, then, the definition for information systems strategy would be "the proper utilization and optimal configuration of the information resources of a corporation, institution, or other organization to produce advantageous conditions in the pursuit of its business or provision of services." Information resources include personnel, hardware, software, communications, or the financial ability to acquire any of them, and information itself. Configuration literally equates with database structures, networks, and the like. It also applies figuratively to scheduling, priorities, timing, and related attributes.

The implied key here is ingenuity. The use of computer technology to automate clerical tasks, if it reduces production costs, inherently contributes to profits or enhances services provided. Yet these applications do not crave corporate ingenuity except in a limited technical sense. The idea of strategy is to go beyond the routine without denigrating the bread-and-butter advantages of the latter. There is no shortage of potential applications.

- *Corporate Marketing*. Capitalism pays the bills of society, but the marketplace has become more of a challenge. It is now less inelastic. When the United States was the overwhelming producer of goods and services consumed within its own borders, one company's loss was another's gain. In the current era of international competition, that is no longer true. The U.S. has lost a significant share of its own market to foreign manufacturers without making compensating gains in their countries. Whatever the flaws might be in the American way of business life, however, a lack of ingenuity and an enterprising spirit are not among them. Computer technology is open to the application of these attributes to enhance international and domestic marketing.
- *Corporate Productivity*. Whether improved market position or efficient production is more important is an unresolvable debate, but no corporation denies the advantages of more efficient production. Just how much further information technology can push production efficiency is problematic, but the greatest untapped resource for most corporations seems to be a failure to make the most of its human resources by letting them make the most of themselves. A number of widely read books attest to this fact, especially Tom Peters' *The Search for Excellence*. Perhaps what is needed, then, are computer models that will persuade less sanguine managers to open their minds to this path.
- *Government "Marketing."* The government has something of a captive market. It puts a few of the people who don't buy its services—tax evaders—in jail, but still roughly $100 billion goes uncollected every year. Conversely, it pays billions to many corporations and individuals, although both often fail to deliver products or provide services as agreed. The documented Department of Defense scandals, the ongoing fraud in Medicare reimbursements, and the savings & loan debacle are only three examples. Clearly, an astute use of information systems technology could be applied to increase the flow of earned taxes and to decrease the abusive financial drain.
- *Government Productivity*. The accelerating budget and trade deficits, combined with the shrinking proportion of wage earners in the population, the increasing demands of the citizenry, the eroding of the physical infrastructure, and the inflationary cost spiral of existing government programs, will undoubtedly generate major dilemmas for the expenditure of available revenues. Decision support systems could prove invaluable for comparing the advantages and disadvantages of hundreds of alternatives.
- *Medicine*. The cost of medical care is the single biggest item in the American economy. It consumes 12.5 percent of the GNP and is increasing. Terminal, but lingering, diseases absorb billions of dollars. Sophisticated computer technology, combined with baselining nuclear magnetic resonance scans and similar techniques, could significantly reduce these costs through low-cost early detection, which in turn would substitute

inexpensive cures for expensive, prolonged, and often futile therapy. It could also be used to restrict reimbursement for excess hospital beds, a factor that seems to be a prime culprit of the cost spiral.

- *Education*. Although machines will never replace teachers, computer technology, in the form of interactive teaching support systems, could greatly increase the effectiveness and influence of a single teacher working with 30 or more students concurrently. Without it, how much individual help can one teacher provide to 30 students in 50 minutes or less each day?

These applications all sound good, and no doubt many of these systems will materialize. Yet caveats intrude. In some cases, the cost of the system might outweigh its benefits. But presuming the requirements are bona fide and the technology is available, the chief danger arises from excess. This excess was foreseen in exaggerated form in Aldous Huxley's *Brave New World* and George Orwell's *1984*—exaggerated, but not mistaken. Consider, for example, the restrictive environment imposed on telephone operators and other employees, whose every iota of work performance is monitored by computers, and whose job, salary, and promotions are primarily dependent on the tabulated results. That is not what is meant by a computer model to demonstrate the productivity of individuals.

A more concrete source of failure is the attempt to integrate systems to achieve strategic goals. The mass of computer systems and databases sitting out there seems ripe for picking. Perhaps 85 percent of all the data that will ever be needed to make the best strategic use of computers is already recorded electronically on hundreds of thousands of perfectly good machines. And most of the information is updated with reasonable timeliness. All that needs to be done is to integrate it, or so goes the theory.

Recent cases suggest otherwise. Billions of dollars have been poured into this effort, often with meager results at best. This doesn't mean all systems integrations are doomed to failure. On the contrary, the three best-known systems in the country are integrations: airlines reservations, electronic banking, and telephone communications. Arguably, however, they succeed because of compelling necessity combined with an understanding—implicit or explicit—of what makes integration work and what makes it fail.

Here then lies a great problem. The integration of existing systems to produce the necessary integration or configuration of data and programming seems a worthy task. If most of the component systems work well, why tinker with them? The adage often cited is "if it ain't broke, don't fix it." That is sound advice, but it confuses ***operability*** with ***interoperability***. A chain of convenience stores can operate at high profit, but they do not lend themselves to integration as a supermarket. The marketing and pricing strategies differ markedly. The former depends, as the name implies, on maximum profit per item in return for convenience. The latter makes its money by mass selling and intense competition, supplemented by higher-profit-margin, impulse-buying displays. Therefore, building the supermarket from scratch is cheaper and simpler, notwithstanding the proven expertise and value of the existing stores.

The point is that an integration of systems, no matter how worthy it might sound on paper, is not always feasible. The logical integrity of the consolidation and its ability to operate efficiently should equal if not exceed the efficiency and operating capability of the best of the targeted components. If it doesn't, it will not work, or at best work only in the Rube Goldberg sense of the word.

## 1.2 FACTORS

To use the discussion of the previous section as a starting point, eight factors appear to intrude between the potential of information technology and reality. Figure 1-1 presents these factors in simplified form. The specific array and intensity faced by each corporation or organization varies widely, but most of these factors operate most of the time.[1]

- *Higher Risks*. The failure rate of many systems is now well documented and has raised the specter of continued failure for new undertakings. As the magnitude of risk increases, the willingness to pursue new paths decreases.
- *The Technological Avalanche*. The progress of computer science and information technology can only be described as an avalanche. The steamroller analogy would be inadequate. Keeping up with this technology is beyond the ability of all but a handful of geniuses.
- *Legal Pressures*. The proliferation of computer-based systems has spawned more than its fair share of abuse and a correspondingly greater share of new legislation to curb the abuse. Although it might never reach the point of mandating an environmental impact study every time a new computer is installed, the potential for even more restrictive legislation is clearly in the offering.
- *The Marketing vs. Productivity Issue*. The contributions of computers to productivity tend to be direct and easily measured. The contributions to marketing tend to be indirect and difficult to evaluate. Still, the market offers the potential for a greater return on investment. Which should take priority?
- *Return on Investment*. Closely associated with the marketing vs. productivity issue is return on investment. Except in a few humanitarian situations, the application of information systems technology should pay its own way and then some. Else why use it? But should that return materialize in the short run or over the long haul?

---

[1]After this book was written, two related events occurred that illustrate the complex factors operating for and against information systems. Eastman Kodak and IBM announced a joint development project for a publishing computer system that will integrate advertising, business, and operations systems, intended for large- and medium-sized publishers. At the same time, eight journalists filed a $270 million lawsuit against the Eastman Kodak subsidiary Atex Publishing Systems, which makes the terminals for these systems. The suit claims the terminals cause cumulative trauma disorders. The plaintiffs include two from *Newsday* and one from *The Associated Press*.

- *The Centralization vs. Decentralization Issue.* Computers operate more efficiently, in the technical sense, when centralized. People and organizations, for the most part, do not. What is the constructive compromise?
- *Security Problems.* As systems proliferate, they are increasingly subject to material failure or damage—perhaps at an exponential rate—to unauthorized access and misuse of data and software, and to crime and abuse.
- *Ethical Issues.* Lastly, as many thoughtful writers have essayed at considerable length, the intrusion of computers into individual lives has been something of mixed blessing, and one that promises to intensify before it recedes.

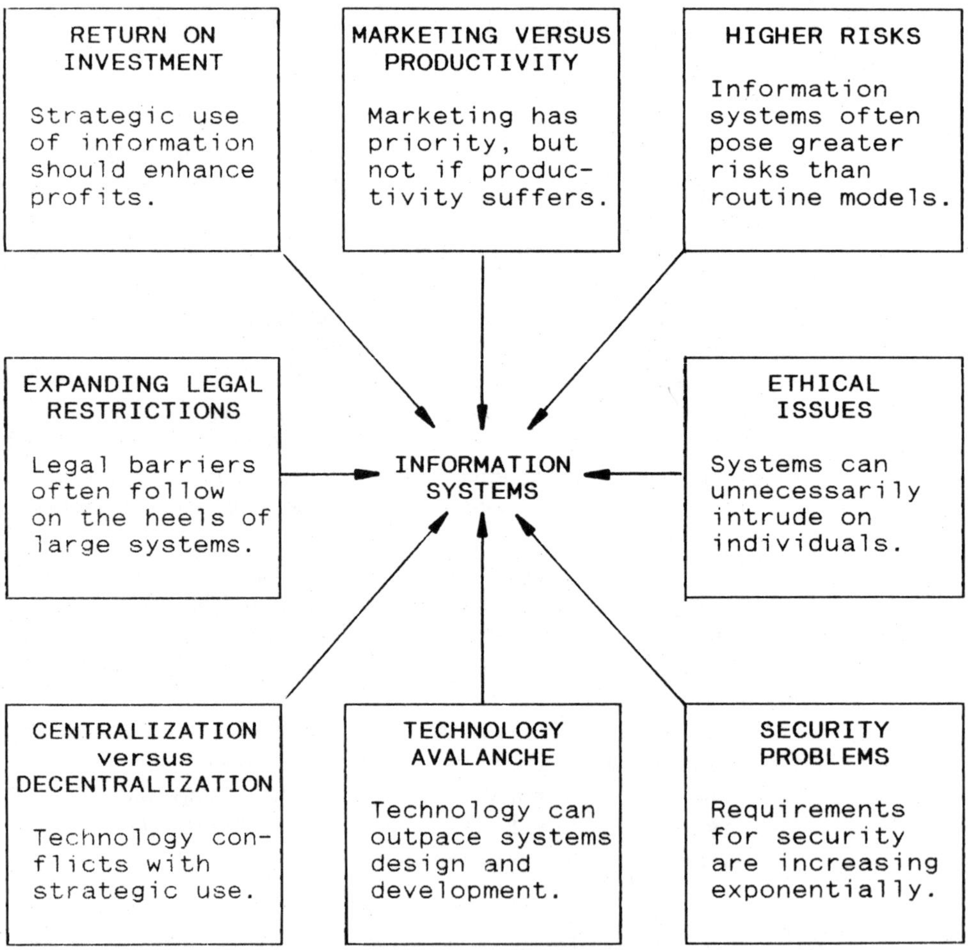


*Fig. 1-1. Factors affecting information systems. The relentless advance of technology has moved the computer from the back room to the boardroom. The information systems it has spawned are being harnessed as instruments of strategy, wielding increasing leverage in the marketplace and in production efficiency. Yet this leverage must also contend with the eight factors shown, which can defeat the strategic intent, if improperly addressed.*

## 1.3 THE MANAGEMENT DILEMMA

The difference in mind-set between chief executive officers and chief information officers, or their equivalent, has grown nearly as perennial as the antagonisms between parents and children, and between management and labor. The CEOs complain that their information managers lack insight and commitment to corporate goals and that they entomb themselves in technological crypts. The CIOs retort that CEOs change goals far too often for technology and systems to adapt. Strangely, most CEO's readily admit to this shortcoming, which perhaps explains why they have risen to the top job.

The influence of this difference in perspective goes beyond mere personality clashes. Figure 1-2 lists some of the implications when priority is given to one or the other. Yet because there are obvious advantages and disadvantages to each point of view, what happens—given the eight factors outlined in the previous section—is that the strategic use of information systems becomes something akin to taming a two-headed octopus.

A *New Yorker* cartoon appearing more than 30 years ago presaged this problem. A young upright technician in shirt sleeves was sitting at the console of a gigantic computer. He had obviously just made a suggestion to his boss standing next to the computer. The boss replied that it would be better if he, the technician, would let him, the boss, do the thinking around there.

Something is needed to resolve the difficulties arising from this task, or at least provide a focal point. Fortunately, the very expression *focal point* provides a clue. It means that point where lines coming from many positions must converge before diverging again into a useful image. If information systems are considered a useful image, they too need a focal point. And a useful way of describing focal points is a term often associated with strategy: *interior lines*.

## 1.4 INTERIOR LINES

The term *interior lines* means the ability to shift resources quickly and without hindrance from one place to another to meet changing requirements. The original application came from military tactics to describe the main advantage of a defender who was surrounded. He can more easily shift his resources to meet attacks than could his attacker maneuver resources to do him in. Figure 1-3 illustrates this phenomenon in general, nonmilitary terms. The informational or knowledge equivalent is a well stocked, well organized library.

Perhaps the best example of the latter occurred at a dinner in the East Room of the White House in the spring of 1962, given by President John F. Kennedy to honor as many living Nobel laureates that would accept the invitation. He rose to speak and intoned that never before had so much intelligence been gathered in that room, with the possible exception of when Thomas Jefferson dined there alone. To restate the case, then, intended strategic information systems should make maximum use of the interior lines of informational resources.

Now interior lines are not all that esoteric or rare. On the contrary, science offers a single word that equates with the judicious use of interior lines: *entropy*.

In thermodynamics, entropy is the inverse measure of the availability of energy. High entropy means unavailability. Lowering entropy means to make energy more available. Energy is made more available by efficient design. Thus, one generator might convert 90 percent of the theoretical energy content to electrical power output; another only 70 percent. The balance is waste and friction.

| | STRATEGIC PERSPECTIVE | TECHNICAL PERSPECTIVE |
|---|---|---|
| OUTREACH | Stresses improving market share, or if nonprofit, provision of services. | Aim is productivity efficiency, both in profit and nonprofit organizations. |
| EXTENT OF DECENTRALIZATION | Maximum emphasis on decentralization of data and systems and perhaps mainframes. | Errs on the side of centralization, for reasons of technical efficiency. |
| USE OF TECHNOLOGY | Technology is secondary to user requirements, though this is often shortsighted. | Often considers the harnessing of emerging technology as a goal in its own right. |
| PROPORTIONALITY OF WORKLOAD | Stress is on new or innovative systems to improve strategic position. | Emphasis is on maintaining and upgrading existing hardware and software. |
| TRENDS IN INTEGRATION | Favors merger-type integrations, notwithstanding the higher degree of risk. | Tends to rely on interfaces, in keeping with the emphasis on systems maintenance. |
| BENEFIT ANALYSES | Benefit analysis is project oriented, though indirect costs can be hard to gage. | Benefit analysis is a secondary consideration. Other analyses are more subjective. |

*Fig. 1-2. Strategic vs. systems perspectives. The strategic perspective looks at requirements and effectiveness. The systems perspective focuses on management and technological efficiency. The two are often at odds, since the benefits of one often operate to the detriment of the other. Striking a balance is perhaps the most difficult challenge for information managers.*

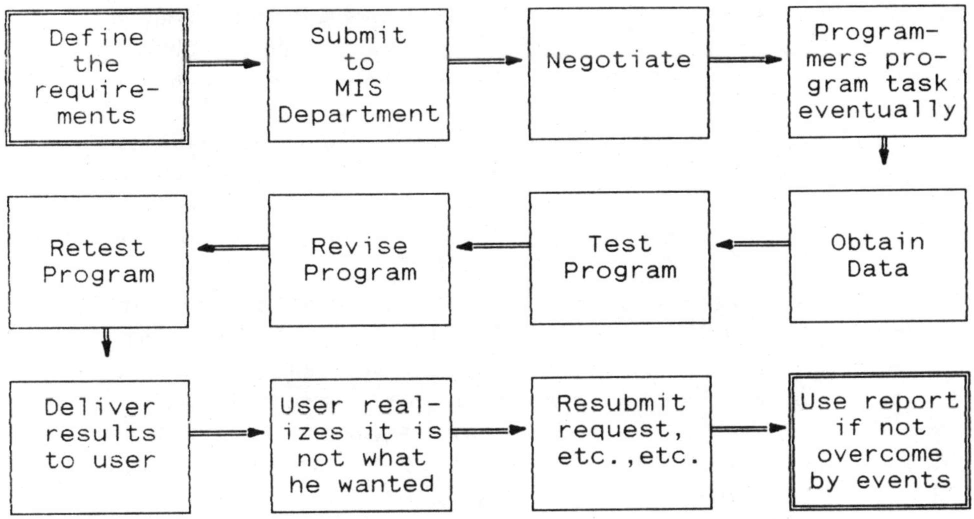


A. THE ABSENCE OF INTERIOR LINES

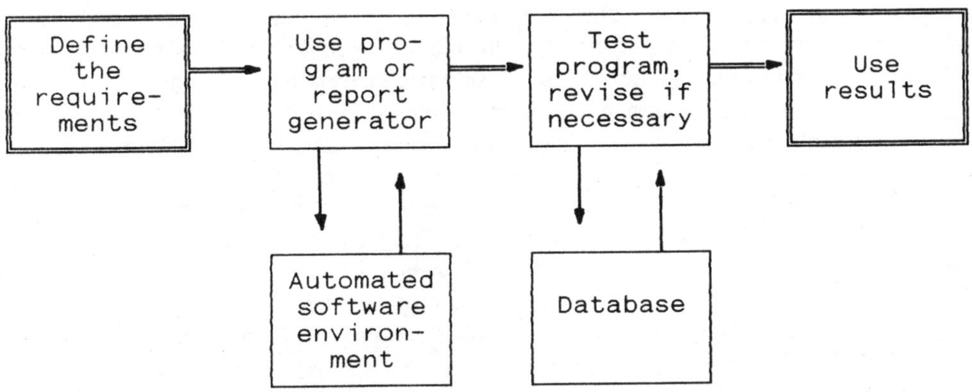


B. THE PRESENCE OF INTERIOR LINES

*Fig. 1-3. The meaning of interior lines. The expression* interior lines *describes the ability to shift resources or information from one place to another quickly and without hindrance. The success of a system, and especially an integration of existing systems, depends on the simplicity of these lines.*

The former eliminates most of the waste and friction; it has higher efficiency and demonstrates lower entropy.

Applied to information theory, entropy measures the degree in which information can achieve its intended purpose. Communications and messages that are lengthy, ambiguous, and confusing have high entropy. Clear, concise messages evince the opposite. Similarly, ponderous information systems suffer from high entropy, while those that quickly yield relevant and terse answers do not. Systems are improved by lowering their entropy. Entropy is lowered by improving interior lines. Interior lines mean creating unhindered paths among data and users. When an operation must be performed on the data before it becomes useful, that process should also have its own efficient set of interior lines.

Before continuing this line of reasoning, however, it should be recognized that only a microcosm of the pattern permeates the whole of logic, mathematics, and physical law. Technical note 1 in appendix B goes into this matter at greater length, but the concept is important enough to warrant a summary discussion here.

The thought process that underwrites all software and the design of hardware traces its roots back 2,400 years, when an obscure Greek mathematician integrated most of the then-known theorems of geometry into one continuous logical stream. Euclid's *Elements* went on to become the second best seller of all time. About 2,000 years later, Sir Isaac Newton, arguably history's most distinguished physicist, roundly criticized himself for not adhering to Euclid's model more closely than he did for integrating the laws of motion and gravitation in his justly renown *Principia*.

The *Principia* then set in motion the quest for the scientific grail, today known as the *Unified Field Theory*. Virtually every physicist subscribes to the hypothesis that all the laws and phenomena of the physical universe are derivable from a handful of simple axioms, logically adhering to the Euclidean model. Further, scientists use the equivalent of decision support systems with increasing frequency to validate or invalidate *trial balloons*.

Yet that isn't even the half of it. The human brain is sometimes considered the ultimate computer. And where does this awesome piece of machinery come from? From a handful of simple but integrated chemical elements, with those in the core of the cell arranged into double helixes. From a single cell, barely perceptible to the human eye, the helixes within selectively grab hold of every resource the cell needs to generate the complex organism known as the human being. The late Nobel laureate Erwin Schrödinger compared the effects of DNA to the weave of a Raphael tapestry, while ordinary compounds fared no better than repetitious wallpaper (though both processes derived from the same laws).

As remarkable as DNA is, however, the granddaddy of empowerment by interior lines of sorts occurs with the stuff used to coat memory storage media in a computer. When an infinitesimal speck of ferrous material is magnetized, the interior lines of its molecular structure are modified to unleash a power to attract other ferrous material. This force is $10^{39}$ times stronger than its gravitational counterpart. This means the magnetic pull of the speck is on a par with the gravitational pull of the entire earth. This phenomenon clearly demonstrates itself every time an ordinary magnet is used to lift a ferrous object in a direction opposite the earth's gravitational pull.

But do not underestimate the precision required to make an integration work well. Some years ago, Broadway staged *The Princess and the Pea*, an old tale that focused on the problem of determining whether a certain young lady was in fact a princess. The doubters put a small pea under seven mattresses, hoping it would cause her to twist and turn all night. "Only a princess could be so sensitive," was the reasoning. Biological cells and systems follow suit. An infinitesimally small mutation to the genes can transform a peaceful cell into a voracious beast medical science calls *cancer*. Correspondingly, a few tiny "bugs" in the first copies of Ashton Tate's dBASE IV triggered major marketing problems for nearly a year, which undoubtedly cost the firm millions of dollars in lost profits. An equally small error in the manned space flight computer programs could send a team of astronauts to the infinity of space.

A profound example of the role of precision is the difference among apes, chimpanzees, and human beings. The genes of the chimpanzee are roughly 1 percent more advanced than the ape's. Accordingly, the former exhibits a higher degree of sophistication than the latter, though not profoundly so. Yet add another percentage point to the technology and the chimpanzee becomes a human being. The difference in this case is profound, although not necessarily in the ethical sense. Similarly, when computer technology achieved the integrated circuit chip, the computer revolution took off and shows no signs of slowing down.

At this point, a question arises. A configuration with good interior lines explains efficiency, but it does not explain the sudden increases to efficiency that result from seemingly minor refinements of that configuration. This is no small point. The implication is that continued refinements to information systems might eventually yield spectacular results.

The answer comes from what physicists call critical mass and a wider range of scientists label catastrophe theory. Most readers are well aware of what happens when a 1/10-ounce, $.10 screw in the fuel system of a 4,000-pound, $30,000 automobile is torqued 1/4 turn too much. Or what happens when a control rod or its equivalent is inserted too far into a nuclear pile used for power generation. If the interior lines are insufficient in number or are not arranged tightly enough, the integration will sputter. Correct the deficiency, and the system hums.

## 1.5 THE INTERIOR LINES OF SYSTEMS

The spectrum of systems arches from the farsighted judgment of great business and institutional leaders to the innards of a machine that at primordial root can do nothing more than channel electrical current and count to 1. Experts at both ends have been trying to bridge the abyss for decades. Business judgment must be translated into practical and usually quantitative directions. Permutations and combinations of simple numbers and their exchange are the building blocks of sophisticated business constructs. When they effectively reach out to each other, the result is that a sufficient network of interior lines has been established. The mini-systems atlas in appendix C tries to illustrate this process.

Improvements among the most popular editions of productivity software offer a simple example of the process. These improvements are largely based on one or more integrations of features, read *the insertion of automated interior lines*, that formerly required manual intervention. In WordPerfect version 5.1, compared to version 5.0, the help menu is now context sensitive. The merge function—itself an example of automated integration—offers a much wider range of options. Complex equations can be entered directly. Tabs adjust automatically to changes in margin settings. Hyphenation draws on the dictionary in lieu of a rule that was wrong 30 percent of the time. All these features give the user greater access to more features with fewer keystrokes in less time. And it sells.

The same could be said for Lotus 1-2-3. Version 3.0 integrates multiple spreadsheets in one operation, allowing the user to relate data in any cell of one spreadsheet to any other cell in another spreadsheet. With database software, the intent to facilitate the integration of data is obvious, but the increasingly sophisticated features also improve interior lines. For example, in dBASE III and later versions, plain English commands are used to instruct the software to perform operations that would require 20 to 30 lines of code in COBOL.

The concept of interior lines also applies to hardware. During the first half of the nineteenth century, and drawing on several centuries of mechanical calculator development, Charles Babbage invented the forerunner of modern computers in the form of an analytical engine. Concurrently but independently, Augusta Ada, Countess of Lovelace and Lord Byron's daughter, developed the fundamentals of programming. At the time, these intellectual landmarks generated only academic interest. On the productivity side, they were too cumbersome and of limited capacity for practical use. On the marketing side, the requirement for automated calculations was minimal. The paperwork load was still manageable and clerks were hired at low wages.

This changed by 1890. Herman Hollerith, an agent for the United States Census Bureau, estimated it would take until past the 1900 census to compile the data of the 1890 census if the old manual methods were used. The 1880 compilation had taken 9 years. Hollerith developed the plans for a more practical analytical engine and persuaded the government to have them built. On a percentage basis, the cost overrun made present-day Department of Defense contracts seem benign, but the machines worked and reduced the anticipated 11-year work load to 7 years. Hollerith then quit his job, formed the Computer-Tabulating-Recording Company, and began manufacturing these machines on a production basis. Today, as every information manager knows, that company is called IBM.

Necessity, as with most inventions, mothered progress from that time forward, almost always compressing more and more capability into less and less space. The first electromechanical models made their appearance circa 1940, followed a few years later by the first true electronic computer. Unfortunately, these machines were still cumbersome, expensive, and of limited capacity. Vacuum tubes quickly gave way to transistors. The interior lines shrunk, and mainframes became a staple of business.

Next came the integrated circuit—the critical configuration—that initiated the nonstop revolution in the data processing industry. The desktop computer

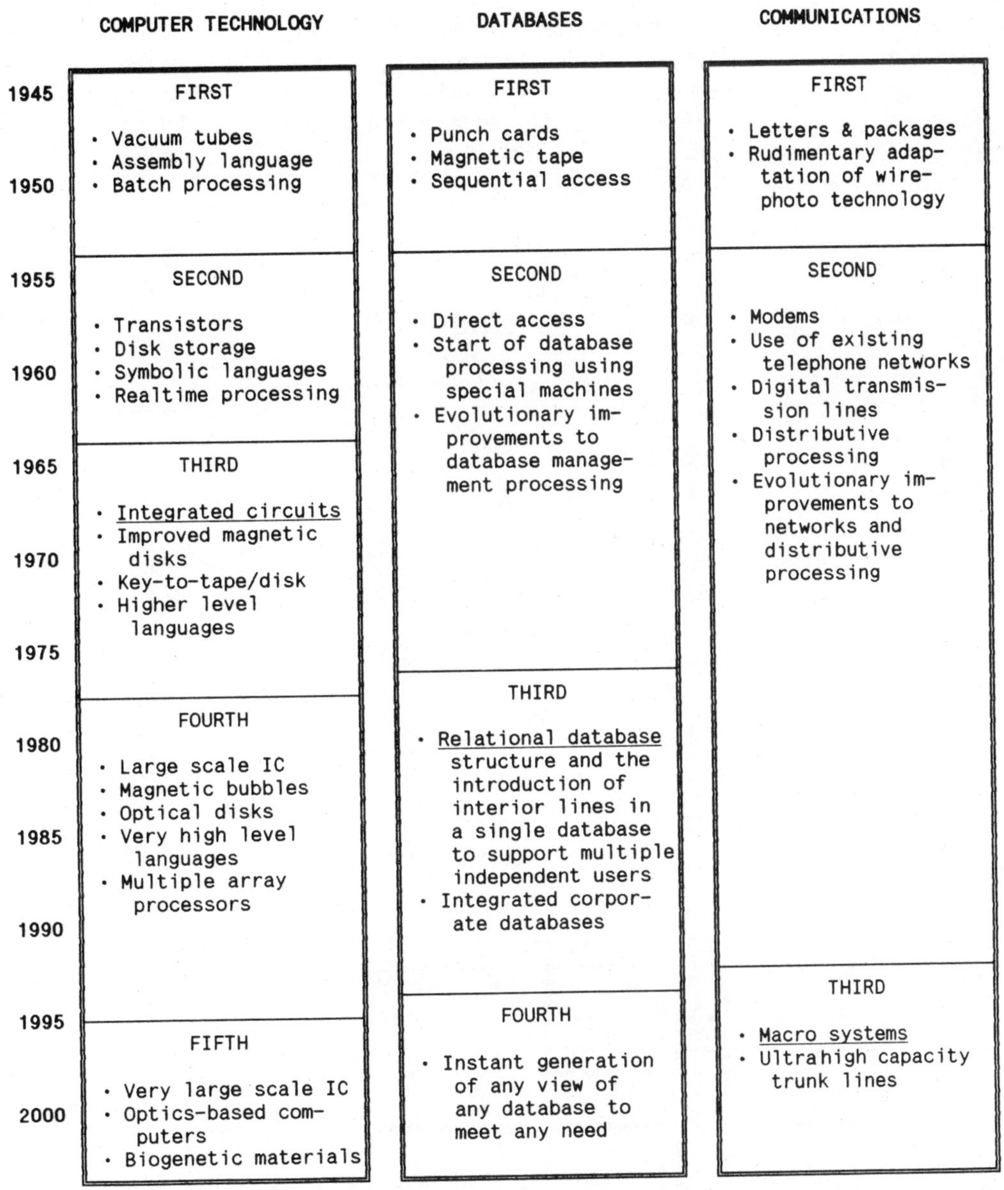


*Fig. 1-4. The generations of information systems. Information systems draw their efficacy from three sources: the computer, a database, and the ability to link the two. Computer technology reached its critical point 25 years ago, with the advent of the integrated circuit. Databases followed suit 15 years later with the relational database management system—integrated knowledge. Linkage is not far behind. It is only a matter of time before a widespread network of computers will be able to operate as if they were one unit—integrated communications. When this point is reached, the potential for radical improvement to information systems will be available to any manager who understands the paradigm.*

of 1990, at one ten-thousandth the price of the original mainframes, offers one thousand times the capacity, efficiency, and reliability. The significance of this turning point was heralded in February 1990, when the National Academy of Engineering bestowed the first annual Draper award, intended to parallel the Nobel prize for more practical developments, to the inventors of the integrated circuit, the late Robert N. Noyce and Jack S. Kilby.

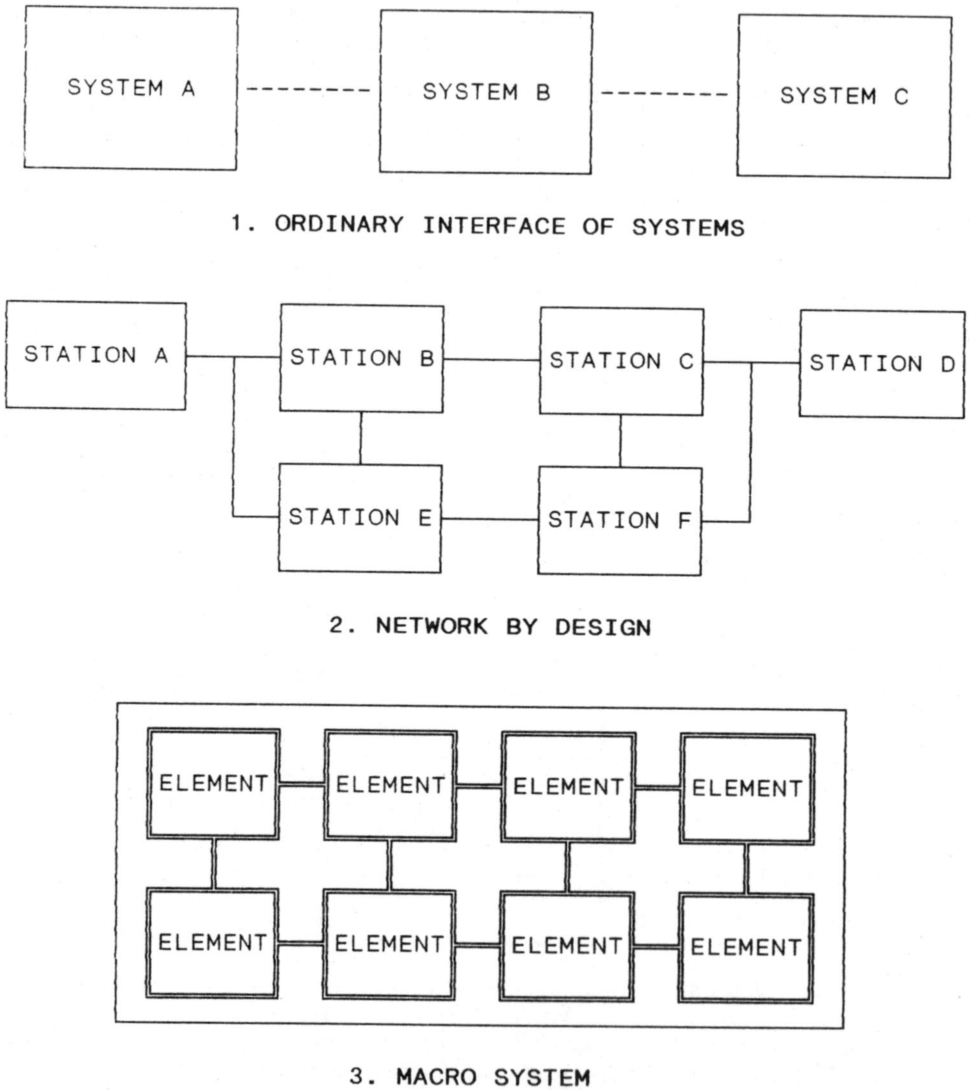


*Fig. 1-5. Macro systems. A* macro system *is a network of fully compatible computers linked by extremely high density communication trunk lines, which is the essence of interior lines, opening the way to extraordinary efficiency for information systems.*

Information systems followed suit, lagging their hardware companion by only 20 to 25 years. Figure 1-4 depicts the history of this movement. Relational database configuration was the key integration, which opened the door to data linkage that was previously available only with specialized technology and esoteric programming rules. In the relational database, each data element is more-or-less immediately relatable to any other element. Thus, a decision support system can: analyze and relate massive amounts of data; generate or find hundreds of alternatives, each with its respective quantitative advantages and disadvantages; list the more favorable alternatives, and do it at one-hundredth the cost and in one-hundredth the time, perhaps faster, than it would take an individual to do, even when supported by ordinary computer-based systems.

This same figure also illustrates the progress in communications technology as it applies to distributed computer systems. Unlike its hardware and database brethren, the network aspect of systems has yet to reach a turning point. That point should prove to be the development of extremely high capacity truck lines, combined with the proper use of relational databases, to enable a network of computers to operate as if they were one unit. Figure 1-5 illustrates this unit in more graphic terms. The significance is that the intractable problem of finding an adequate compromise between centralized and decentralized systems might be overcome. A physically centralized host computer in one of these networks can be operated in a highly decentralized mode without losing the technical advantages and interior lines of centralized systems.

A major question of efficient software and programming still remains. Often overshadowed by its hardware and communications cousins, software is what now consumes the bulk of the information systems dollar, and is where the strategic use of information technology will eventually succeed or fail. All of the other elements will likely be pushed into adequacy by the sheer force of technology. Fortunately all this technology strips away the baggage that accompanies software development so that information managers and their senior systems analysts can concentrate on meeting the logic of requirements.[2] Figure 1-6 depicts this evolving situation.

---

[2]In this arena the infamous term *object programming* comes to fore. Surely no term in computer science and information systems, save the word systems itself, has more definitions. One person will claim it means defining variables in software programs by their purpose—their *object*—rather than computer data structure, such as numerical or character variables. A second person will disagree violently and posit that object programming refers to database systems. A third person will chime in that it really means a library of software subprograms that can be templated for a wide variety of applications. A fourth will argue his colleagues have lost their senses. Object programming, so he will claim, means the use of program generators that eliminate most programming in the first place.

In a sense, all views correct. The object of object programming is to make programming techniques as close to human logic and definitions as possible and to get rid of all the artifices necessitated by the computer's mechanical nature. All programming, of course, must eventually be reduced to this level, but sophisticated programming environments can make the translations all but invisible.

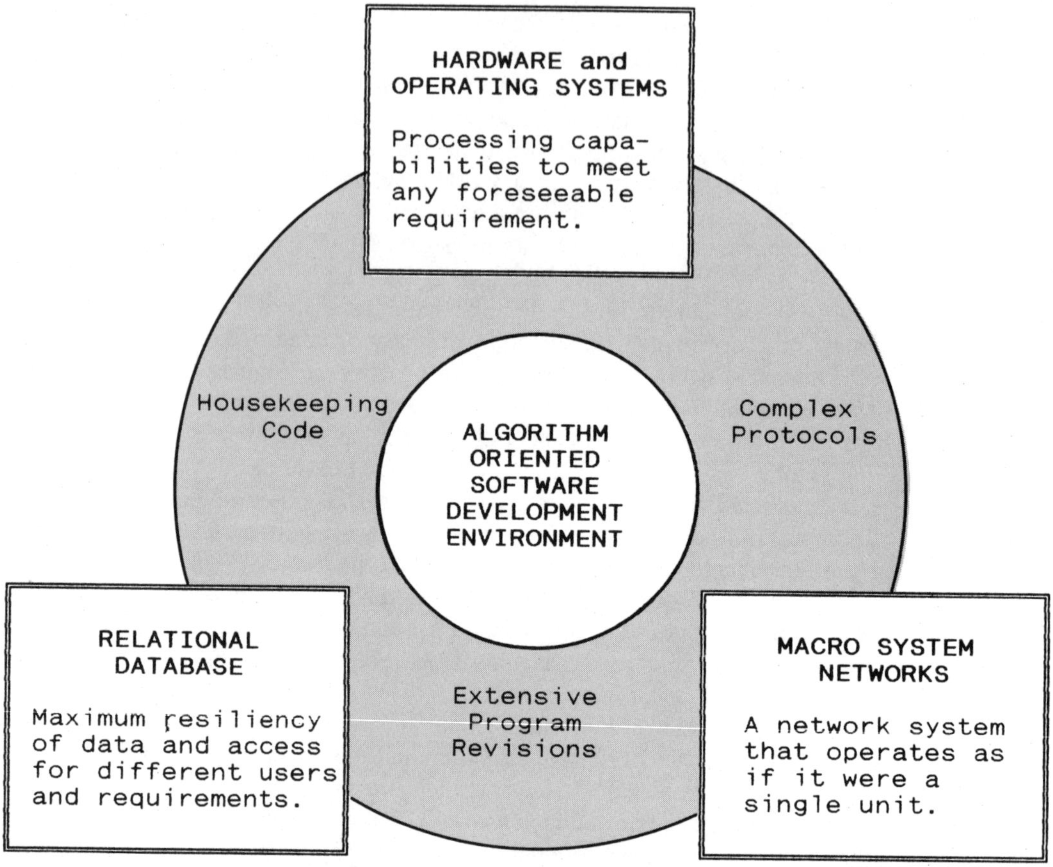


*Fig. 1-6. The triad of computer technology. The integration of the triad of computer technology—computers, databases, and networks—eliminates the roughage from the software environment. Increasingly, analysts and programmers can concentrate on the logic of requirements and on developing productivity software to simplify even that task.*

## 1.6 THE THREE FACES OF INTEGRATION

As stated in the introduction to this part of the book, an integration of systems differs from a singular system only in that many of the interior lines of communications are added after the fact. Figure 1-7 illustrates how the adding of those lines can be accomplished with one of three intents.

- *Merger*. The intent of a merger is to eliminate the separate identity of all or part of the targeted systems, with the product of the merger operating as if it were originally designed as a singular system. Because of the phrase "all or part," merger-type integrations can take one of several forms.
- *Interface*. The intent of an interface is less ambitious than a merger, and limits itself to getting separate systems to communicate with one another, without detracting from their separate identity. As such, an

interface has only one basic form that can vary widely in degree and number of computers linked together.

- *Standardization*. The usual intent of a standardization is either to facilitate another model of integration or to effect cost savings. In some cases, however, the standardization per se yields the same effect as an integration.

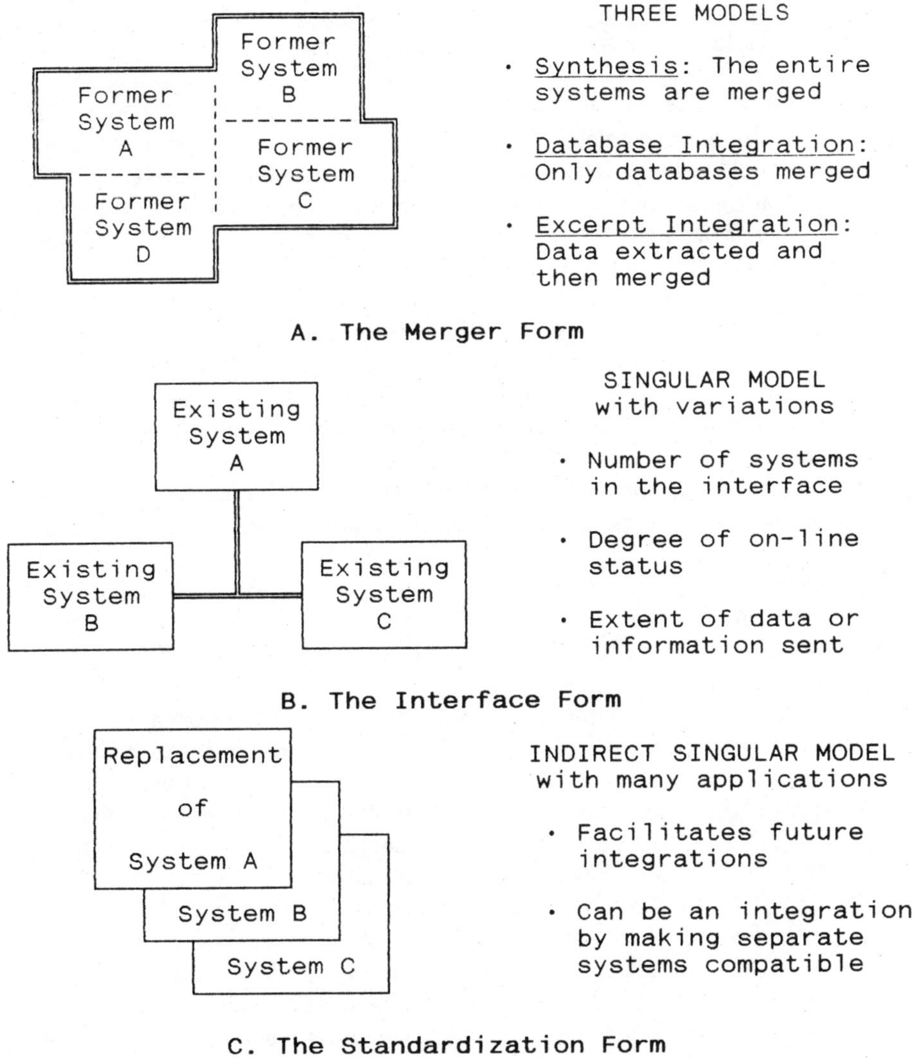


*Fig. 1-7. The three faces of integration. The* integration of systems *is a sweeping term that describes three distinct forms. The merger form aims at symbiosis, where the sum is greater than its parts. The interface form is less ambitious and focuses on the exchange of data or software between existing systems. The standardization form seeks to make the other two more efficient, although when incompatibility is the only obstacle to a latent integration, this form becomes an integration in its own right. The merger form comes in three models: a total synthesis, a database integration, and an excerpt.*

## 1.7 INTEGRATION MODELS

The intent to integrate by merger yields three models: a complete synthesis, a database integration, and an excerpt integration. The interface and the standardization intents are their own singular models. Figure 1-8 provides a summary of descriptions and the key advantages and disadvantages of each. The potential for improving interior lines is strongest in the merger-type models and weakest in the standardization model, except in those cases where the standardization alone solves the problem.

- *Synthesis*. The synthesis model is a new system that encompasses all of the functions and databases of the targeted components. Some elements of the old systems might be salvaged, especially hardware and systems software, but those decisions are made only after the new system is designed. The chief advantage of this model is that it affords maximum opportunity to integrate all aspects of a system, that is, to improve the interior lines markedly. The chief disadvantages are the predictable high cost and the high risk of failure. However, when lesser models of integration will not meet requirements, or will meet them only with excessive electronic plumbing, this option, or alternatively the integrated database, could be the model of choice. Case study C in appendix A, which compares several systems, provides more background.
- *Integrated Database*. The integrated database model does exactly what the name states. All or part of the data of separate systems are integrated into a logically singular unit. From that database, different departments or agencies continue to run their programs, with little need under most circumstances for extensive coordination. A logically singular database does not require a physical integration. The use of distributive processing can compensate for physical separation. Its great advantage compared to a complete synthesis is that the entire development effort can be concentrated on just one objective. As such, it is the *e pluribus unum* of integrations, although in practice applications of this model are rare. The few that exist are in reality originally centralized systems that expanded, sometimes with satellite databases. Still, the potential remains high and is the basis for the hypothetical case study in chapter 21.
- *Excerpt Integrations*. The excerpt model is the simplest and the easiest of the five models to implement. It consists of excerpting data from targeted systems and entering that data into a high-level decision support system or into a centralized management information system. This model qualifies as an integration because either a standardized data element dictionary must be imposed or utility software must be written to convert the input into a uniform layout. The disadvantage is that the higher-level users must accept the degree of quality in the underlying databases. As discussed in case study D in appendix A, this limitation is often acceptable.

| | DESCRIPTION | ADVANTAGES | DISADVANTAGES |
|---|---|---|---|
| SYNTHESIS | Essentially a new system to replace targeted systems. Hardware, software and databases are salvaged only to the extent they still "fit." | Opportunity: (a) to redesign the systems and revise outdated software, (b) to integrate a database, and (c) reduce operating costs. | Normally has the highest development cost and risk of failure. Many projects tend to become ambitious beyond resources and capabilities. |
| DATABASE INTEGRATION | A synthesis limited to databases. The resultant data base might be distributed, but it can be accessed as if it were located at one site. | An optimal solution in most cases. Excepting for uniform data element definitions, each user can write programs independently. | Not useful in the absence of significant overlap among the targeted databases or at least meaningful relatability. |
| EXCERPT INTEGRATION | This model accepts copies of selected data from targeted databases, on a periodic basis to support higher-level management. | Minimum cost, and little need to coordinate the integration with operators of the targeted systems. | The quality or its lack of the data in the existing databases must be accepted "as is," notwithstanding exhortations to the contrary. |
| LIAISON INTERFACE | Often called an interoperable integration, this model joins systems by way of extensive electronic "plumbing" and protocols. | Probably the most efficient means of linking parallel transaction-type functions, where transmission time is critical. | Except for linking parallel functions this model is expensive, cumbersome, and usually inefficient. |
| STANDARDIZATION | Imposes a requirement that all parties use the same type of hardware, systems software, and/or communications networks. | This can lead to both direct and indirect cost savings, and also facilitate future integrations using any of the other four models. | The cost of converting some functions could prove too expensive, or alternatively, require unacceptable compromises. |

*Fig. 1-8. Advantages and disadvantages of integration models. Each integration model offers its own distinct advantages and imposes its own set of disadvantages. The requirements for an integration project, and the condition of existing systems, usually suggest which model will work best.*

- *Interface Liaisons*. The interface liaison model of integration is sometimes called an interoperable integration. It stresses communications among existing computers in order to transmit data, software, and/or outputs among the constituent members. As such, negotiations and ongoing liaison are required to make it work in both the technical and the informational sense. The efficiency of this model depends on how well the interior lines of each component system are linked. If the connecting lines speed up former transactions without introducing offsetting delays, the model will be useful. Case study E in appendix A describes some examples of interfaces, although the potential of applications is vast.
- *Standardizations*. This model makes no pretense of integrating systems directly. It aims only at requiring all or most users in an organization to use the same computers, the same programming languages or other systems software, or the same communications network. As stated, the objective is often cost savings. If so, the savings can be by way of mass purchasing or by reducing the complexity of maintenance or training. Alternatively or concurrently, the objective can be to simplify integrations of a higher-order model in the future. A few examples are described in case study G of appendix A. The Ada programming example in the case study is the largest attempt to date.

## 1.8 SYSTEMS INTEGRATION HURDLES

All five models of integration encounter hurdles between concept and operational status. Figure 1-9 depicts them in general terms. The key to understanding most of these hurdles is the common theme of this book—the sought-after interior lines among divergent systems to effect strategic advantage. Collecting odds and ends in one location or under one umbrella system is not an integration. To earn that name, the pieces must relate to one another logically or physically. For an integration to work well requires clear interior lines of logic, relatability, and transmission. The former without the latter is usually too circuitous.

- *Establishing Strategic Objectives*. An integration, like any system, should produce advantageous conditions in the pursuit of business or provision of services. The integration of the various airline reservation systems, primarily an interface superimposed over a high degree of standardization, offers obvious advantages to all parties, as do most criminal information data banks developed by different police departments.
- *Determination of Necessity*. Systems integration is never a necessity in its own right; not today, not tomorrow, not ever. Necessity should be derived from requirements external to the targeted systems and, further, that can be met only by some form of integration. Unfortunately, the lure of integration for integration's sake permeates many organizations.
- *Functional Disparities*. The necessity of integrating systems with different functions is also questionable, except for an excerpt integration or where they share a common database. Even then, the quality of the data

among the respective systems could vary too much for the integration to be useful. The attempt to merge independently designed single-function programs into one master program typically results in excessive compromise, unwieldy software, monetary waste, disgruntled executives, and disappointed users.

- *Hardware and Software Compatibility*. The integrating of existing systems almost always encounters major technological hurdles, usually in the form of incompatibilities, which include hardware, systems software, data storage formats, database systems, networks and protocols, available times when the components are on-line, and different definitions or legal ranges of values for the same data elements. Every one of these hurdles can be overcome, but as the repairs mount in scope and cost, the resulting integration can price itself out of the market.
- *Management and "Turf" Battles*. Integrated systems, especially those set up as an interface, are inherently more difficult to manage than existing systems. First, the project manager might not have adequate control over the components. Second, all the utilities developed and hardware obtained to facilitate communications are added to the sphere of responsibility. Third, the users of the components can, and often do, grow uncooperative.
- *Implementation*. The most common hurdle here is implementing the integration concurrently with using the targeted systems in their original configurations to meet here-and-now requirements.

Collectively, these hurdles present an obstacle course of sorts for managers intent on integration. To draw on the metaphor of Rudyard Kipling, it is not a matter of filling "the unforgiving minute with 60 seconds worth of distance run." It is more like compressing 300 seconds worth into that unforgiving minute. Ask any manager who has tried it.

## 1.9 POWER CURVES AND TRADE-OFFS

Power curves and trade-offs are, or should be, strongly related. The generalized power curve means that a few elements, measures, factors, contributions, or whatever tend to account for the bulk or essence of any achievement, and that additional effort adds only increasingly small increments of improvement, eventually reaching the point of diminishing returns. Diminishing returns can mean either a decrease in return of investment or a decrease in overall efficiency. Figure 1-10 illustrates the generalized power curve model.

A major application of this curve signifies that only a relative handful of issues need to be resolved to give an information system or integration a fighting chance for success, that is, correct decisions on these kingpin issues will usually prove sufficient to absorb a horde of lesser problems. Conversely, bad decisions prove resistant even to sustained excellence at the working level. Other applications cover the inclusion of data in databases, the number of stations in a network, the number of features to buy in computers, and the scope of a prototype to test a systems concept.

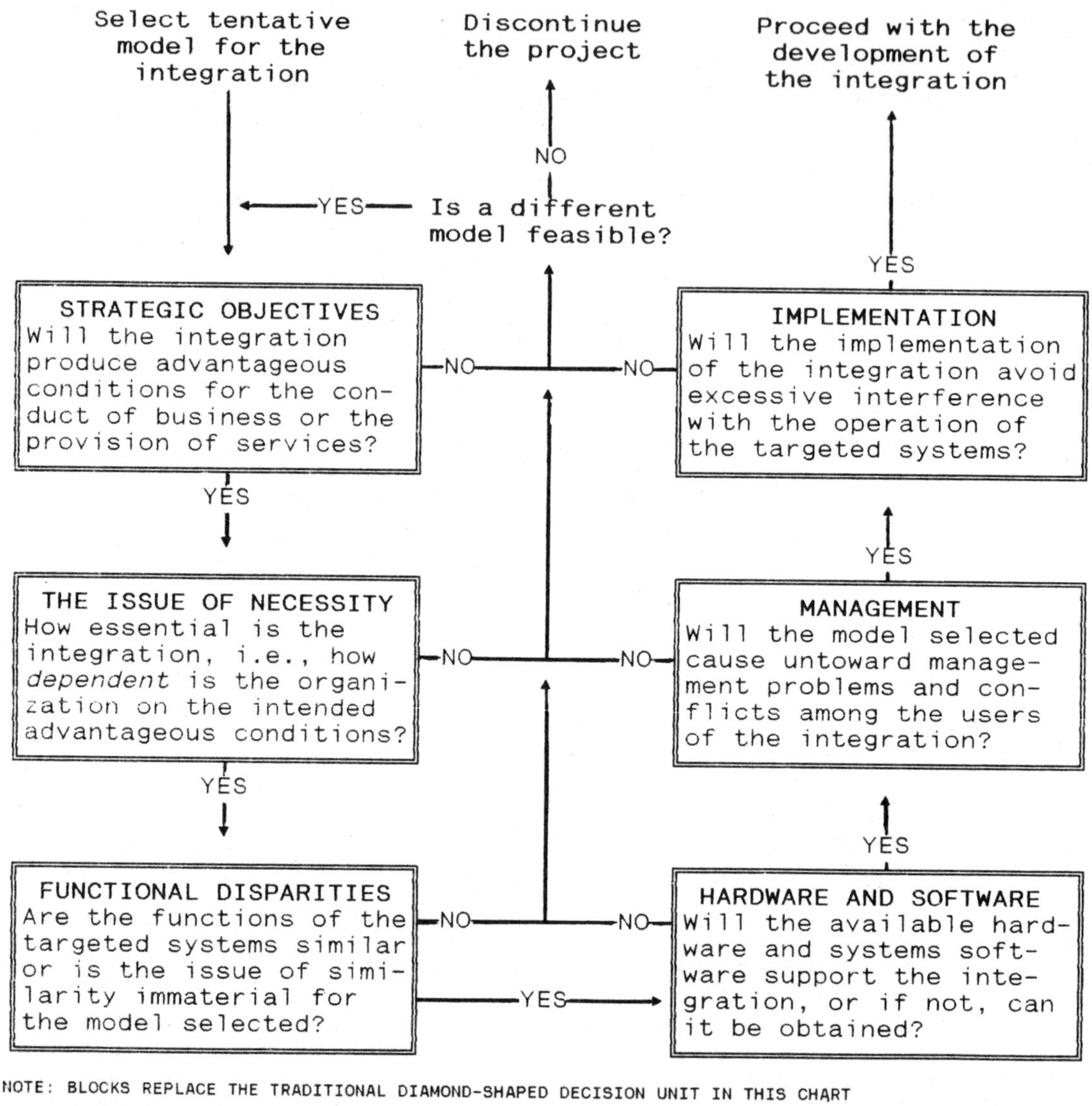


*Fig. 1-9. Systems integration hurdles. Most attempts to integrate existing systems must negotiate six hurdles between concept and implementation. If the project cannot or probably will not clear any one of these hurdles, the planning should start over with a new model.*

The colloquial expression here is "being behind the power curve," meaning the consequences of bad decisions pound the manager into the ground two feet every time he backfills the hole one foot. The implication is that information managers should first determine and then concentrate on the kingpin issues and factors inherently underwriting any major decision, which will reap benefits when it comes to trade-off considerations. Every system mandates one or more compromises. The idea is to avoid comprising on what is important or critical. And so the question becomes: "What dictates the slope of the power curve?" The steeper the slope is before tapering off, the fewer the elements that really count. Hold on to those elements for dear life, and trade on the balance.

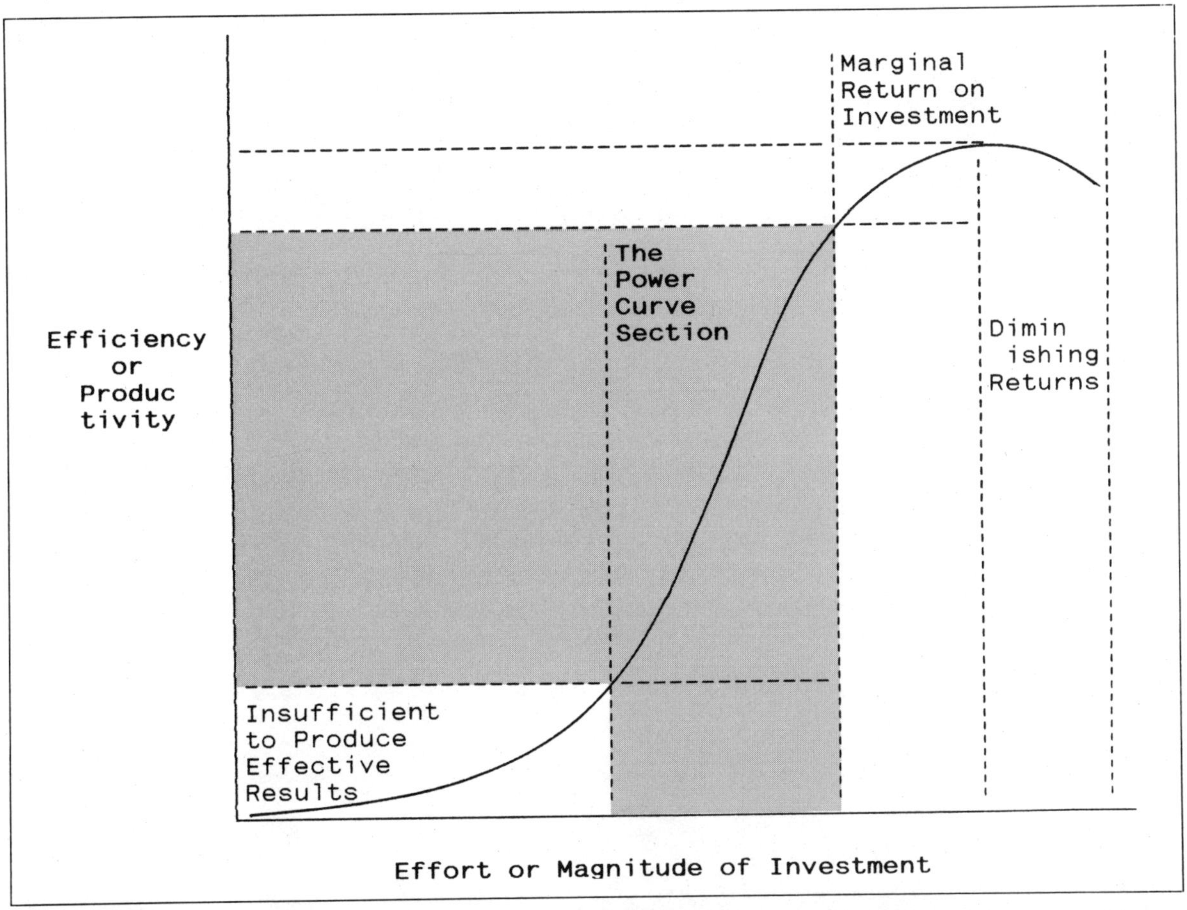


*Fig. 1-10. The general power-curve phenomenon. The relationship of productivity or efficiency is seldom a linear function of effort or investment. That relationship is curved, and though the curve has many forms, each form usually has a steep segment, called the* power curve. *Marginal increases to effort or investment, while on that segment, yield major dividends. Conversely, minor slippage can invite disaster. Beyond that segment, additional investment yields only marginal, and sometimes negative, benefits. The power curve phenomenon dominates computer technology and information systems.*

# 2

# The Application of Strategy

*There are no astonishing ways of doing astonishing things.*
*All astonishing things are done with ordinary materials.*

—Benjamin R. Haydon

Chapter 1 defined strategy for information systems as "the proper utilization and optimal configuration of the information resources of a corporation, institution, or other organization, to produce advantageous conditions in the pursuit of its business or provision of services." It then argued that the central idea of strategy is to obtain better results with existing resources or alternatively, to achieve the same results with fewer resources. But can it be done in practice? Would it violate an organizational equivalent to the law of the conservation of energy? In short, can energy be created?

The questions beg the issue. Energy is not created by strategy. The efficient use of energy is what counts. With that in mind, this chapter posits that the concept of logistics is the key to understanding the application of strategy to information systems. From this concept, six principles are derived. This is followed by five sections that look at: factors affecting strategy, levels of consideration, the issue of necessity, the meaning of functionality, and some issues on technology vs. systems.

## 2.1 THE LOGISTICS OF INFORMATION

Twenty years ago, Peter Drucker stated that developed countries were evolving into information-based societies, a thesis that in part accounts for the proliferation of computers. Information equals permutations and combinations of data and interpretations of it. Hence, data is the core of most, if not all, information systems. If the data in a system is always relevant, correct, complete, and accessible, the system will likely prove worthwhile. If that data is further configured by way of an efficient integration, the results might rate superlatives.

This ideal state is a form of logistics. The term *logistics* may connote the movement of supplies, but conceptually it also applies to information, that is, the important thing is to get the right amount of stuff, material or information, to the right place at the right time. Ironically, one of the best examples combines a particularly insightful application of strategy for information systems with a physical logistics problem. This is the Uniform Product Code (UPC).

This seemingly innocuous bit of technology has nearly revolutionized the retail trade and has permeated many other endeavors. The obvious advantage of the UPC is that it greatly speeds up handling and improves accuracy at checkout counters. Fewer personnel are required to work with the same number of customers. Further, the collection of data has led directly to better inventory control and review of pricing policies. Finally, efficiency has increased to the point where some competing grocery stores have closed.

Beyond the retail trade, many other uses for UPC-code technology have been discovered. For example, some organizations use UPC strips to track paperwork, such as, the Army Reserve Personnel Center in Saint Louis, Missouri. This agency has responsibility for more than ten million records and processes hundreds of thousands of noncomputerized transactions every year (and millions of computerized inputs). It affixes a UPC-like adhesive-backed strip to complex manual transactions and logs them into an automated system. Every subsequent handler again logs the document, so that whenever necessary its status can be determined instantly.

## 2.2 SIX PRINCIPLES OF STRATEGY FOR INFORMATION SYSTEMS

There are no established principles for strategy. This applies equally to geopolitics and information systems. The closest thing would be the principles of war used in defense and military planning. The present wording would not fit systems strategy, but the underlying concepts are tangible enough to cover a wider array of applications. The reason stems from the basic requirement to put the right resources in the right place at the right time, or what the previous section pictured as the logistics of data. The rewording, then, falls into three sets of two principles each. In each set, the second supports the first. Figure 2-1 depicts these three sets.

### 2.2.1 Objective

The defense principle of the objective states that one should "direct every [application of resources] toward a clearly defined, decisive, attainable objective." As terse as that statement might be, it is often violated in practice with disastrous consequences. For example, many historians attribute the ignominious failure of the United States in Vietnam to a failure to formulate precise objectives that were both attainable and decisive.

A computer system that adheres to this principle should make a difference compared to the absence of that system. Further, the organization must have the means to see the project through, that is, the goal must be within practical reach. The principle of the objective thus can be restated, "direct information resources toward objectives that will make a significant improvement in the implementation of policy, at an acceptable cost." Automated systems are a perfectly acceptable form of indentured servitude. They should be made to do exactly what the organization needs done. Case study B in appendix A describes three examples of using computer technology to improve market position directly.

**PRINCIPLES RELATED TO PURPOSE AND STYLE**

OBJECTIVE. Direct information resources toward objectives that will make a significant improvement in the implementation of policy, at an acceptable cost.

SIMPLICITY. Design systems with the simplest possible configuration and directives for use.

**PRINCIPLES RELATED TO INTEGRATION AND INTERIOR LINES**

CONFIGURATION. Configure the elements of a system to facilitate attaining the objectives without undue risk of compromising information to the detriment of those objectives.

RESILIENCY. Organize and direct the application of resources to effect a resilient superiority of information sufficient to prevail in the marketplace or in the provision of services, as the case may be.

**PRINCIPLES RELATED TO MANAGEMENT AND LEADERSHIP**

RESPONSIBILITY. In the planning, development, or operations management of any system. fix general responsibility on one individual, and vest him or her with sufficient control over the necessary resources to effect the objectives.

INITIATIVE. Ensure that a system provides a sufficient and timely view of information to make a significant difference in the conduct of business.

*Fig. 2-1. Six principles of information systems strategy. Six principles, grouped in three sets, affect the success or failure of information systems. Each set comprises a primary and a supporting objective. Most of them are related to interior lines.*

### 2.2.2 Simplicity

Objectives benefit from simplicity, and therefore it is no surprise the defense version of this principle states "prepare clear, uncomplicated plans and clear, concise orders to ensure thorough understanding." One apocryphal tale relates that during the Civil War, General Grant had a mildly retarded clerk review all his orders. If the clerk understood the orders, the probability was high his commanders also would understand them. Restating the principle, then, would yield, "design systems with the simplest possible configuration and directives for use."

Now computer science is a complex field. Thus, it is easy to become enamored of technological dazzle and to seek to incorporate as much as possible of it into a system, overlooking the fact that the "dazzle" itself comes from permutations and combinations of simple roots. The UPC is an excellent example of adhering to the principle of simplicity. Yet for the Nature Conservancy, it was not.

This private organization, which is directed by individuals who pride themselves in being altruistic, hard-headed businessmen, buys land that should be returned to natural or wilderness status. It obtains a small part of its funding from sales in gift shops maintained in some of the preserves. Tracking the sales by way of UPC-type code stickers might have led to increased revenues, but the idea was rejected. The cumbersomeness of it would have detracted from the more important responsibilities of the managers and staff at the preserves.

### 2.2.3 Configuration

This principle is drawn from two closely related defense principles and is the essence of integration. The defense principle of *maneuver* at one time stated "position resources to favor accomplishment of the mission." The principle of *security* is the complement, which advises against letting the opponent get the upper hand. As previously suggested, the opponent in business is the competition. For nonprofit organizations, the opponent is some problem to be overcome or challenge to be met. Whatever the case, these principles suggest arranging resources optimally without significant loss to the advantages existing before the strategy was applied, which implies risk taking.

Not surprisingly, there are times when an organization is justified in "rolling the dice," but at least the decision maker should fully understand the risk he is taking. Therefore, the rewording of the principle should be, "configure the elements of a system"—hardware, databases and programs, and communications—"to facilitate attaining the objectives without undue risk of compromising information to the detriment of those objectives." Police criminal-information systems can be worth ten times their cost, provided they are not readily accessible and updatable by criminals. Even more common are raids on corporate databases and the more destructive alternative of inserting viruses.

### 2.2.4 Resiliency

Resiliency lends both stretch and clout to configuration. The principle advises empowering a system with the necessary capabilities to prevail under difficult operating conditions, and like its mate is also derived from two defense principles. The first is *mass*, which advocates concentrating resources at the decisive (or effective) place and time. The second is *economy of force*, which is the complement of mass, advising that only minimum essential resources be allocated to secondary objectives. These principles follow closely on the heels of the objective, namely that once critical objectives are recognized, the boss is advised to concentrate resources on them. Economize on the balance.

The problem with resiliency is that information systems are established for the long haul and thus compare with what are called military operations. Successful operations tend to discount the value of specific military victories, and instead concentrate on prevailing over time. The difference was once highlighted by Napoleon's lament the day before he evacuated Moscow: "I beat the Russians every time, but that does not get me anywhere." This is no different from business. Successful businesses don't make every sale, but they prevail in the marketplace.

They do this because they have resiliency—the necessary resources, concentrated and expended at the more critical points—to succeed in a sufficient number of efforts. All successful organizations make mistakes, sometimes monumental mistakes. But they seldom make those mistakes by failing to spend sufficient resources on critical objectives, or by betting the farm on a single objective, at least once past the entrepreneurial phase. Hence, this principle can be stated, "organize and direct the application of resources to effect a resilient superiority of information sufficient to prevail in the marketplace or in the provision of services, as the case may be." The telephone communications systems in the United States exemplify this principle in spades.

### 2.2.5 Responsibility

The first four principles addressed systems, the next two focus on the management of systems. The first principle is derived from what defense calls *unity of command*. It states, "for every objective, ensure unity of command under one responsible commander." This principle presumes that the individual has sufficient control over the necessary resources to effect the objective. Thus, to the extent this principle applies to information systems, it can be restated as, "in the planning, development, or operations management of any system, fix general responsibility on one individual, and vest him or her with sufficient control over the necessary resources to effect the objectives." The "amens" will be audible at any distance.

Unfortunately, the tendency in many organizations is to spread responsibility for a project over two or more departments or committees, especially within the government. The consequence is that individual responsibility does not surface until very high on the organization table. At that level, the incumbents usually have greater responsibilities than overseeing a specific project.

### 2.2.6 Initiative

Initiative enhances the effect of assuming responsibility, and as a principle is once more drawn from two defense counterparts. The principle of the *offensive* advises seizing, maintaining, and exploiting the initiative. The principle of *surprise* advises striking the opponent at a time or place or in a manner in which he is unprepared. The application of the former to information systems is nearly self-evident. It almost always takes a certain amount of initiative to create or improve advantageous conditions on a long-term basis. The application of the latter, surprise, taxes the imagination at first glance, except criminal investigation systems and the like.

A deeper look suggests a different perspective. When a business is competing in the marketplace, it should try to beat the competition. In a nonprofit environment, a system should help to resolve problems before they become intractable. For example, as mentioned in the introduction, the faster that computer technology can be applied to the early detection of cancer, the sooner more lives will be saved and medical costs reduced. Thus, the principle of initiative can be stated, "ensure that a system provides a sufficient and timely view of information to make a significant difference in the conduct of business."

## 2.3 FACTORS AFFECTING STRATEGIC PRINCIPLES

At least five factors affect the operation of the derived principles of strategy applied to information systems.

### 2.3.1 Resiliency vs. Flexibility

The principle of resiliency, which advises investing in sufficient heft to prevail in the long run, should not be confused with flexibility. Flexibility implies that objectives can be modified to accommodate shortfalls to resources. By contrast, resiliency means ensuring sufficient resources or alternatives are on hand to meet most contingencies, at least those that would otherwise prove fatal to the organization.

Resiliency does not compromise objectives, although it might shortchange the peripheral odds and ends. A good example of this difference occurs in database design, discussed more fully in section 5.5.

A flexible approach to a database design might employ the network model. This model permits accessing the data in several logical routes. However, when a contingency occurs that cannot be addressed by one of those routes, problems surface. By contrast, the relational database is intentionally structured to permit any logical route into the data, irrespective of the contingency. It does takes somewhat more programming to use it for known requirements, but the return on that investment is extensive resiliency to meet future needs.

### 2.3.2 Improvements to Efficiency

Efficiency seldom adheres to a linear relationship with system improvements. As discussed in the introduction, a series of major changes to a system configuration might produce only minor improvements to processing. Then a final change can yield a major improvement. So it behooves information managers to concentrate on the configuration of a proposed system, including hardware selected, database design, structure of software, and organization of the system with respect to users. Boilerplate corrections to a poorly designed system will seldom remedy its defects, but fine tuning well-designed circuits is an art worth the candle. Chip manufacturers have been doing this for decades.

### 2.3.3 Ergonomic Gap

Scholars have long studied the general problem of man vs. machine, coining the term *ergonomics*. Thousands of dollars have been spent to figure out that data entry error rates at bank teller machines could be reduced by eliminating the push button for the decimal point. Yet little of the research seems to motivate improvements for the much larger problem of dovetailing user requirements with systems design. If anything, the mass of the literature suggests that the single greatest failing of information systems and their managers is insufficient attention and consideration given to users.

This gap is as wide as the cartoons depicting it are numerous, and can only be closed by recognizing that information system managers are managing information more than systems. The latter is only a means to the end of the former. As information increasingly dominates the work of general management, the individual in the center should begin to think more like the man at the top and less like a software engineer, worthy and necessary as they are.

### 2.3.4 Cost Accounting

Good strategy does not exempt an information manager from cost accounting. On the contrary, strategy should lower costs for the same effect, or alternatively provide more effect for the same dollar, which means cost accounting, and cost accounting usually means projecting life-cycle costs. Unfortunately, these long-term costs are difficult to gauge. The factors are often indeterminable and sometimes interminable. Besides, system costs are inevitably underestimated, and benefits overstated. Finally, in large governmental agencies, the price of systems is sometimes disregarded altogether. Perhaps the better approach would be to limit the financial analysis to return on investment, a point that is emphasized in chapter 4.

### 2.3.5 Approaches to Systems Development

In theory, systems should be developed, operated, and maintained systematically. The definition of *software engineer* in the American National Standards Institute/Institute of Electrical and Electronics Engineers (ANSI/IEEE) Standard 729 – 1983 says as much. Yet major exceptions can and do occur during initial planning. It could be a mistake to take too much of a systems approach to formulating the concept and macro configuration for a new system. Albert Einstein, answering the question how he worked, responded simply "I grope." More to the point, the article by Frederick P. Brooks "No Silver Bullet: Essence and Accidents of Software Engineering" (*Computer*, April 1987) convincingly argues that really capable individuals and not rigid procedures are responsible for the best system designs.

Project managers often lament the short-sightedness that discounts the value of a first-rate mind brought on board to create the general architecture for a difficult system. Sometimes the reason is the unwillingness to pay the high salary these few individuals command. Sometimes it stems from an abiding faith in the systems approach. And sometimes it is forced on managers by restrictive directives. Whether these configurationalists are men of genius is beyond the scope of this book to address, but they earn their pay.

## 2.4 LEVELS OF CONSIDERATION

Any system that contributes to organizational goals, particularly if it reduces costs or provides more service for the same cost, has strategic value. This value can be achieved at any or all of the three levels. At the highest level, the strategic benefits typically accrue by using decision support systems (DSS) or high-level simulators. At the lowest level, which is usually transaction-oriented, the return on investment comes from using less expensive computer technology to replace more expensive resources, particularly labor. At the middle level, the application usually depends on interactive programs lacking the scope of a decision support system but a quantum jump ahead of routine automated processing.

Figure 2-2 illustrates these three levels in terms of their respective contributions to strategy. Figure 2-3 then blocks case examples of the three levels with respect to the principles of information strategy. The simplest example of the mid-level application is a spreadsheet configured with "what-if" logic. More sophisticated programs would include executive information systems (EIS). Although the dividing line between EIS and DSS is not clear, the former concentrates on more immediate issues and usually takes far less software development than the latter, which entails sophisticated programming.

Irrespective of these higher levels, it would be a serious mistake to discount the lowest level. A well-designed routine processing system in the long term can contribute more to corporate profits or attainment of nonprofit objectives than the most sophisticated information system. Arguably, the airline reservation systems fill corporate coffers more than the piggyback programs that optimize route planning, although both contribute to profits.

In some situations, the strategic success of a system depends on the integrated use of the same data at all three levels. Perhaps the best example of this was the first application of operations research to a major, indeed a survival-intensity problem. At the time, computer technology was too embryonic to support the work, but the history of the case served as an impetus for the subsequent development of expert systems technology.

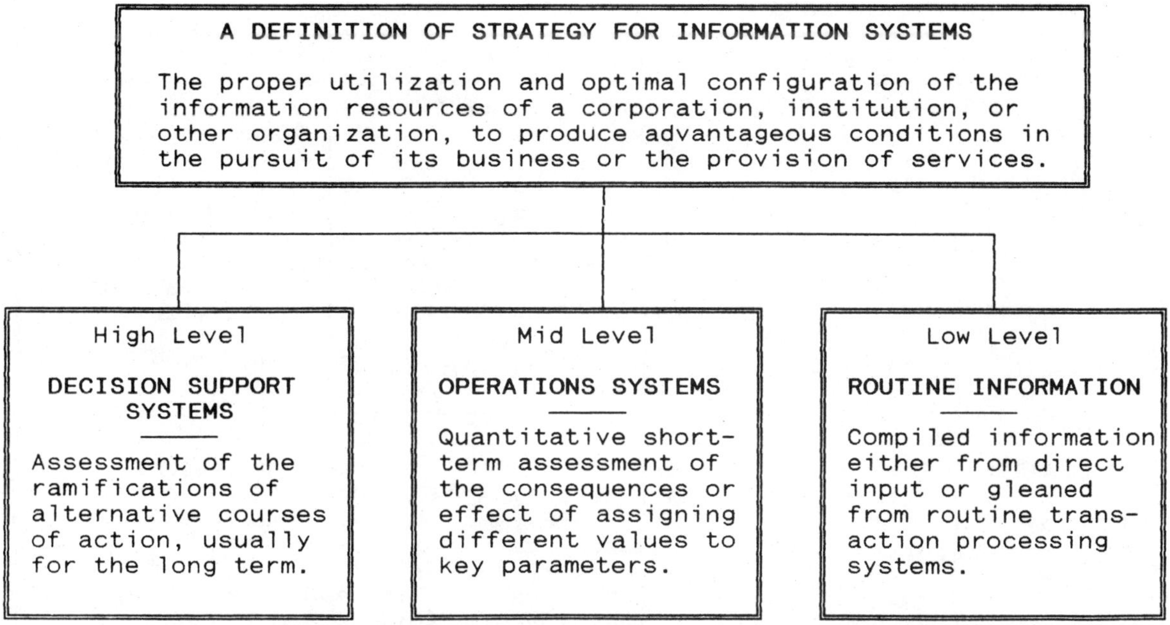


*Fig. 2-2. The three levels of information systems strategy. Information systems strategy operates at three levels: high-level decision support systems, mid-level operations management systems, and low-level routine information gathering, often as an adjunct to transaction processing. The middle level is also known as* executive information systems, *or* executive support systems.

This unusual case occurred during the Battle of Britain in 1940–1941. Winston Churchill said of the Spitfire and Hurricane pilots in that battle: "Never before have so many owed so much to so few." Yet, as F.W. Winterbotham relates in *The Ultra Secret*, underwriting that remarkable performance was a control center working with a level of detail seldom processed even today except by mainframes. Of necessity, every gallon of aviation fuel and every hour of flying time, and from what bases, was rationed, allocated, and reallocated, to effect an optimal defense against the determination of the *Luftwaffe*. When the onslaught was finally turned, Sir Winston had few resources left with which to defend. Great Britain had stood at the edge of her grave. Without this human-powered, three-tier information system, she might very well have fallen into it.

### 2.4.1 High-Level Decision Support Systems

Decision support systems are typically interactive. They present quantitative responses, which might be exact or rated in terms of probabilities, to challenge the user's judgment. This is the current focus of much applied research, which has resulted in computer simulations to hone the skills of chief executive officers by bouncing their ideas against facts and probabilities associated with various business endeavors. The techniques grew out of the basic research in expert systems, and have largely supplanted it outside academic circles. Chapter 12 addresses this at greater length.

<table>
<tr><th></th><th>HIGH LEVEL</th><th>MID LEVEL</th><th>LOW LEVEL</th></tr>
<tr><td>OBJECTIVE<br>Directing resources towards explicit objectives</td><td colspan="2">The various strategic and operational investment buy-sell systems exemplify this principle, though in some circumstances, the collective effect has contributed to "panic selling." The algorithms—not the application of the principle—may be in need of revision.</td><td>This principle is almost automatic at lower levels. Requirements are normally clear-cut and nearly equate with objectives.</td></tr>
<tr><td>SIMPLICITY<br>Designing a system with the simplest environment</td><td>Some of the medical diagnosis and many of the executive decision making simulators operate with maximum simplicity.</td><td>The system used by the Otis Elevator Company for customer support, with its high degree of responsiveness, is a good application</td><td>Automated bank teller machines are a wide-spread example; programming a VCR is not.</td></tr>
<tr><td>CONFIGURATION<br>Arranging resources to facilitate attaining objectives</td><td>The Worldwide Military Command and Communications System, developed 25 years ago, was once a clear leader on this point.</td><td colspan="2">The airline reservation systems, most notably Apollo (United Airlines) and SABRE (American Airlines), exemplify configuration, serving both the low level requirement to book seats, and the operational requirement to evaluate schedules and routes.</td></tr>
<tr><td>RESILIENCY<br>Maintaining resiliency of resources sufficient to prevail</td><td>The ASAP system of the American Hospital Supply Corporation seems to stay on top of a constantly changing marketplace.</td><td colspan="2">Clearly, the telephone communications industry takes top honors here. The systems operate with remarkable efficiency, and do so under peak loads, quickly assessing the situation and rerouting millions of calls over different routes. Failures are rare.</td></tr>
<tr><td>RESPONSIBILITY<br>Fixing responsibility on one person with control of resources</td><td colspan="2">Though Frontier Airlines, Inc., has subsequently been absorbed in a merger, the accomplishments of Lowell R. Shirley, an information systems director, demonstrated the great influence for the good a single individual can exert by accepting responsibility.</td><td>Had not FAA systems managers assumed responsibility despite antiquated equipment, air travel would be dangerous.</td></tr>
<tr><td>INITIATIVE<br>Ensuring sufficient and timely information</td><td>USAA and Chrysler Corporation, among others, have shown a high degree of initiative in systems with long-term benefits.</td><td colspan="2">Systems using the Uniform Product Code technology have proven the utility of taking the initiative for both the low-level function of checkout-counter tasks and for the mid-level functions of optimizing inventory from the mass of data entered by using the UPC.</td></tr>
</table>

*Fig. 2-3. Systems strategy at different levels. The application of the principles of information strategy varies markedly with the level of processing, as indicated by these examples.*

### 2.4.2 Mid-Level Management Operations Systems

Management operations systems respond to simple inquiries. As previously mentioned, the "what-if" spreadsheet can fill the bill, but the Internal Revenue Service offers two complex examples. One has worked with extraordinary effectiveness, the other has yet to prove itself. In the first application, income tax returns are analyzed against related criteria (related to data entered on the return) to identify returns that will likely yield the most additional tax upon audit. Chapter 6, section 1 continues the discussion on this application.

### 2.4.3 Low-Level Routine Processing

The higher levels might enhance the market position or sphere of influence, but they are no substitute for a base of dull but solid information. Probably more than 80 percent of the total computer systems dollar is invested in this level of processing. Therefore, the would-be information systems strategist should ensure that these less glamorous bread-and-butter programs are working at top efficiency.

### 2.4.4 A Hypothetical Case Example

The national budget provides an excellent case for illustrating the three levels of information management:

**Low-Level.** James Miller, the Director of the Office of Management and Budget in the later years of the Reagan administration, kept the essence of the national budget on a Tandy laptop model 200, which had a storage memory of only 72K bytes. As far as can be determined, he used this automated information frequently. Yet most of the analysis was his; the information system provided only organized information.

**Mid-Level.** A mid-level information system could take this information and put it on a spreadsheet to project the national deficit for the next 30 years. These projections would be based on adjusting ten or so critical parameters, such as the amount of the annual deficit, prevailing interest rates, the unfunded share of government pensions, the costs of Social Security, Medicare, environmental controls, the trade deficit, various bailouts, and so forth. Depending on the values assigned to these parameters, the deficit could reach up to $20 trillion in 30 years, or roughly $320,000 per family of four. If the output were used to remind decision makers what needs to be done now to head off the consequences of that large a deficit, the information system would be operational or short term.

**High-Level.** If this program were developed as a decision support system and then used to allocate shrinking resources against increasing requirements with the idea of optimizing the expenditures over a period of many years, it would qualify as a high-level information system.

## 2.5 THE ISSUE OF NECESSITY

Necessity, like beauty, is often in the eyes of the beholder. It can range from a system that is obviously imperative to one that is necessary only for the Chief Information Officer (CIO) to keep his staff and his job. The systems required for the manned space program have been an indisputable example of the former. The editorial in the Winter 1990 issue of *Information Strategy*, appropriately titled "You Bet Your Job," provides a ludicrous example of the latter. The case cited involved a CIO who was told that if he didn't find new work, his staff would be cut by 75 percent and his job abolished. Amazingly, a sizable amount of necessary work was suddenly discovered. Sad to say, the tone of the editorial implied admiration for the CIO.

Resolving issues of necessity can be a tough decision for the information manager. His boss, or his boss's boss, might dictate what is necessary and what isn't. Or the manager might be, and usually is, trying to satisfy the competing demands of different departments. The following subsections discuss some points that might be helpful in this arena.

### 2.5.1 Necessity vs. Risk

Necessity and risk are two different concepts. Necessity measures the extent to which a system compels its own development, i.e., the extent to which policy objectives will fail of implementation or achievement without the system. Risk, by contrast, concerns itself with the probability of success or failure. A necessary system might fail. A totally unnecessary system might succeed, at least in the mechanical sense.

An automated property inventory system for a small firm entails little risk. An inexpensive desktop computer and some equally inexpensive proven software will meet the requirement. Still, the necessity of the system might be questionable, especially if the firm has only 30 pieces of equipment worth inventory status. By contrast, an interactive system to regulate traffic during rush hour in major cities, using continuous update inputs from all traffic areas, could be considered necessary for many sound reasons, but whether it would work well or not is debatable.

Restated, risk is an extenuating or an aggravating factor that can influence priorities, but it is not an aspect of necessity, per se. The sources of this factor vary, but the common denominator is that planners have insufficient cognizance of the environment affecting the problems the system at issue aims to ameliorate. For this reason, building a prototype, as discussed in chapters 16 and 17, might be in order.

### 2.5.2 Necessity vs. Cost-Effectiveness

*Cost-effectiveness* is the measure of the return on investment; that is, how much did the system contribute to the profits, a larger share of the market, or a reduction in the costs of producing the same item. For nonprofit organizations, cost-effectiveness is usually measured in terms of reduced costs in providing the same service or the corollary of providing more service for the same dollar.

Unfortunately, there are many cases where cost-effectiveness is a moot consideration beyond the question of finding the least costly alternative to meet a need. For example, questioning the cost-effectiveness of a system designed to increase the chance of survival for patients in intensive care hospital units might imply an insensitivity to what really matters in life, but the effectiveness of alternative techniques can and should be measured. If the system proves prohibitively expensive, the entire program might have to be scrapped. This is a complex problem. Chapter 19 tries to develop a useful perspective.

### 2.5.3 A Model Scale-of-Values

Necessity does not lend itself to a universal rating scale as does, for example, the pH scale for measurement of relative alkalinity or acidity in chemistry. Thus, the manager that wants a rating scale must develop it himself. Figure 2-4 provides a simple model, one that would have to be tailored to the criteria for success in each organization.

The model in FIG. 2-4 has three scales. The first measures necessity, and ranges from 1 to 7. A "7" rating marks a compelling necessity. No room for doubt can be entertained. At the other end, a rating of "1" means the intent of the system is facetious and could prove debilitative to other policy goals, if only by absorbing funds that should be spent elsewhere.

| DEGREE OF NECESSITY | RISK INVOLVED | COST EFFECTIVENESS |
|---|---|---|
| 7 Imperative, Compelling | A Negligible | $ Highly Cost Effective |
| 6 Urgent | B Moderate | ¢ Reasonably Cost Effective |
| 5 Essential | C Calculated | = Break Even |
| 4 Gainful | D Precipitous | – A Loss Situation |
| 3 Marginal | F Insurmountable | ? Unknown or Unpredictable |
| 2 Hollow | | |
| 1 Facetious | | |

*Fig. 2-4. A scale of values for determining necessity. The issue of necessity is too subjective to warrant an objective rating scale applicable to all situations, but organizations can develop their own scale based on the generic model shown here.*

The second value is a letter grade, ranging from A to F, to indicate the risk involved in fielding the system. A rating of "A" indicates only negligible risk of failure if any, and usually applies to those systems that have proven themselves in similar situations. A "B" represents a moderate risk, and a "C" a calculated risk. A moderate risk would suggest a much better chance of success than failure, but the potential for failure cannot be discounted. A calculated risk means that although the chance for success still outweighs the risk of failure, it will likely take sustained management skill to avoid that failure. A "D" grade means a precipitous risk. Here, failure beckons more strongly than success, suggesting that only the most persevering leadership and sharp judgment can avoid failure. An "F" grade indicates failure is all but certain.

The third value is a symbol. The "$" means the system is or will be highly cost-effective. A suffix of "¢" suggests a modest return on investment. An "=" indicates a break-even situation, with the value of the system measured more in convenience than any discernible dollar savings. A "–" would mark a net loss on the investment in dollar terms, irrespective of the amount. In cases where the return on investment was indeterminate, a "?" would be used.

## 2.6 FUNCTIONALITY AND LIMITS

The term *function* has many shades of meaning. In mathematics, the meaning is precise. Given the precise logic required by most systems, the mathematical definition provides a good starting point. In this definition, a dependent variable is said to vary based on the values of one or more independent variables. Thus, the flow of water from a faucet is a function of the valve opening, the water pressure, and perhaps a few other variables. Similarly, the outputs or products of a system are a function of the data and the programming that operates on that data.

### 2.6.1 Hunchers, Bunchers, and Crunchers

Most systems are based on one of three functions. Systems designed primarily to support decision making can be thought of as *hunchers*. Routine data processing systems, which usually rely on masses of data, are *bunchers*. Scientific models and expert systems that require massive mathematical calculations round out the categorization as *crunchers*. In theory, two or all three general functions can be mixed in the same system, although in the past these functions seldom proved compatible in one system.

The problem lay in how data was used. Decision support systems, at a minimum, required direct-access data files, whereas some management information systems worked on the old batch processing model. When direct-access data was required, a sequential run through the database extracted what was necessary and placed it temporarily in a direct-access file. Scientific programming tended to run the same way, except it was common to copy all the data from a sequential file into a direct-access file.

Further, different programming languages were used for the different functions: typically Cobol for management information (and Cobol still accounts for about 70 percent of all business programs), Fortran for scientific uses, and Pascal plus specialized languages such as LISP and Prolog for decision support systems. The upshot of all this was that programmers tended to specialize in one of the three functions, which created staffing problems for managers.

Fortunately, the compartmentalization of functional programmers is slowly changing. Relational database design can support all three functions at essentially the same time. Different programs can use copies of the same data as appropriate to requirements, although this doesn't mean every system must support two or all three functions. However, certain design efficiencies might work best for specific functions.

### 2.6.2 The Limits of Systems

Pushing a system beyond its design limits is usually a mistake. By way of analogy, entrepreneurs tend to be jacks-of-all-trades. Successful practitioners have some idea of manufacturing, finance, personnel, marketing, and public relations. In most cases, however, these across-the-board abilities eventually prove inadequate. As the company grows, the entrepreneur fails and is replaced by a general manager with a better understanding of the marketplace and the division of labor. The fate of the likable Steve Jobs at Apple Computer, Inc., is a classic example. His technological prowess ranks him among the top two or three computer giants in the country. Apparently his general management ability does not follow suit.

Systems are not much different, especially when managers continuously boilerplate an older, simpler system with many extensions, add-ons, and enhancements. This applies even when the added features are all the same functional type. The original set of interior lines in the system just cannot handle the overload efficiently. It either gridlocks or works only after a fashion. The cost of maintenance and further additions can double or triple. Wisely, the ANSI/IEEE standard definition of software engineering includes the expression, "and the retirement of systems."

## 2.7 TECHNOLOGY VS. REQUIREMENTS

As a rule, existing computer technology will meet any systems requirement. Even the need for ultrahigh processing speed can be met by ganging supercomputers in parallel, multiple-processor arrays. However, these technological field expedients might not be affordable yet, or alternatively the required technology might not be packagable under user-specified size constraints. The "Cray laptop," at $4,995, is still a few years in the future. Three points can be made about technology and requirements.

1) *Distributive Processing.* Macro systems, a network of computers that operates as if it were a single computer, are well within the reach of

available technology today, but the price, in most cases, is prohibitive. As such, many distributive processing networks are substitutes for the ideal macro system until it becomes affordable. Chapters 10 and 14 discuss the implications of this paradigm.

2) *Computer Sizes*. Although computer hardware by itself is the least expensive item in the life-cycle costs of most systems, the choice of mainframe, mini, or microcomputer (including desktop), can have major cost consequences. As will be discussed in sections 3.1 and 9.1, a mainframe computer system entails major personnel and maintenance expenses, whereas desktops absorb the fewest additional dollars. The minis are somewhere in between, closer to the micro than the mainframe. The penalty for buying too small a computer is obvious. The consequence of buying too much is the swelling of the management information budget to take advantage of the excess capacity, the modern equivalent of Parkinson's Law.

3) *Technology vs. the Short-Term Future*. Computer technology is often outdated shortly after it hits the market, although the outdatedness usually applies to the sophistication of the next advancement rather than meeting requirements. Most programs today are run on machines 5 years or older and work admirably well. Some of these machines are 25 years old. Therefore, the manager should ''unfascinate'' himself with technology and instead concentrate on what is required to do the job. Yet, occasionally circumstances warrant an exception to the rule of matching technology to requirements. If anticipated projects will eventually overtax the hardware, buying the next size computer might be worthwhile. On the other hand, if the next lower size computer will shortly attain the capabilities of the targeted size, major cost savings are in the offering. For example, a few firms needing the capabilities of a low-end minicomputer in 1989 waited until micros equipped with the Intel 80486 64-bit-bus chip became available. More on this subject in subsection 8.2.3.

# 3

# The Parameters of Systems

*Then suddenly from the hills,*
*the Harpies swooped down upon us.*

—Virgil
*The Aeneid*

The term *parameters* implies limits, but those limits arise from the action of values nested in functions. A system is a function. Its limits are determined by decisions on a handful of critical values or parameters. Gauging parameters correctly in the planning process means the development and operation of a system has a good chance of adhering to estimates and meeting expectations. Failure to gauge parameters correctly leaves a project wide open to untenable fluctuations. This chapter focuses on the how and why.

Perhaps the best way to understand the operation of parameters is to refer to an ordinary household budget. A budget supposedly sets limits on expenses. What really happens is that a handful of key decisions, or parameters, directly or indirectly set the stage for about 90 percent of household and family items. The budget then becomes a game plan for determining how to buy everything else with the remaining balance. Those decisions are: the price of the home and the attendant mortgage terms, the attitude toward cars and their replacement, the number of children (which is not always a decision per se), and the debt ceiling beyond the mortgage.

The price of the house influences taxes and insurance, and how much is spent to fill it. Next, cars now cost what homes used to cost. Then, the cost of raising children, including college, can easily reach $250,000 each over a period of 22 years. Finally, the high interest on debt, if it were invested instead, would reach sums in the hundreds of thousands of dollars over a period of 30 to 40 years. These parameters do not apply to all families, and sometimes high expenses motivate individuals to seek higher incomes. Nevertheless, the model illustrates the role of parameters.

In systems, parameters are derived from magnitudes, configuration, and priorities. To figure out those parameters, the life of a project, once conceptualized, can be divided into three phases: planning, development, and operation. This breakdown compresses the ANSI/IEEE standard phases for software, which includes requirements, design, implementation, testing, installation, and operations/maintenance. Planning equates with requirements plus the front end of design. Development encompasses the balance due on design, and all implementation, testing, and installation. The operations phase remains unchanged. The front end of design work might be considered macro design, and the balance considered micro design. Figure 3-1 depicts the three phases.

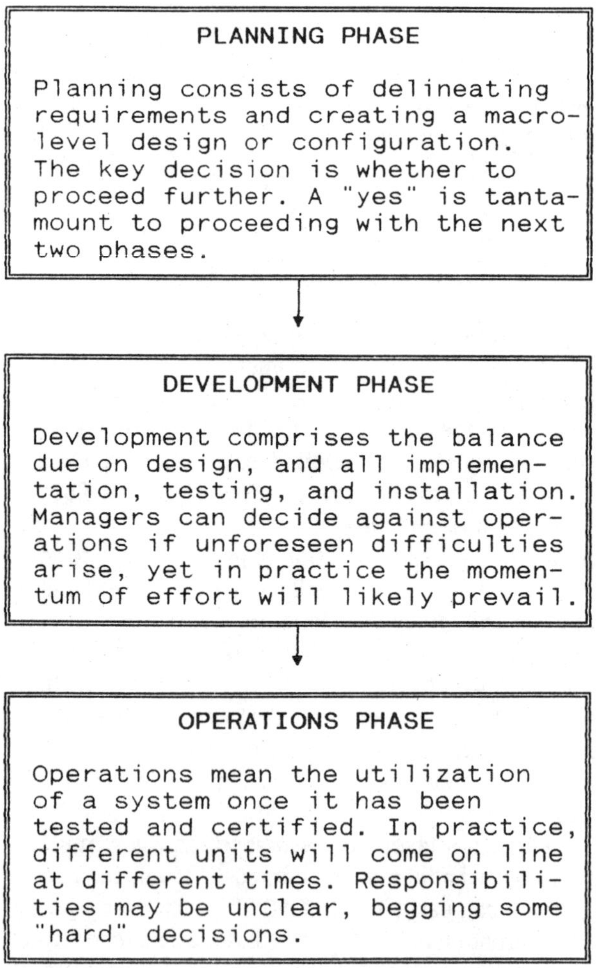


*Fig. 3-1. The three phases of a system. Although many texts and directives break the gestation of a system into several phases, there are only three from a senior management perspective. Each of these phases begins with a pivotal decision.*

Macro-level design clearly defines the parameters implicit in the requirements, although the process can be more of a struggle than the orderly ANSI/IEEE standards imply. Besides, to think of the subsequent development as a pure sequence of micro design, implementation, testing, and installation is a mistake. First, large systems are typically implemented in units, so that the phases overlap. Second, testing begins in the final stages of design, and usually continues in one form or another through the end of installation. Third, the sequence of phases can vary markedly depending if the project is new and self-standing, an extension of a new system, a replacement system, or an integration of systems.

The *keel* of a system, its macro-level design, is laid out from documented requirements. Unfortunately, the word ''documented'' often understates the case. The real world is feast or famine. The information systems manager will either have to pry the requirements out of prospective users, or conversely, fight back hordes of I-want-the-moon-and-I-want-it-now claimants. So the work on the macro-level design often begins without first nailing down the requirements, coupled with a naive belief that the details can be negotiated as the project gathers momentum. The sad consequences of this naivete have been published in many horror stories.

The successful information manager should insist the requirements are delineated in sufficient detail to support calculation of the system parameters. Failing that, he should maintain an active conversation with future users. Figure 3-2 graphs the consequences of inappropriate system requirements. This is the first application of the power curve phenomenon cited in section 1.5, and needs little explanation beyond FIG. 3-2.

- *Computer Capacity and Sizing*. Because of the major cost consequences of mainframe vs. minicomputer vs. micro/desktop computers, determining the appropriate computer size(s) as early as possible is the first order of business. Many systems will require more than one computer, but not necessarily dedicated computers. Some networks will require a mix of different computer sizes. If existing computers are to be used, estimating the processing requirements is even more critical.
- *Number of Stations*. The second item is to establish the minimum number of stations required to make the system work. As the number of stations increases, communication and control tasks tend to mushroom, at least compared to fewer stations for the same processing and database magnitudes.
- *Software Development Requirements*. Packaged software might seem expensive, but it is cheap compared to the cost of developing programs from scratch, which includes extensive costs of testing and validation. Therefore, determining the degree to which programming requirements can be met by existing software is important. The savings can mean the difference between a ''go'' and a ''no-go'' decision.

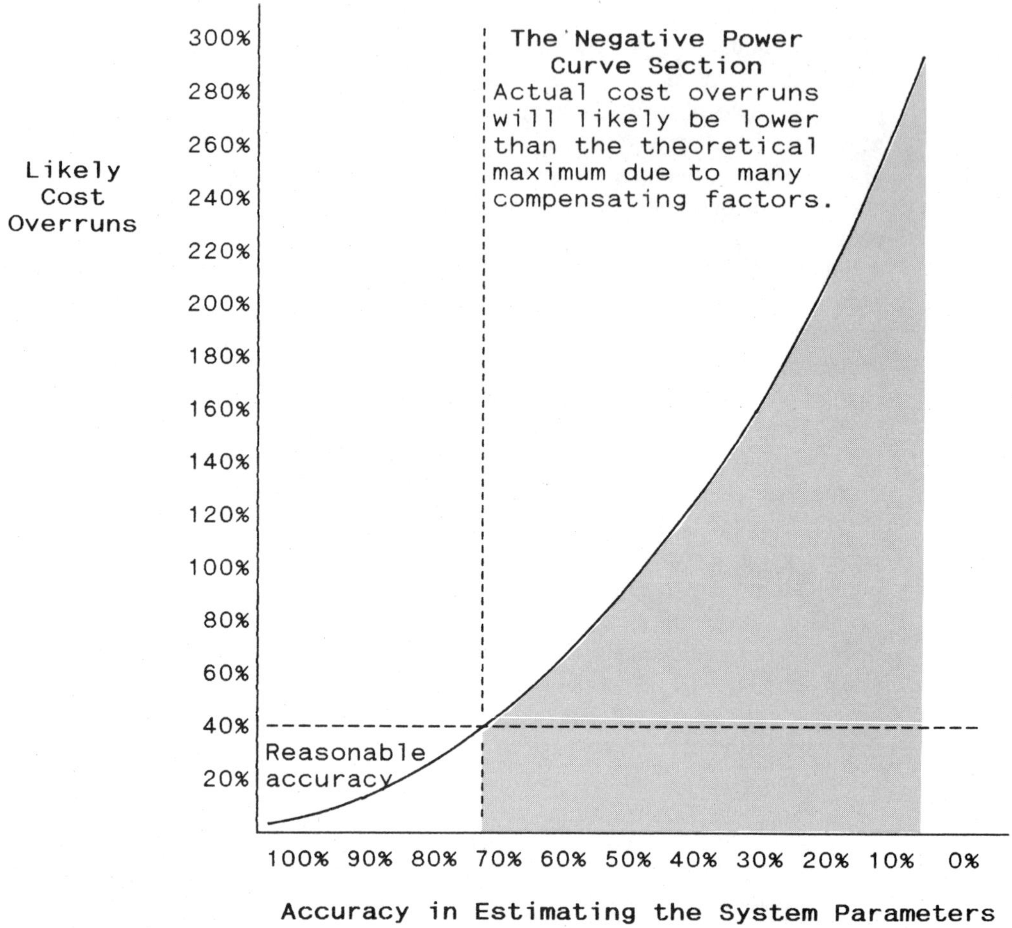


*Fig. 3-2. The power curve of estimating. Good estimating and planning requires an early recognition of key parameters, but the payoff is an accurate projection of costs. Conversely, failure to gauge these parameters correctly can result in cost overruns of up to 200 percent, or even higher.*

These parameters lead to the preliminary estimate of costs and return on investment. Ideally, this estimate should be based on life-cycle costs. Failing that, the minimum requirement would be the estimated development costs combined with the net operational return on investment for the first three to five years. These bottom line answers can be derived from a macroanalysis of magnitudes, configurations, priorities, and constraints.

## 3.1 MAGNITUDES

The determination of magnitudes answers the question "how much?" or "how often?" For planning phase purposes, 90 percent accuracy will suffice. The margin of error can be offset by adding 10 percent for cost overruns. If the system will replace what exists in manual or semi-automated form, obtaining this information might require some digging but at least the information exists. For systems that have no existing manual counterpart—not as uncommon as popular belief would have it—some form of modelling, testing, or prototype might be required. Figure 3-3 summarizes the six types of magnitudes and their relationship to system parameters.

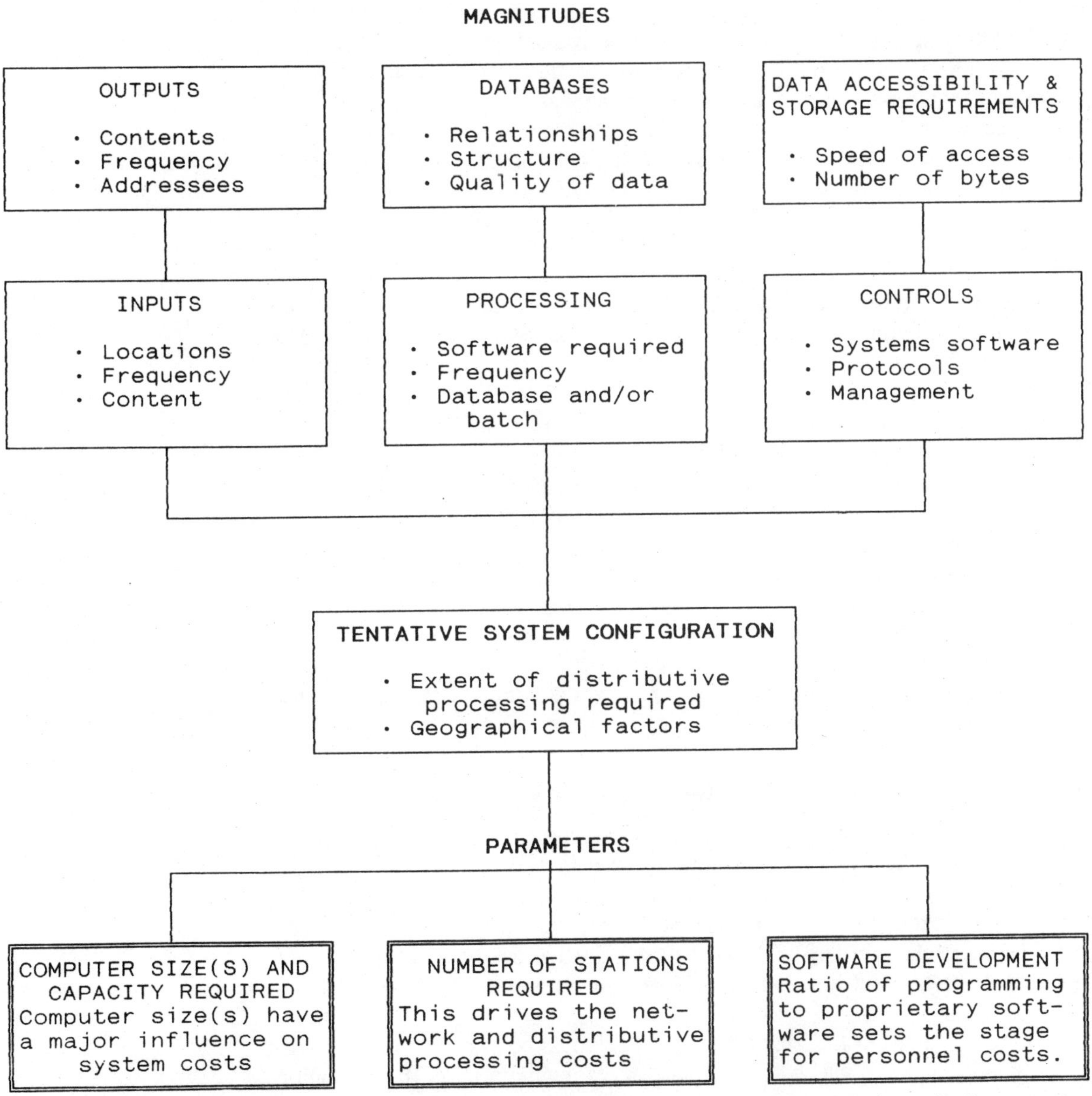


*Fig. 3-3. Magnitudes, configuration, and parameters. Estimating the magnitudes of six items leads to a tentative system configuration, which in turn sets the values for the three parameters common to most systems.*

### 3.1.1 Outputs

Although outputs are the last item in the train of processing, they are the first consideration in planning. Without outputs, a system is futile, although they could consist of nothing more than viewing parts of a database. So, if there is any one place where a minor excess of detail is worthwhile in the planning phase, this is it. Requirements very nearly equate with outputs. The detail includes: the contents of those outputs, the frequency of production or access, and the locations where these outputs must be transmitted.

Unfortunately, some potential users have a tendency to make a wish list for the output requirements. This increases the database and processing requirements, but not necessarily in proportion to existing processing. In other words, a few elements added to an already substantial database can significantly increase the number of outputs at a marginal cost.

### 3.1.2 Databases

Outputs are generated from data, although some of this data can be entered at the time the output is produced. Therefore, this item asks how much data must be *resident* in the system to generate the required outputs. The physical distribution of the data is equally important, albeit as a configuration, not a magnitude item. The quality of the data required is also important, but higher degrees of quality usually entail higher costs.

The common measure of the data storage requirement is the *byte*, which equates with one character of data (or 1/4 of an ordinary precision decimal number). The data storage requirements of the largest systems are measured in trillions and sometimes quadrillions of bytes of data, but they are not always *on-line*. To this total must be added the bytes for the software that accesses and processes that data. This requirement seldom increases in direct proportion to increases in the size of the database. The significance is that as the database increases, and with it the number of users, a larger computer size might be necessary, which can increase costs disproportionately.

### 3.1.3 Data Accessibility and Storage

Data accessibility means the speed and frequency by which data can be accessed. This in turn breaks down into five levels of data storage. Figure 3-4 illustrates these five levels. The higher the level, the higher the expense per byte of data. As the price of the higher levels decreases with time, the tendency is to put more data on line. Yet without an effective database structure, the result could be an electronic McGee's closet.

- *Programming Level*. This means the data must be available within a program; that is, it will be stored in the operating memory of the computer whenever the system is active. The alternative to this is to store the data in *read-only memory*, which is usually an extension of the operating memory. This alternative is common in imbedded programs, such as missiles.

This use is increasing with erasable, programmable read-only memories (EPROMs), admittedly something of a contradiction in terms.

- *On-Line Direct Access Storage*. This usually equates with disk drives that are open when the system is operational. The access time is 10 to 20 times slower than operating memory data, but this is improving.
- *Back-up or Archival Electronic Form*. This means magnetic tapes, which might or might not be mounted and open at the time the system is active. As will be discussed in section 5.1, batch processing with magnetic tape input is much faster than interactive processing with direct access files, except for random updates, which is best done with the direct-access system.

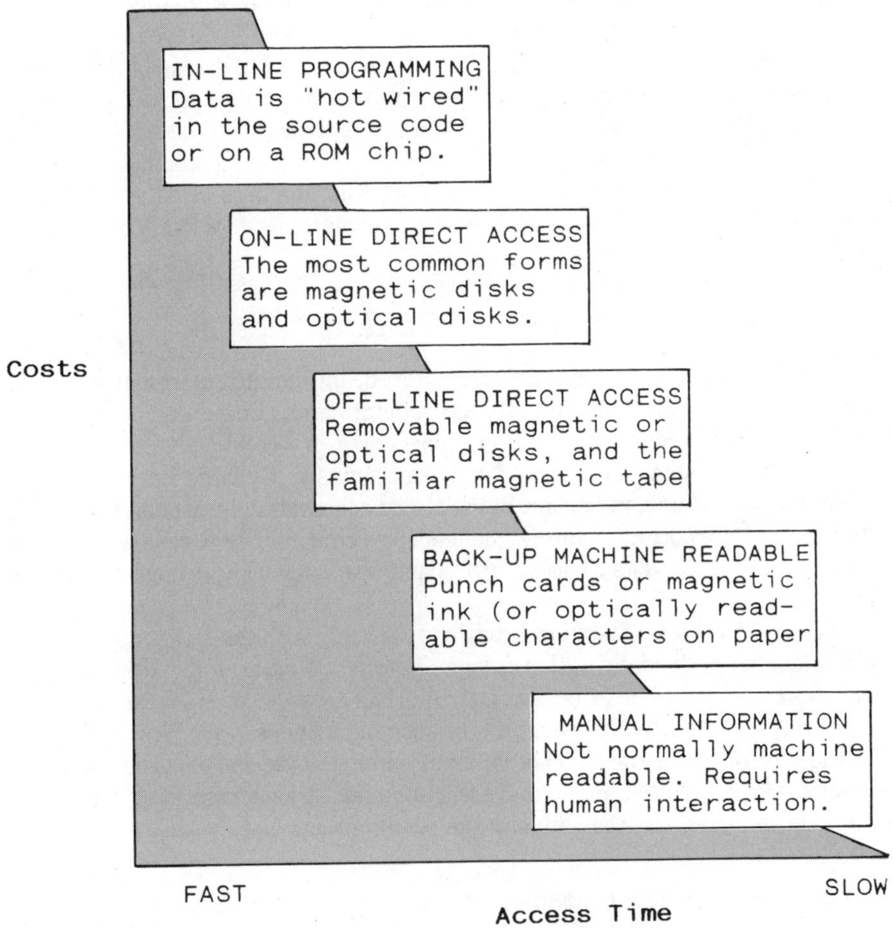


*Fig. 3-4. Levels of data storage. In general, the faster the access, the higher the cost. Probably the widest cost (and access time) range occurs at the off-line direct-access level. At the lowest level, emerging technology increasingly can* read, *or digitally record from oral input, what was once thought as manual information.*

- *Back-up Machine Readable Form*. Strange as it may seem, the punch card and its scan card successors are still used, sometimes as the equivalent of a *hard copy* backup for critical software. The more advanced forms of backup readable data storage include the UPC code and its many spin-offs, as well as ordinary typewritten pages that use state-of-the-art input scanners.
- *Manual Form Only*. This lowest category means either the data is never entered electronically into the system, or is entered only on an exception basis and then usually temporarily. Medical records are a good example, although the trend today is to enter notes directly in digital form.

Optical disk technology and EPROM is changing this picture somewhat, especially for data and information that is seldom updated except to add data. Irrespective of the technique selected, however, the total byte storage requirement is factored upward by specialized formatting and high-speed accessing requirements, and factored downward by storing numerical data in binary format or by *packing* the data. Sometimes the former is due to supplementary index files (as described in technical note 13 in appendix B). The latter sometimes occurs when information managers are forced to use these techniques because of limited storage capacity, although packing vast amounts of data can significantly increase processing and access time, and perhaps denigrate the potential for using relational database structures.

### 3.1.4 Input Requirements

All data in a system must first be entered, but input requirements do not necessarily correlate with data storage requirements. Some data is more-or-less permanent, requiring only a one-time entry or occasional update. At the other extreme, some data is updated continuously. Updates between these polemics fill the entire spectrum. In the airline reservations systems, the names of cities with airports are rarely changed. By contrast, seat reservations are updated continually. The available flights and seats per flight occupy the middle ground.

Also, the volume of input can vary considerably with the location and therefore affect network configuration design. Nearly 600 cities in the United States offer scheduled airline service, but just 10 urban areas account for 30 percent of the U.S. population and an even greater slice of business, which itself accounts for the bulk of airline travel. That is, input estimates are as concerned with the number and distribution of input transactions and the average time it takes to enter those inputs, as it is with storage requirements.

### 3.1.5 Processing Requirements

Processing, apart from that immediately associated with inputs and accessibility, is perhaps the most difficult magnitude to gauge. Sometimes the processing that supports outputs is done in batches before the outputs are generated. In other systems, processing is done only at the time of the output.

The amount of processing can be monumental compared to the size of the output, which is common to many scientific models, or the processing can be minimal, such as in the generation of rosters. Whatever the case, the output requirements dictate how much existing or available software can be used, and how much software must come from original programming. A decision leaning toward maximum use of proprietary software could prove to be the single best means of reducing development costs.

### 3.1.6 Controls

As systems grow in complexity, control, or automated management of the components of the systems, can expand to a major consideration in its own right. Some controls are inherent in various operating systems, database management packages, network software, and the like, but others must be programmed from scratch. The estimate is likely to prove the most technical of the six magnitudes, and the one least understood in detail by general management.

## 3.2 CONFIGURATION REQUIREMENTS

After a preliminary estimate of magnitudes is developed, the next step is to draft a tentative configuration for the system, at least for those involving more than one site. The configuration used will not normally change the magnitudes, but it could have a significant impact on estimated costs. The reason is that as the number of stations and the lines of communication increase, the cost per transaction usually rises. Additionally, the more complex the configuration, the higher the costs of controlling the system. Finally, the slower response times could mandate expensive compensating *fixes*.

On the other hand, if the magnitudes are estimated with reasonable accuracy, subsequent changes to the tentative configuration will not likely cause major changes to costs, unless the increase in the number of stations and lines is major. For example, an increase from 200 to 250 stations will not likely raise total system costs by more than 5 percent, but an increase from 200 to 600 could quadruple the total price. This unwieldy relationship comes from three factors: the effervescent concept of distributive processing, the attempt to substitute communications for good design, and geography in the broadest sense of that term, not to mention the astronomical increase in the number of possible paths of transmission.

### 3.2.1 Distributive Processing and Its Variations

Distributive processing exists whenever two or more computers, separated by more than a few yards, are electronically linked. Even when the second of two units is only a *dumb* terminal, and all the data storage and processing occur in the first unit, distributive processing occurs. In practice, the term is used to describe shared processing among multiple sites.

Accordingly, no single model of distributive processing exists. On the contrary, each application beyond the simplest models displays its own uniqueness.

This variety stems in part from the worthy goal of distributing data and outputs to users rather than have the distributions queue up at a few centralized locations. However, this maximum decentralization loosens the internal lines of the system from an organizational perspective.

### 3.2.2 Communications vs. Processing

Communication networks have become so versatile that at times the ability to transmit is substituted for more efficient processing that could reduce the total system requirements significantly. For example, transmitting extensive data for a local scientific computation is less efficient than computing the result at the storage site of the input data and then transmitting the answer.

A less obvious situation occurs when personnel records are decentralized to plant sites and maintained at the site. Copies of these records, or at least selected data, are then transmitted to the central location of the company headquarters for corporate planning and management purposes. Yet in organizations where transfers are common, a suggestion might be made to consolidate the records in one location and to distribute copies of applicable records to sites where the individuals are located. Some updates could continue to be made locally, but only to transmit the transaction to the central system, except data that is used only locally.

Unfortunately, users might become dissatisfied, which could lead to another try at decentralization. Repeated changes of this kind are expensive and can eventually exceed the initial cost of the system. Therefore, you should think through the optimal configuration while considering the magnitude and inherent distribution of the estimated transactions. The rock refuses to budge; the hard place does not grow softer.

### 3.2.3 Geographical Factors

When the configuration of a system is measured in degrees longitude and latitude, and especially when it crosses national boundaries, a host of additional factors come into play, some of which might result in greater costs. A few specifics illustrate the point.

**Time Zones.** If a system operates only during normal business hours, and several time zones are bridged, then at least the central control point must operate for longer than normal business hours, which can mean higher personnel costs.

**Climatic and Weather Conditions.** This item might seem far fetched, but when a system stretches into regions where weather extremes exist, hardware and communications equipment require specially controlled environments.

**Customs of Foreign Countries.** This source of problems can range from an "unwritten" rule to use the host country's facilities at high prices, to unusual laws, or to language problems, such as employing local personnel who cannot speak English sufficiently to operate the system. Many nations have imposed severe restrictions on transborder transmission of electronic data.

## 3.3 PRIORITIES AND HIERARCHICAL REQUIREMENTS

Priorities might or might not have a major impact on the general scope and cost requirements for a system. What is important is to determine which priorities will have that impact. The next six subsections describe the wide range of situations where issues of priority arise.

### 3.3.1 Database Hierarchies

Database structures are described at some length in sections 4.2 through 4.5. For reasons outlined in that discussion, the relational database model should be used unless there is a compelling reason to use another model. Other models tend to restrict the utility of the system and can increase the cost of processing any requirements that are at variance with the built-in hierarchies.

### 3.3.2 Processing Priorities

When all requirements have equal priority and there are no time constraints, processing can proceed in the order entered, and outputs distributed whenever the queue permits. In practice, systems are not set up this way. Elevators in office buildings provide a good analogy. Delayed elevator service can result in an exodus of lessees, hence elevators must be designed to handle peak load demands within certain time constraints, which require overcapacity.[1]

Similarly, most systems will have priority requirements. In a personnel system, the entry of a record for a new hire or an update to show an employee has left the firm will have a higher priority than an update for a service award. If this seems like an irrelevant point, consider the personnel system for a major corporation or government agency. The active records number in the hundreds of thousands and sometimes exceed a million. In these large systems, processing priorities loom large. A failure to get a handle on these priorities can result in expensive changes later.

### 3.3.3 Computer Usage Priorities

Except for microcomputers, few systems have dedicated computers. Accordingly, even if computers are made available without a constraint on the amount of time, when the computer can be used, or the waiting times generated by higher priority users, can create problems.

---

[1]The issue of impatience can be severe. Research at the University of Texas measured the effect of delays with interactive data processing on both so-called type-A and type-B personalities (who are supposedly more calm and serene than type-A people). The results proved the latter lose their patience just as intensely as the former. The only difference was the amount of time it took.

The implications of this research for management are that all executives will likely become impatient when they must wait too long to obtain results from a computer terminal, which is another reason to hedge bets on potential interfaces intended for management information purposes. Many, if not most, of them increase waiting times.

The Pentagon offers an extreme but not uncommon example. Top Secret clearances are required by all personnel using some mainframe computer systems in that building, even if the work being done is unclassified. As such, a user cannot leave a terminal until the log-off is accepted. At times the wait can be up to 45 minutes. When this involves nonexempt employees of a contractor, the government is billed time-and-a-half. The point is, a system should be configured with respect to time, as well as with respect to space. If the intended computers are overloaded at the critical times, some processing might have to be done earlier.

### 3.3.4 Communications Priorities

The problem of communications priorities is closely associated with the problem of computer usage priorities, except that alternative routing is usually available, even if it is on an ad hoc basis. More significantly, if crucial messages or outputs are not routed timely, the worth of the system could be called into question. Perhaps the quintessential example from precomputer days was the delay in transmitting from Washington to Hawaii on December 7, 1941, the warning of a possible Japanese attack. Less dramatically, companies have lost bids on major contracts because of delayed transmissions.

### 3.3.5 User Priorities

Conflicts among users for priorities can be serious. More than once, participants have ceased using a system because of its inadequacies, and withdrawn their funding for it, overtaxing the remaining users. Even when this does not occur, shifts among user priorities will likely prove the rule more than the exception. Accordingly, the project manager needs to build as much resiliency into the system as possible. Resiliency is the byproduct of interior lines.

### 3.3.6 Resource and Implementation Priorities

Every experienced information manager is acutely aware of the conflict over priorities for resources to implement a new system. Further, certain phases of a system can have a priority for implementation, although this sequence can introduce major inefficiencies from a systems viewpoint. Thus, if certain data can be computer generated after all the required data is entered in the completed system, and a higher priority phase must be implemented before that supporting data is entered, the required data must be collected and entered on an interim basis.

## 3.4 THE EFFECT OF CONSTRAINTS ON SYSTEM ESTIMATES

More often than not, systems are developed under one or more major constraints. A constraint can require the use of truly antiquated computers, even buying an additional computer or replacing the old one would be cheaper. Air traffic controllers have had to live with this constraint for years. Or the organization might require a specific programming language be used, even though the available programmers might not be adept in that language. Or perhaps the system must fight for communications time on already overloaded circuits.

Overall, these constraints will tend to raise costs and cause the system to work with less efficiency than specified. Some managers cede the argument, but claim the constraints simplify the planning process and can lower the total costs to the organization. Perhaps so, but to the individual responsible for a specific system, these constraints will impose some of the following problems.

**Effect on Magnitudes.** Constraints tend to affect the calculation of magnitudes in several subtle ways instead of one extraordinary obstacle. For example, if on-line direct access data storage is limited, a slower form of access must be used or the processing will have to be routed to another location.

**Configurations.** If established communication nets must be used to compensate for insufficient hardware capacity at critical points, the result could be an expensive and cumbersome distributive processing configuration.

**Priorities.** Priority constraints take many forms. They can include a generation of reports for senior management, although the value of those reports is questionable. Priority constraints can overload a system and cause the manager to seek alternative and perhaps unnecessarily expensive means of meeting more important needs.

As computer equipment proliferates and networks become established, constraints are more likely to increase than decrease. Thus, the information manager will inevitably be faced with the need to make trade-off decisions, which is something of an art and a science.

## 3.5 ADDITIONAL FACTORS AFFECTING SYSTEM REPLACEMENT

Managers who discount reincarnation have never replaced an existing system. In theory, a replacement system should eliminate the inefficiencies of the old one and make room for new features. In practice, some of these procedures will have assumed Brahmin status: they creep back into the new design and must often be accommodated at high cost.

**Magnitudes.** The most common problem with magnitudes is retention of data and reports that have lost utility. If necessary, uses will be invented to retain them, although it might be possible to downgrade the storage media for the data. On the other hand, certain ancient data can remain valid. A recent attempt to eliminate the system of payments to Civil War widows was challenged. The manager explained that a few drummer-boy veterans, upon reaching their 80's, had married very young girls for the sole and legal purpose of bestowing the survivor pension on them. Some of these girls have lived into their 80's and are still entitled to those pensions. A few might live past the beginning of the twenty-first century.

**Configurations.** A common problem is the relocation of personnel who manage the various stations of an older system. A replacement system might work best with an entirely different configuration, but relocating these personnel could entail an expense out of proportion to the benefits of the replacement system.

**Priorities.** The most common problem with priorities is the schedule for replacing the old system with the new, particularly when the same hardware and software must be used. Converting existing systems, for example, can take as much work, if not more, than the original programming.

## 3.6 ADDITIONAL FACTORS AFFECTING SYSTEMS INTEGRATIONS

The planning process for an integration is no less difficult than for a new system or replacement. The work saved on determining all the requirements is replaced by the tedious adjudications for new priorities. Next, the configuration itself can prove to be a major task. Lastly, if the necessity for the integration is not compelling, turf battles will likely consume an inordinate amount of the information manager's time.

### 3.6.1 Syntheses

The planning phase for the synthesis model encompasses the equivalent of a design for a new system plus the drawn-out discussions over what can be salvaged and what can be kept, and of the latter, how much modification will be required. The tendency to salvage as much as possible is psychologically stronger than the cost-savings arguments that can be marshaled against it. Therefore, the best thing that an information manager can do is to develop a comprehensive design that salvages nothing, then compare alternatives to that ideal as a baseline, and lastly to identify the optimal trade-off points.

### 3.6.2 Database Integrations

In database integrations, the magnitudes should be reduced by way of decreasing redundancies, but if distributive processing is used, the configuration is apt to be complex. For example, the existing hardware and systems software could prove inadequate to handle the consolidated load. If constraints bar obtaining the necessary technology, the old stuff must still be used, and that will mandate compromises that can severely denigrate the efficacy of the interior lines essential to making an integrated database work well. The point is, as harped on in section 1.7, most integrations entail aggravating circumstances, if for no other reason than targeted components are seldom designed with integration in the forefront.

### 3.6.3 Excerpt Integrations

Excerpt integrations are the easiest to plan. Usually the integration will be built from scratch, and therefore the only pressing issues will be the media used and the frequency for obtaining updated copies of the necessary data. However, if the sum of the excerpted data accumulates beyond the capability of available hardware and software, new technology might be required. And if logical compatibility among the targeted databases is a problem, the cost of the necessary translation utility software also needs to be included.

### 3.6.4 Interfaces

Integrations using the interface model will increase magnitudes and introduce a host of configuration requirements. The largest magnitudes will likely be the conversion or transmission software that enables the systems to communicate with each other. The configuration will be the network that enables communications. Even when all this is workable and affordable, priorities must be established, even if none previously existed.

As implied in subsection 1.6.4, attempts to interface existing systems take on heroic proportions, unless the functions evince a high degree of compatibility, given a compelling necessity for integration. If the planning phase fails to show this amount of work, the information manager should start raising questions.

### 3.6.5 Standardizations

Planning for a standardization project should proceed in two steps. The first step is to select the tentative hardware, software, communications, or data element dictionary that can accommodate existing functions and programs. The second step is to gauge the cost of transforming each item of what exists into the standardization. Usually a few exceptions will be necessary. No single way of doing business is likely to satisfy all requirements. The Department of Defense's imposing the use of the Ada programming language on its new systems has been a significant and far reaching attempt at standardization, but to date the exceptions and aging of older programs outweigh the programs written in that language.

## 3.7 OPTIONS WHEN A PROJECT APPEARS INFEASIBLE

The odds are that any proposed system will prove more expensive and difficult to implement than anticipated, even if the return on investment can still make a project worthwhile. When the planning work suggests the return will be negative, and there is no compelling reason to accept that loss, five options are available:

1) *Alternative Financing.* Alternative financing means either placing other projects on a lower priority or increasing debt.

2) *Scale Down.* This option eliminates lower priority features. Unfortunately, too many cuts to reach an acceptable price might leave the resulting system short of the stated requirements.

3) *Stretched Implementation.* Stretching out the project could be the best solution. This option retains the required features and puts the cost within range over the long haul.

4) *Redesign.* In cases where alternative funding is unavailable, neither cuts in features nor delays in implementation are acceptable, and the project is imperative, the only practical option is to redesign the system or integration to make it work within the constraints.

5) *Postponement or Cancellation.* This option is the simplest solution, although in most cases, postponement beyond a short time is tantamount to cancellation. Most projects that can be postponed indefinitely tend to have marginal necessity. The exception would be those few times when the required technology is not yet available.

Irrespective of the option selected and for reasons detailed in section 20.2, the end of the planning phase marks the last real chance an organization has to redirect its efforts. After the development stage begins, a system picks up momentum, even with major cost overruns. The kill fee is too high in psychological terms.

# 4

# Return on Investment

*A billion dollars here, a billion dollars there,*
*and pretty soon you're talking about some real money.*

—A Congressional aide for the Appropriations Committee

Life-cycle costs for any system designed to last more than a few years are difficult to estimate. Too many uncertainties and unknowns operate on systems to warrant long-term analysis. Nevertheless, because costs tend to be underestimated and benefits overestimated, it behooves managers to pay closer attention at least to development costs and the operating costs for the first three to five years.

The anticipated return on investment for the same period also needs to be calculated. For profit corporations, if the net return on investment doesn't cover the development costs within the same period of time, the long-term financial effectiveness of the system is questionable. For nonprofit organizations and administrative systems within profit-oriented companies, the same criterion applies, except that return on investment usually means the net value of the improvements obtained compared to having had invested the cost of development in other projects.

Restated, every system should return in savings or in profits more than it consumes, unless there is a compelling humanitarian reason or reason of state to accept the loss. Even in these cases, the goal should be to reduce the cost or increase the influence of the means previously employed. Otherwise, the funds should be invested in more beneficial projects.

Unfortunately, although the concept of return on investment is clear enough to calculate for fungible securities and perhaps for organizations as an entity, it is anything but easy to calculate for a system within an organization. First, the allocation of costs against specific systems is not always well defined.

Second, gauging lost opportunity costs, the losses from not having invested the money elsewhere, is difficult. Third, the contribution of the system to future profits, or expanded or improved services, is hard to project and difficult to untangle from other factors. These uncertainties plague every large business, and permeate their nonprofit counterparts.

Chapter 19 addresses this and other related subjectivity problems, suggesting that a manager is obliged to quantify alternatives as far as possible before attempting a qualitative judgment or trade-off decision. Yet systems can affect costs in ways that defy any form of plausible quantification. For example, what is the proper cost-accounting entry for the backlog that accumulates in information systems departments because of back-filling excess computer capacity with less-than-essential work? Or how does one value the "hunch" of an insightful manager when it proves successful, or conversely the poor judgment of another manager when the company outgrows his perspective?

At this point, the irked systems manager could throw in the towel, with the proviso an organization should simply invest in systems that appear to offer the greatest potential and dismiss detailed cost estimates "as not worth a hill of beans." Don't tell that to a cost accountant. The latter will ask how high the hill is, and if you say "15 feet," he will respond, "Assuming a conical shape, a 1-to-3 slope, 42 pounds per cubic foot, and 75 cents to the pound, those beans are worth approximately $1,001,971.71 retail." In the process he will imply your attitude about that precious hill is entirely too casual and perhaps flippant, and that if it's coffee beans you're talking about, it's a whole new ball game.

By all means, throw him out of your office, but do not fire him. His intent is to save your skin and to keep the company coffers in the black. In other words, irrespective of how difficult gauging costs can be, the manager must persist in doing so, at least to the point of calculating the anticipated return on investment. There is no other way to compare alternatives. With that justification in mind, this chapter examines direct costs, the dominant cost factors for systems, indirect costs, return on investments, special considerations for integrations, and a quick look at computer models for cost estimating.

## 4.1 THE DIRECT COSTS OF PHASES

Delineation of costs must begin by eliminating one category that many planners are inclined to include: investment-to-date. Prior investments are sunk costs and have no place in this form of cost analysis except the salvage value of equipment on hand or personnel costs that might be reduced in the future. The lamentation, "we have already invested thus-and-thus dollars in this system" is altogether too common. Yet beyond the minor exceptions noted, there is no way to recoup that investment. It is gone. The only legitimate data for a projection is a future cost.

A comparative analysis compares the cost of continuing with a system with one or more alternative courses of action measured from that same date forward. Further, most planning costs should be considered as sunk costs. A certain amount of planning is necessary before a cost estimate is feasible, and after that point is reached, the costs that led to it are gone. Therefore, direct costs should be divided into the latter two phases outlined at the beginning of chapter 3: development and operations.

One last general point. Estimating costs is not a prelude to preparing for the Certified Public Accountant examination. Estimates are just that, estimates. They do not require ledgers, audit trails, double entry bookkeeping, or other procedures that go with good accounting practice. Objectivity, more than the proverbial green shade, is what counts.

### 4.1.1 Development

The costs of development equal the translation from the macro-level design derived from the requirements in the planning phase to a system that works to meet those requirements. It does not normally include maintenance expenses or corrections to minor errors identified after the system is certified as operational. This bracketing is plain enough for operating expenses (not to be confused with systems operations), but it can squirm when it comes to capital investment.

For example, if a computer must be purchased to implement a system but must be obtained during its development, what portion of it should be attributed to that phase, especially if it will be used for other programs? Should it be based on a periodic depreciation figure or on the full cost? If the project fails, will the computer be used elsewhere? Unfortunately, there is no universal rule. Every organization has its own cost allocation rules of thumb. What is important is to avoid making a project look better or worse than a fair application of those rules would yield. Also, the conscientious information manager need not be too concerned with detail, as long as his cost accountant is.

### 4.1.2 Operations

Accounting practices for identifying operating costs vary somewhat from development costs, because of the wider net that working systems sweep. Development costs are usually restricted to a specific department in an organization (or alternatively contract costs) plus any capital investments. Operations costs can intrude into every department in an organization, down to and including the cost of personnel entering data.

Yet the cost allocation practices of each organization will probably work for the operations phase as it does for development. Again, the manager need have little concern with the details. What remains important is that the costs included are as honest an estimate as possible. Even at that, estimates should be increased by some factor developed from organizational experience. The tendency is to overlook some items and underestimate others. Fortunately, if the estimates are conscientious, then notwithstanding occasional bias, the bias should apply evenly to the cost estimates of the alternatives.

The one really difficult issue is setting the point in the future to end the estimate. For very large systems, a period longer than five years to regain development costs might be justified, especially if the capital investments are heavy. Again, the organization is likely to have its own rules of thumb. Yet each year added to the length of time necessary to reach the break-even point is a vote against launching the project.

### 4.1.3 Expansions and Enhancements

Systems rarely operate more than two years, if that long, before they are modified, expanded, or enhanced. Minor changes come under the heading of maintenance, which is usually considered part of the operating costs. By contrast, overhauls are major changes and should be considered as equivalent to a new system. When the project falls under the latter category, the cost estimating procedure should differ from a new system only in one respect. The operating costs are the net costs after subtracting the costs of continuing to operate without the changes. Estimating the development costs would not differ, except perhaps if the development work impinged on current operations.

## 4.2 THE DOMINANT COST FACTORS

At one time, computer hardware was the dominant cost factor for systems. The earliest programs consisted of setting switches in the computer. Software did not exist and communications went by mail or by telephone. Also, personnel costs were only a fraction of the hardware. These costs have changed dramatically.

Today, hardware costs are reaching toward a mere five percent of the total information systems budget. A $60,000 minicomputer, which is a one-time capital expense, barely exceeds the annual salary plus benefits of one senior programmer, and the former is dropping while wages increase.

Yet the old notion that remains is surprisingly strong. Antiquated computers are often maintained, even if they lead to extremely high operating costs. For example, a minicomputer priced between $40,000 and $100,000 and requiring little operating expense can easily exceed the capabilities of an old mainframe, which requires full-time operators and entails many indirect costs. Sometimes continued reliance on these relics could double or triple the systems budget.

In short, and with one major exception, cost estimates for projects should not be too concerned with the computer and its peripherals. What runs the bill up on systems are personnel, software, and in many cases, communications. Contract costs also can be high, but that is misleading. Break the bill down, and what you see is personnel and software. Moreover, these costs are interrelated. Reliance on older programming languages or programming from scratch can significantly increase personnel costs. By contrast, reliance on higher-level languages and packaged software can greatly reduce them.

The exception to hardware occurs when too large a computer is obtained. As mentioned, mainframes and some minicomputers require operating personnel, whereas the smaller minis and essentially all micros do not. Also, systems software can cost 100 times or more for a version designed to operate on the bigger machines compared to the desktops. For example, a Cobol compiler for a mainframe or mini costs a minimum of $50,000. A desktop version can be bought for $500. Finally, mainframes and minis have a way of encouraging the development of large information systems departments, whereas decentralized micros can be serviced by contract.

Communication costs give the appearance of being more orderly, which is misleading. Excessive reliance on distributive processing, which is sometimes necessary due to constraints to continue using outdated computer hardware, can obviously increase communication costs unnecessarily. It can also increase the requirement for operating personnel and the software to make it work.

### 4.2.1 Personnel Costs

Except small systems, personnel and other labor costs will dominate the analysis. Labor intensive software is becoming increasingly sophisticated in what it can do, and skilled personnel rate higher and higher salaries, partly because the demand is outpacing the supply. As mentioned in the introduction, the average size of the management information departments in the second 500 companies of the Fortune 1000 is 50. If the mean cost of paying, benefiting, and equipping one skilled individual is $90,000 per year, then the average annual total personnel cost (direct and indirect) for these departments is $4.5 million. Added to this cost are the personnel costs of users and the personnel slice of any contracts. For the companies in the upper half the Fortune 1000, you are talking about some real money.

### 4.2.2 Software Costs

Purchased software, for applications and systems, is comparatively cheap. A language compiler for a mainframe is priced in the $75,000 range, but the cost to develop and maintain a first-rate language compiler would be at least $10 million. The development of Cobol over the last 30 years probably represents a total investment well in excess of $250 million. Few organizations make that mistake, but many fall into the trap of writing applications programming from scratch when proprietary software is available at a much lower total cost. Even when the former course must be taken, higher-level languages, and the systems software that generates applications software, can significantly reduce these costs. Yet personnel costs will remain high, if only for the tasks of design, coding, and testing. Whether the manager chooses to call these costs software or personnel is immaterial.

### 4.2.3 Communication/Network Costs

Pure communications costs, apart from any software and protocols necessary to make networks and interfaces among computers work, can vary from an occasional telephone call using a modem to millions of dollars per month. A few companies own satellites and a larger number sign long-term leases for part of a satellite's relay capability. Other companies install their own fiberoptic cables.

The cost of transmitting one byte of data over a fixed distance has been falling in absolute terms for the past 30 years, but this is offset by an even greater increase in traffic. It has been said that making the communications industry work today using the manual procedures of 50 years ago would take the entire work force of the United States. Some analysts restrict that calculation just to telephone communications. For the information manager this means that communications for systems, especially integrations of systems, are both tempting and expensive; not per byte, but per user.

## 4.3 INDIRECT COSTS

By definition, most indirect costs are costs that cannot in part or in whole be directly attributed to a specific activity, department, or cost center. Yet these costs do exist and, in the absence of the activities or departments at issue, would not occur or at least would be lower. However, what might be an indirect cost to a specific department is usually a direct cost to the organization as an entity. For example, subdividing precisely the costs of a personnel department to all other departments in an organization is difficult. By contrast, those costs are direct when it comes to an organization's profit line.

A special category of indirect cost is *lost opportunity*. Money spent on a system is money that cannot be invested elsewhere. At a minimum, organizations can invest funds at 8 to 10 percent interest. They also can be invested in new capital equipment or perhaps additional advertising in an attempt to increase market share. Lost interest should be factored into the return-on-investment calculation, unless the system must be developed and all the alternatives cost roughly the same.

## 4.4 RETURN ON INVESTMENT

The return on investment equals the benefits gained minus the cost of obtaining those benefits. The cost of obtaining those benefits equals the operating costs plus the investment or development cost necessary to start earning a return. Figure 4-1 shows this calculation. The development cost should be factored by the lost opportunity cost of potential interest. That is, if the development funds have not been expended, they could have been invested and would have increased in value by the time the system becomes operational, and would continue to increase until the return repaid the investment. Actual projects present a more complex picture because of inflation, varying costs, changing profits or benefits, and so forth.

### 4.4.1 Proprietary vs. Nonprofit Perspectives

The central processing unit of a computer doesn't have the foggiest notion of profit. It controls the storage of data, the execution of logical instructions, and the generation of outputs. What an organization does with that data and those outputs is immaterial to the CPU, but the cost of that work can be measured.

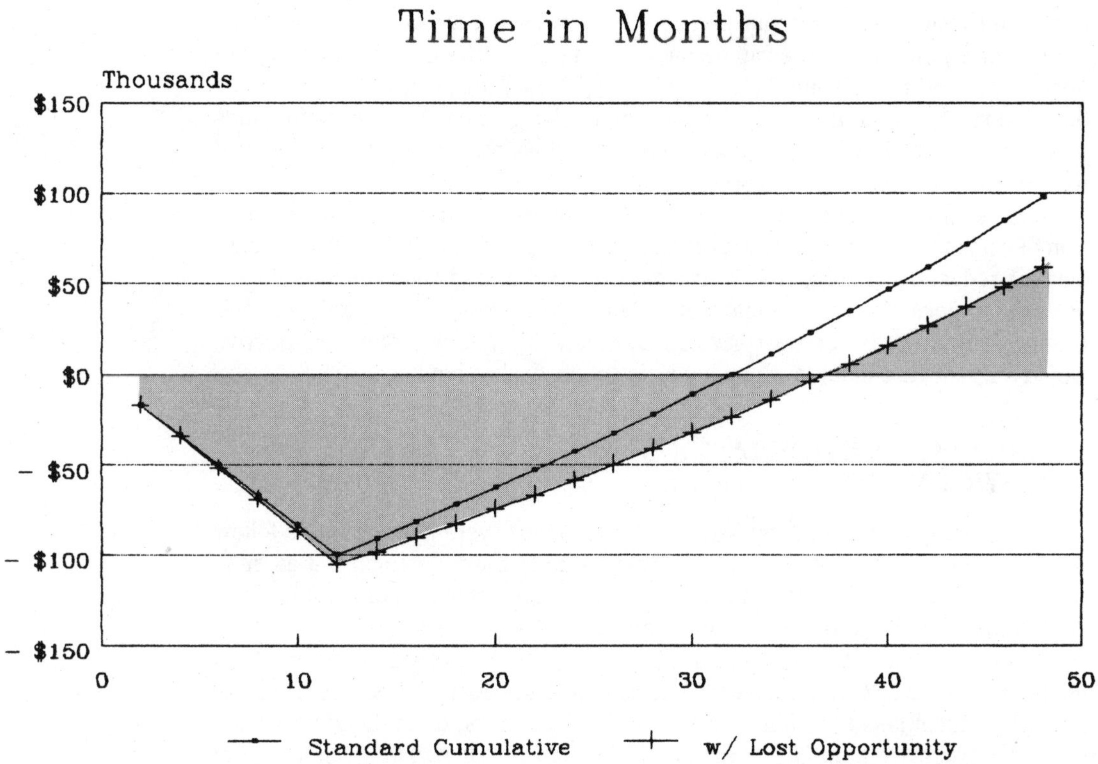


*Fig. 4-1. Return on investment. Calculating the return on investment for information systems is little different than for any project, but lost opportunity costs are often overlooked. In this example, the system costs $100,000 to develop and implement over a period of one year. Operating costs are set at $300 per month, and the gross return or benefit—starting after one year—of $5000 per month increasing at a rate of 1 percent per month. Lost opportunity cost is set at 10 percent per year, applied against the cumulative cost balance. This delays the break-even point about five months and reduces the net return on investment by a factor of about 40 percent at the end of four years.*

The question then becomes, "Is it worth it?" For a profit-oriented corporation, *worth* usually relates to the proverbial "bottom line." For nonprofit organizations, the cost of a system should not exceed the de facto savings achieved by replacing old ways with the new system, unless there is a compelling reason to accept the loss. The term *nonprofit* might be indispensable with reference to tax law, but it is often a lame excuse for avoiding good business practices. Even in the case of humanitarian causes, getting the most for the dollar still makes sense.

### 4.4.2 Direct vs. Indirect Earnings

As always, profit is gauged by a profit-loss or income-expenses statement. From this statement, measuring the impact of a specific cost factor can only be done by comparing two statements—one without the factor in operation, the other with it—holding all other costs steady. In practice, this comparison is nearly impossible. For example, if a computer system improves the processing of insurance policies, profits can be said to increase to the extent the costs are decreased over and beyond the costs of the system. However, if the computer-based service also improves the processing of claims, and that reputation adds to a firm's goodwill, which is a legally recognized asset, the system can be said to contribute indirectly to additional profits.

For nonprofit organizations, a direct return is usually measured by a reduction of costs to provide the same service. If only time is reduced, without a concurrent reduction in staff, then earnings are moot unless those resources are directed to performing additional work. The federal government, for example, grants many awards for cost-savings suggestions, but a larger perspective would suggest that much of the savings is theoretical at best.

## 4.5 SPECIAL CONSIDERATIONS FOR SYSTEMS INTEGRATIONS

In general, return-on-investment calculations for system integrations follow the same logic as new systems. The existing units must be regarded as sunk costs, but the cost of continuing to operate without change compared to the cost of integrating them is a legitimate and essential concern.

What is peculiar to an integration is the typically severe underestimate of costs, and the overly generous estimate of benefits. Most of these errors stem from the difficulties of merging the targeted components, as outlined in section 1.7. The excessive benefit estimate then comes from discounting the effect of the predictable compromises that evolve in the process of bridging the discontinuities. It is a viscous if not a vicious cycle.

Perhaps the best analogy is the planning process for a new marketing strategy. This process can start when the chief executive officer calls in a product manager. Pointing to some territory on a large-scale map he says, "I want you to expand into this area." The product manager then calls a meeting, and with the aid of more precise demographic-type maps, begins to consider what it will take. Hurdles the CEO did not consider begin to surface. Still, the boss wants it, so the effort continues. Finally, the salesmen begin to comb the territory and discover even more hurdles. Snow tires are not a big seller in Arizona.

And so it is with systems integrations. Higher-level managers tend to overlook details. Mid-level managers might find a way of "white-washing" those details, but the computer will not. Computers feed on the most minute details, and it costs a lot of money to change a computer's diet.

## 4.6 COMPUTER MODELS FOR COST ESTIMATING

Computerized cost-estimating models first came into widespread use in the construction industry, where a few minor errors can mean losing a bid or conversely losing the company. This type of software has been extended into every major cost accounting and estimating application, although no single program seems to have gained industry standard status. Unfortunately, many of these programs are little more than ledgers.

What is needed are executive information programs, tailored to the way each organization conducts business, that will calculate the financial consequences for the range of options that act as parameters. Programming a model of this caliber would not take much effort, and it could pay for itself quickly. A good analyst, using ordinary spreadsheet software, could produce a workable model in two to four weeks. Most of that time would be spent verifying the program against the organization's historical data. Refinements to the model might take another six months, but the prototype will likely have encompassed the lion's share of crucial data and algorithms.

# Part II

# The Database and Its Environment

In most systems today, and for most integrations, the database is the dominant concern. The reason is simple. Information depends on data. If adequate data is present and accessible in a system, then required answers can be generated as far as the logic to do so is known. Conversely, the extent the data is unavailable, inaccessible, or inaccurate is the degree to which generated answers are no better than guesswork.

On the other hand, organizing and structuring data is no easy task, especially when different users have entirely different ideas what a system should do to support their respective responsibilities. In these situations, the information manager has two basic choices: to build a system for each user, or to build a one-size-fits-all system. The former is usually a waste of resources, and the latter is often an ambitious task that falls by the wayside. Fortunately this is changing. Advances in technology increasingly favor development of large corporate databases that nonetheless can serve many divergent requirements, which leads to an exemplary case to lead off this part of the book.

The company is USAA, a diversified insurance and financial services institute headquartered in San Antonio, Texas. Nonprofit, and without a single salesman, it has developed a customer base of over 2 million policyholders and investors. In the process, as gauged by independent consumer surveys, it has earned and maintained the highest client satisfaction among all major insurance companies in the country.

Like all financial companies, it utilizes data processing extensively, but with a difference. The Chairman of the Board, retired Air Force Brigadier General Robert F. McDermott, makes a point of frequently visiting every department and office in his far flung organization. Over the years he has spurred the development of one of the world's showcase data processing departments. Although the entire corporate database is located in one building (plus a separate backup facility), it serves its members worldwide with few complaints. IBM routinely brings teams through every month to demonstrate how things should be done. But to McDermott and his extraordinary staff, the system and the reputation wasn't enough.

On one of his visits some years ago, McDermott noticed the vast amount of paperwork on desks, and quietly marked samples of it with an X. Returning a few days later, he found that many of the papers were still there. He then declared the company would work towards a paperless organization. In addition to the extremely well-structured automated databases, most correspondence and other paperwork is captured on optical disks, and can be transmitted anywhere in the building or in the world within five seconds.

This operation was not implemented solely by General McDermott, and he is the first to admit it. The list of the contributors is extensive, and many have since retired from USAA. The individuals in the second photograph comprise only a small fraction of those who worked so hard to achieve the record. At the same time, it is doubtful if that pinnacle would have been reached without the insight and judgment of the man at the top.

With this fine example as a starting point, then, the next four chapters examine databases from four perspectives, under the general assumption that data and its input comprises a system in its own right nearly apart from any user

*Fig. II-1. Pictured here is Mrs. Joan Holguin, USAA policy service representative, working at a correspondence image processing terminal. Behind her are Robert F. McDermott, chairman of USAA, and John Akers, chief executive officer of IBM.*

*Fig. II-2. The team effort at USAA. Shown here are Janice Marshall, Regional Vice President; General Donald R. Lasher (US Army, retired), President of the Information Services Division; James A. Patterson, Executive Vice President of Property & Casualty, Systems & Support; Doris Dent, Assistant Vice President, P&C Operations Analysis; Renae Summerour, Executive Director, P&C Operations Analysis; and Sheila Jackson, P&C Operations. Many others, since retired, have contributed to the USAA information systems.*

applications. Chapter 5 reviews the structure and mechanics of effective databases, with emphasis on the deceptively simple relational database model. Chapter 6 focuses on the complex meaning of *good* data. Good data is a catch-all term that encompasses seven different criteria. Failure to deal with any one of them can lay waste to any database, no matter how well it is managed.

Chapter 7 looks at the procedural system that surrounds an automated database, namely audit trails, access controls, and other quality control measures. Chapter 8 then portrays management as an outer ring, encompassing both the procedural and the automated systems. It covers a wide range of subjects, with the emphasis on designing the environment before a system is implemented, and trade-off considerations.

# 5

# Data and Database Structures

*The mechanic should sit down among*
*the levers, screws, wedges, and wheels,*
*like the poet among the letters of the alphabet,*
*considering them as the exhibition of his thoughts,*
*in which a new arrangement transmits a new idea to the world.*

—Robert Fulton

Data dominates systems, although it wasn't always so. As late as 10 years ago, information managers could regard data on a par with hardware and software. Today, that would be a serious mistake. Systems are increasingly configured around databases instead of the older batch process. This seemingly innocuous change has enormous significance for systems. Managers cannot afford to gloss over it.

As mentioned in section 1.4, the biological equivalents of a system are cells and organisms. The ability of cells and organisms to operate is largely attributable to the genes. Genes are the constituents of chromosomes. Therefore, the former equates with data, the latter with the software that executes the instructions inherent in the gene data. A few bad genes can readily weaken if not destroy the efficiency of the cellular system or organism. Similarly, bad data, or even poorly configured and hence unaccessible data, can mean the failure of an information system.

This problem became apparent to insightful thinkers in the academic world more than 10 years ago. Their solution has been formalized into the concept of the *relational database*, although the term is something of a misnomer.

Unfortunately, relational database software packages, such as SQL and dBASE IV, can be used without regard to the rules that make relational databases particularly effective. Worse, these rules are shrouded in exquisite jargon that obscures the significance of the structure. For example, the literature sometimes refers to records as *tuples* and comparative adherence to the rules as *degrees of normalization*. These terms might have apt and clear meanings to mathematicians and logicians, but they confuse practical businessmen and management information students.

The essence of the relational database is a direct application of the concept of *interior lines*. Data is arranged so that any element can be quickly linked to any other element or elements without interference, meaning that any number of users can work the data without regard to how any other user works it. The deceptively simple configuration has the resiliency to allow each manager to take on responsibility and exercise the initiative to meet his or her own information objectives. In *Hamlet*, Shakespeare has the hero lament, "I could be bounded in a nutshell and count myself a king of infinite space, were not that I have bad dreams." The relational database eliminates many software-type "bad dreams," and in the process condenses the strategy of information systems into something of a "nutshell."

Still, the model does not supplant all others. Some of the older models still offer advantages that outmaneuver the clean interior lines of the relational database in some situations, of which the famed airline reservations system is a major example. Yet the tendency of many system managers is to veer toward these older alternatives before fully considering the advantages of the relational model. Alternatively, when the latter is adapted, the rules are not followed. Avoidable inefficiencies are thus introduced. This chapter emphasizes this structure and its ramifications for efficient design. The issues of database distribution and distributive processing are covered in sections 8.1 and more extensively in chapter 10.

## 5.1 THE SIGNIFICANCE OF DATABASE PROCESSING

Early processing consisted of simultaneously entering data and programs to obtain the required output. Business systems depended on masses of input data stored sequentially on punch cards and later on magnetic tape. The minuscule computer operating memories limited the processing to small programs. These limitations did not hinder the requirements for payrolls, credit cards, other billing systems, and periodic updating of records. Thus, these functions became established computer applications more than 30 years ago.

Other requirements gave the impetus to direct-access technology. With that came massive improvements to operating and rapid-access storage. For example, the 64K operating memories and 192K floppy disks common to microcomputers/PCs 7 years ago have evolved into multimegabyte memories and hard disks up to 600M (a 300,000% increase). Figure 5-1 depicts the upshot of this evolvement, namely the supplanting of the batch process with database management technology.

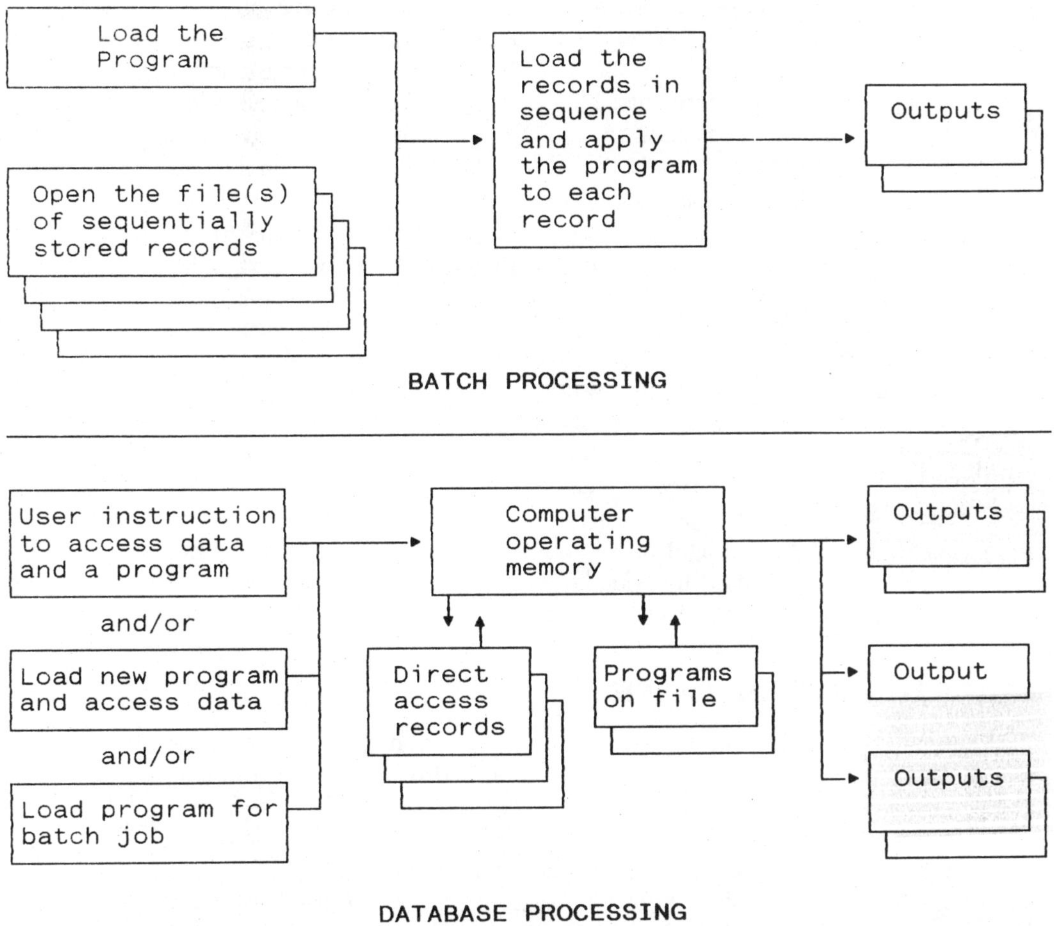


*Fig. 5-1. Batch vs. database processing. Batch processing runs records through repetitive processing in the sequence found in the files. Database processing can access one or more records directly and limit the processing to those records selected, although it can also be used for batch processing. The only advantage batch processing retains is high speed when millions of records must be processed, but even that edge is being eroded by emerging technology.*

The great significance is that the internal lines of information handling transferred from executives, acting like file clerks, to the computer. Properly used, database processing can free decision makers of their clerical chains, and permit them to focus attention on what is important. Even the well-known high-speed advantage of batch processing might wash out within the next five years. A summary of the advantages and disadvantages follows.

- *Advantages*. As stated, the major advantage of the relational database design is that different users can use the same database for different purposes without the need to coordinate with other users, and with fewer programming requirements to access the data. This in turn simplifies the integration of separate databases. Another advantage is that sophisticated decision support systems can be developed using relational database software instead of the specialized computers and programming languages developed more than 30 years ago. These admirable relics permitted both direct access to, and linkage of data. The most well known of these setups was LISP (LISt Processing) and the French equivalent Prolog. They are still in use today, albeit mostly in versions that operate on ordinary computers. Yet expert systems in the form of decision support programs are equally amenable to the relational database approach and ordinary programming languages.

- *Interim Disadvantages*. The primary disadvantages of database processing: it is more expensive, and it is slower than batch processing. Fortunately, the second of these disadvantages is being overcome by technology with transaction processing speed wars. Sales of on-line transaction-processing systems surpassed $27 billion in 1987 and are expected to reach $50 billion by 1992. Thus, the lack-of-speed disadvantage of running sequential batch processing from a direct-access database will be short-lived. The cost might remain higher, but this will be offset by the leverage to be gained from having both transaction processing and information systems feeding off one trough.

## 5.2 THE DATABASE HIERARCHY

Most data is stored by hierarchy. The notable exceptions are text files common to word processing and some expert systems. In discussing this hierarchy, however, one point needs to be stressed. The word *set* can range in value from 0 (not 2) to any number the user can think of, subject only to hardware and software limitations. When the value is 0, this is known as a *null* condition, meaning that a set has been established within the system, but no entries have been made (or all existing entries have been deleted). A null set is sometimes called an *empty* set.

The fact that a set can contain only one entry is self-evident. The upper limit is reached when the system runs out of data to store (now common) or media on which to store it (increasingly uncommon), whichever occurs first. Upper limits are large. Both the Internal Revenue Service and the Social Security Administration maintain hundreds of millions of records, although not all of them are active.

The logical management of this mass begs hierarchy. Figure 5-2 depicts how this hierarchy combines data elements into records, which are arrayed into files, which are grouped into a database. Unfortunately, the term *file* is used in several contexts within the data processing lexicon, and this generates confusion. The *hierarchical file* is more of a logical than a physical concept. By contrast, the *systems file* is a discrete unit of media space allocated to store any type or amount of information a user wants to store on it, subject only to the physical limitations imposed by hardware or software. Worse, many users still refer to a record as a file, as in, "Let's take a look at so-in-so's file."

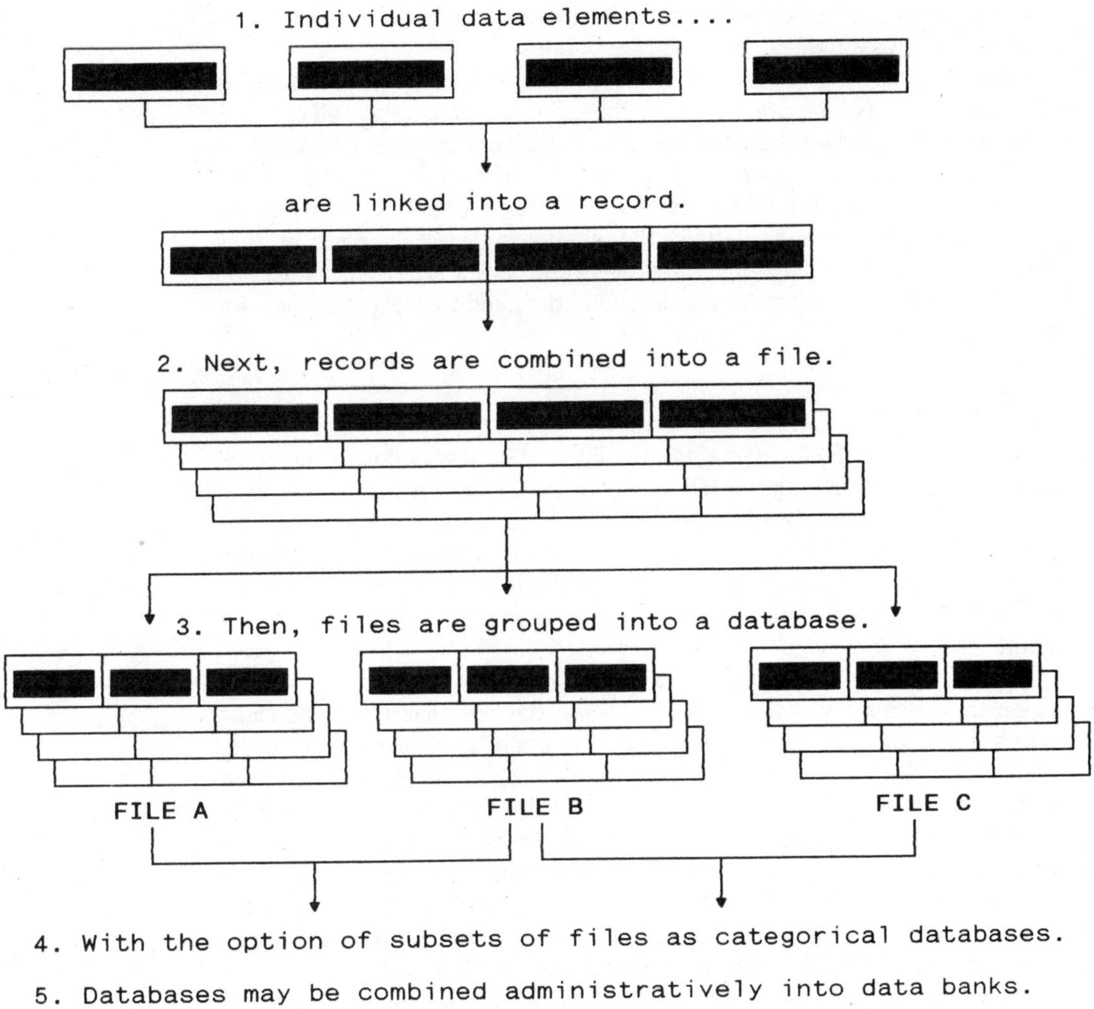


*Fig. 5-2. Generic file structures. Except for some expert systems and for text/word processing, organization of data follows a nearly universal hierarchy.*

### 5.2.1 Data Elements

The data element is the lowest form of useful information with respect to the intent of the database. When an atom or molecule is broken down into its constituent particles, it no longer resembles the element or compound of which it was originally a part. If the digits of a Social Security number are separated, it is no longer recognizable as a Social Security number, although the individual digits could be used in a different context.

Some data elements have their own internal hierarchy. For example, a name can be subdivided into first name, middle name, last name, and suffixes. This is a matter of convenience. When this is done, the user chooses whether to call each component a data element or alternatively a subfield of a larger element. Some software packages restrict the options.

Data is normally stored byte for byte. That is, each character is stored in one byte of storage (which can represent 255 different characters, half of which have been rigidly standardized, and the other half nearly so unless a substitute set is used in a particular system). However, numerical data can be stored in *binary format*, which means that a set of 4, 8, 16, or occasionally 32 bytes are used as an entity to store the value of the number in lieu of its digits. In very large systems, this alternative might or might not have a significant impact on storage requirements and processing time, due the need to convert formats for outputs.

### 5.2.2 Records

A *record* is a set of data elements, usually but not always describing some entity. An example of an entity would be a personnel record for an individual or at least the data relevant to some aspect of an individual, such as payroll data. In this sense, a computer record is no different from an ordinary manual record jacket stored in a file cabinet. Even when the record is pure text, the text can be considered a single data element and therefore the record comprises that one element.

However, not all data elements in a record are equal. One or more of the data elements are usually designated as *key fields*, the field that determines how records are accessed. Personnel records are typically accessed either by the Social Security number or the individual's name. Ideally, the key field for each record in a specific file should contain a unique value. For the Social Security number, this is almost automatic. The numbers are recycled but only after a previous holder has been deceased for a specified number of years.[1]

Besides entered data, a record also can contain computer-generated control data elements. The most common control element is a *pointer*. A pointer contains the location of additional data pertaining or related to a primary record, and is often used when records of unequal length need to be stored in one file, or when only certain information must be immediately accessible and *on-line* storage capacity is tight.

### 5.2.3 Files

A *file* is a set of records. This parallels a file cabinet filled with records, although as mentioned above, referring to a manual record jacket as a file is not uncommon. As an ideal, all records in the same file should have exactly the same number and definitions of data elements. This is not essential, but to the

[1]The decision to recycle Social Security numbers, in lieu of expanding them to ten digits or alternatively to start using letters in addition to digits, illustrates the high price of making even minor changes to large computer systems. The cost estimate to modify the data fields and outputs for more than 100,000 users who use Social Security numbers in automated systems is in the billions of dollars.

extent that files veer from this standard is the extent to which database management systems entangle their interior lines and run up the bill on programming.

### 5.2.4 Databases

A *database* is a set of files. The degree in which these files are logically related is immaterial, although in practice the term connotes sufficient relatability to support comparison or combination of information from different files in the database to meet user requirements. The question remains if databases themselves can be grouped into an even higher rung on the hierarchy. Informally, the answer is yes. This top rung is sometimes called a *data bank*, but its use is intended for data storage management in the mechanical sense rather than processing relatability.

### 5.2.5 Categorical Databases

*Categorical databases* are arbitrary subsets of a database. Hence, this designation is not a tier in the hierarchy. Instead, it is used to simplify or restrict access to the files in a database. Thus, if an organization's database has 50 files, all of which have at least some semblance of relatability, the files used by personnel might be considered as the personnel categorical database. Similarly, the files used by payroll could be considered as the payroll categorical database. Figure 5-3 shows how two or more categorical databases can share common files. The significance is not academic. Control of that much data is not a simple matter. Granting authority to update files must be carefully allocated, while considering which departments depend on them.

### 5.2.6 Relationships Among Files

The relationships among files determine how databases are, or should be, structured. The temptation is to organize files for ease of access. Yet different users have different ideas of what constitutes ideal access routes, or even how they should be subgrouped as categorical databases. This issue is seldom resolved by a totally logical approach. It usually takes a concerted management effort, which in turn requires the manager involved to have a good grasp of the consequences of various courses of action.

Nevertheless, the ideal is to establish files that have the highest degree of logical tightness to them. Schools of all types, proprietary or nonprofit, afford an excellent example. The minimum files would be students, faculty (or instructor staff), courses, classroom facilities, and usually programs. This breakdown applies to public schools, technical schools, colleges and universities, and any other school except the school of hard knocks. The latter has only students. Requirements can then be met by relating data in one or more files without affecting how any other user relates the data.

Still, accessibility of data to different users might require limitations. Specific users rarely need to draw on all possible relationships among the data elements. For example, a scheduler might need to extract copies of data on

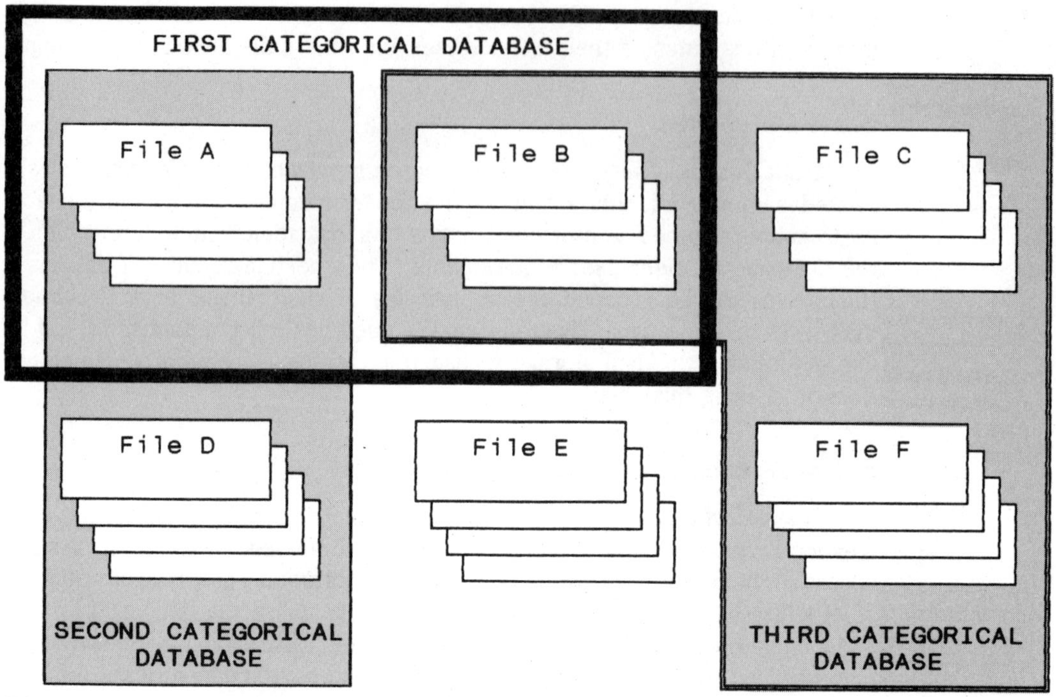


*Fig. 5-3. Categorical databases. Categorical databases are arbitrary, and often overlapping, subdivisions of a corporate database. The idea is to limit access on a need-to-know basis without detracting from the logical integrity of the database as an entity.*

students that includes the program they are enrolled in. He can relate this information to the program file to figure out what courses the student will take during the next unit of time, based on checking the program file. He can then relate this to the available instructors and facilities available, and in the process generate alternative schedules. Because the scheduler does not need to review student grades or other private information, his access to these fields should be blocked.

### 5.2.7 Access Techniques

Computers can operate at extraordinary speeds compared to human processing, but they lack perception. They cannot visualize an entire database in one glance as the human eye can. Processing occurs sequentially, checking one item of information at a time. Thus, accessing a specific record among millions at an acceptable speed requires special techniques. Normally, these techniques are of little concern to users, but the choice can have major consequences for the efficiency of very large systems. The three most popular techniques are: hashing, indexing, and binary search, as described in technical note 13 in appendix B. In large systems, the choice can be significant enough to warrant the attention of the chief information officer.

## 5.3 A THEORETICALLY IDEAL DATABASE

Because trade-offs are common to database design, a standard to compare alternatives is worthwhile. This ideal database would be impractical in all but a few isolated environments, but as a point of reference it can prove useful. Figure 5-4 shows this point. That is, the extent the ideal is impractical is the extent to which database management problems will increase. A trade-off analysis seeks to minimize those problems. The next four subsections discuss the three criteria of the ideal base, followed by a look at its use as a baseline.

### 5.3.1 Absolute Singularity

*Absolute singularity* means that there is only one database, and that every data element relevant to any record occurs once and only once. As an extreme hypothetical example, if the databases of all government agencies were consolidated, an individual's Social Security number and name would be recorded only

| | Theoretical Ideal | Disadvantages |
|---|---|---|
| Absolute Singularity of each Piece of Data | No element of data for any individual, entity, or item represented by a record can be duplicated except as a non-upgradable copy or view of that data. Eliminates inconsistent data. | The cost of maintaining the ideal is often a cumbersome network or interface integration, though to the extent compromises are made, the integrity of the database will decline. |
| Maximum Relatability of all Data | Any logical relationship between or among data elements or records is always checked at the time of entry, update or deletion, in order to ensure maximum data integrity. | This may require excessive centralization of data or alternatively cumbersome interfaces, Further, the errors detected may exceed the design level of database accuracy. |
| Maximum Generation of Data | No data is stored if it can be generated from other data available in the database. This compresses the database to the smallest possible size and enhances logical integrity. | Constant regeneration of frequently used data may be counterproductive, and further it may encourage adding otherwise immaterial information to the database. |

*Fig. 5-4. The theoretically-ideal database. The ideal database never duplicates data, and is structured for maximum relatability of data it holds. Also, it never stores data that can be computer generated from other data. In practice, these criteria are impractical, especially in distributive processing systems, but they serve as a baseline for evaluating options to the extent those options deviate from the ideal.*

once in one record. This singularity would perforce increase the number of categorical database designations because many of them would have to share the same kingpin record, but all problems associated with duplicated data would be eliminated.

This criterion does not prohibit copies of data existing in multiple locations. Where this occurs, whenever the primary location is updated, the copies also must be instantly updated. Besides, in the ideal situation, only the primary location can be updated directly.

### 5.3.2 Maximum Relatability

*Maximum relatability* means that all possible logical relationships among all data elements and records in a system are imbedded in the database design and its controlling software. Thus, all relationships among data elements must be clearly identified and capable of being readily checked. If the relationship is absolute, it would serve as a bar to an invalid or incorrect entry or update. If it is relative or probable, the relationship would maximize the opportunity to verify updates interactively.

### 5.3.3 Maximum Computer Generation of Data

The theoretically ideal database also would place maximum reliance on computer generated data. That is, any data that could be computer generated from the logical relationships among other data would never be stored. Instead, it would be generated when needed. For example, the number of records stored in a file would not itself be stored as a value. The number could be computer generated by counting the records every time the count is needed.

In practice, maximum generation of this data is not only impractical but unwise. A field containing the number of records can serve as a check on the records actually in the file. Further, when computer generation is itself a complex process, as occurs in some expert and decision support systems, the repeated computer generation is inefficient.

### 5.3.4 As a Baseline for Actual Systems

When evaluating the advantages and disadvantages of practical alternatives, use the following measures:

**Consistency of Duplicated Data.** Because absolute singularity is impractical, some duplicated data is inevitable. The criterion for keeping duplication at a minimum is the point where the cost of correcting duplications exceeds the cost of eliminating them in the first place.

**The Integrity of Data.** *Data integrity* refers to the degree to which all the data in the database maintains logical relationships, and therefore equates with the criteria for maximum compatibility. To the extent data grows distended is the extent a database suffers a loss in utility. Furthermore, because singularity helps compatibility checking, this criterion should be considered only after the manager has established a tentative degree of singularity.

**Accessibility.** Accessibility, which usually reduces to questions of how much time it takes to access and link data, is usually the most important attribute to users. However, if the problems arising from bad data accumulate, quick accessibility is lost. Unfortunately, this criterion is often the driving consideration, and therefore the systems manager might have his hands full attempting to strike a workable compromise.

## 5.4 DESIGN FACTORS

In addition to the criteria exemplified by the ideal database, several factors significantly impact on the selection of a database structure and the specifics of its organization.

### 5.4.1 Hierarchical Priorities

Some systems operate on a fixed sequence for accessing data. For example, airline reservations are made by first checking for available routing between cities, then by the flights available between a specific pair of cities, and finally by the seats available on the flight selected. By contrast, and drawing on a previous example, a school system might maintain separate but logically equal files on students, faculty, courses, facilities, and programs.

The critical decision is whether to structure and link the files in the priority of logical use, or opt for the relational database structure and let the software "do the walking." This can be a tough decision. Information managers who do not have a bent for matters technical would still be advised to make an exception for database structures.

### 5.4.2 Data Inclusion

The ideal database refers to its structure, not to the completeness of all relevant data. Certain data is more critical than other data. As data becomes less used, the issue of whether to include it is raised. Systems can clog up with too much data and often force an organization to upgrade their system to a larger size, which entails a major increase to the costs of operation with few additional benefits. Figure 5-5 depicts the power curve in generalized form. It will probably vary with the organization, but it usually exists.

For borderline cases, the cost of using an alternative storage or retrieval method should be carefully considered. One executive, after much soul searching, decided the best way to obtain one seldom-used item was to call the individual involved and ask him. He was nearly fired for this, of course, but the solution worked.

### 5.4.3 Distribution of Data

Complete centralization of data in one location is usually impractical. Moreover, the technique of distributive processing permits a database to be developed in several locations, giving the appearance of a singular database to users and subject only to reliability errors in transmissions among the primary locations. But it should be noted that the rate of transmitting data—and accesses require transmission—is somnambulistic compared to the density of information that can be bounced around inside a single computer and its peripherals. This problem often leads to the most far reaching decision required in network systems, namely, how to arrange the "furniture."

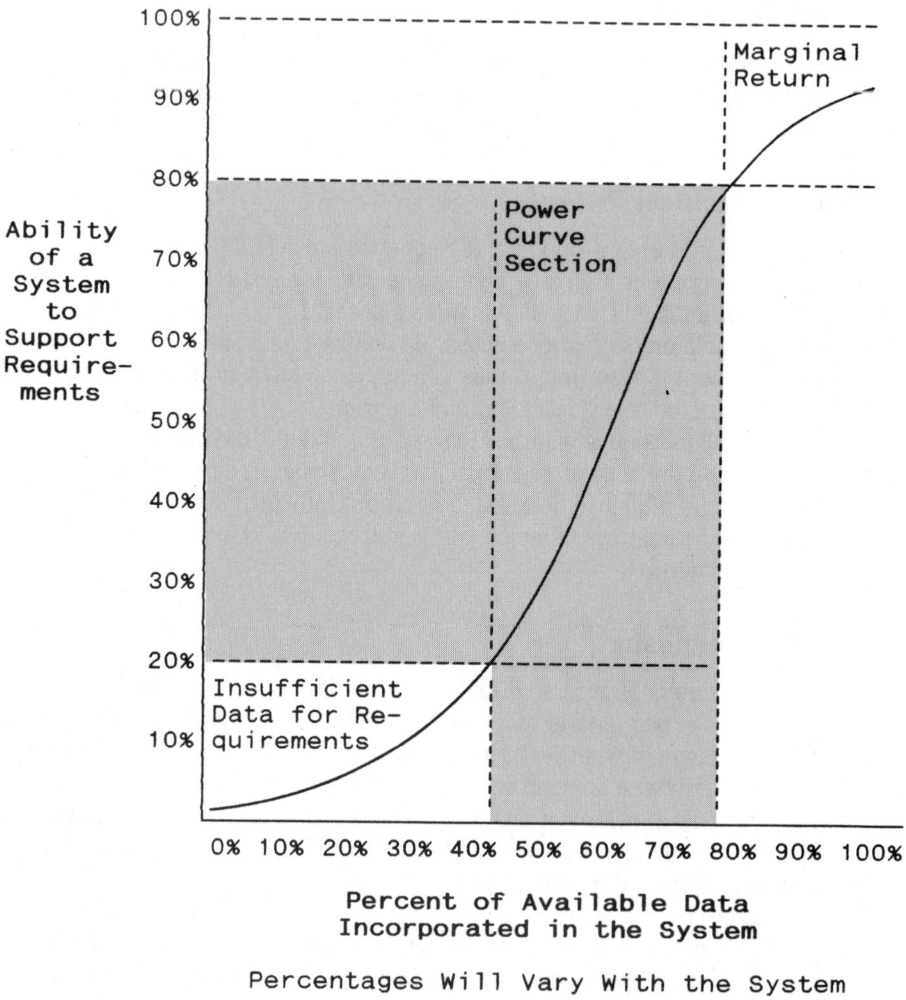


*Fig. 5-5. The power curve of data inclusion. Adding data elements to files in a database sharply increases its utility up to a point. Beyond that point, the return on investment is marginal and perhaps negative. The argument that the additional data might be needed for future requirements holds less water today. The relational database structure lets this additional data be added at a later date without affecting existing programs.*

## 5.5 THE THREE MODELS OF DATABASE STRUCTURE

Essentially all database designs use one of three structures: the relational database, the hierarchical database, and the network database. The hierarchical database came first and until recently was the most prevalent in large systems. The network design added flexibility to the hierarchical design to overcome its fixed priorities; alternative routes through the data are possible. The relational database, as mentioned previously, does away with all pretense of hierarchy and network, leaving those considerations to the programmers who will access the data. Figure 5-6 depicts these three models in terms of the routing.

### 5.5.1 The Relational Database

At this point in the text, you should have a good idea of what a relational database is. In practice, there are relational databases and then there are relational databases, meaning they are not all equal in efficiency. Theoreticians have identified five sets of criteria, called ***degrees of normalization***. Each degree includes all the restrictions of the degree preceding it, and then adds new ones. Strange as it might seem, these restrictions serve the best interests of the information manager.

Technical note 12 in appendix B discusses the cumulative criteria for the five degrees of normalization. For the moment, the key to understanding the virtue of these criteria is that the rules improve the interior lines of the database with respect to programs that must use it, and for the database administrator who must maintain this database. Unfortunately, the task of organizing data into these formats is irritating, onerous, and vexatious. Programmers, particularly those in departments beyond the responsibility of the information manager, will fight tooth and nail on the grounds it entails unnecessary work on their part. Yet here, at least, the academicians really know what they are talking about.

### 5.5.2 The Hierarchical Database

The hierarchical database, as the name implies, starts with one key file and then places all subordinate files in a strict hierarchical relationship. An entire subordinate file might be linked to just one record in the key file. The airline reservations system previously mentioned offers a good example. The primary file is keyed on all cities from which flights originate, and contains data on all destinations for which a single ticket will suffice.

After the proper record is found, pointers direct the search to a subordinate file containing information on each flight in the stated direction. Then for each flight, there is a tertiary file with records for each seat on that aircraft. In practice, the structure is even more complex than this because flights must be broken down to subflights between all stops. Also, artificial seats must be created to intentionally overbook passengers to compensate for the no shows.

The principal disadvantage of this model is that the subordinate files cannot

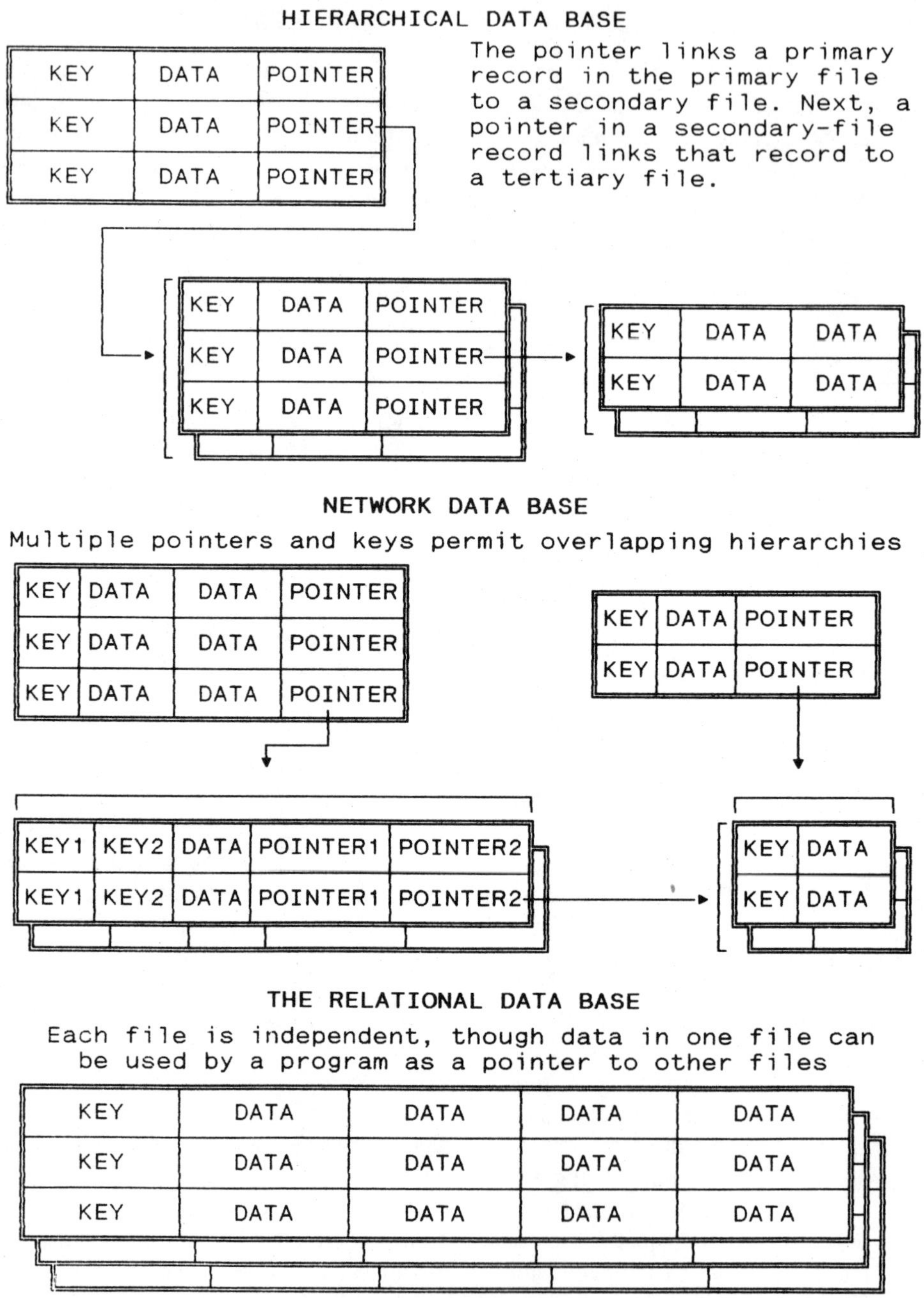


*Fig. 5-6. The three standard database structures. The hierarchical structure links subordinate files to pivotal or basic files. The network file is a form of cross-hatched hierarchical structure. The relational model backs off from those structures and puts all files on an equal footing, which means that programs must do the linking. The trade-off is that different users can use the same database for different purposes without coordination.*

always be directly accessed, and when they can, the structure of the data might not lend itself to general processing requirements. The second disadvantage is that fundamental changes to the hierarchy are difficult and expensive to implement, and might be impossible if the existing users cannot dispense with the existing order.

The reason the hierarchical database gained early popularity was that older computer systems had restricted memory, which required maximum programming efficiency oriented to the function for which the system was built. If the function remained unchanged, the disadvantages were irrelevant. In an age of information systems, however, those disadvantages loom large. Moreover, the relational database model lends itself to hierarchical processing without denigrating its inherent advantages, although a little more programming is required.

### 5.5.3 The Network Database

A network database structure should not be confused with a communications network. Instead, it is designed to let the user work into a singular database from different directions. In effect, the network structure superimposes several hierarchical structures into one net when those hierarchies must access common files. It is complex, but it can and does work, vaguely analogous to a *Monopoly* game. In Monopoly, the roll of the dice determines where the player will stop, but where he stops can result in a secondary command to advance or retreat elsewhere. Or the player might have to consult one of several files of cards, which themselves might direct additional movements. The computer version of that game could, but doesn't, use the network model.

The disadvantages are nearly the same as those for the hierarchical model, only worse. The network model does permit several hierarchical structures to operate concurrently, but after set up, fundamental changes or changes to certain record layouts are even more difficult. Further, similar to the hierarchical structure, the relational database structure also can be adapted to any requirement for a data-network structure.

## 5.6 DATABASE VIEWS

A *view* of data is any selection, rearrangement, or generation of values extracted or otherwise computed from a primary database. The view can be temporary or permanent. The latter is a common practice in distributive processing, although this makes updating complex. Further, views can be generfrom preceding views an infinite number of times, which provides the basis for many decision support systems. The significance of this feature is that an organization can maintain its primary database with few changes, while also satisfying any user requirement if the data is available.

Views can be generated from any database model—relational, hierarchical, or network—but the relational model simplifies the programming required. Figure 5-7 depicts an oversimplified example of a two-step view sequence. Still, the pressure to remold a relational database design into a hierarchical model remains strong. Database programmers try every which way to insert pointers into records, in order to relate files directly. The information manager would be wise to avoid this technique unless the database at issue has a singular purpose. Instead, the manager should rely on views and software to relate data.

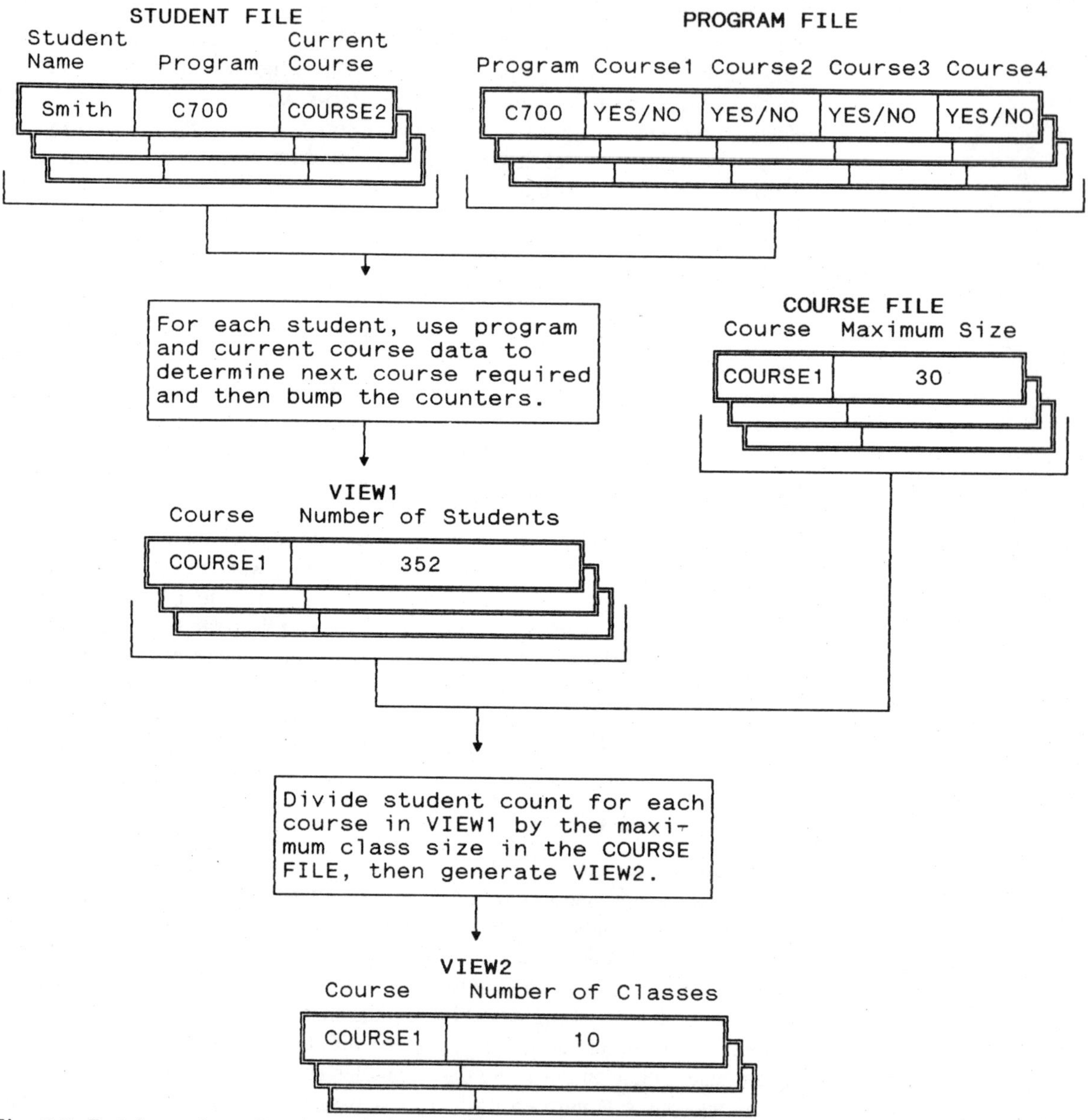


*Fig. 5-7. Database views. Database views are either excerpts of a primary database or a computer-generated revision of all or part of it. Views also can be generated from preceding views. If the primary database is built with the most primordial form of information available, then an infinite number of views can be excerpted or generated to meet any possible requirement without any changes or updates to the primary database. The class scheduling process shown here is a simple example of two sequential views.*

## 5.7 THE DATA ELEMENT DICTIONARY

Data element dictionaries are to systems what conventional dictionaries are to language, grammar, and syntax. As information systems increase in complexity, the data element dictionary becomes truly indispensable. Figure 5-8 illustrates how a single page in the dictionary can provide an extensive amount of information. None of this information is superfluous. All of it will at sometime or another affect a decision in the design, development, operation, or possibly the subsequent integration of a system. Other points to consider are:

- *As a Legal Anchor.* The legal range of values should be recorded in the dictionary. More important, however, would be the authority to enter or update the information in the system itself, and any audit trails required (discussed in section 7.1).
- *As a System in Its Own Right.* As a system grows, creating an automated system just to manage the data element dictionary is not unusual. The advantages of an automated dictionary include drawing on the files to support validity and compatibility checks in the main system itself. When this is done, however, update access to the dictionary must be severely restricted.
- *As a Means of Resolving Disputes.* One of the major problems in systems integrations, or even when capturing data from an old system as input to a new one, is to ensure that the data elements will meet the same criteria. The complexity of this information warrants reference to data element dictionaries. If the targeted systems use separate dictionaries, the decision makers—the information manager will rarely have sufficient authority to make the decisions alone—can adjudicate issues only by comparing those dictionaries for the data elements at issue. Attempts to impose an entirely new dictionary almost always fail.

## 5.8 DATABASE ADMINISTRATORS

The complexities of databases and the dictionary mandate the position of database administrator for large systems, and at least as an added responsibility to an existing job for smaller ones. The title, connoting something of a clerical position, belies its importance. Pressures to add, change, or delete data to a corporate database are immense. Simultaneously, the administrator must keep the organization's general informational needs in mind. Too much rigidity can defeat bona fide user requirements. Too much flexibility can generate problems that will eventually defeat the system or at least incur major costs. For integrations, this position can be the most important job in the information systems organization.

## 5.9 SPECIAL PROBLEMS WITH SYSTEMS INTEGRATIONS

All models of systems integration, except standardizations applied to other than databases, must reconcile differences among the constituent databases.

The problems will vary with the model of integration, but they are usually irksome. Any time independent entities are required to accept a common way of doing business or even a common way of communicating with one another, compromises must be made.

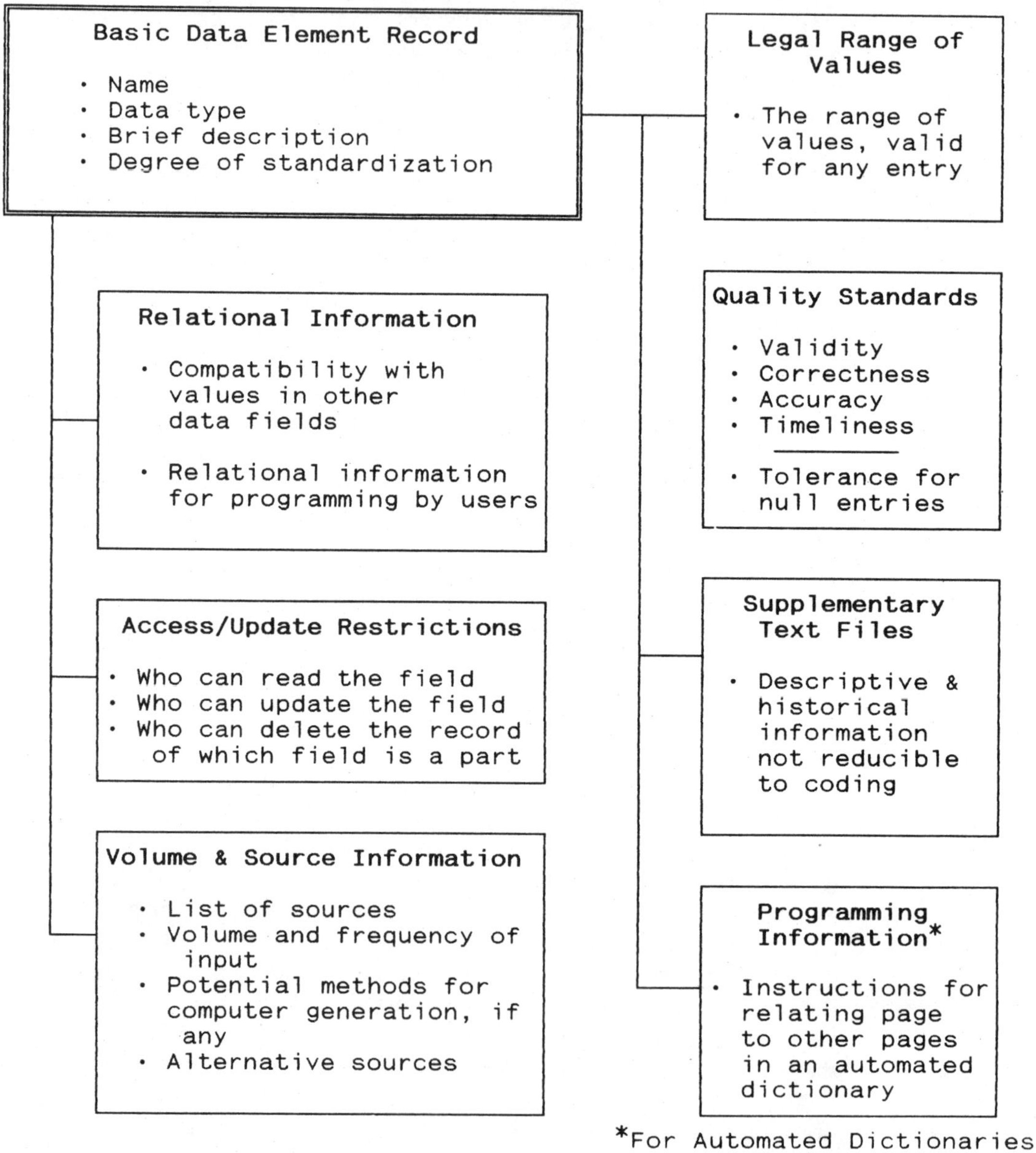


*Fig. 5-8. A page from a data element dictionary. Data element dictionaries can be as simple or as comprehensive as requirements warrant, but the growth of database systems suggests that these dictionaries will become more, not less, comprehensive. The page shown here is an example of that, yet it is not exhaustive. The dictionary, in turn, can be automated and linked, in part, to the system or systems it supports.*

These compromises center on what statisticians call *degrees of freedom*. Degrees of freedom roughly measure how tightly or loosely statistical data is interrelated. With any given set of data, greater degrees of freedom mean that measures of correlations are less reliable, that is, less probable for the identical sample sizes. Similarly, when computer systems targeted for integration display their own tight databases, too many loose ends in the merger can entangle the hoped-for interior lines. Four reasons apply:

1) *Conflicts with Required Data*. An integration that requires all the data resident in the targeted systems is rare. The users of the original systems might continue to need it, but not the other users. The issue then becomes how much of the data to merge into one database, or at least how much of the separate databases to make interoperable or of uniform format, as the circumstances warrant.
2) *Conflicts with Priorities*. After systems are made interoperable or the respective databases are integrated, conflicts for priority of access will arise. At the extreme, this can lead to a major court case. For example, Frontier Airlines sued United Airlines because the latter had manipulated its shared Apollo reservation system to its own advantage. Frontier won the case.
3) *Conflicts with Degrees of Accuracy Required*. This seemingly negotiable problem has been the death of more attempted integrations than any other single cause. The general rule is that the degree of validity, correctness, accuracy, timeliness, reliability, compatibility, and completeness in the integrated database must meet the criteria of the most demanding user. Compromise might be a way of life for 99.9 percent of all managers, but here it spells failure, rather than relief. See case study E in appendix A.
4) *Implementation Problems*. Even when all the details for an integration of systems are worked out, the task of phasing it in remains. In large active systems, this task can be a major hurdle, for the same reason that improvements to major highways are sometimes three times more costly than new highways built from scratch on vacant land.

# 6

# The Complex Meaning of "Good" Data

*Get your facts first, and then you can distort 'em as much as you please.*

—Mark Twain

The question, "How good is the data?" is probably the most oversimplified question in data processing. This misunderstanding stems, in part, from the adage "garbage in, garbage out." Although this presumes data is either garbage or it is not, the truth is, data is not that black or white. In fact, a few small errors in crucial data can produce results that are worse than garbage. Conversely, cumulative errors in a system can mutually compensate each other, and thus permit generation of valid outputs in terms of the objectives for which the system was designed. To understand how and why requires an understanding of how data itself operates.

The ordinary checkbook, simple as it might be, shows almost all the factors, somewhat reminiscent of why Adam Smith was able to explain economic theory in *The Wealth of Nations* by reference to a pin factory. Most checking account holders receive monthly statements from the bank operating the account. Each of these monthly statements should be reconciled with the user's ledger. Discrepancies in the data are common, and most of them are due to errors by the account holder rather than the bank. Failure to reconcile the two accounts might or might not lead to disaster, depending on the type and number of errors, but as a minimum the accuracy of the checkbook as a record of expenses will degenerate.

The point is, a checkbook is a system. It might be a manual system for the account holder, but inevitably it is part of an automated system for the bank. If the bank permitted as many errors to creep in as account holders do, it would soon be in very deep trouble. Put another way, useful information systems veer closer to the standards of a bank system than to account holder ledgers. Presume, therefore, for the purposes of this chapter that the manager is creating a simple automated system for his or her checkbook. If the potential array of errors seems aggravating in this simple case, imagine what it is for a complex database.

## 6.1 SPECIFIC CRITERIA

The quality of data depends on seven criteria. A single data element is rarely subject to all seven, but the cumulative data in most records is subject to at least five and sometimes all seven. The meaning and significance of these criteria are discussed in the following subsections. Figure 6-1 summarizes these criteria.

### 6.1.1 Validity

*Validity* has two meanings for data: data represents what it purports to represent, and values entered are within a *legal*, or acceptable, range. For a checkbook entry under "description of transaction," the acceptable range of values would be any combination of letters, numerals, and symbols. But it still would not be valid unless the entry described a transaction. For example, the name of the payee, the source of the deposit, or the reason for transaction such as a service charge all describe a transaction. If the date of transaction is entered in that column, it would pass muster in terms of legal range of values but not in the larger meaning that the data represents a "description of the transaction."

A second example is the entry of the amount of a payment or debit in the appropriate column. In most checkbooks, the legal range of values is a positive number with two decimal places (for U.S. currency). But whether or not a system accepts a null entry in the decimal positions, as an input for zero cents (or a single digit as an indication of tenths of a dollar), is an option with the designer of the system. Forcing the user to enter both decimal places would tend to reduce truncated entry errors, but it also would make the system less user friendly. Alternatively, the system might respond with a question to the user asking if the truncated value was intentional.

A negative number would inevitably create an error, as all numbers in the debit column are subtracted from the running balance. For the larger meaning of validity, if the entry is a dollar amount, correct or incorrect, it is valid. If it represents anything else, such as the check number, it is invalid.

The problems associated with validity increase with complex databases. For example, the difference between "number of dependents" and "number of exemptions" (for tax purposes) is significant, although the two values are the same more often than not. The first relates to people who are dependent on an individual for their support. They might or might not qualify as tax exemptions.

| CRITERIA | DESCRIPTION | COMMENTS |
|---|---|---|
| Validity | The data represents what it purports to represent and is within the legal range of values. | Information that is misrepresented is useless, and in no case should it fall outside the legal range of values. |
| Correctness | The data *correctly* represents what it purports to represent. | Probably the most common source of error in automated databases. |
| Accuracy | Accuracy means the extent to which data is precise; usually applies to mathematical data. | Inaccurate data often gives the appearance of being accurate, usually due unavoidable quirks in software. |
| Timeliness | Timeliness asks the question, "as of when was the data correct?" | Outdated information can be equally troublesome as incorrect data. |
| Reliability | The degree that data in a database is identical to the input or output of it. | Most reliability errors arise from malfunctioning equipment and communications. |
| Compatibility | The extent to which logical relationships among data elements dovetail in terms of the actual data. | Some compatibility errors are based on absolute rules, others indicate only the possibility of an error. |
| Completeness | The extent to which all data fields in a record have been updated. | Incomplete data can be as harmful as incorrect data, though at least the status is known. |

*Fig. 6-1. The criteria of good data. The expression, "good data," is a catch-all term that covers seven criteria. All seven apply to most databases, although rarely to each data element.*

By contrast, tax exemptions refer to units by which tax liability (and withholding) is reduced and do not always equate with dependents. For example, some state income tax systems permit additional exemptions for being over the age of 65 or legally blind. (Federal tax law now provides tax relief for these individuals by way of a larger standard exemption.)

The consequence of a validity-type error depends on the circumstances. In the checkbook debit example, a negative number will increase the running balance by twice the amount of the check. If it were the check number rather than the amount, the difference between the actual amount and the check number would be the measure of the error entered into the running balance.

A more subtle case of validity occurs when the information in a data field is misinterpreted, notwithstanding the data element dictionary definition of its contents and purpose. The January 1990 issue of *Consumer Reports* pointed out that the data field labelled "number of inquiries" in credit reporting is often used to estimate credit risk, even though many inquiries can accumulate for good credit risks.

### 6.1.2 Correctness

*Correctness* of data is the most straightforward criterion. It simply means the extent to which data is correct for the record to which it pertains. For the checkbook transaction example, correctness means that if a payee entry was made, the payee named is the payee to whom the check was written. In the example of the debit amount, a correct entry means the dollar amount is correct. In the former case, the error is total. A misspelling would be an accuracy error. In the latter, the error has degrees, that is, the amount by which the entered data differs from what was written on the check.

Incorrect data is probably the most common form of error in most systems, and needs no further example to make its meaning clear. The consequences depend on the use to which the data is put and the magnitude of the error. A checkbook entry error of $2 is not normally as serious as an error of $2,000 (although exceptions do occur).

In more complex systems, serious errors can lead management to make bad decisions on incorrect and misleading information. An example would be the interpretation of data from an aircraft/missile detection system as an attack when the object detected is entirely peaceful (what is called a false positive). The shooting down of an Iranian passenger plane over the Persian Gulf in 1988, based on a mistaken interpretation of the signal data as an Iranian combat aircraft intent on war, was a grim example.

### 6.1.3 Accuracy

*Accuracy* follows closely on the heels of correctness and is nearly synonymous with the term *precision*. The correct value of the mathematical symbol $\pi$, the ratio of the length of the circumference of circle to its diameter, is 3.14, or 3.142, or 3.1416, or 3.14159, and so forth, depending on the degree of accuracy required. For character data, such as a name or payee in a checkbook, accuracy relates to spelling, unless the data is no longer recognizable or is mistaken for another name, in which case it is incorrect rather than inaccurate.

Sometimes, the dividing line between correctness and accuracy gets fuzzy. For example, a diagnosis recorded on an automated medical records system. In those cases where the difference is distinct, the systems planner should be aware of it. The Department of Defense ran into an extensive problem as it converted from the 6-byte, 6-bit word structure of the old Honeywell computers in the Worldwide Military Command & Communications System to the standard 8-byte, 4-bit word structure. The conversion of 36-bit longitudes and latitudes (in radians) to the 32-bit format lost enough accuracy to render some programs useless. Accordingly, the old data had to be stored in double-precision format (which took 64 bits). The system was not overtaxed, but the number of labor-years required to convert the software that used this data was another matter.

The criterion of accuracy does not apply to all mathematical fields. For checkbook entries, the standard input is in dollars and cents, which for all practical purposes can be stored as an integer value of cents, and converted to dollars and cents in reports. Unfortunately, this is not a complete remedy. The maximum integer version of a dollar-and-cents entry in a 4-byte field is just under $21.5 million, which is small change in large financial institutions. Therefore the system must be able to store this data as long integers, or as character data, both of which consume more memory.

### 6.1.4 Timeliness

Correct data carries with it the implied question, "correct as of when?" The value of the mathematical constant $\pi$ hasn't changed since the beginning of time, although the accuracy of its known value increases each year. Nor does the debit value of a check change. However, the checkbook balance is correct only as of the last entry made, presuming all previous errors have been corrected. Failure to record subsequent transactions renders the checkbook increasingly out of date, irrespective of how correct the existing entries might be.

If data changes frequently, the failure to update results in incorrect and untimely data. Yet the incorrect data was correct at one time. For the checkbook system, omission of a debit can be corrected by adding it to the file. For an incorrectly entered amount, the correction requires either a debit or credit transaction, or alternatively, recalculation of the balance from the point the error occurred, depending how the data is stored.

The problem of timeliness in some systems is measured not in months or days, but in tiny fractions of seconds. For example, an embedded system to control missile flights, particularly manned flights, requires extreme timeliness of data and the best in real-time processing. The same is true with computers installed in automobiles to regulate fuel and environmental control devices, although the consequences of an error for a driver are seldom equal to the fate that would await an astronaut.

Another problem arises with different time zones, especially when daylight saving time is in effect in some but not in all areas. Contracts have been lost because these time differences were overlooked. The cartoon character of Lucy in *Peanuts* once surmised that today could not possibly be the Judgment Day, since it was already tomorrow in another part of the world.

### 6.1.5 Reliability

*Reliability* refers to the degree to which data accessed is identical with data in the database, or as a corollary, to the degree that entered values are stored exactly as entered. Most reliability errors come from problems with hardware, especially communications hardware, but they also can result from bugs in the software, or by a user attempting to enter data of greater length or accuracy than the system is designed to accept.

The simplest way to demonstrate reliability is to snip one or more of the 25 wires in an old parallel printer cable. Depending on which wire or wires are snipped, the quality of the printout would range from a few errors to absolute gibberish. For the checkbook system, if the user tried to update the checkbook by way of a modem from a distant location, the transmission could be *nicked* electronically, meaning that one of the bits of information would be dropped or an extraneous bit added.

The consequences of reliability errors are roughly the same as for incorrect data, with one major exception. Most but not all reliability errors are obvious and suggest the data be retransmitted. But when the errors are not easily detected, the source of the problem can continue to operate on masses of data. For this reason, many techniques have been developed to monitor the quality of transmissions. The two most prevalent are *parity* and dual *transmission*.

**Parity.** This technique computes control information as a mathematical or logical function of the data, and adds it to the transmission. If the original data is changed during transmission, the transmitted parity calculation will no longer dovetail with a rerun of the calculation at the receiving end (in most but not all cases). The most common example of this is the ninth or parity bit added to 8-bit bytes on magnetic tapes. More sophisticated techniques are available and others can be uniquely formulated to meet the needs of an organization.

**Dual Transmission.** This technique transmits the same message at least twice over the same or separate lines and then compares the results at the receiving end. A common example of this occurs in the familiar copying commands in microcomputer disk operating systems. These commands offer the option of verifying the data transmitted (or recorded) is identical with the source. Some systems run sample dual transmissions as a quality control measure.

### 6.1.6 Compatibility

*Compatibility* refers to the correctness of data with respect to values in other data fields. The checkbook offers yet another example. The balance is equal to the algebraic sum of all previous transactions. For this reason, the running balance is inevitably computer generated in automated systems. In a personnel record, a date of birth too close to the date of employment is an obvious compatibility error. This error occurs more frequently than imagined. Individuals often enter the current year on an application blank for date of birth.

If all data is valid, correct, and current in a record, then in theory it should display perfect compatibility, which is not an original source of error. This is true in most occurrences, but there are exceptions. Rules affecting relationships among different data entries can themselves be incorrect, which, for example, sometimes occurs when major changes to income tax laws go into effect. Thus whether a deduction for such-and-such an expense is allowable under such-and-such conditions is subject to interpretation. In practice, however, most compatibility errors are not errors, but conditions used to detect other types of errors.

These errors can be absolute or only probable. Both types are part and parcel of the Internal Revenue Service (IRS) income tax return audit procedures. Virtually all computational errors are absolute compatibility errors. The more significant compatibility checks evaluate improbable relationships among data entries. For example, an individual reporting a gross income of $28,000 per year and claiming a mortgage interest deduction of $20,000 might be suspected of filing an incorrect return. This does not mean the return is incorrect, only that there is a greater probability of its being incorrect compared to another return showing the same gross income with only $4,000 mortgage interest claimed.

The IRS directs much of its auditing capability, which is limited with respect to the number of taxpayers, to the more questionable returns. For all the horror stories about IRS agents, the occasional abuses are outweighed by the dishonesty of some taxpayers 1,000 to 1. The estimate of the tax liability of unreported income and invalid deductions is $100 billion in 1990 (projected to rise to $127 billion in 2 years), plus a documented portfolio of unpaid tax bills in the amount of $87 billion. To compensate for this loss of revenue, honest taxpayers pay the existing rather than potentially lower rates, for the same reason retail stores must charge higher prices to cover losses from shoplifting. If it weren't for these computer-generated compatibility checks, we might all be paying even higher taxes.

### 6.1.7 Completeness

*Completeness* means the degree to which the collective data fields in a record, file, or database have entries, correct or incorrect. A null field that should be updated is inherently incorrect. With one exception, the error is obvious. The exception occurs when numbers are stored in binary format. A null field is identical with the value zero, which could be the correct value, although software can be programmed to differentiate between a null field and true zero by way of a flag that marks the field as null. An example of this feature occurs in the familiar Lotus 1-2-3 spreadsheet package.

To one degree or other, incomplete records are more the rule than the exception in most systems. But the consequences of incomplete data vary with: the amount of data missing, the purposes to which that data is put, and the frequency of the error among all records in the file or database. Omitting the payee in a checkbook record would seldom create problems, especially as the omission can be corrected during reconciliation. In a personnel system, omitting data could result in an employee's missing a chance for a promotion and a possible lawsuit.

## 6.2 THE RELATIVITY OF "GOOD" DATA

What comprises "good" data in general depends on many factors. A checkbook with a few errors not exceeding $.50 will rarely cause any problems, but the omission of a $1,000 check can cause later checks to bounce, which can trigger penalties and perhaps a bad credit rating. Elsewhere, a personnel system can tolerate errors in data on total hours worked when that data is used for management information purposes. But when that data is used for payroll purposes, most errors will result in time-consuming and expensive corrections, not to mention morale problems among employees.

### 6.2.1 The Power Curve of "Good" Data.

Figure 6-2 graphs the power curve, which is the complement of the power curve for inclusion of data discussed in subsection 5.4.2. The point of diminishing returns is reached when the costs are higher to keep the data in good shape than to exercise corrective actions when errors are detected. The key relationship between the two curves stems from the fact that automated data lends itself to quality control better than information strewn about an organization's precincts.

### 6.2.2 Variable Criteria

Some data in a record can require more accuracy than other data. In a payroll, an incorrect Social Security number or an incorrect rate of pay would be an intolerable error, but excessive income tax withholding would not normally be as serious. The employee can obtain a refund when he or she files a return for that tax year. In fact, more employees than not have too much tax withheld, averaging about $1,000 per return.

The data in some records in the same file can require a greater degree of accuracy than the same data in other records. Thus a 5 percent error in a transaction for $1 million is a far more serious error than the same percentage error in a petty cash reimbursement for a taxi cab fare. Therefore, the criterion for accuracy should be stated in both percentage and absolute terms if necessary. This dual application also provides an example of the technical difference between *precision* and *accuracy*.

## 6.3 CUMULATIVE SHORTCOMINGS AND ERRORS IN DATA

The adage, "a chain is only as strong as its weakest link," is not necessarily true in data processing. A chain is a poor analogy for complex data. Some errors are not only tolerable, they are sometimes encouraged to avoid reaching a point of diminishing returns. Other errors must be accepted as inevitable.

The effect of cumulative errors depends on the source and the purpose to which the results are put. When each specific data item must be correct, the contribution to error reduction by way of cumulative calculations is immaterial.

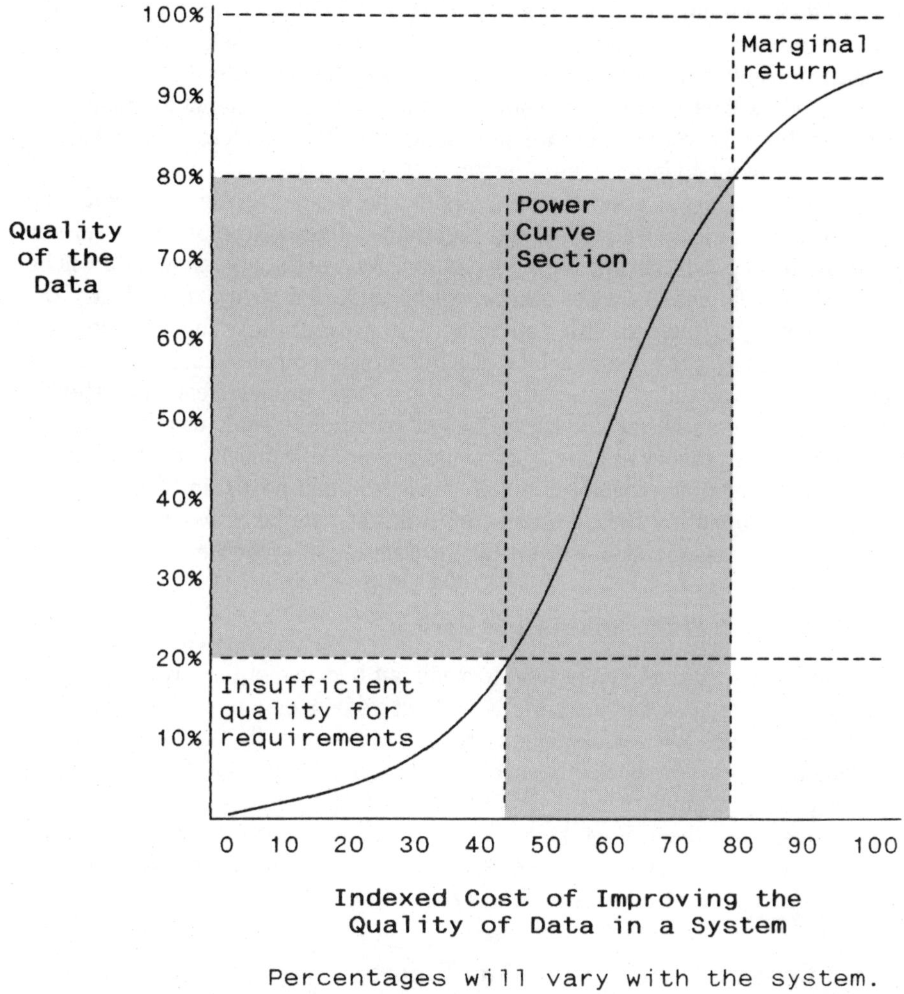


*Fig. 6-2. The power curve of good data. Similar to the curve for data inclusion (Fig. 5-5), good data also follows a power curve. As usual, the shape of the curve depends on the intent of the information system. Irrespective of that shape, minor improvements to quality control yield major benefits up to a point. Beyond that point, the return on investment is marginal. With rare exception, the attempt to ensure 100 percent good data is not only futile, it is easier and cheaper to correct a few errors after the fact.*

But where data is evaluated only in totals or averages, the error reduction phenomenon is an important consideration. The key to understanding this effect is the difference between random and biased errors.

### 6.3.1 Random vs. Biased Errors

*Random errors* are errors that occur by chance and are likely to occur with predictable frequency. They are rarely attributable to negligence or other human shortcomings, or to errors in software or equipment malfunctions. On the contrary, random errors are inevitable within the limits of accuracy established for maintaining data, which is the same reason the precision of manufactured goods will vary within the established limits of dimensional tolerance. By contrast, biased errors can be traced to a fundamental shortcoming, which can include the intent to introduce the error.

Genetics offers a good analogy. Under the best of living conditions and medical care, random variations and mutations of the chromosomes will still occur both at conception and during gestation. As a result some children will be born with tragic defects while others will be endowed with extraordinary talents. Short of abstinence, little can be done to prevent these inherent defects.

By contrast, poor health habits or a lack of good medical care can increase these genetic variations—generating what are more properly called congenital defects. As far as is known, these biased mutations result in problems not endowments. In theory at least, they are preventable. Similarly, random errors in databases are unavoidable, although measures can be taken to reduce the intensity and quantity. Biased errors, by contrast, can be prevented, although only at an increasingly high cost for higher degrees of error-free data.

### 6.3.2 The Effect of Cumulative Errors

Cumulative random errors tend to wash out because of the law of averages. This does not mean a random error is without its consequences, but that when totals or averages are calculated, the results will be nearly the same as if the individual entries were perfectly correct. The same is not true of biased errors. Biased errors accumulate in the direction of the bias. If errors do not occur with every entry, then the average error for all records will not be of the same magnitude as the typical error for those records where the errors exist. TABLE 6-1 provides comparative data on the two types of errors.

### 6.3.3 Compensating for Random Errors

Random errors are compensated by increasing the number of entries and taking an average. A good example occurs in high-order topographic survey work. Available instruments do not offer the necessary precision in one shot. Hence, the calculations must be based on the average of several readings. Higher orders require a larger number of trials. The same is true for most experiments in the sciences.

A variation on this technique occurs with the option on income tax returns to enter data to the nearest dollar. Amounts less than \$.50 can be ignored, provided any amount equal to or exceeding \$.50 is rounded to the next highest dollar. In a few cases, this will result in a tax liability \$1 or \$2 more or less than would have been calculated by using exact amounts, but for 80 million returns the effect is essentially zero. More significantly, the reduction in data entry work for IRS processors saves millions of dollars in personnel costs.

*Table. 6-1. The effect of cumulative errors. Random errors tend to wash out as they accumulate; biased errors do not. In this table, each number represents the cumulative error for both types of errors for the number of entries listed in the left-hand column.*

| Number of Entries | Cumulative Random Errors all Records Error=±($1 to $10) | Cumulative Biased Errors all Records Error = +$5.50 | Random Error as a Percent of the Biased Error |
|---|---|---|---|
| 10 | +$51.00 | $55.00 | 92.7% |
| 25 | -$62.00 | $137.50 | -45.1% |
| 50 | +$51.00 | $275.00 | 18.5% |
| 100 | +$329.00 | $550.00 | 59.8% |
| 250 | +$361.00 | $1,375.00 | 26.3% |
| 500 | +$708.00 | $2,750.00 | 25.7% |
| 1,000 | +$108.00 | $5,500.00 | 2.0% |
| 2,500 | -$129.00 | $13,750.00 | -0.9% |
| 5,000 | +$1,179.00 | $27.500.00 | 4.3% |
| 10,000 | +$1,483.00 | $55,000.00 | 2.7% |
| 25,000 | -$347.00 | $137,500.00 | -0.3% |
| 50,000 | -$3,378.00 | $275,000.00 | -1.2% |
| 100,000 | -$5,539.00 | $550,000.00 | -1.0% |

The random numbers were generated using QuickBASIC 4.0, looping for 100,000 trials after reseeding the generator. Each trial generated a random number between -$100 to +$100 of at least $10.

### 6.3.4 Compensating for Biased Errors

Compensating for *biased errors*, which sometimes go by the name *Kentucky windage*, requires that the error rate is known, and known to be biased in a certain direction. Here, an average correcting value can be applied. The airline industry uses this technique every day. Most flights intentionally overbook to compensate for the statistically biased error of no-show reservations. Occasionally, this results in actual overbooking, and one or more passengers must be bumped (with compensation) from a flight. Yet the total compensation paid is much less than the lost revenues that would occur without intentional overbooking.

Another fascinating case was the Army's officer evaluation rating scheme. In the former system, which was in effect until 1981, the key indicator reduced to a single number with a maximum value of 200 points. Within seven years of its implementation, 200 points had become the norm. A score of 199 was considered a nick; 198, a severe warning; and 197, a disaster. Previous rating schemes had suffered the same fate.

The problem was solved with a computer system that kept track of the endorsement ratings given by senior raters (the rater's rater). Each senior rater is annually confronted with his or her distribution of ratings. The pressure generated has been sufficient to lend a modest degree of discrimination—in the positive sense of the word—between the merely outstanding officers and the true "water walkers." In other words, the inflation persists, but an adjunct computer system successfully compensates for the biased errors that otherwise would make the ratings almost useless.

### 6.3.5 Data "Roll Ups"

Data roll ups differ from totals. The intent is to gauge the implications of the results instead of calculating sums, thus payroll totals should be exact. However, gauging trend lines in company payrolls, as a means of managing general costs in the future, does not depend on exact calculations. Restated, the cumulative effect of some biased errors can be tolerated in roll ups more so than exact totals. Also, applying corrective factors might be easier. This is of particular significance for the excerpt model of integration.

The efficacy of roll-up data is pervasive. The January 15, 1990, issue of *Newsweek* reported a far-reaching, if distressful, example. James Aiken, the recently appointed Commissioner of Corrections in Indiana, found he could project penitentiary cell requirements by analyzing student socioeconomic data as early as the second grade. This result does not mean that socioeconomic status is destiny for an individual, but for the purposes to which the data was put, it was destiny enough.

## 6.4 DESIGN CRITERIA

Chapters 7 and 8 discuss the management of input, from the procedural and the managerial design perspectives. In theory, the information manager should lay down the threshold level of data quality required in a system before the perspectives are put into focus. In practice, the level required can significantly affect the costs associated with managing a system. It also can restrict the configuration options for distributive processing, especially how inputs are distributed with respect to where data is stored.

Unfortunately, the issues associated with the quality of data are often overlooked in the design process, which leads to expensive corrections. Many techniques are available to reduce this problem. The next two are nearly universal to one degree or other.

### 6.4.1 Automated Identification of Errors

Certain types of errors lend themselves to automated quality control. Legal-range-of-value checks, compatibility checks, degree-of-accuracy checks (although not necessarily indicating correct data), and techniques for gauging reliability can reduce if not eliminate many of these errors. By contrast, qualitative validity and correctness, apart from compatibility relationships, can seldom be ensured by automated means, except in the limited sense of computer generating sampling reports intended for manual verification.

Errors related to timeliness can sometimes be checked automatically by requiring effective dates to be included in the inputs, and then developing sophisticated software that audits this data for likely cases of outdated data. Incomplete data can be controlled in part by disallowing record inputs without sufficient data in them, or disallowing outright deletions of information in certain data fields.

The important point is to design the system with the maximum amount of automated checking and verification of data, on the grounds that the cost of automated checking will rarely exceed 1 percent of the cost of human labor, which is true even when a few additional elements of data must be entered in the system with no utility other than verifying required data. The reason is a matter of taking advantage of automated interior lines.

### 6.4.2 Quality Control Measures

Most organizations maintain records of detected errors, ranging from input rejections to the number of corrective actions required for data accepted. Other organizations conduct random sample audits. Still others develop unique ways of verifying data. For example, at least one firm intentionally entered errors in selected records, and then waited to see how long it would take before they were detected. Not all errors lend themselves to being corrected or overcome by the same measures. What is important is to identify and isolate the source of the errors.

## 6.5 CONSIDERATIONS FOR SYSTEM INTEGRATIONS

Every system has some measure of bad data. When separate systems are integrated, opportunities arise to eliminate some of the errors. However, they are often offset by the task of dealing with a wider range of errors and the problem of finding an acceptable degree of quality for different users.

Unfortunately, compromises can generate more problems than they supposedly eliminate. For example, the attempts by the Army to interface its pay and personnel systems failed, notwithstanding the potential to eliminate a mass of duplicated data elements. Part of the reason was the finance section had to maintain a higher degree of data quality than the personnel section was willing to concede. (See case study E in appendix A.)

**Syntheses.** A synthesis integration offers the maximum opportunity to reduce errors for at least five reasons. First, most cases of duplicated data will be eliminated. Second, management resources can be sharply focused on the larger but singular system in lieu of a multitude of smaller systems. Third, the lessons learned from experience with the targeted systems should improve the efficiency of the design. Fourth, the integration should yield a singular data element dictionary and thus a uniform legal ranges of values. Fifth, compatibility checks should prove more extensive and easier to execute. However, unless the targeted systems bear a great deal of relatability, the value of these advantages is negligible and perhaps harmful to corporate interests.

**Database Integrations.** In terms of the database, a database integration is nearly the same as a synthesis. Therefore, the same advantages accrue and the same problems tend to occur. The exception is when the software used to screen and evaluate data by some users is not shared by all the users in the organization. This problem can stem from legal restrictions or from less distinguished reasons. The weeds of turf battles can work their way into a system faster than a virus.

**Excerpt Integrations.** Unfortunately, the advantages of a synthesis or database integration do not apply to the excerpt model. Only copies of existing data are integrated, in excerpt integrations. Hence the data comes with all the errors generated in the separate systems. This result is acceptable when management is concerned primarily with approximations and trend lines, but not anything else.

**Interfaces.** Interfaced systems can be likened to fiefdoms when discussing the quality of data. Ancient kings knew they could levy their respective fiefs for troops and money up to a point. Beyond that point, they could not control the details by which the chieftains ran these fiefs. Similarly, in interface integrations, the managers of different systems must usually rely on the quality control of other managers if they want to make use of data beyond their own system. Unfortunately, not every individual puts organizational good above local interests. Information managers cannot eliminate this problem, or even make much of dent in it. What they have to do is deal with it.

**Standardizations.** The standardization model of integration seems to have the least impact on the quality of data, except at those times when a uniform data element dictionary is imposed on diverse groups. Still, an improved communications network could reduce reliability errors.

# 7

# The Procedural System

*The government is very keen on amassing statistics.*
*They collect them, add them, raise them to the nth power,*
*take the cube root and prepare wonderful reports.*
*But you must never forget that every one of those figures*
*comes in the first place from the village watchman,*
*who puts down what he damn pleases.*

—Sir Josiah Story
Inland Revenue Department
Great Britain, 1896-1919

The database of an automated information system extends beyond its electronic components. Entering data into a system is only the final step in a large operation. Conversely, accessing that data is only the first step in another one. The only difference between the *internal* and the *external* aspect of a system is: in an internal system, the mechanics are managed by the machine itself, in an external system, the procedures must be managed manually. Because these procedures are routine, they comprise a system in their own right and sometimes are partly automated by a secondary system.

An information manager might argue that because these procedures extend beyond the machinery, they are not his responsibility. Not so. As discussed in chapter 1, the information manager is managing information more than systems. If the automated core of a system falls short of sufficient data, quantitatively or qualitatively, the organization must resort to obtaining it manually. That takes time. If the problem stems from inadequate procedures, the manager has failed in his responsibilities as much as if he certified faulty software as operational. Or if an individual from a competing firm gains unauthorized access to proprietary information, which in turn affects the company's profits, the value of that manager's computer expertise is moot.

More significantly, good procedures can improve the efficiency of any system, and conversely a well-designed automated system can simplify manual procedures, which can reduce operating costs. The reason is the prevailing theme of this book—the opportunity to maximize interior lines throughout every tier of a system, that is, ensuring the fewest interruptions along the most direct and fastest paths of information flow, except when the intent is to block that flow.

The specifics of internal lines for input differ from output. With inputs, the requirement is to identify errors before they get into the database, which means avoiding procedures that add to the potential for errors as well as streamlining the process of stopping errors that existed before. The former are ergonomic considerations; the latter, audit trail procedures. For outputs, the main considerations are clarity and simplicity for the user, assuming the access is authorized. When access is not authorized, the task is to impose enough obstacles between the individual and the system to discourage most attempts and nail the balance. Figure 7-1 presents the general picture.

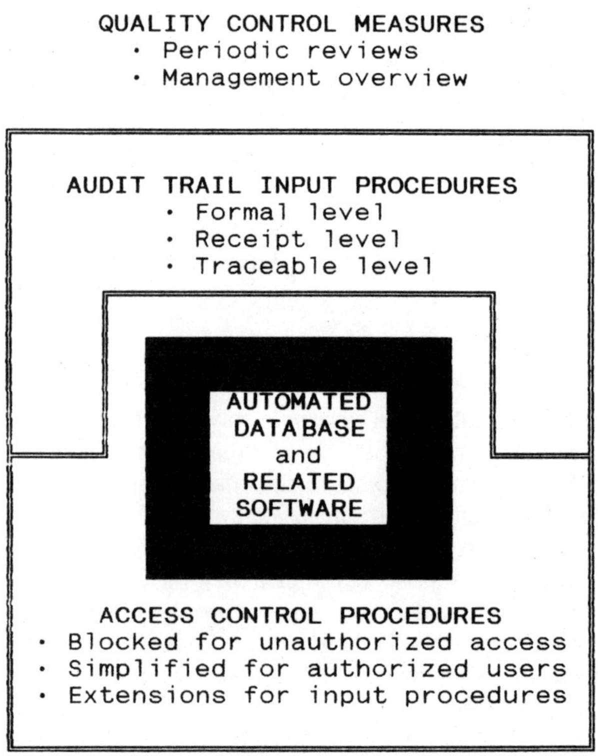


*Fig. 7-1. The procedural system. Procedures for managing input and controlling access to a database comprise a system in their own right. The former relies on one or more levels of audit trails; the latter relies on procedures to block or simplify access appropriate to the situation. Both should be encompassed by general quality control measures and management overview.*

This chapter looks first at the more technical of these requirements, namely audit trails and access control. The focus then shifts to an overview of quality control measures for both input and output, followed by a brief look at partial automation of control procedures. The chapter concludes with three sections on input problems associated with the various models of systems integration.

Are the procedures for an information system fundamentally different from a simple transaction or routine record-keeping function? If the former merely extracts data from existing systems, then the question is irrelevant. As discussed in section 6.3, the accuracy of the source data will normally suffice for higher-level information purposes. If the information system is developed along more original lines, the answer is no, although the extent of the procedures could be less.

The last point here is that most procedural systems follow the familiar power curve, that is, a few measures tend to account for the lion's share of quality control. The balance will fill in the blanks. The procedures that do the most good will vary with the system, and they might or might not be the most expensive ones.

## 7.1 AUDIT TRAILS

Good data does not get into a system by accident. Many factors operate to denigrate data from the time it originates until it is recorded electronically. When errors have financial consequences, audit trails are essential to trace the sources. Management must be able to pinpoint them, not only to correct the entries but to take corrective actions to reduce the incidence of future errors. In more specific terms, most audit trails require that the data entered in a system be exactly the same as on the document, except for coding equivalents. Thus if for some reason male and female gender were entered as A and B respectively, the A or the B would not have to be on the audit document.

The mechanics of audit trails operate at one of three levels. To the extent data in a system imposes pecuniary liability on one or more individuals is the extent which the system will employ a higher level. The three levels of audit trails are listed in descending order.

1) *Formal*. This level requires formal, authenticated documentation before data is entered into a system. This audit trail is common for most payrolls and many accounting systems, especially in government agencies. It is roughly analogous to registered mail.
2) *Receipt*. This level permits direct entry of data and then provides a computer printout of the input to be verified and stored. The immediate output is the audit trail. A simple but prevalent example would be cash register tapes at checkout counters, both on behalf of the retailer and the customer. This receipt backs up the data transmitted to inventory

control. The source documentation can then be disposed of. In theory, this technique should be no less accurate than the formal level, but in practice it is all too easy to verify incorrect data after the fact. The analogy here would be certified mail, and there is a difference. Registered mail is often used to ship diamonds and even classified documents (within the United States) up to the level of Secret. Not so with certified mail.

3) *Traceable*. This level documents the routes and paths of data in general, but does not log each document. This is analogous to insured mail. In some cases, a lost parcel can be traced, but the idea is to provide compensation if it cannot. The cost of the insurance is cheaper than a higher-level audit trail to prevent loss in the first place.

Irrespective of the level of audit trail employed, information managers should avoid creating unnecessary paperwork. Fewer forms, and the fewer times data is transcribed from one form of media to another, translate to a more efficient system and dollar savings. If this efficiency mandates redesigning existing forms to improve the interior lines, then the expenditure is a solid investment.

Related to this problem is the tendency of some managers to accept written requirements and rules literally. In these situations they might resist these modifications on the grounds the revision would fall short of specifications. The information manager might have to spend considerable time persuading these pedants to look at matters differently.

### 7.1.1 Legal Requirements

The requirements for most audit trails are established either by law or by commonly accepted practices within a profession. Some of these laws are at the federal level, although normally in a general form that requires implementing regulations. When designing a system, audit trail requirements and their intent must be considered as part of the system.

Further, legal requirements do not end with statutes. On the contrary, the doctrines associated with civil law can in effect mandate extensive audit trails, to prevent or at least reduce the risk of abuse or damage. An organization can be held liable if it is negligent in permitting incorrect data to be entered in a system, if it subsequently results in harm or actionable damage to an individual. In a litigious society, this is no small point. Note how every software manufacturer explicitly limits warranties against incidental or consequential damages from the use of their software.

### 7.1.2 Professional Imperatives

Even without explicit or implicit legal requirements, systems that employ audit trails do so with the support of most of the personnel involved. They might occasionally express dissatisfaction with an irksome provision, but a suggestion to do away with the documentation will usually be met with strong resistance. Whether the reasons are psychological or organizational in origin is immaterial. The attitude is usually justified by professional standards.

The significance to managers is that any attempt to eliminate or degrade the standards is improper and largely futile. This is particularly applicable for system integrations, as discussed in sections 7.5 through 7.7. If anything, integrations can require more extensive trails to cover the possible loss of control over the data after it is entered into the system or to compensate for delays in tracing errors as a result of the larger database.

## 7.2 ACCESS CONTROL

Organizations control access to data for three reasons: to adhere to legal requirements, to protect or advance organizational interests, and to simplify access for those individuals who must or should use the data. As shown in FIG. 7-2, the contradictions are built-in and will likely be compounded by the security provisions covered in chapter 13. As access terminals evolve into work stations, the conflicts will only increase. The easier gleaning intelligence from an organizational database becomes, the more severe the security problem is to prevent unauthorized access.

In many cases, controls can indirectly reduce the quality of data or alternatively increase costs. On the other hand, these problems are not new. Few restrictions apply solely to computerized databases. If an organization is entitled to collect and maintain certain data, it is almost always entitled to record that information in a computer system. Similarly, if an organization is barred

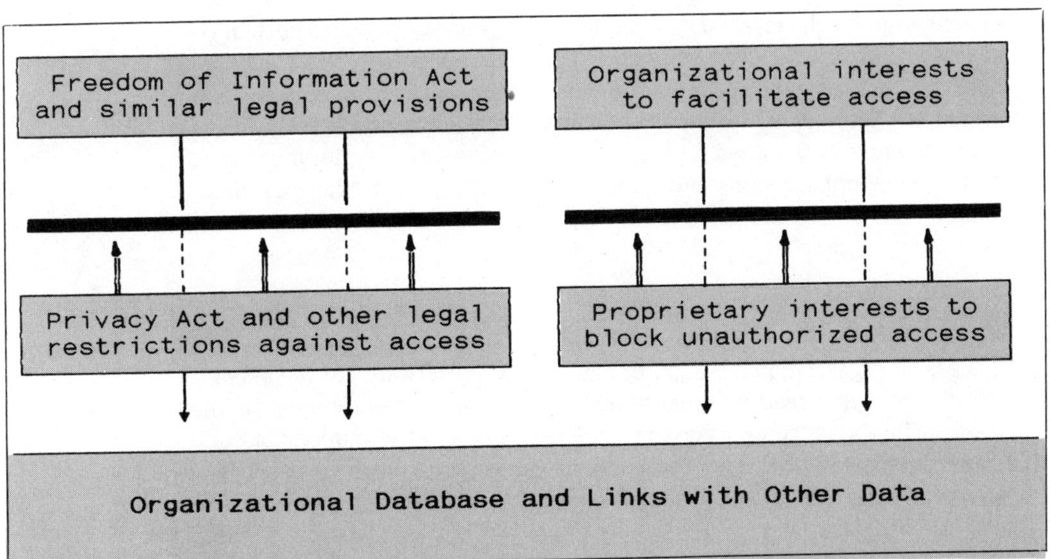


*Fig. 7-2. Contradictions with access controls. Access to databases must be controlled, due to legal restrictions and organizational interests. It must also be facilitated for individuals who require access, and to support other laws. Striking the right balance is a difficult task.*

from distributing certain data from its files, it almost certainly will be restricted from circulating that information from an automated database.

However, the ease with which data can be accessed in some systems compared to information in locked file cabinets presents a different problem. An organization might have to take special measures to prevent an unauthorized access, a matter of security, rather than a legal consideration. In very large systems, the ease of access also can incur major ethical issues, as is described in chapter 21.

Other control requirements stem from the increasing potential for illegal duplication or use of copyrighted software. Sticky cases arise when proprietary software is *paraphrased* to avoid paying a license fee. At what point does harnessing logic, which is always in the public domain, devolve into plagiarism sufficient to invite a legal suit?

### 7.2.1 Privacy vs. Freedom of Information

The Privacy Act restricts access to data; the Freedom of Information Act opens it. In theory, each applies to different types of data. In manual systems, documents that contain both kinds of information can be distributed by first blacking out the information that cannot be released, and then making photocopies of the balance. The same procedure should be followed with automated systems, but technical reasons often make this difficult. The federal government has recently admitted that computer databases have forced many of its agencies to restrict access under the Freedom of Information Act, primarily because it is too easy to concurrently access information covered by the Privacy Act.

Attempts to block certain data elements to certain users under certain conditions involve complex programming. The alternative is to restrict access to the data and let those individuals decide what can and what cannot be released. Unfortunately, that option reduces the practical efficiency of a system. This is one more example of the need for trade-offs. As information systems expand to permeate entire organizations and their customers or clients, the existence of automated data access brings together diffuse problems that were dealt with piecemeal in the past.

### 7.2.2 Proprietary Rights and Obligations

Unless an organization's computers and systems software are owned in fee simple, the manufacturers will likely have placed major restrictions on their use, especially the software. The principal restriction is the number of copies that can be made and what uses those copies can be put to without paying additional license fees. In practice, illegal copying of software occurs more frequently among amateurs than organizations, except perhaps in academic environments where the violations are intended primarily for educational purposes.

This situation has led some manufacturers to protect software from being copied by including a few instructions—vaguely analogous to a "controlled virus"—that prevent copies of the software from executing. Earlier versions of Lotus 1-2-3 and most versions of dBASE are examples. Unfortunately, these instructions can be nullified by expert programmers and by other software designed to overrule the instructions. The capabilities of the latter technique are blatantly advertised. Although using this type of software to make copies is illegal, developing, selling, and owning it is perfectly legal.

Another interesting case arose in IBM's attempt to create and patent unique central processing units for their series 2 personal computer line. The highly popular PCs, XTs, and ATs were designed to be imitated and to encourage maximum software development. The ostensible reason was to prevail in the PC marketplace, notwithstanding the head start won by Apple, Tandy, and others.

This tactic worked only too well. Compatibility with IBM quickly became the largely unpatented standard. Collectively, other manufacturers were able to regain the majority share of the PC market. IBM, apparently assuming its name would carry the day, then created a new architecture for its series 2 products. This strategy didn't work. The older design had become too standardized. Eventually the company was forced to return to the prevailing architecture to make their PCs—the irony was not lost on most observers—IBM-compatible.

In all of this legal tangle, however, one point must be made clear. With rare exception, any applications software or databases created within an organization remain the property of that organization. To the extent they require systems software to execute, the owners should still abide by the restrictions placed on that software, such as the number of computers the systems software is allowed to utilize. But the data and the applications software can be copied an infinite number of times and sold, licensed, or distributed to anyone the organization selects, without violating the manufacturers' license agreements. The recipients, of course, should also abide by the those agreements, plus any new restrictions imposed by the intermediate party.

### 7.2.3 Official Security Restrictions

Special restrictions sometimes apply to data in government databases that seldom apply to commercial equivalents. The most common situation is classified data. The laws and regulations that affect access to classified information fill volumes. Standards applied to contractors tend to be even stricter than for government agencies, probably because the increased opportunities to access that data illegally. Further, the number of specialized security levels above Top Secret is itself classified. Next, the doctrine of "need to know" permeates access rules for most classified information. Finally, security clearances for different government departments are not interchangeable.

The point on "need to know" has major significance for information managers. Individuals who work on hardware, software, and communications, where classified information resides or is transmitted, must have the same clearance and permission for access as those who use the information. The trend, especially in the Department of Defense, is to reduce the number of individuals cleared for access to highly classified information, even though the proliferation of systems mandates an increase.

Other factors to consider here are the high cost of any system that uses classified data, especially if it is distributive; the long delays in obtaining the appropriate security clearances for the requisite number of personnel; and increases in the time necessary to develop and test software compared to a nonclassified environment. Furthermore, as data accumulates, its sheer mass often warrants a higher classification, which in turn increases the cost of a system and reduces the number of individuals who can access it. As a corollary, after data is integrated, the entire database must assume the highest classification of any data resident in it.

## 7.2.4 Organizational Interests

Organizational interests are probably the strongest factors affecting access to data. Legal requirements and restrictions might tip the scales in a courtroom, but short of that, an organization tends to operate based on what decision makers perceive as the organization's best interests. These interests might or might not coincide with personal interests.

The information manager should confront organizational interests early in the planning process. Section 2.5 argued that perceived necessity for a system was in part a subjective factor. Subjective factors are usually based on organizational interests. The interests that direct a system to be developed also will suggest the interests that will be served in setting the rules for accessibility. This is no small point, especially when an information system can support major decisions. The tendency to record crucial but damning information and then restrict access to it forced one U.S. president to resign from office. Twelve years later, the same tendency fueled the Iran-Contra scandal. The parallels in lesser offices might not be as dramatic, but they exist.

## 7.2.5 Simplifying Access

Assuming the issues of legal requirements and organizational interests have been resolved, the work of the information manager then turns 180 degrees. The process of accessing data should be simplified, irrespective of the number of users. In effect, the users should become end points in the interior lines of the information system. Now, keyboard access is done with the fewest keystrokes and the fewest iterations to obtain the necessary information. This approach usually goes by the oversimplified name of user-friendly systems.

User friendliness can be nothing more than polite messages flashed on a monitor. For example, "Please review page such-and-such of the guidelines" in lieu of the usual, "Stop. Error code number umpti-umpt." Unfortunately, this gingerbread approach will seldom make systems user friendly. Anyone who has ever worked with even simple spreadsheet or database management programs knows that mastery of any type of decision support system does not come easy, especially when complex logic must be applied to compare data in successive iterations. If crucial decision making can be done too easily, chief executive officers can be replaced with computers. Therefore, strive to simplify the mechanics without discounting the intelligence and experience necessary to make use of a good decision support system.

## 7.3 QUALITY CONTROL

Quality control traces its roots back to the early nineteenth century. The motivation, however, was the opposite of what it is today. As the industrial revolution spread and mass production became popular, the skill and care of artisans had to be restrained to meet production schedules. Today, industry and government seldom confront excessive quality. The inevitable intent is to improve quality by reducing slipshod work.

Technically, audit trails can be considered a form of quality control, but the latter connotes a wider spectrum of activity. Audit trails are precise documentation requirements pegged to every specified transaction, or at least so most of them can be retraced. By contrast, quality control measures can be routine or occasional, exhaustive or sampling, or penetrating or superficial. The goal of quality control is to ensure that procedures maintain the intended design level of quality. Without quality control, the criteria will not be met. If the criteria are not met, the system either will fail of purpose or fail to generate the anticipated return on investment.

The level of quality control will vary with the circumstances, so much so that suggesting guidelines would be a mistake. However, if the procedural system is simple, ensuring it works also will be simple. Quality control is the bridge between formal repetitive procedures and management overview. It is as much an attitude on the part of managers, as it is a way of doing business. A horde of procedures will not substitute for quality control. The information manager should bear this in mind when designing a system.

If the design level of quality control then proves too difficult or expensive, four options are available: accept the higher costs, accept a lower standard of system efficiency, find a different way within the system to reach the original objectives, or abandon the system as impractical.

## 7.4 AUTOMATION OF PROCEDURES

One of the more interesting turnabouts in computer applications is their use for quality control of databases and processing that remain manual. The procedure cited in section 2.1 used a UPC-type sticker to monitor complex paperwork. By extending all or part of a formal audit trail, procedure itself can be automated. The problem, however, is the automation might require its own audit trail.

In the example, no requirement for the trail existed. The system was developed to provide management with a tool where there was none. This would not be true for a formal audit trail. To avoid a secondary trail, the automation must be restricted to simplification. The option of downgrading a formal-level audit trail to a receipt-level is often a compromise solution, if the additional errors are tolerable.

Some managers and many textbooks advocate a formal *information resources management system*, implying that most procedures can be mechanized. Perhaps so, but one caveat applies. The attempts to automate quality control of air controllers have shown that the quality control managers become less immersed in the action. As a result, they are less able to react in those crises requiring human intervention. Automation of quality control procedures can be pushed too far, a fact that supports the thesis that quality control and procedures are fundamentally different.

## 7.5 PROBLEMS WITH SYNTHESES AND DATABASE INTEGRATIONS

In theory, audit trails and other quality control measures for targeted systems and databases should suffice collectively for the intended integration. The key word here is "collective." The separate measures do not always neatly collect. Consider the following points:

**Audit Trails.** If the integration makes no change to existing input stations or in the ability of each existing station to access data, and accessing is within the times it originally had, then the integration should have no impact on the audit trails. Yet, as mentioned several times in previous chapters, after a database is integrated, the criteria of the strictest user must usually be adopted by all users, at least with respect to each data element.

**Access Control.** The most likely problem with integrated databases is the exponential increase of opportunities for unauthorized access, or inherently simplifying illegal access to accumulated data that would have required a more difficult effort when the component databases were separated. This problem can be overcome in part by categorical database structures (subsection 5.2.5), electronic controls, and geographical access restrictions where applicable. The phrase, "in part," should be emphasized. The pace of integration seems to outdistance the speed with which controls can be developed to curtail eavesdropping.

**Quality Control.** Quality control of integrated databases might or might not be easier than the sum of the measures exercised over the components. The elimination of duplicate data fields will tend to reduce review requirements, but the mass of the system or database can encounter new problems, especially if it is distributed. A good analogy would be the difficulty of managing a chain of stores in three states compared to managing a similar chain in one city.

## 7.6 PROBLEMS WITH INTERFACE INTEGRATIONS

Because interface integrations can take many different forms, the impact on procedures can vary from negligible to significant. On the other hand, no matter how sophisticated these procedures are, they cannot compensate for an interface design that lacks necessity or attempts to integrate incompatible functions. When the interface is feasible, the procedural problems tend to be a less intense version of those associated with database integrations.

**Audit Trails.** The most common problem occurs when two or more separate systems are linked and the data from one is transmitted to another, instead of entering it at the original location. Audit trails of the system with the higher standards must now apply to both, irrespective of the cost. Relocation of the personnel and offices responsible for maintaining the audit trails might be necessary.

**Access Control.** If the design permits a formerly separate station to use the software operating at another station to access the data, the limits of licensing agreements can be violated, particularly if any part of that software is transmitted to the using station. The obvious solution is to negotiate new license agreements, although this provision might be more expensive than anticipated.

**Quality Control.** These requirements will usually increase. Each component will continue to need its own quality control, while all the hardware, software, and communications nets installed to implement the integration will add to the load. Further, pinpointing errors in the network can prove troublesome, even in the best designs. Consider the nationwide breakdown of the famed AT&T long-distance network on January 16, 1990. The problem was traced to a new piece of software in one location. Yet it took about 12 hours to identify and fix the bug, during which time several million dollars in net profits slipped into oblivion.

## 7.7 PROBLEMS ASSOCIATED WITH STANDARDIZATIONS

Standardization of hardware, software, or communications can introduce any number of unique problems, but they seldom fall under a few generic categories. Perhaps the most serious problem is when a uniform data element dictionary is imposed on separate systems. In some cases, the new legal range of values for specific data elements will no longer accommodate all requirements. See technical note 11 in appendix B for one solution to the problem.

From a higher perspective, the Department of Defense decision to implement Ada as its standard programming language (to include database management software) has been, among other objectives, an attempt to improve software quality. Whether these implementations have reduced quality control for entering and accessing data remains to be seen. It is the old problem of attempting to replace human skills with machines rather than supplementing them.

# 8

# Managerial Design of the Database Environment

*There is a kind of sympathy in honest minds, by means of which they give an easy credit to each other.*

—Henry Fielding

The previous chapter focused on the procedural system that surrounds an automated database. One of the points was to structure as many of the procedures as possible. Unfortunately, no procedure can fit all situations, and even the best procedures will fail on occasion. The reasons can range from a crucial piece of paper accidentally being pushed into a trash can, to a disgruntled employee entering incorrect information into a system.

Good management should superintend the database environment, both the inner-automated part and the outer-procedural ring. Yet even here, the environment can be designed to simplify its own management. The steps taken will tend to mutually reinforce each other. The design should aim for this optimal mix.

The means of simplifying management are: understanding the relationship between inputs and the database configuration, establishing tiers for quality control, maximizing automated inputs, recognizing special problems with complex or unique inputs, and keeping the factor of human motivation in the foreground. The first five sections of this chapter respectively address these points. The sixth section covers integrations, which summarizes the related comments in the previous three chapters. The last section is a wrap-up on trade-offs, with a concluding reference to the principles of strategy for information systems.

## 8.1 RELATIONSHIP OF INPUTS AND THE DATABASE DESIGN

The database model chosen for a system—relational, hierarchical, or network—depends largely on the nature of the processing required. However, the specific organization of the records, and the distribution of data among files, should be based on the pattern of inputs, unless a compelling reason suggests otherwise. For example, in a complex distributive processing system, record structure might beneficially parallel input records, which simplifies the input process, and leaves the generation of specific database views to software. Access to specific files during input can be limited, which reduces processing time and the potential for error. More significantly, this could reduce the cost of distributing data on a periodic basis and improve the barriers to unauthorized access.

The variety of relationships between the system and the organization and its input sites is too vast to illustrate the situation with a single chart. Yet every information manager should ensure that a chart of this nature is prepared to map the situation for each system under his or her responsibility, especially for systems in the design phase. Solving problems that arise from these relationships has led some decision makers to separate the database from the system, that is, the database and its input become the primary system. Access is restricted to data essential to process updates. Users of the data are then "piggybacked" on the primary system, with corresponding restrictions on updates, except to generate and modify views.

### 8.1.1 Input Demographics

Ideally, data should be entered at its point of origin. The processing might not occur until after the input has been transmitted over thousands of miles, but at least it is in the system and no longer subject to degradation except by unreliable transmission media. In practice, this is seldom the case. What happens is that some data originates in outlying offices or field stations, some data originates at points beyond the immediate reach of any terminal, and some data originates at central locations. The question then becomes whether to centralize or to distribute the input, or more accurately the proportion for each location.

If the resident locations of the database are decentralized, then top-loaded inputs must be distributed downward before many of the input checks can be run. If the database is centrally located (with copies or views distributed as appropriate), locally entered data must often be transmitted to the central location before final acceptance. Whatever the case, an ideal solution seldom offers itself to the planner. Inevitably, major trade-offs will be required. Further, a design to improve accuracy of input might be inappropriate for a system where accuracy is less important than processing. For example, a management information system that washes out errors by the law of averages, or by using corrective factors seldom depends on the accuracy of each item. See subsection 6.3.4 for an example.

### 8.1.2 Dominant or Critical Inputs

Occasionally, a sports announcer ruminates that while a football game comprises 150 plays or so, only eight or nine decide most contests. Similarly, in most systems only a fraction of the inputs updates the dominant or critical parts of the database. These kingpin data fields or pivotal records drive the rest of the database in a logical sense, but these items will vary with each system. For a transactional personnel system, which requires many updates and records kept of those updates, the kingpin elements would be: name or Social Security number, current or new status, the effective date of the change, and the elements in the record that are updated the most frequently, or are most often used for compatibility checking.

Understanding this logical hierarchy can lead to an efficient database structure. This efficiency stems from reducing the number of logical paths, which improves the interior lines. Users that depend on different paths can rearrange the database by way of views. Restated, decisions on the structure of the database should veer toward simplifying the input process, which will likely improve the quality and quantity of the data. Let the software accommodate user requirements. Figure 8-1 shows a generic transaction-code input data field that can be used to control input processing, which in turn might suggest how a database should be structured.

### 8.1.3 Input Mechanics

When input mechanics become too stringent or too difficult, users might rebel and perhaps torpedo the quality of the input. An interesting example of this occurred in 1984, when the Internal Revenue Service installed a new tax return processing system. The well publicized flaws greatly overtaxed the patience of clerks. Some of them disposed of returns to meet quotas. Piles of these returns were later found in the ceiling panels and other hiding places. The IRS did a commendable job of correcting the errors within a year, but this does not gainsay the problems that can arise when input mechanics present major difficulties.

Most systems break down at transfer points or the equivalent, somewhat analogous to most plane crashes occurring during take-off and landing, and most automobile accidents occurring at intersections. Debugging software, aggravating as it can be, is easy compared to eliminating or even reducing ergonomic interface problems. Academic courses tend to belabor the former and gloss over the latter, yet experienced managers know full well where the chronic headaches come from.

## 8.2 QUALITY CONTROL TIERS

Quality results from the combined effect of: the attitude of managers, general quality control measures, specific audit trail procedures, and the automated

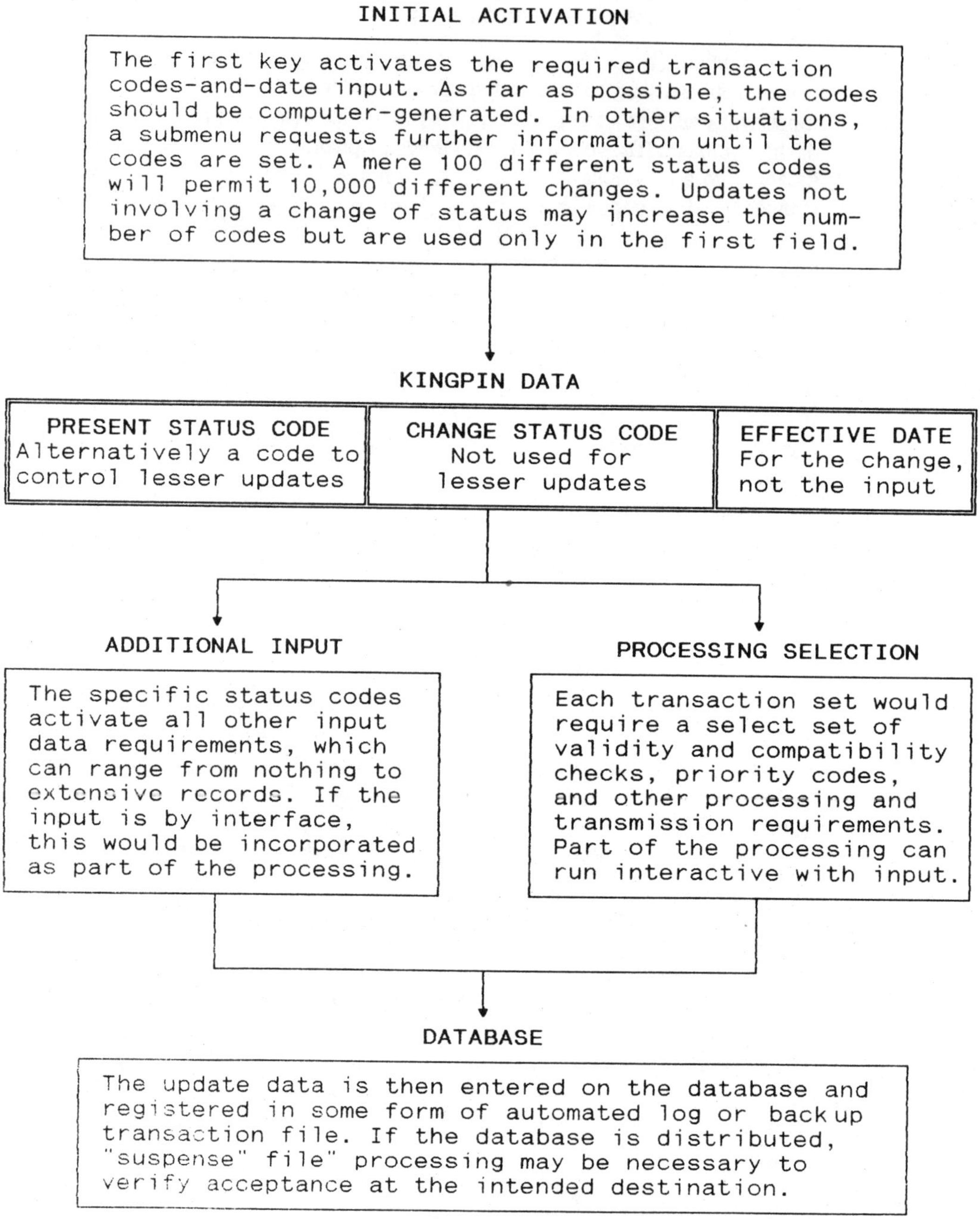


*Fig. 8-1. A generic transaction code setup. Transactions that involve a change of status would be updated by entering the present and changed status codes, plus the effective date. This information would activate all other required input on an interactive basis. The codes themselves could be plain-English terms or even selected from a menu or chain of menus.*

checks in the system itself. The manager or planner must then decide how much reliance to place at each level or tier, analogous to a series of increasingly fine screens or sieves. Figure 8-2 shows this process.

As a rule, the proportionality should favor the tiers in the reverse order. Maximum reliance should be placed on automated checks, followed by an emphasis on the applicable level of audit trails, then by general quality control

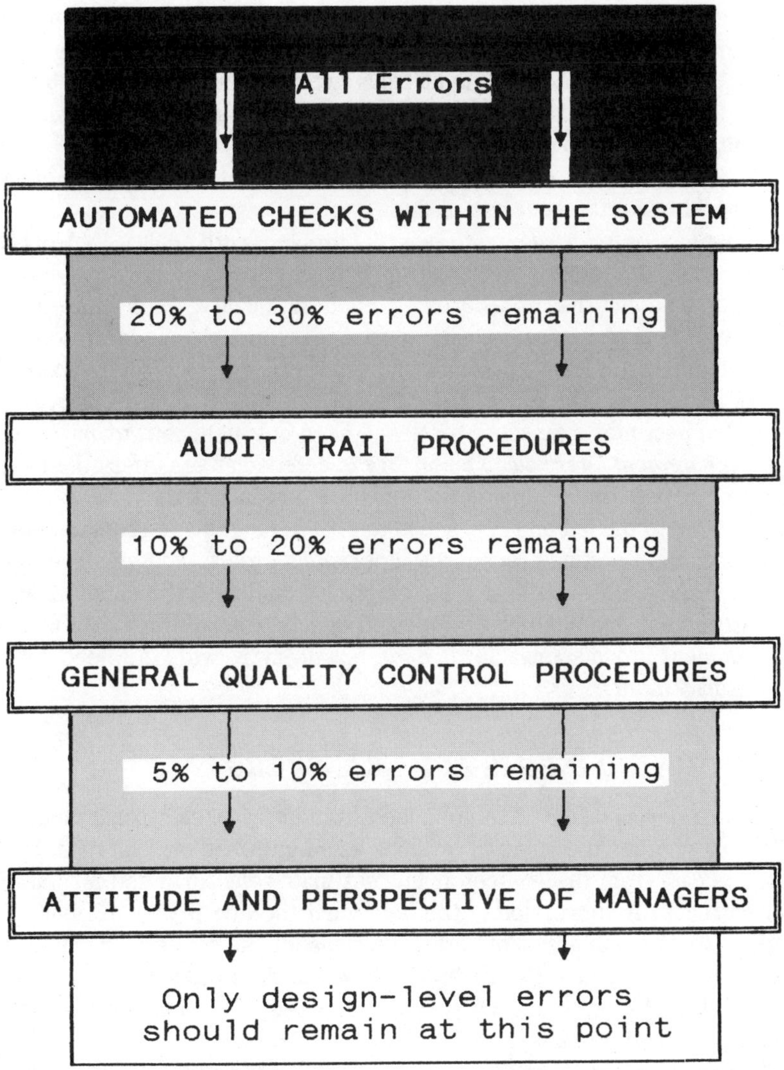


*Fig. 8-2. The sieve of input quality control. The design of the input environment should reverse the chronological sequence of input processing. Priority should be given to automated checks, next to audit trails, then to general quality control procedures, and finally to the attitude on the part of measures. This yields the maximum return on the least investment.*

measures, all of which leaves managers to work with exceptions and to oversee the general efficiency of the entire set-up. The reasons are lower costs and higher efficiency.

- *Automated Checks*. Automated checks are the most inexpensive form of quality control and are usually applied to all inputs. These checks can be enhanced by a good database structure, primarily by improving the compatibility checks. This is another reason for going the extra mile when designing the most efficient structure under the circumstances.
- *Audit Trail Procedures*. Audit trails are far more expensive than computer checks because of the labor required. But like the former, computer checks also cover all transactions and can be streamlined. Further, many of them are more or less mandated. The information manager should make the best use of them.
- *Quality Control Measures*. The great problem with quality control is that, by itself, it is nearly meaningless. Systems are by definition systematic, and so should the procedures for ensuring quality. As discussed in section 7.3, to the extent quality control measures are an extension of procedures, or at least a periodic audit of them, they will likely prove more efficacious. To the extent they are not, the quality control director's job often becomes a sinecure for a well-liked but inefficient manager.
- *Management Overview*. The history of defense affairs offers the best lesson. Since time immemorial, military organizations have been regimented to the hilt and encased in tons of regulations, directives, policies, standard operating procedures, operations orders, and whatever. Yet no profession puts as heavy an emphasis on leadership and managerial attributes. Although proceduralized quality control for a database environment is indispensable, it does not do away with the need for good management.

## 8.3 AUTOMATED INPUTS AND TRANSFERS

Data for one system is often obtained from external electronic media, irrespective of whether the transfer qualifies as an interface or a merger. In many cases, the data from the sources might not match the form and format of the target database. A conversion of the data must then be made, manually, automated, or some combination of both. The rules for the conversion can be absolute or they can be probable, or they can have absolute rules for some elements and probable rules for others. Or perhaps the rules will be absolute under some circumstances and probable under others.

To make matters more complex, the issue of absolute vs. probable rules can hinge on a compatibility check. For example, consider check processing, which is a billion dollar industry. What decision should be made when the dollar amount in digits does not match the text amount written on the same check, or when one of the paired entries is illegible? This happens several million times every day. Should the check be rejected? That would add to processing costs.

Should the text amount govern? If so, does it govern only when the apparent discrepancy is within certain limits? What if the check isn't signed, but has been accepted by several intermediate processors? Alternatively, what decision is proper if an endorsement on the back falls below the $1^1/_2$-inch margin, but has been accepted by other institutions in the chain?

These problems are spurring the proliferation of bank teller machines, especially in retail stores and gas stations, which significantly reduces the input processing load, and cuts back the incidence rate of bounced checks. As advised in section 2.4, never underestimate the strategic value of good low-level processing. The same is true for credit card purchases, where the receipt level of audit trail is slowly replacing the formal level. That is, the items charged are entered directly into a machine (using a laser scanner when possible), which produces a receipt the customer signs. The transaction itself is then activated, albeit sometimes before the signature is obtained.

## 8.4 SPECIAL PROBLEMS WITH UNIQUE INPUTS

A small percentage of input transactions tend to account for the bulk of data in a database. Similarly, a small percentage of inputs can generate requirements for most of the software, although the problems associated with the latter often get short shrift by information managers. Yet as input processing at decentralized sites increases in complexity, the situation mandates more highly trained personnel. At a certain point, and after considering the following points, the information manager should find centralizing the processing of unique or complex transactions more advantageous.

### 8.4.1 Sources of Complex or Unique Inputs

Complex or unique inputs tend to come from one of three circumstances:

1) *Previous Errors*. A long chain of previous errors, particularly when undetected until some catastrophe occurs, is perhaps the most frequent source of these inputs. The entire chain of errors must be unravelled, which usually requires intense manual review and perhaps research.
2) *Ad Hoc Exceptions to the Rule*. Every rule has its exceptions, and sometimes these exceptions are intricate, a problem satirized in the novel *Catch-22*. In practice, the Department of Defense *Joint Travel Regulations*, which focuses on reimbursement of expenses, makes the intricacies of that novel seem tame by comparison. The DOD is still debating whether completely automating the process would be more economical than reducing the rules to utter simplicity and accepting the price of an occasional excess reimbursement.
3) *Unusual Events*. Most organizations experience unusual circumstances that tax the capabilities of its management. They stem either from a particularly intricate set of requirements or from an infrequent but simultaneous massing of less troublesome problems—mental gridlock.

For example, Mr. and Mrs. Jones want to fly from Des Moines to New Zealand to celebrate their twenty-fifth wedding anniversary. Unfortunately, work schedules force them to travel within a tight time frame, which means all but one hour of the anniversary date itself will be lost when crossing the International Date Line. So they would like to have a special meal and champaign served at midnight, in the economy section. Also, a delayed take-off of up to one hour would mean cutting into the 60 minutes or perhaps missing the anniversary date altogether. In this event, they want a backup reservation on Koala airlines to solve the problem. Finally, they insist on talking with Mrs. Smith, the supervisor who was so friendly and helpful with a special requirement when they took a trip to Bora Bora to celebrate their tenth anniversary 15 years ago. Does this sort of thing really happen? You bet—and a lot worse.

### 8.4.2 Problems with Input Processing

The difficulties of writing programs in advance to handle unusual traffic are: the nature of that traffic cannot always be foreseen, the permutations and combinations are usually too numerous to write sufficient programming to cover all contingencies, and even when the software can be written, the effort might not be cost effective. For example, most exception processing requires an exception to compatibility checks. If these checks are written to permit input of questionable items in complex situations, they also could permit excessive inaccurate data to be entered under routine circumstances. On the other hand, if all the exceptions are written into the software, the software can prove too intricate and prone to errors.

### 8.4.3 The Centralized Adjudication and Input Option

The complexity of unique inputs might warrant specialized central processing facilities. In this alternative, unusual cases would be routed to one or more specialized centers: staffed with the experienced personnel, stocked with the necessary references and granted the authority to override various automated checks in the system. The reason is the opportunity to cut costs, shown in a graph in FIG. 8-3. The audit trail documentation required in these centers would accordingly be more stringent, but the number of cases handled would be small compared to routine inputs.

This alternative obviates the need to: distribute and maintain extensive software, train station personnel in the special procedures, distribute copies of necessary references, and establish extensive quality control measures to ensure everything works well. The disadvantage is that forwarding the necessary information to the centralized facility can take too much time. Further, this alternative could be abused by local clerks unwilling to do a little research within the reach of their resources.

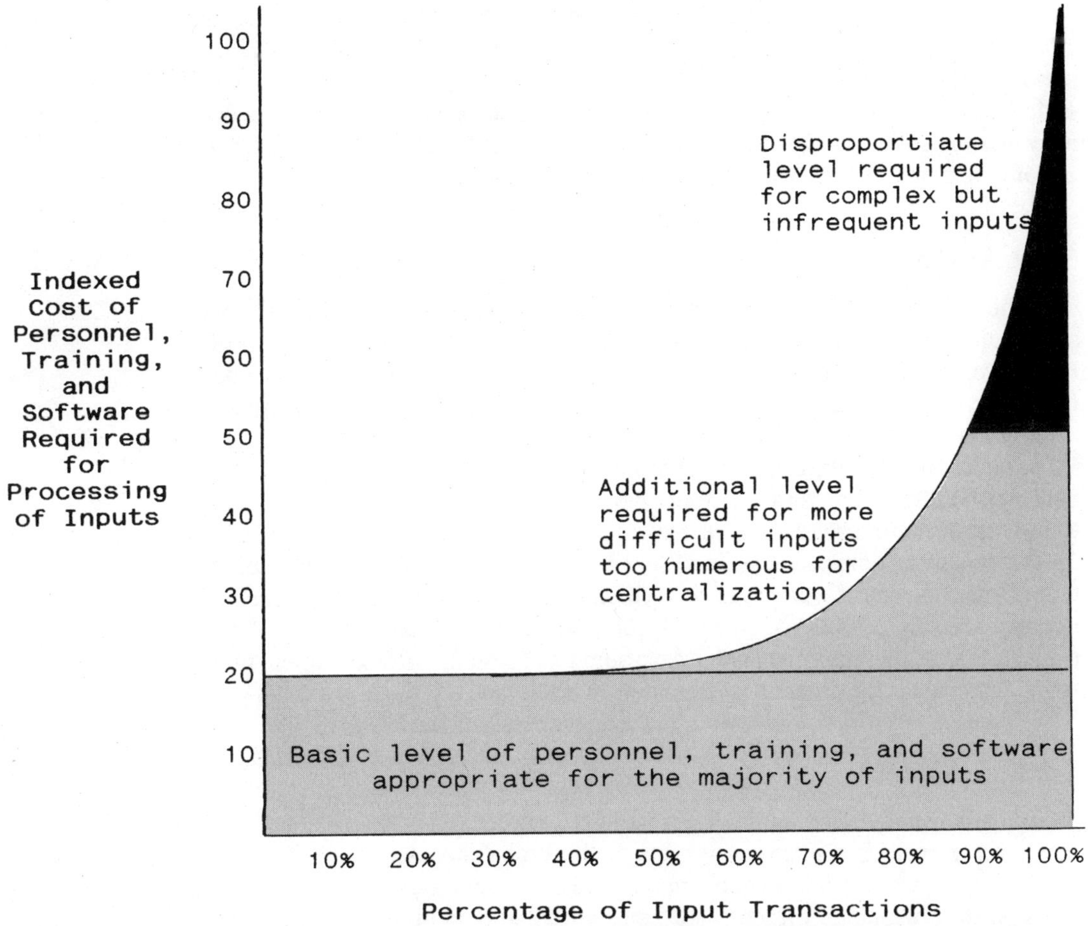


*Fig. 8-3. Centralized adjudication for complex inputs. Although distributive processing rates strong praise, centralized adjudication of complex or unique updates warrants serious consideration. The cost of processing these inputs tends to rise exponentially with the degree of complexity. If not centralized, the cost must be duplicated at each station, compounded by the cost of additional quality control measures.*

## 8.5 HUMAN FACTORS

If economics is the dismal science, ergonomics can be outright lamentable. To a data processing professional, working with a keyboard and monitor poses about as much concern as turning lights off and on. For other users, the anxiety levels can be significant. The anxiety might be irrational, but it can and does occur. Systems planners must deal with these anxieties, until the individuals affected overcome them.

When the problem stems from mere unfamiliarity, training and experience will usually suffice. But when the machine represents an intrusion on what is commonly regard as the prerogatives of human judgment, the problem is more serious. Many senior executives will not touch computers, although they endorse and even champion their use for routine processing. Many professionals will avoid some proven computer applications, for example, the reluctance of some doctors to work with expert-system diagnostic aids.

### 8.5.1 Anxiety

The only practical remedy for inexperience is experience. Whether this accrues in formal training sessions or informal on-the-job training is immaterial. If the workers are already experienced in working with some form of input machinery, the task is that much simpler, but presuming all anxiety will be removed is a mistake.

The anxiety can stem from workplace problems, or from fears that continued radiation from monitors will affect health. The research on this issue continues. In the former situation, management should take corrective action. In 1985, accounting employees at Fort Belvoir, Virginia, filed a class action suit in federal court against several agencies within the Department of the Defense to improve working conditions. Although the computer input tasks were not the primary task at the time, the addition of them to an already sardine-like environment aggravated the situation to the point of intolerance.

### 8.5.2 Resistance

Whether professional-outlook resistance to a proposed system can be overcome will vary with the circumstances. If the probability is low, perhaps the project, or at least the part in question, should be scrapped. If it is only a matter of adequate presentation, then a little salesmanship is in order. But when the resistance centers on a fundamental belief, management has a bear of a problem.

For example, the rising cost of medical care and the questionable efficacy of investing billions of dollars to prolong the agony of dying for the terminally ill will likely bring about a system of rationing health care, formally or informally. This rationing already exists in Great Britain and other developed countries, and not just for the terminally ill. Kidney transplants and dialysis are often denied the elderly, on the grounds that limited resources are better invested in the young.

Yet it is one thing to permit a doctor to make a judgment call in close cases, another to require him to enter data into a computer for a decision. To look at matters another way, the ethical considerations of automated billing for a credit card are minimal; for health care rationing, maximum. Ethical considerations will be exacerbated to the extent the entire decision process is automated, yet it might be impractical to permit too much leeway within the health-care profession. Any leeway will inevitably be interpreted in the most liberal possible manner.

### 8.5.3 The Relationship of Quality and Motivation

It almost goes without saying, motivated personnel work better than unmotivated personnel. The research on this point is conclusive and exhaustive. Unfortunately, the leadership capabilities of managers vary too widely to depend on research to any great extent. What can be systemically implemented is to tie the quality of input with benefits to the users, or at least to the practical consequences of failing to meet standards. Thus, payroll systems inherently motivate users to ensure greater accuracy than personnel files.

## 8.6 SPECIAL PROBLEMS WITH SYSTEMS INTEGRATION

Integrations pose additional factors to be considered in the general design of the input environment. Figure 8-4 summarizes these factors, which might or might not offset the efficiencies intended by the integration.

- *Syntheses and Database Integrations*. Both models should improve the effectiveness of compatibility checks and reduce if not eliminate duplicate data, which will permit an increase of automated checks at the price of more expensive and time consuming quality control procedures. Nevertheless, compromises are likely to be made on the design of the database and its input checks. Accordingly, the information manager will find himself immersed in many trade-off decisions.
- *Excerpt Integrations*. Most inputs to excerpt integrations will be automated. Because the data must be accepted "as is," the design tasks will tend to focus on conversion software to the extent the targeted databases are incompatible.
- *Interfaces*. The impact of an interoperable integration on the management of input can range from negligible to severe. If the interoperable features are restricted to a better distribution of outputs, then the management of the input should not be affected. But if the interoperability means data from one system will serve as the input to another, instead of original input in that other system, then the management of the latter will of necessity become interested in the quality control of the former. The ensuing turf battles might, and often do, defeat the project.
- *Standardizations*. The most common problem with standardizations stems from a uniform data element dictionary that does not meet all user requirements, which often can be solved using the technique described in technical note 11 in appendix B. Beyond this, and as suggested in section 7.7, standardization as a direct means of improving quality control can be pushed too far. The more important issue is compatibility.

## 8.7 TRADE-OFFS

This chapter has emphasized that trade-offs are a way of life in database design. What those trade-offs prove to be will vary considerably with the system, although several points are common to all of them.

| | Advantages to Utilize | Disadvantages to Overcome |
|---|---|---|
| Syntheses and Database Integrations | By reducing duplicate data and massing formerly separate databases, compatibility checks can be expanded and accelerated. | The concentration of data invites unauthorized access, albeit offset by management's ability to focus on fewer databases. |
| Excerpt Integrations | The limited nature of an excerpt integration allows attention to be focused on transmission and data conversion software as required. | The disadvantage is similar to syntheses, though compounded by the massing of data with the most strategic significance. |
| Liaison Interfaces | Similar to syntheses, interfaces can reduce duplicate data and thus can increase compatibility checking, if the network can sustain it. | In addition to retaining existing quality control procedures, the resultant expansion of the network will need additional measures. |
| Standardizations | Standardizations *might* facilitate some aspects of quality control by reducing the range of expertise necessary to manage systems. | Imposing a uniform data element dictionary can fail to meet all user requirements and hence lead to rejection or to too many exceptions. |

*Fig. 8-4. Database management for integrations. Integrations can both simplify and exacerbate the quality control requirements of the database environment. The specifics vary with the model.*

**Points of Diminishing Returns.** Any measure designed to improve or ensure the accuracy of input can be pushed to the point where it becomes cost ineffective, and also can incur resentment among the users of the system. The literature is full of case histories and analyses.

**A Baseline for Trade-offs.** The design threshold criteria for acceptable accuracy is the baseline for establishing guidelines for the management of input. At that point, the trade-off considerations focus on the mix of features to use, from record formats and automated input checks to the degree of centralized vs. decentralized inputs. This baseline should be changed only when maintaining the design level appears to be too expensive or impractical.

**Minimizing Input.** The management of input can be simplified by reducing the man-machine interface input to a minimum, both in quantity and in frequency of occurrence. This point is obvious but often overlooked by designers and planners. The information manager should press it.

Another way of looking at trade-offs is to consider the six principles of strategy for information systems outlined in section 2.2. Figure 8-5 depicts the application of these principles to database design, emphasizing what seems to be important. Trading away these attributes could be a serious mistake.

PRINCIPLES RELATED TO PURPOSE AND STYLE

OBJECTIVE. Direct information resources toward objectives that will make a significant improvement in the implementation of policy, at an acceptable cost. *In virtually every case, the objective of an integration is to improve resiliency. Any other objective should be questioned.*

SIMPLICITY. Design systems with the simplest possible configuration and directives for use. *Every trade-off decision that compromises on simplicity is likely to incur more costs than it saves.*

PRINCIPLES RELATED TO INTEGRATION AND INTERIOR LINES

CONFIGURATION. Configure the elements of a system to facilitate attaining the objectives without undue risk of compromising information to the detriment of those objectives. *In practice, this mean a balance between centralized and decentralized data bases.*

RESILIENCY. Organize and direct the application of resources to effect a resilient superiority of information sufficient to prevail in the marketplace or in the provision of services, as the case may be. *Patchwork is not resilient. Massing or networking of data must stretch not twist to better meet requirements.*

PRINCIPLES RELATED TO MANAGEMENT AND LEADERSHIP

RESPONSIBILITY. In the planning, development, or operations management of any system. fix general responsibility on one individual, and vest him or her with sufficient control over the necessary resources to effect the objectives. *Integrations tend to eschew singular responsibility, just when it is most needed.*

INITIATIVE. Ensure that a system provides a sufficient and timely view of information to make a significant difference in the conduct of business. *Excessive networking and distributive processing can offset the intended timeliness of the integration.*

*Fig. 8-5. Trade-offs vs. the principles of strategy. The application of the principles of strategy for information systems, when applied to the database environment, offer a number of considerations for trade-off decisions.*

# Part III

# Technology and Wherewithal

Computer technology might be where the action is at, but it is seldom the source of system failures. If anything, few managers take maximum advantage of the technology that does exist, and most general managers have too many other priorities to afford the time to understand technology in detail. Yet until there is a common understanding between general management and the managers of technology, the potential to utilize technology will not likely be realized. For this reason, the six chapters in this part of the book attempt to bridge that gap.

Chapter 9 addresses hardware, with an emphasis on matching size to requirements. It also looks at freedom of choice in different situations when acquiring hardware, the advantages of minor overbuying of capability, and considerations for systems integrations. Chapter 10 carries the discussion into communications, with special emphasis on the significance and implications of the Open Standards Interface Agreement.

Chapters 11 and 12 discuss software; the former with a focus on general programming, the latter on artificial intelligence (AI) and decision support systems. For most systems, software is the dominant cost factor and also the most common cause of failure. But for information strategy, after the bread-and-butter transaction systems are in place, the view is increasingly towards AI and expert systems. Now AI is probably the most overrated aspect of computer science, but at the same time, the most underused. Chapter 12 tries to explain why.

Chapter 13 turns to the more mundane subject of security, a subject which has finally gained the attention it deserves by way of the computer virus (although these viruses account for less than 1 percent of all the devastation experienced by systems). It is true that too much money and effort can be spent on securing systems against all possible sources of damage and destruction, but the facts suggest that few companies have erred in that direction.

Chapter 14 is a bridge into the final part of the book: management. It focuses on emerging technology, specifically how management should consider what is being developed in the labs with reference to projects and systems on the drawing board.

Identifying a company or organization that best exemplifies the use of computer technology proved to be an impossible task. For some, communications made the difference; for others, efficient routine processing was the money maker. Yet in terms of information processing, expert systems offer the most potential. The corporation that exemplifies this is E.I. du Pont de Nemours & Co., Inc.

It has been said that the best companies earn their reputations not so much by being exceptional at every aspect of their business, but instead by being excellent in everything they do, and it is as true for departments as for organizations. The artificial intelligence department at DuPont is a good example. This small shop, headed by Dr. Ed Mahler, has fielded in excess of 800 expert systems to date, and has an equal number in progress or on the drawing board. Most of these systems are characterized by the following attributes.

- *Low Cost and Low Risk*. By relying heavily on expert-system program generators (called shells), PCs, and prototyping, the average cost of each system is about $25,000, including labor. Approximately 90 percent of the projects succeed of intent.
- *High return*. On average, each system has resulted in savings or new business at a ratio of $10 earned for every dollar invested.
- *Training*. The training of personnel to use these systems might be called relentless, for without end-user satisfaction and ability to operate these systems, Dr. Mahler knows his work would largely collect dust. This end-user orientation has permitted a decentralization of processing to the field, while keeping the corporate strategy foremost in mind.
- *Simplicity*. Expert systems can be generated from different shells, but each is oriented to a specific data relations methodology. Most of these models are maintained in the DuPont software library, and each is used for its intended purpose and no other. More significantly, the department has rarely made the mistake of trying to field a system more sophisticated than was necessary.

A track record of this caliber can only arise from a combination of good management ability, sound judgment, and an acute sense of what technology can do and what it cannot do. Many other corporations have used expert systems to great advantage, but finding another that has done it as well is difficult. Already the subject of a Harvard Business School case study and portrayed in chapter 7 of the book, *The Rise of the Expert Company*, there is little that can be done to amplify the well-deserved accolades of DuPont, except to emphasize the crucial role played by an individual who can bridge the gap between corporate strategy and technology.

*Fig. III-1. Ed. G. Mahler is the manager of artificial intelligence at DuPont. His work has been featured in a number of business publications.*

# 9

# Hardware

*Machinery . . . is when the poet introduces*
*the use of machines or brings some supernatural*
*being upon the stage, in order to solve some difficulty,*
*or to perform some exploit*
*out of reach of human power.*

—Encyclopaedia Britannica, 1771

Among the many elements of systems, hardware takes the lion's share of publicity while contributing the least to life cycle costs. It wasn't always this way; 45 years ago, hardware was 99 percent of the bill. Now it rarely accounts for more than 10 percent, and often less than that. Further, the capacity of today's best computers exceeds that of their electronic Abraham by a factor of at least one trillion. Finally, the cost of this computing power will continue to decrease, or to look at matters a different way, the same dollar will buy an increasing amount of it.

The reasons for the decrease in costs are similar to those that account for other forms of technology: increased demand that accelerates the pace of research, marketplace competition, and physical reduction in the size of the equipment combined with increased reliability, which lowers both capital and operating costs. The reasons for higher capability are attributable to a combination of factors, as described in technical note 2 in appendix B. Most of them are variations on the trend to compress more circuits into less space, thus improving the interior lines, at least in the electronic sense.

Unfortunately, the significance here is not always favorable to management. Although the costs might be going down, the expanded capabilities invite increasingly sophisticated systems. The more sophisticated the system is, the higher the costs of personnel, communications, and software. If these costs are offset by a better return on investment, fine. When not, as described by example in case studies C and G in appendix A, the results are often Quixotic. The collective cost of these failures might have exceeded $10 billion.

Without question, the best approach is to concentrate on what is necessary in a system, and assume that with few exceptions—primarily where high capacity in very small spaces is required—the computer or computers necessary to support that system exist. In cases where a new system must be superimposed over existing, antiquated computers, the problem is not hardware at all, but one that needs innovative software, efficient configurations, and productive scheduling to work around a difficult situation. With that in mind, the balance of this chapter looks at using the right size computer for a system, the advantages of buying excess capability within the correct size range, decision options in practice, the increasingly important aspect of peripherals, and concludes with impacts on integrations.

These discussions present one apparent inconsistency. The cost of hardware, as a percentage of total costs, continues to shrink. Concurrently, a bad decision on what size or how many computers to use can lead to expensive consequences, a bona fide tail-wagging-the-dog situation. Johnny Carson put this matter in perspective on his *Tonight* show. He mentioned he had read that weddings now cost about $13,000. After a pause, he surmised such an amount would barely pay his lawyer's photocopy bill.

## 9.1 COMPUTER SIZES

Any computer can be used to meet any requirement if time is no object and it has access to as much memory as necessary. The same is true for programming languages with respect to software development, as discussed in section 11.5. Further, any number of computers can be linked together to pool resources, again if time is no object. The efficiency would be deplorable, but in the logical sense at least, the system would work.

The analogy would be the ability to move a houseful of furniture across the country with a subcompact car. It would take some ingenuity, much time, and many trips, but it could do the job. Conversely, moving vans are inappropriate for local delivery of pizza, although that too can be done. Choosing the right size computer is a critical decision, notwithstanding the comparatively low acquisition cost. Figure 9-1 illustrates the consequences of missing the target.

### 9.1.1 Mainframes, Minis, and Micros

Roughly speaking, computers come in three sizes: mainframes, minis, and micros or desktops. These sizes overlap, and the upper part of the mainframe range is often considered as a separate category, namely supercomputers. Supercomputers, of which there are less than 300 in existence worldwide, often rely on supercooling technology to eliminate electrical resistance. The relationships among these sizes depend on three parameters.

1) *Trend Lines*. As time progresses, miniaturization compresses the capacity and the price of each size into the next lower size. Figure 9-2 depicts this trend.
2) *Capacity and Price Ratio*. The median model in each size offers roughly 10 times the capacity, at 10 times the price of the next smaller size. The only exception occurs when micros are compressed into laptops. Here, in return for maintaining the same computer power in a tighter package, the price can double.
3) *Interior Lines*. Besides the higher capability of larger sizes, the physical configurations provide a more efficient arrangement of interior lines for the interchange of massive quantities of data and information. This feature cannot be duplicated by networking computers of a lesser size, at least not in the immediate future.

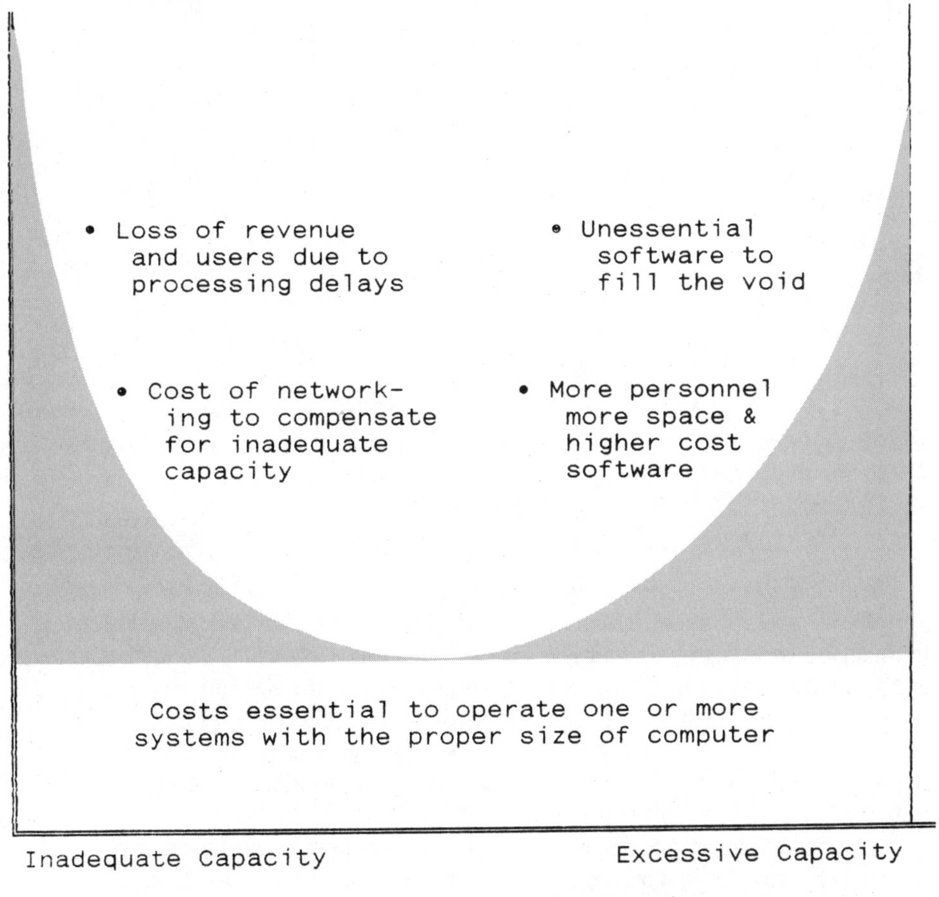


*Fig. 9-1. One size doesn't fit all. The wrong size computer, whether it is too small or too large, adds to the cost of information systems, both directly and indirectly. The amount will vary with the circumstances, but it is usually significant.*

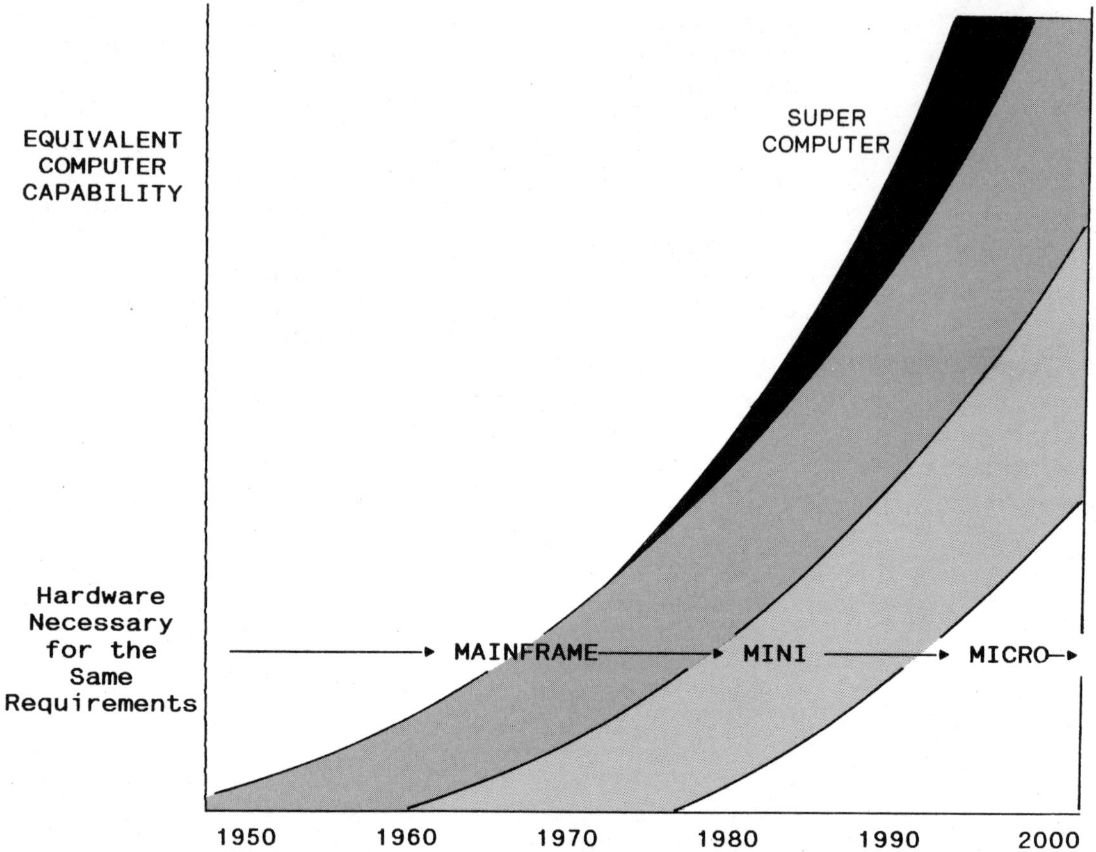


*Fig. 9-2. Trend lines in computer capacity. Miniaturization is compressing hardware into smaller sizes. Yesterday's mainframe is on a par with today's mini, and today's mini will undoubtedly be on a par with tomorrow's micro.*

The last item, interior lines, is where the issues of multiple users and peripherals are strongest.[1] Micros, except at the high-price end, do not lend themselves to concurrent multiple access. All other sizes do. Median-point minis handle from 10 to 20 users concurrently; mainframes, from 100 to 200. Supercomputers can handle even more, although in practice these behemoth number crunchers are used more for extremely high execution speed rather than increasing the number of users. The latter requirement is more economically met by linking mainframes.

The difficult aspect of dealing with these parameters occurs in the overlap zones. For example, in a borderline situation, would it be wiser to obtain a low-

[1]Case study K in appendix A provides an example of simultaneously applying interior lines and the power curve of diminishing returns to the design of hardware, which is the reduced-instruction-set chip (RISC). By eliminating the seldom-used hard-wired logic circuits, general processing efficiency has been improved markedly.

end mainframe or a high-end mini? Usually, the arguments favor the latter. The total cost will be less. However, if future programs and expansion of the database will severely overtax the mini, then a mainframe might be the better choice. Parallel reasoning applies to the choice between a micro and a mini.

### 9.1.2 Cost Leverage

The ability of the computer size to influence total costs significantly derives from both direct and indirect factors. In the case of overbuying, the direct factors include: the number of personnel necessary to operate the computer, the space and environmental conditions required, and the cost of systems software. The indirect cost would be the pressure to make use of the excess capacity for less-than-necessary programming.

For underbuying, the direct-cost increase is due primarily to the necessity of linking computers to compensate for inadequate capacity, although this can be offset by reduced personnel and operating costs. The indirect costs include the increased costs of decentralized procedural systems and problems arising from delays in processing. The consequences of somnambulistic processing range from mere annoyance to intolerable loss of profits or degradation of services. Figure 9-1 graphs the power curve effect of these factors. Figure 9-3 outlines the reasons in more detail.

### 9.1.3 Hardware Compatibility

As stated at the beginning of this chapter, any piece of hardware can be linked to any other piece of hardware to support logical relationship. As

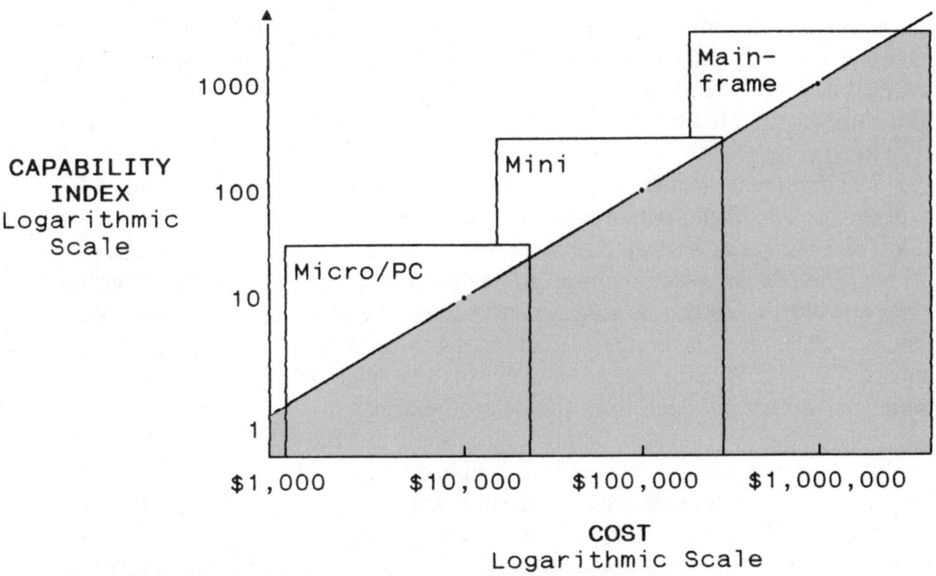


*Fig. 9-3. Cost factors of computer sizing. On the average, each upgrade in size increases the price of a computer ten-fold, in return for a similar increase in capacity. However, the wide range of capabilities within each size can change the factor considerably.*

thrashed out in chapter 11, the bridge between the hardware and the logic is software. To the extent the hardware components fail to dovetail is the extent to which software must substitute. The toll on this bridging is more time and less reliability. Substituting software for hard wired compatibility is a rudimentary prosthesis. See section 10.6 for more detail on this, and section 14.7 for the evolving long-term implications.

### 9.1.4 Mixing Sizes

Systems with a mix of computer sizes have become the rule rather than the exception, even excluding those mainframe and minicomputer systems linked to *dumb* micro terminals. Yet how to link different size computers is seldom the issue. The technology for doing this has been reduced to a science that improves continually. The more likely issue focuses on distribution of data and processing as a function of existing capacity, instead of what would be more efficient from a user viewpoint. Further, attempts to link an inadequate mix of computers could raise costs and reduce efficiency, which in turn can mean reduced profits greater than the short-sighted savings gained by making do with what exists.

## 9.2 OVERBUYING CAPACITY WITHIN A SIZE RANGE

Whenever an organization buys a computer, it should always consider buying more capacity than it needs within the size range it selects. The additional capacity: will not raise personnel costs, will not require more expensive systems software, will not create a major vacuum to attract unnecessary programming, but will provide mechanical resiliency at an insignificant marginal cost. This is in marked contrast to the consequences of buying hardware one size too large. It is the difference between buying a house with one more bedroom than presently needed (to provide for another child) and buying a mansion when you only need a house.

The argument against this position is that future requirements tend to be underestimated. Thus, within a few years, an organization might have to buy a larger size computer anyway. Although this is true, the reasoning overlooks two factors. First, if and when the time comes for upgrading, most of the programming and data bases can be salvaged with little additional expense, provided a model is selected that is upward compatible with a larger size. Second, the apparent sunk cost of the interim model would be offset by the return on investment, or interest not paid, from the delayed purchase.

Someone once said that compound interest is "the eighth wonder of the world," but even two years worth of simple interest, when delaying the purchase of a major item, is worth considering. TABLE 9-1 provides data on the savings. Additionally, the delayed purchase would likely result in obtaining even more capacity for the same dollar as a result of the trend lines in computer technology.

*Table 9-1. Quick recovery on lost opportunity cost. The sunk cost of buying a smaller computer while waiting for requirements to emerge that would warrant a larger size, can be recovered rapidly by the return on the interim investment of the difference in cost.*

| | | | |
|---|---|---|---|
| Mainframe cost | $1,000,000 | $1,000,000 | $1,000,000 |
| Sunk cost of the minicomputer | $50,000 | $100,000 | $200,000 |
| Amount for temporary investment | $950,000 | $900,000 | $800,000 |
| Interest @ 8% for 1 year | $76,000 | $72,000 | $64,000 |
| GAIN/LOSS | **+$24,000** | *-$28,000* | *-$136,000* |
| Interest @ 8% for 2 years | $158,080 | $149,760 | $133,120 |
| GAIN/LOSS | **+$108,080** | **+$49,760** | *-$66,880* |
| Interest @ 8% for 3 years | $246,726 | $233,741 | $207,770 |
| GAIN/LOSS | **+$196,726** | **+$133,741** | **+$7,770** |

THE COST OF THE MAINFRAME DOES NOT INCLUDE HIGHER OPERATING COSTS, AND THE SUNK COST OF THE MINICOMPUTER DOES NOT INCLUDE THE SALVAGE VALUE.

## 9.3 OPTIONS IN PRACTICE

William James liked to tell of his personal experience deciding between the doctrines of free will and determinism. Upon application to the *Determinists' Club*, the question, "Why?" was asked. He replied, "I choose to." They threw him out. So he went across the street to the *League of Free Will*. The same question was asked. He responded, "I didn't have any other choice." His application there was also declined.

The information manager faced with decisions for a new system confronts a similar Hobson's choice. In theory, he is free to choose. In practice, those decisions are often hemmed in by pressure to make use of what is available, which is especially true in government agencies and very large corporations. In more detail, then the options are:

**New Computer.** This is the ideal situation, but it arises infrequently. Yet if the situation suggests that no other option will work, then the information manager should concentrate on convincing his superiors of the consequences of compromise. There is a good reason why ox carts are prohibited from travelling on interstate highways.

**Replacement.** The cost savings that accrue from replacing old computers with new ones increase almost exponentially as a function of the age of existing computers. Sometimes, an ancient mainframe can be replaced by a top-of-the-line microcomputer. Even if some software must be rewritten, the one-time cost could be paid for by elimination of operating staff and maintenance.

**Upgrade.** This means increasing the capacity or capability of existing computers, often done by replacing the existing central processing unit with new boards or upgrading data storage devices with faster-access technology. When the alternative of replacing hardware is out of the question, and the machinery on hand cannot bear the load, the choice is between an upgrade and the next option, expansion.

**Expansion.** This option differs from the preceding one by adding additional hardware instead of upgrading the innards. The effect is often the same, but the comparative simplicity and lower cost of add-ons often sacrifices the advantage of the more efficient electronic interior lines of a good upgrade. Although the choice appears to be technical, performance capability is first a concern of management.

**The Make-Do.** Supposedly, this option should be considered only when existing hardware has the capacity to handle the new requirements. In practice, compromises are made. The on-line time for existing programs can be cut back, or longer queues can be imposed on all users. A potential offset here, in a few cases, is that information managers have the opportunity to persuade users to rid the organization of outdated programs, or at least downgrade their venue to independent and inexpensive micros.

## 9.4 PERIPHERALS

Peripherals are hardware components linked to the central processing unit. Besides monitors, the most common peripherals are input interfaces, data storage devices, printers, and communications equipment. Most peripherals provide the means of input, storage, and output. By itself, in a manner of speaking, the computer only "hums."

The range of capacities and capabilities of peripherals is as diverse as computers themselves. For example, the slowest printers (at little more than $100) crank out only 10 lines per minute, perhaps fewer. The fastest printers (at $50,000 to $150,000) can rack up 20,000 lines per minute, perhaps more.[2] The ranges among data storage devices and transmission components are equally dramatic. For example, data can be transmitted at densities anywhere from 300 characters per second to more than 125,000. However, density is not what should be of primary concern to management.

In parallel with computers, the technology of peripherals is sufficient to input, store, and output any amount of the data and information. The object is to do so efficiently. Efficiency is the byproduct of two objectives: the reduction of

---

[2]As discussed in case study K in appendix A, the laser printer is another fine example of applying interior lines to hardware design. The design of this printer substitutes maneuverable rays of coherent light for mechanical fonts. In the process, one machine can substitute for a range of printers. For PCs, the price might seem high, but for mainframe applications, these printers compete with their mechanical equivalents at one-third the price.

the input, storage, and physical output to a minimum; and a design that yields the optimum electronic interior lines possible for the balance. Yet the awesome technological progress in computer science is too often perceived as the giant maw of an angry god to be appeased by endless feeding with data. Put the idol on a diet, and sometimes the interior-lines problem will take care of itself. In more specific terms:

**Data Storage.** The more data that is resident, the more difficult ensuring its integrity and its accessibility becomes. The ability to store data in ever-shrinking tight spaces and to reach for it with lightening speed seldom ameliorates the problem. Distributing it to field locations, unless propelled by bona fide management considerations, won't help either. As belabored in sections 4.3 and 4.4, when integrity of data becomes the primary consideration, and the point of diminishing returns for including data is given fair consideration, the volume that must be stored will tend to compress. On the other hand, data that is stored can benefit from a good understanding of the hierarchy of storage media. See technical note 3 in appendix B on this point.

**Input Peripherals.** As the task of entering data becomes increasingly mechanized and automated, as described in technical note 4 in appendix B, the quality and correctness of the data is likely to improve, and so too will the quantity. This ergonomic technology sometimes only serves to aid and abet the temptation to store as much data as possible.

**Printers.** In winter, 25 percent or more of the fuel used to heat the Pentagon is waste paper produced in the Department of Defense. Most of that paper spews from computer-linked printers. On a larger scale, environmentalists claim that 50 percent of all waste dumped into landfills is paper or paper products. And more than one senior-level executive has decried the reams of computer printout given them by information managers, when all they wanted was a few concise answers to a few precise questions. It is no coincidence, therefore, that many organizations long ago implemented maximum electronic transfer of funds, and now aim at creating paperless work environments.

Summing up these points, a greater sensitivity to users might result in a more restricted use of peripherals. If a paperless environment is the goal for a transaction-based work environment, information systems could benefit even more. Whether the information manager chooses to call the means executive information systems, intelligent work stations, or artificial intelligence, is unimportant. The idea is to use the computer to supplant the printer and the photocopy machine, if for no other reason than that printers (and copiers) break down about 50 times more often than computers.

## 9.5 HARDWARE AND INTEGRATIONS

If the technology exists to meet the needs of almost any system, then technology also exists to meet any requirement for an integration. Unfortunately, the factor of efficiency looms even larger, and the costs of reaching the desired

| | PHYSICAL INTEGRATION | LOGICAL INTEGRATION |
|---|---|---|
| SYNTHESES and DATABASE INTEGRATIONS | Unless the setup is revamped in parallel with the logical merger, the former will be little more than a cumbersome physical interface. | To qualify as a merger, the logic and/or data of the systems must be integrated to the point where the old systems are barely recognizable. |
| EXCERPT INTEGRATIONS | This model entails the least amount of physical integration, as that task occurs only in the receiving computer and database. | The logic of an excerpt integration is almost exclusively that of ensuring a common definition among the common data elements. |
| LIAISON INTERFACES | An interface, almost by definition, falls short of being a physical merger, and no amount of additional interfacing can overcome the lack. | When the intent is to transfer data between systems, the lack of a physical integration is not detrimental. Beyond that objective, it is. |
| STANDARDIZATIONS | Strictly speaking, a standardization is not an integration, but it can facilitate one by reducing electronic incompatibilities. | Except when applied to standardizing the data element dictionary, the logical obstacles confronting an integration must still be addressed. |

*Fig. 9-4. Considerations for integrations. Physical and logical integrations are two different matters, at least for some models of integration. The former are not always capable of supporting the latter.*

level of it are greater in comparison to systems built from scratch. As discussed more fully in section 10.5, the problem is linkage. Figure 9-4 and the following points summarize the problems in terms of the different models for integration.

- *Syntheses and Database Integrations*. The dominant problem with merger-type integrations, except the excerpt model, is that the logical merger and the physical means of that merger are two different things. Unless the network of computers and peripherals can be configured to act as if it were a single computer, the logical merger will be superimposed over a physical interface. To the extent the interface network imposes tangled webs of communications is the extent to which the intended symbiosis will likely retort with informational sludge. As simple as this observation might be, failure to recognize it is an invitation to disaster, as is described in case study C in appendix A.

- *Excerpt Integrations*. The excerpt model of a merger-type integration overlooks the logical vs. physical dichotomy. Most of the traffic is one-way periodic transmission in which speed is not critical. Thus, most applications of this model can accept the limitations of a physical interface. The only hardware requirement is to ensure the central computer at the receiving end can handle and park the traffic.
- *Interfaces*. The interface integration by definition depends on a linkage of computers, and makes no pretense of reaching for a merger of the supporting hardware. If the available transmission lines and networks can bear the anticipated traffic under peak loads, the primary issue devolves into ensuring the peripherals can generate and receive the volume. This is not normally a problem unless too much software must be substituted for hardware compatibility.
- *Standardizations*. The dominant force driving standardization among computers is the ability to link them. Without this need, the only motivation would be cost savings. Yet, in the volatile, highly competitive marketplace for hardware, taking advantage of market prices probably would result in higher savings than mass purchases. Restated, the information manager with foresight will push for maximum compatibility—read *standardization*—among the bulk of hardware acquired, which will pay massive dividends in the future.

# 10

# Communications

*Well, if I dialed the wrong number,*
*why did you answer the phone?*

—James Thurber

If the gods on Mount Olympus in Homer's time had had an efficient communications network, it's problematic if the mortals plying their ambitions below would have had an easier or a rougher time of life. The powers that be were always infighting and had a different set of priorities. In the *Odyssey,* Minerva lectures Ulysses' son Telemachus at great length. At the end of this diatribe, she concludes with an afterthought, "One more thing I need to tell you about. Your father's enemies intend to ambush and kill you tonight."

Modern corporations and other organizations do not always differ from this environment. The decision makers at the top are sometimes less concerned about bankruptcy and failure than the members of the middle estate. So-called "golden parachutes" can be arranged in advance, like the tens of millions of dollars distributed as bonuses among senior executives at Drexel Burnham Lambert a few months before it went belly up. This attitude often translates into a major conflict between centralization and decentralization of authority and the information systems deemed necessary for either alternative. The centralized approach tends to control information to support explicit corporate or organizational goals; the decentralized approach, to facilitate field operations. The two do not always coincide.

Many organizations require a complex mixture of both. The *Wall Street Journal* directs its editorial policy from a central location. The reporters and investigators work individually and file their stories from distant locations. This information is routed to a central data bank, which is then typeset on computers and distributed to seventeen printing plants strategically located throughout the United States and to several other plants worldwide. These locations add local advertising, and the international editions add content. The sales and distribution of the paper is even more decentralized, yet continual feedback to the main editorial offices affects policy, which in turn can affect the degree of centralization or decentralization.

The macro systems envisioned in section 1.5, where a network of computers and systems operates as if it were installed on one computer, will not necessarily solve the centralization vs. decentralization conflict. It can help, however. The physical centralization of the database enhances logical integrity and accuracy, while the mechanics ease decentralization of operations as appropriate. Until that time, the information manager must make the most of available communications and distributive processing technology. The idea is to create the optimum configuration of interior information lines for the needs of his organization.

The scope and complexity of this task is not to be underestimated. The options are many, and the technological steamroller can turn a currently infeasible option into a good solution a few years hence. On the other hand, banking on the future can risk changes to requirements that negate the potential. As described in case study A in appendix A, even the best information systems managers realize that this task is a tough nut to crack. All that can be done here is to provide some idea of the factors and parameters that normally affect these decisions.

The balance of this chapter begins with a section that reviews the gap between computers and distributive requirements, including a look at the *Open Standards Interface Agreement*. Next come three sections on the specifics of networks and communications, and another section on implications for integrations. This is followed by a short discussion of the current war between IBM and AT&T on operating systems, or why the ideal of the open standards agreement is not fully in sync with business realities. The concluding section summarizes the chapter in terms of issues that are likely to have the most significance for information managers.

The superintending point to all this information is that communications are a poor substitute for good systems design and a user-oriented database structure. As a rule, the cost of excessive communications will eventually outweigh the interim savings gained by keeping existing but inadequate designs. Further, if the compromise is inefficient, it will denigrate production and marketing strategies.

## 10.1 THE LOGIC VS. SYSTEMS GAP

At the requirements end of the spectrum, the necessity for more sophisticated systems, or alternatively the integration of existing systems, increases each year. At the hardware end, the capabilities increase markedly each year. Between them, the connecting elements do not always keep pace.

The analogy is the requirement of two people trying to communicate with each other. If both individuals speak different languages but have equivalent background and are on the same wave length conceptually, only a translator is required. If they speak the same language, but are on a different wave length, an adjudicator would be appropriate. If they lack only equivalent background, an educator or explainer of sorts might be required. If two common elements are missing, then two of these intermediaries are necessary, and those two must be able to work with one another. When all three are missing, then three intermediaries are necessary. This situation would be exacerbated by the need to have all three work with one another.

The same happens with bridges among systems. The more systems lack compatibility, the more translators and other intermediaries—read software—will be needed to bridge the gaps. In practice, the situation is more complex. Like the poor chap in a popular song lamenting he has seven women on his mind, the compatibility gap operates at seven levels, each of which was formally delineated in the *Open Standards Interface Agreement*. Figure 10-1 depicts these seven levels, and FIG. 10-2 shows the negative power curve arising from the cumulative use of too many software bridges. The following points summarize the seven levels:

- *Physical Compatibility.* This level addresses the physical design and electrical supply requirements of hardware. The standardization of cables and plugs for ordinary home telephones is a parallel example. As an exception to the need for software bridging, most incompatibilities must be resolved either by redesign or by insertion of electronic circuitry.
- *Reliability.* This level concerns the uniformity or lack of uniformity among the means to ensure reliable transmissions, or at least to identify errors. The parity method described in subsection 6.1.5 is an example. Standardization makes parity techniques uniform.
- *Packet Length.* Data is normally transmitted in units or packets of so many bytes each, vaguely analogous to standard size paper envelopes. The agreement recommends a standard size packet.
- *Pacing.* Standardized packet lengths are useful only when the sending and receiving stations are designed to work with those specifications, and includes sufficient flexibility to encipher and decipher sensitive messages. This is the communications equivalent of a dismounted drill combined with the ability to change into and out of camouflage uniforms without missing a beat.
- *Synchronization.* Even when packets are fully regimented, their transmission must be synchronized in any network that is more complex than one-way traffic between two nodes, and is a far more difficult problem. Synchronization is the equivalent of managing 10 parades marching at the same time in the same town, each following its own route. In the film *Patton*, one scene has the famed general directing traffic between two columns of tanks crossing paths, in effect synchronizing the crossing of the tanks of one column between the gaps in the other.
- *Formatting.* Even when transmission of data works well, if that data is formatted differently among different users, it remains incompatible for practical purposes. An applications example would be a memo written

with one brand of word processing software being revised by another person using a different brand. Utilities exist to make the conversion, but they are time consuming and do not always work with 100 percent accuracy.

- *Accessibility.* This final level addresses the task of regulating access among many users. One simple example is deciding among simultaneous attempts to access, update, or transmit the same item of data. If three plants order the same critical part, but only two are left in the inventory, which plant will wait? Will it be first-come-first-served, or will priorities based on comparative production be imposed? The agreement does not attempt to answer that kind of question directly, but it does recognize that the electronic means of doing this within a complex system should be more uniform.

| | Problems Overcome by the Open Standards Agreement | Software Bridges in the Absence of the Agreement |
|---|---|---|
| Physical Compatibility | Units in a network or integration can be connected physically without conversion units. | Software bridging here is uneconomical and inefficient. |
| Reliability | Reliability-type errors due to incompatibilities are eliminated or at least reduced. | Reliability checking, such as parity, must be used, or alternatively dual transmissions. |
| Packet length | Standard packet length (bytes per "burst") facilitates pacing and synchronization. | Software to subdivide traffic into standard packet length is simple but must be agreed upon. |
| Pacing | With standard packet lengths, pacing the transmission is greatly simplified. | Each node must have pacing software for each other node to which it sends traffic. |
| Synchronization | Compatible packet length and pacing must still be synchronized in all but a few simple networks. | Without standard packet lengths and compatible pacing, software is far more complex. |
| Formatting | Standard formats eliminate the need for hundreds of all-too-common conversion utilities. | Existing conversion utilities are themselves nearly standardized but they are troublesome. |
| Accessibility | Facilitates the development and operation of protocols to regulate network traffic. | Without standardization here, protocols can prove too intricate and inefficient. |

*Fig. 10-1. Compatibility levels for communications. Compatibility between computers, including software, operates at seven levels. The Open Standards Interface Agreement addressed all of these levels as a goal for the future. In the interim, information managers need to consider the software bridges essential to bridge the gaps.*

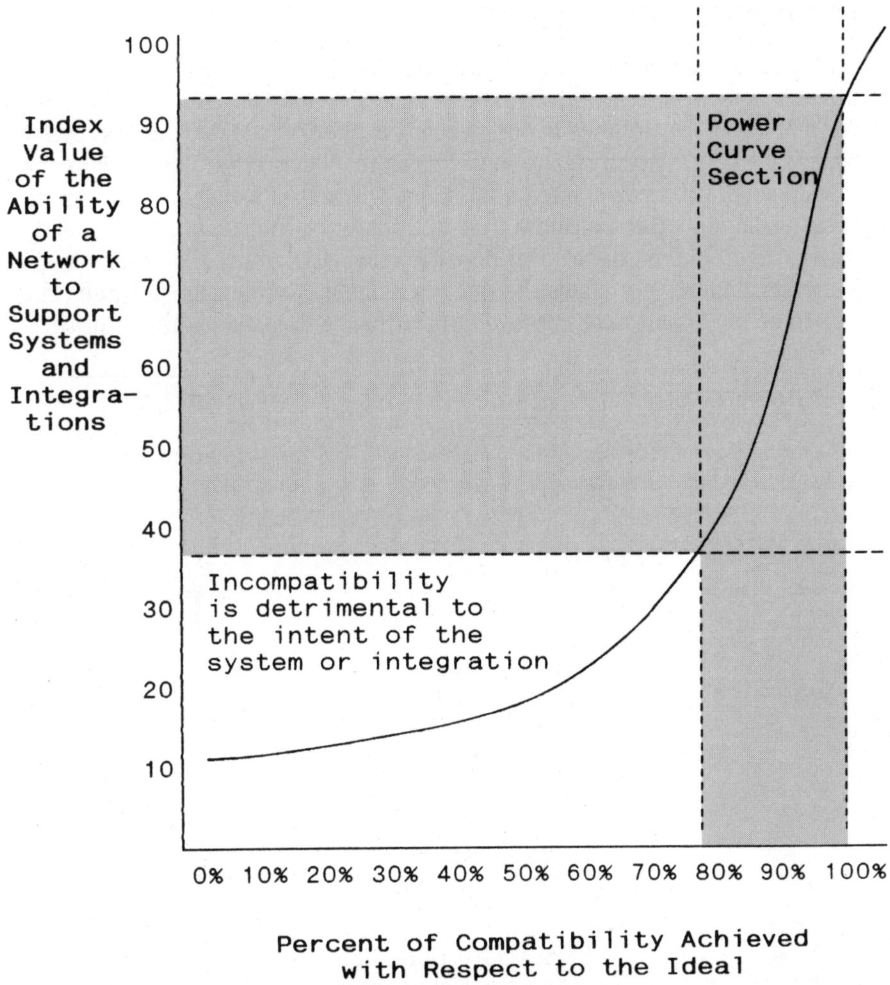


*Fig. 10-2. The power curve of improving compatibility. Although any and all problems of incompatibility can be overcome with software bridges, too many of these bridges will encounter a point of diminishing returns, especially by way of introducing delays with heavy communications traffic.*

The Open Standards Interface Agreement is a very significant milestone in the unfolding history of computer science and information systems. Yet, even when fully implemented, with every element of a network or integration meeting these standards, the task of designing an efficient configuration will remain. Among other problems, the interfacing of the logic and of applications software will still intrude. For this reason alone, the ideal remains to reduce communications traffic to a minimum consistent with requirements. Unfortunately, these requirements are likely to expand as organizations increasingly come to rely on computers as the only practical means to prevent drowning in paperwork.

## 10.2 TRANSMISSION OF DATA

Electrical transmission of data, whether by wire or by radiation, travels at nearly the speed of light, which means that a signal can circumnavigate the globe more than seven times in one second. In theory at least, the first byte of any message sent from any point on earth can reach any other point in less than 1/14 second. In practice, it takes a tad longer. Traffic is usually routed through several mediums, which consume time in transfer or translation. Still, speed is not a problem. The problems are: density, reliability, and waiting times to use the circuits. Figure 10-3 shows the interrelationships among these three problems. To no one's surprise, improved performance demands a higher price.

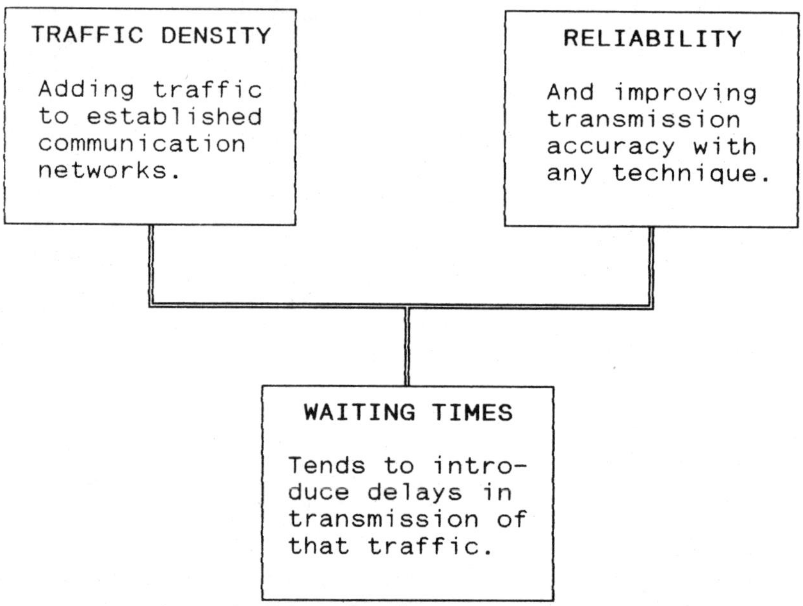


*Fig. 10-3. The three parameters of communications traffic. In an era of increasingly larger systems and integrations, the ability to communicate between computers assumes greater importance. Good communications are a function of three parameters: density, reliability, and acceptable waiting times. Advantageous improvements to the first two increase the third disadvantageously, all other things being equal. That problem can be overcome with higher capability, more expensive equipment, or by cutting back on the traffic. Trade-offs loom large.*

### 10.2.1 Density

Density measures how much information can be transmitted per unit of time, usually under ideal conditions of one-way traffic without breaks, buffers, or interference. It varies from 1200 bits per second, commonly called *bauds*, to over 500,000 bits per second. As a byte usually has eight bits, and it takes one byte to represent one character, these numbers equate with a range of 150 to 62,500 characters per second. Transmitting 10 double-spaced pages of informa-

*Table 10-1. Significance of comparative transmission densities. Transmission of data varies from about 150 characters per second to more than 63,000. The table here depicts the theoretical significance of these differences with reference to different traffic loads. In practice, delays and switching add to the times required for complete transmission when there is no slack.*

| DOCUMENT: | | 1-Page Letter | 5-Page Report* | 100-Page Document* |
|---|---|---|---|---|
| Number of Bytes: | | 1500 | 16,000 | 300,000 |
| TRANSMISSION DENSITY | | TRANSMISSION TIME REQUIRED | | |
| Baud | Bytes/Second | Seconds | Minutes/Seconds | Minutes/Seconds |
| 1,200 | 150 | 10.0 | 1 46.7 | 33 20 |
| 2,400 | 300 | 5.0 | 53.3 | 16 40 |
| 4,800 | 600 | 2.5 | 26.7 | 8 20 |
| 9,600 | 1,200 | 1.3 | 13.3 | 4 10 |
| 25,000 | 3,125 | .5 | 5.1 | 1 36 |
| 50,000 | 6,250 | .3 | 2.6 | 48 |
| 75,000 | 9,375 | .2 | 1.7 | 32 |
| 100,000 | 12,500 | .1 | 1.3 | 24 |
| 200,000 | 25,000 | .06 | .6 | 12 |
| 300,000 | 37,500 | .04 | .4 | 8 |
| 400,000 | 50,000 | .03 | .3 | 6 |
| 500,000 | 62,500 | .02 | .2 | 5 |

*SINGLE-SPACED

tion will take about 2 minutes at slow baud rates. A fast transmission will do the job in about 3/10 second.

Increases to traffic within design limits do not normally introduce significant delays. If anything, the increased traffic takes maximum advantage of the theoretical maximum density. Yet like rush hour on urban freeways, specific transmissions can take more time to get through. TABLE 10-1 provides some comparative data on transmission rates, as factored by various delays.

The wide range of transmission densities comes from a combination of factors. These factors exert a cumulative effect, meaning that the efficiencies of each are multiplied. Thus if there were only four elements, and the performance index of each element ranged from 1 to 5, the combined effect would range from 1 to 625 (equal to 5 raised to the fourth power). The ratio between 1200 baud and 500,000 baud is about 1:417. In practice, the factors don't combine this neatly, and there are more of them. Perhaps the three most important factors are:

1) *Analog vs. Digital Transmission.* Analog transmissions convert bits of data into modulations of amplitude or frequency, like nodding one's head more (or less) vigorously, to signal approval or disapproval. Modulation

is the basis for common radio transmissions. By contrast, digital transmissions send a pulse of current one per bit of information (with gaps to signify the absence of bits in byte patterns). The former is slower, cheaper, and as close as the telephone. The latter is faster, generally more expensive, and usually requires subscription to, or control over a line set up to transmit digital information. The innards of a computer rely almost exclusively on digital transmission, with up to 128 (or more) parallel circuits. To a computer, then, even the best of external communications are Neanderthal.

2) *Serial vs. Parallel*. Data can be sent serially, which means one bit at a time. Or bits can be grouped in sets and sent in parallel. Printer cables are a common example. Sending 32 bits of data simultaneously increases the density by a factor of 32. But the technology requires more than just multiple lines. Each group of bits must be continually lined up. Because they travel at nearly the speed of light, a small electronic burp can bring about total chaos. For example, when a parallel cable is bent in order to follow a curved path, the outer wires are stretched and the inner wires are compressed. The bits in the inner wires will therefore arrive first and be mixed with bits on the outer wires that were from a previous group. Intermediate relay stations can realign the bits into their respective groups, but that chore must take place every 10 to 25 feet. For this reason, ordinary printer cables are rarely longer than 12 feet, and even they can be rendered useless by tight coiling.
3) *Number of Lines*. The more lines that are packed into the same physical space, or alternatively the more modulations or pulses that are sent over the same transmission, means the more messages or data that can be sent within the same time period. Thus, a fiber optics cable can offer 100 to 1000 times more lines than a similar diameter standard electrical transmission cable. This practice has a parallel in optical disk vs. magnetic disk storage of data. However, multiple lines differ from parallel transmission, in that each message is sent over only one line.

Beyond these simple ideas lies a welter of technology, which includes multiplexers, concentrators, front-end processors, satellites, simplex vs. half-duplex vs. duplex transmissions, broadband transmissions, and so forth. Yet what remains important to management are the questions of available density, reliability of transmission, and inherent delay times.

### 10.2.2 Reliability.

As discussed in subsection 6.1.5, reliability is the measure of how closely the information at the point of reception resembles what was transmitted at the point of sending. Absolute 100 percent reliability is an ideal rarely attained. The degree of reliability usually requires some form of checking that identifies transmission errors and activates some means of correction, if only a retransmission.

The alternative is to accept a threshold amount of error, either in percentage terms of total data transmitted, or in the accuracy of units of data. Whatever the case might be, information managers are usually faced with trade-off decisions. Increased reliability means increased costs. Decreased reliability means lower direct costs, but higher costs in terms of after-the-fact corrective actions, or perhaps lost business.

### 10.2.3 Delays

Waiting for a response to, ''Good morning. How are you today?'' sent to a resident on a planet circling the nearest star (Alpha-Centuri) beyond our solar system, would take about seven years. Senior executives begin to lose their patience after about seven seconds.

Delays are critical. Further, more users, a heavier traffic load, or a greater number of nodes will perforce introduce or lengthen queues. Information managers have several options: accepting these delays, upgrading the network, or finding alternative means for transmission of less important traffic.

Closely associated with this issue is the on-line vs. on-call setup. *On-line* means that computers are connected and either transmitting/receiving data or waiting to do so. *On-call* means that communications are available, but before a transmission can be made or at least accepted into the targeted system, something must be turned on at one or more computers. The signal itself can sometimes do this, but it takes more time than if the system were already on-line. In some cases, the messages might accumulate in a large buffer until users at the receiving end can get to them.

The apparent solution of putting all affected systems on-line simultaneously is not always feasible. In some cases, this could require operating personnel around the clock, or the computers themselves might become so overloaded that users must be scheduled. Although any computer can be rigged to support any number of concurrent users, the delays increase at an exponential rate when the number begins to exceed the design limit. The geometry of it is no different from rush hour gridlock.

## 10.3 NETWORK CONFIGURATIONS

Nearly every textbook in computer science makes a point of describing the three network models. The *star* model has a central host computer with lines radiating out to multiple computers. The *ring* model places computers at different points on a ring. Transmissions flow through each computer until the last party that needs the information is reached. The *bus* model operates like a bus line, with different stations adjacent to different points on the line. Traffic stays on the bus until it reaches an intended station.

These ideal models are all very neat, but most networks are combinations of them, and if the organization relies on a network service, how that service is configured is seldom of concern. The important item is the distribution and flow of data to meet requirements. Whatever the requirements might be, some model or combination exists to meet them.

### 10.3.1 The Four Orientations

Two factors spawn four basic orientations of information processing. The first factor, *commonality*, is the degree to which data is: common among different users, or the degree to which data must be massed at one or more locations as a prerequisite to meet requirements. The second factor, *centrality*, is the degree to which data originates or first enters the system centrally. Figure 10-4 portrays the four orientations.

The orientations mandate more caveats than advice. Data can originate worldwide, but as occurs for the insurance and investment firm USAA (case study A in appendix A), the information remains manual and is transmitted by mail or telephone to a few central locations, where it first enters the system. Because all input must be related immediately to a comparatively few tables, the commonality is also high. As a result, the computer system at USAA is highly centralized, successfully so.

| Degree of Centrality | Degree of Commonality: LOW | Degree of Commonality: HIGH |
|---|---|---|
| HIGH | <u>Low Commonality</u><br><u>High Centrality</u><br>Data originates at one or only a few sources, but each distributed user needs only a small slice of it. | <u>High Commonality</u><br><u>High Centrality</u><br>Data originates at one or only a few sources, and it is needed by by widely distributed users. |
| LOW | <u>Low Commonality</u><br><u>Low Centrality</u><br>Data originates from many sources without the need for distributed users to access much of it. | <u>High Commonality</u><br><u>Low Centrality</u><br>Data originates from many sources but with the need for distributed users to access its mass. |

*Fig. 10-4. Four orientations of data networks. The configuration of most networks depends on two factors:* commonality *and* centrality. *Commonality is a rough measure of the extent to which all users rely on the same database. Centrality is the degree to which data, common or not, must or should be centralized in one or a few locations, perhaps for reasons of technical efficiency. These two factors mean that networks have four possible orientations.*

For the Chrysler Motor Corporation (in case study A), the data in at least one component originates and is processed in a decentralized mode. Other components originate and operate in a few locales, but with little direct database relationship to the decentralized one. In the former case, a centralized summing up of the data from all components is critically important for ensuring that the intended strategic use of computer technology remains on track. For further examples of this and related problems, see case studies I and J in appendix A.

Taking these cases as a starting point, then, few information systems fit neatly into one of the four orientations. Thus, systems decisions are among the most difficult faced by information managers and are probably the source of the biggest and most costly mistakes. Perhaps the only way out, as summarized in section 10.7, is to start with the ideal database and data flowchart, and from that point figure out the network and distribution configuration that would best meet that need. This task is no small undertaking and might warrant a computer model, something that is discussed further in technical note 6 in appendix B.

### 10.3.2 Defined Nets

A variety of commercial or user-installable nets are available. The decision whether to subscribe to an external net vs. installing one is a little different in a fundamental sense than the choice between subscription commercial telephone service for internal communications vs. buying an internal set up. The financial advantage of the latter tends to improve as the geographic area served compresses and the number of users increases.

**Wide Area Networks (WANs).** The function of WANs can range from mere inquiry/response systems to distributed data processing, funds transfer, or reservation-type systems. The amount of traffic, the frequency and degree of peak loading, the security risks, and any uniqueness of requirements are some of the factors that ply on the decision to subscribe or to develop.

**Local Area Nets (LANs).** Conceptually, local area networks are micro WANs, and the linking of LANs in a wide area network is not unusual. The best-known example comprises cellular telephone nets that are linked to long-distance telephone services. However, in most LANs there is a greater emphasis on groupware (multiple access software), as well as commonly accessible data and text files, used at many stations. Office systems are a good example, although the productivity and savings gains often fail to materialize.

**Common and Value-Added Carriers.** These carriers are the best-known means of communications. Value-added carriers typically lease lines from common carriers and convert them into specialized circuits to meet the communications needs of subscribers. In this way, for example, the subscribers can be ensured—for a price—of having higher priority, unique distribution requirements met, or whatever.

**Information and Database Service Networks.** These systems are analogous to proprietary software. Everything is developed and managed externally. Similar to browsing in a bookstore, the subscribers can scan the data as necessary. Credit bureaus are perhaps the largest application. Another common use occurs in research and development, where duplicating files of published documents developed by others would be cost inefficient. That is, when the information available nearly coincides with requirements, there is no need to go elsewhere, although this is seldom the case for all organizational requirements.

## 10.4 NETWORK CONTROL AND DEGRADATION

As the number of stations and paths in a network increase, the difficulty of controlling traffic increases at a high exponential rate. TABLE 10-2 shows the situation in simplified form. The problems compound when the traffic flow is uneven, when synchronous traffic flow can no longer be maintained, or when any other factor operates to imbalance the traffic pattern, which is especially true with peak loads. Few if any communication networks are adequately designed to process these loads directly. When they occur, either randomly assigned delays are encountered, or a predetermined sieve of priorities is activated.

*Table 10-2. Transmission degradation factors. Most complex networks have the ability to reroute traffic over alternative paths. When some of the paths are down, the remaining paths must take up the slack. This table provides a simplified example of the effect of an increasing number of lines out of operation under a sample of traffic loads. In practice, many factors operate to make the situation worse.*

| Percentage of Traffic Paths Available | Maximum Traffic That Will Get Through On Time<br>Actual Load as a Percentage of Maximum Load<br>50 Percent | 70 Percent | 90 Percent |
|---|---|---|---|
| 90% | 100% | 100% | 100% |
| 80% | 100% | 100% | 89% |
| 70% | 100% | 100% | 78% |
| 60% | 100% | 86% | 67% |
| 50% | 100% | 71% | 56% |
| 40% | 80% | 57% | 44% |
| 30% | 60% | 43% | 33% |
| 20% | 40% | 29% | 22% |
| 10% | 20% | 14% | 11% |

(light shading) Traffic is problematic in the 50-to-80% range

(dark shading) Networks often break down below the 50% mark

As an alternative, some form of backup communications can be used. Each of these alternatives has advantages and disadvantages. The litany that follows is intended only as an overview of the problems and the inherent conflicts and difficulties of applying solutions.

### 10.4.1 Protocols and Priorities

*Protocols* are rules by which communications traffic is routed and managed among computers and stations. Normally, they are programmed as an adjunct to operating systems, but a few languages, notably Ada, permit protocols to be written within applications programming. Information managers are prone to underestimate the intricacy of protocols in complex systems. The reason seems to be that although an individual can perceive a network in its totality at one glance, the computer must grope in the dark, as it were, never knowing from where the next byte of data is coming, or knowing in advance where it is going.

### 10.4.2 Network Degradation

Network communications tend to degrade for one basic reason—traffic overload. This problem can arise from an unusual amount of traffic, or from a breakdown of some lines, which overloads the balance. The reasons for breakdowns vary, and include: atmospheric conditions (for wireless transmissions), physical damage to telephone lines (such as a construction bulldozer ripping up a trench filled with fiberoptic cables), or a flaw in the control software. The latter was the cause of the January 15, 1990 breakdown of AT&T telephone communications. Figure 10-5 presents a graphical view of the degradation function, one of sharpest power curves in the field of computer and communications technology.

## 10.5 IMPLICATIONS FOR INTEGRATIONS

The significance of the preceding discussions essentially duplicates the implications for hardware, as discussed in section 9.5. The points here merely restate the commentary in terms of communications.

- *Syntheses and Database Integrations*. A logical merger superimposed over an interfaced set of computers means the intended synthesis is dependent on how well and how fast the supporting machinery communicates. The issue thus becomes how close the network comes to mimicking a singular, albeit very large computer.
- *Interfaces*. The logical and the physical requirements coincide. The objective is to transmit or access information and software over lines of communication that are intended to do just that. The issues are efficiency and reliability. Can the message get through to Garcia, so to speak, in time to do what has to be done?

- *Standardizations.* Almost without exception, the intent of standardization is to facilitate interfaces, which is the motivation behind the open standards agreement, and it is the most pressing problem in distributed information systems. Standardization is also the most difficult; users are at the mercy of what's available on the marketplace, combined with the investment in capital equipment to date. A significant increase in standardization often entails both a major capital investment and a different paradigm for the storage and flow of information. That's a tall order with a short fuze.

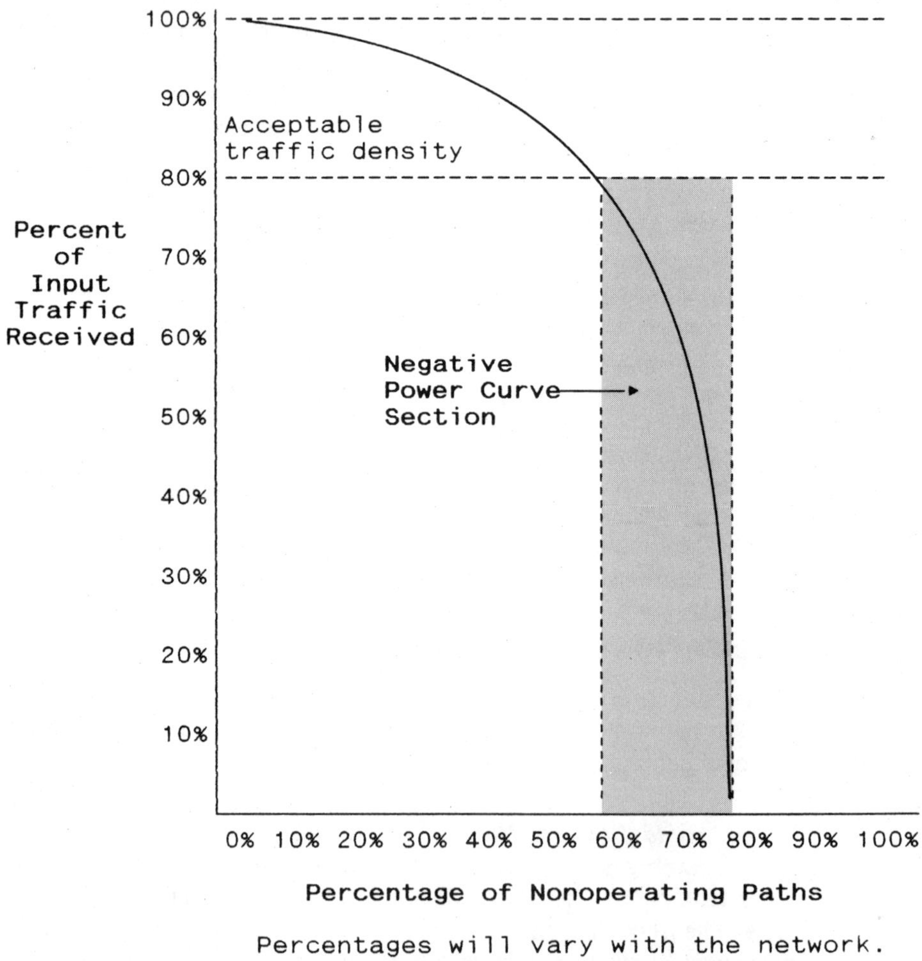


*Fig. 10-5. Network degradation. Networks demonstrate an acute application of the power curve phenomenon. Most of them provide considerable resiliency to handle peak traffic loading or to reroute routine levels of traffic when some of the lines are nonoperational. But after the saturation level is reached, the curve of performance turns down sharply, almost vertically. In short, information overload is an invitation to temporary disaster.*

## 10.6 THE OPERATING SYSTEMS WAR

Although 13 manufacturers signed the *Open Standards Interface Agreement*, the two giants in that group are engaged in a war over operating systems for micro computers and some minis.[1] IBM favors Microsoft's Disk Operating System (DOS), and its enhanced revisions such as Operation System Two (OS/2). AT&T is pushing for UNIX, a system that it developed before divestiture removed the legal restriction to engage actively in this market. Thus, the war shapes up between a company that notwithstanding a chronic tapering off of sales, is still the market leader by any measure, vs. another giant of a company, albeit with comparatively minimum experience and history on this particular battlefield. AT&T's advantage is the fungibility of UNIX. UNIX comes closer to adhering to the ideals of the agreement.

IBM's ally, Microsoft, is the world's leading supplier of software, while AT&T relies on Sun Microsystems. The latter is no slouch, but the IBM/Microsoft alliance wields most of the clout. Further, while UNIX might give the appearance of greater uniformity or standardization, it still must be adapted to operate on different machinery. AT&T has been less than successful at getting other hardware manufacturers to meet it at least half way. Accordingly, AT&T has tried to redesign UNIX to work on a wider range of machinery, which is somewhat like designing a vehicle that will serve as a taxi, a pickup truck, and a luxury sedan in one model. Still, AT&T remains the dominant force in the communications industry, and communications are the wherewithal that makes widespread information systems feasible.

So who will eventually prevail in this war? Probably IBM/Microsoft, although given the tactics, the victory could prove Pyrrhic. As stated, the IBM/Microsoft team has the clout and is fighting on its own turf, against an opponent who's primary weapon has an intractable flaw: It doesn't work well enough to win over a contending share of the market. UNIX is something of a strategic hamlet, yet one continuously reinforced—bankrolled—by a company who understands the pressing need to communicate efficiently, better than its overpowering opponent.

History offers a hint of what could be done here. As World War II wound down, and the United States and its Western European allies began to realize that the Soviet Union would become the force to reckon with, Churchill sat down with Stalin for a brief conversation. Accepting the inevitability of Soviet dominance in eastern Europe, Churchill took a map and drew a line down it. What lay to the east, he admitted, would come under the influence of the Soviet Union. What lay to the west, would be off limits. Stalin nodded agreement. That line became, as Churchill himself later coined it, the iron curtain. Unarguably, it was psychologically devastating to millions, and more than a thousand individuals were slaughtered trying to cross over. Still, it was a case of good fences

[1]The 13 companies were: IBM, AT&T, Control Data Corporation, Data General Corporation, Digital Equipment Corporation, Hewlett-Packard Company, Honeywell-Bull, Inc., Sun Microsystems, Inc., Unisys Corporation, Wang Laboratories, Xerox Corporation, NCR Corporation, and Telenet Communications Corporation (which is a subsidiary, via US Sprint Communications, of GTE).

making good neighbors for a period that droned on for 45 years in a less-than-ideal world.

IBM and AT&T could profit from the lesson. If the former would concentrate on hardware and the operating systems, and the latter on more effective communication trunk lines that would enable distant computers to operate as if they were one unit, both would stop wasting resources, and their respective customers might become more satisfied. Enough said.

## 10.7 TO REVIEW THE BIDDING

Communication decisions are the most complex in information systems, and the options and alternatives are the most extensive. The technological considerations are intensive and improve at an uneven pace among themselves. Most users find they have inherently conflicting requirements when attempting to balance the needs of transaction-based systems with information management. Tackling this problem begs some priorities:

- *The Data Issue*. How much data is needed? To what extent is it mutually relatable? Where does it originate and where and how is it used? Draw the map, understand the informational topography, and work from there.
- *Transmission Density and Reliability.* What are the magnitudes associated with the storage and the flow of this data? What degree of accuracy between senders and receivers is required, and to what extent can errors be corrected after the fact?
- *The Distribution Issue*. What are the practical options for the storage and flow of data? What disadvantages does each present with respect to the logical ideal, that is, what is the price of redistributing information circuitously?
- *Network Resiliency.* What network configuration will yield the most resiliency? Given the inevitability of compromise for all but the simplest networks, what design offers the most stretch to accommodate future requirements, peak loads, and changing marketing strategies?
- *Security.* Where are the weak points? How far can potential damage be prevented? For damage that cannot be prevented, how much can be limited? For what cannot always be limited, what standby plans and procedures can be set up?

These questions do not yield easy answers, and the difficult answers that eventually surface tend to be more expensive and demand more compromise than originally presumed. Yet this is the price of attempting to substitute electronic storage and flow of data in an era when information has become too massive and too complex for the human mind to manage and use with any efficiency. To ask the issue another way, what set of internal lines will provide decision makers with the best chance to exercise their judgment and acumen and the least chance of propelling them further into the status of overpaid clerks?

# 11

# Software

*Ask and you shall receive;*
*seek and you shall find;*
*knock and it shall be opened to you;*
*provided: you know what you are doing,*
*you ask, seek, or knock correctly,*
*and the requisite data is available.*

—Matthew 7:7
Murphy's Revised Version

Software is a set of instructions that tells a computer and its peripherals what to do. This was true when Augusta Ada Lovelace set down the rules for programming in 1840. It is true today. And it will be true countless millenniums from now. The trend, however, is to let the computer and its operating (or workhorse) software absorb the drudgery. The information manager can then concentrate on logic and data to meet user requirements.

Software development is the single most expensive element of information systems, and it is the most prone to error. The potential for error increases exponentially in proportion to the amount and types of instructions, or *code*, that must be written. Finally, as programming requirements expand, the tendency is to concentrate on *housekeeping* code. Housekeeping code manages the format of input and output, the hierarchy of files, the storage of data, and the structure of the applications software itself. In an era of expanding knowledge-based information systems, this humdrum work is unavoidable. Yet it short-changes the logic, or *algorithms*, that can put that knowledge to work to meet the strategic objectives of corporations and other users.

The central idea of software development is to delegate the housekeeping work to the computer and its workhorse software. This stuff goes by many names: *systems software, database management packages, language generators,* or *computer assisted software engineering* (CASE). Whatever the case might be in a particular environment, the chief benefit is the elbow room it gives the information manager to maneuver his resources and concentrate on user requirements. Software development is the difference between orchestrating concertmeister-quality musicians vs. spending a lot of time on music lessons.

A system in development often employs hundreds and perhaps thousands of personnel for many years. More than 479,000 people make their living as programmers. Put another way, the development of a system is nearly synonymous with software. If it gets out of hand—something that occurs too often—the consequences can be disastrous. General management and information managers should have a better understanding of the context in which software development proceeds. It is the language of systems. Illiteracy on the part of general management invites failure. Six guidelines for software development apply:

1) *Minimize Original Programming.* The goal is to reduce the amount of new software written. Instead, try using proven, off-the-shelf programs, which are generally called *proprietary* software. When that option is questionable, make maximum use of software that automates the housekeeping code, which is usually called *productivity* software.
2) *Recognize Interior Lines.* The decision maker should not underestimate the potential of software to generate critical intelligence from masses of data in a short time. Good software lays out efficient interior lines, what some writers prefer to call *linkage* or *structure,* between what users need and what resides in the computer.
3) *Document and Test Software before It Is Written.* This anachronism is less facetious than it appears. Many successful systems have been developed in record time because the requirements were first reduced to user manuals, complete with examples of what the processing should yield under certain conditions. In this way, the required logic can be thoroughly tested, perhaps by prototype, before the code is written. After the logic is clear, programming reduces first to engineering and then to highly skilled clerical work.
4) *Decide Early on the Database Structure.* An awareness of the advantages and disadvantages of various database options and models, and of potential network configurations, can exert a positive impact on the planning phase.
5) *Slacken Rigid Development Procedures at the Front End.* Software development environments have become increasingly structured in the administrative sense, which tends to stifle the initiative, ingenuity, and creativity essential for a good macro configuration. But after the music is written, so to speak, its orchestration will likely benefit from tight conducting.

6) *Balance Accuracy with Requirements*. Many projects aim for excessive mathematical and statistical precision that is not warranted by the data or the requirements. This precision consumes unnecessary software development costs and is more prone to error, and also takes inordinate processing time. Senior managers, who are asked to have patience with this approach, won't.

The balance of this chapter starts with an overview of the software development process, followed by sections on documentation and testing, structure, systems software, programming, considerations for integrations, and concludes with a brief look at programming environments. Case studies G and L in appendix A are the best bets for seeing the consequences of good and bad software development environments, except with integrations. For the latter, see case studies C through F in appendix A.

## 11.1 FROM CONCEPT TO CODE

The advice to make maximum use of existing programming and productivity software has a major drawback and a subtle but prevalent management dilemma. The drawback is that the attempt to shoehorn requirements into the systems setup can result in damaging compromises. The dilemma asks what to do with the excess personnel among the nearly 500,000 skilled programmers currently employed. The answer goes beyond the scope of this book, except to say that any decision to opt for original programming, when existing software will do the job well, begs higher costs and increased errors.

The shoehorn problem is easier to address. The ease stems from two mutually reinforcing trends. First, existing programming refers to complete systems that have proven their worth in similar situations, not to software modules collecting dust in the organization's library. Second, productivity software, especially database management systems, are the rule more than the exception. The mutual reinforcement comes from the inclusion of productivity software in proprietary cousins, which, incidentally, is what gave Ashton Tate trouble when the initial version of dBASE IV had major bugs. Solitary users could fall back on the older dBASE III+ version until the bugs were worked out. Not so for software vendors; they depended on the new version to craft updated versions of their proprietary software.

When proprietary software uses the same database management software that an organization uses, it can be piggybacked on the existing database. Carried to its logical end, a well-stocked, well-structured, well-distributed organizational database will lend itself to any number of new requirements with only a minimum of additional housekeeping code.

The significance for management, then, is to exit the concept-structure-programming sequence at the earliest possible point. Figure 11-1 illustrates this sequence, although it oversimplifies the general situation. Many if not most system requirements are met with a combination of two or three types of software.

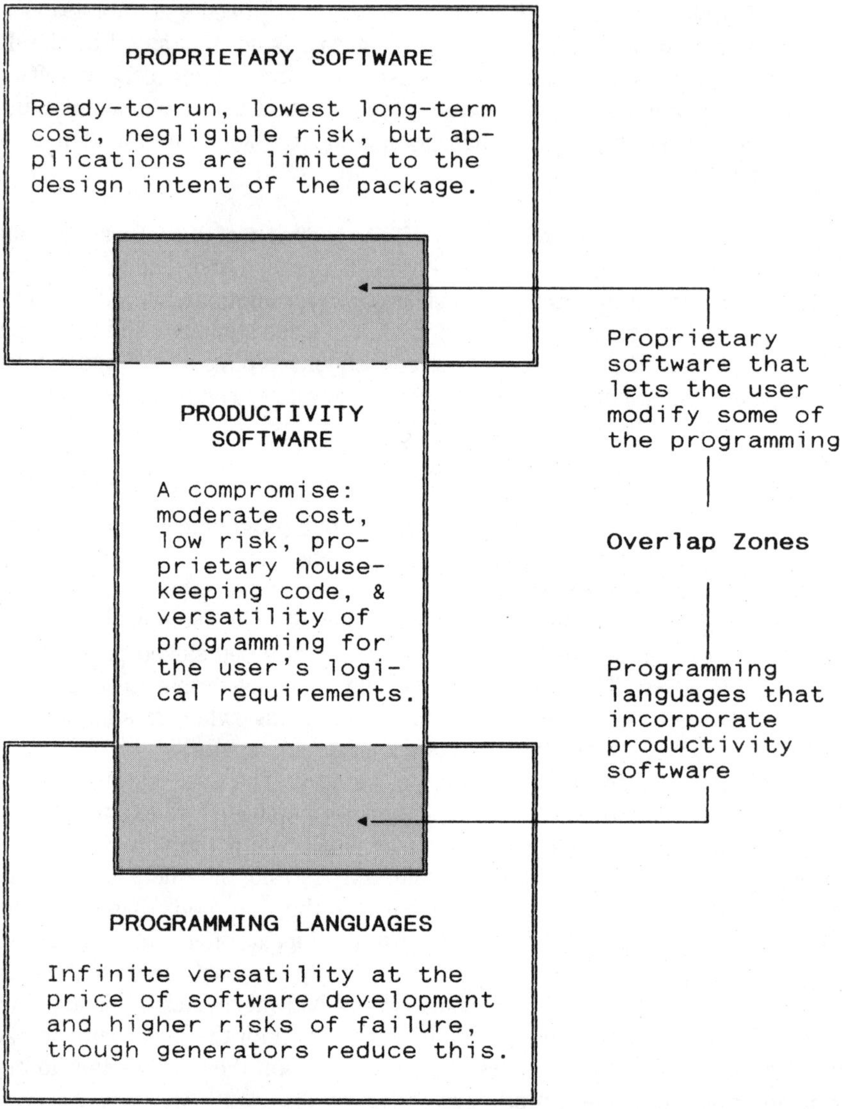


*Fig. 11-1. The three categories of applications software. Applications software can be divided into three categories: proprietary, productivity, and original programming. The dividing lines are not clear, but most information managers have recognized that the use of proprietary and productivity software can generate major cost savings, produce programs with fewer errors, and deliver the products earlier.*

Nevertheless, the information manager would be wise to get rid of as much software development baggage as possible, in more detail:

- *Concept or Macro Level.* This equates with determining the parameters of an intended system (which were described in chapter 3). During this phase, the experienced manager will begin to consider software alternatives, concentrating on potentially useful proprietary software and database management packages. To avoid the shoehorn problem, the emphasis should be on identifying comparative advantages and disadvantages, not decision making. The decision making should focus on the logic necessary to meet the requirements.

- *Structure or Modular Level.* This roughly equates with micro configuration work. Because the next step will be programming, the kingpin software decisions must be made here. The alternatives identified during the macro configuration phase now need to be thrashed out: is there an existing software package that will meet requirements without shoehorning, and if not, how much productivity software can be used to reduce the housekeeping code?
- *Programming or Micro Level.* If forced into original programming, the manager is not without means of reducing the work. New programming languages and program generators can sometimes cut the number of lines of code by a factor of 10 or more. For example, 100 lines of Cobol programming can be replaced by 10 to 20 lines of code, sometimes fewer, written in a higher-level language. Alternatively, Cobol language generators can be used with the same favorable ratio. More on this in section 11.5, as well as case study G and technical note 7 in the appendices.

All of this brings up a major point. Many new programs are tacked onto existing systems. The information manager is then faced with a difficult decision, namely: reprogram the entire package, boilerplate older systems, or find an ingenious method to link new programs written in more efficient languages, with existing code written in older tongues.

This task is no small matter. Approximately 70 percent of the business programs in use today are written in Cobol, comprising about 70 billion lines of code, and represents an investment in excess of $1 trillion. When information systems are superimposed over these largely transaction-based models, what course of action is best? If an existing system operates primarily in a direct-access database management environment, the choice is usually between parasiting the information system directly on the database or alternatively on copies or views of that database. Otherwise, with the increasing use of computers for strategic ends, the advantages of a complete overhaul should at least be considered.

## 11.2 DOCUMENTATION AND TESTING

If there is anything on which computer professionals agree, it would be the necessity of thorough documentation and testing of software. In theory this can be carried to an excess, but the number of times that managers have complained that a system was too well documented or too thoroughly tested are rare enough to make them candidates for the Smithsonian Institution. The tale is told of one senior programmer testing a sophisticated piece of expert system software. He was nearly in tears. When a co-worker inquired why, he replied, "I can't get this program not to work." He was convinced, and rightfully so, that all programs have errors. Unless he found his share, the program would likely fail at a critical time, and with it, his reputation.

Apocryphal? Perhaps, but consider the AT&T communications breakdown on January 16, 1990. The problem arose in a peak-load communications traffic management program. In times of peak loads, the excess traffic must be redirected over alternative routes. On this occasion, the load became heavy enough to give the logic itself a case of overload. For all practical purposes, the software simply stopped, which triggered a chain reaction. When communications traffic could not get through that node, copies of that same program at other nodes tried to reroute it, and in turn immediately overloaded the copies, which therefore caused their operation to "hang up."

In a period of less than 12 hours, approximately 65 million calls did not get through. That's a lot of lost business, and perhaps it damaged AT&T's reputation to the benefit of other long-distance carriers. In fine, an inadequately tested algorithm might eventually cost that corporation tens of millions of dollars in lost revenues. Chapter 2 advised against underestimating the strategic value of sound routine processing. The author rests his case.

### 11.2.1 Testing

The informal 20/80 – 80/20 rule suggests that 20 percent of software development is spent writing programs and 80 percent debugging them. Of the bugs, 80 percent will prove to be simple errors that should have been foreseen, while the remaining 20 percent will have been beyond reasonable foresight. The significance to management is that if the debugging load can be reduced, the software development costs and the time required also will be reduced. One means of doing this is to nail down the criteria for testing before the coding begins. Most managers will agree that programmers who do this, produce the most trouble-free programs. They always keep in mind what the system must do.

### 11.2.2 Top Down vs. Bottom Up

The two general approaches to programming and testing are *top down* and *bottom up*. The top-down approach consists of writing the main module (or *driver*) in full, plus stubs for subordinate modules. This skeleton is tested to make sure it is capable of controlling the modules, irrespective of what those modules might be later programmed to do. Then the succeeding layers are programmed and tested in hierarchical order, until the lowest level is reached.

The bottom-up approach is the exact opposite. The lowest modules are programmed and tested on a stand-alone basis. Then the next level is programmed and tested with emphasis on using the lower-level modules. This process continues until the main module is reached. Figure 11-2 illustrates these two approaches. One compromise version would build the top-down framework, and then program modules from the bottom up, using the framework as a

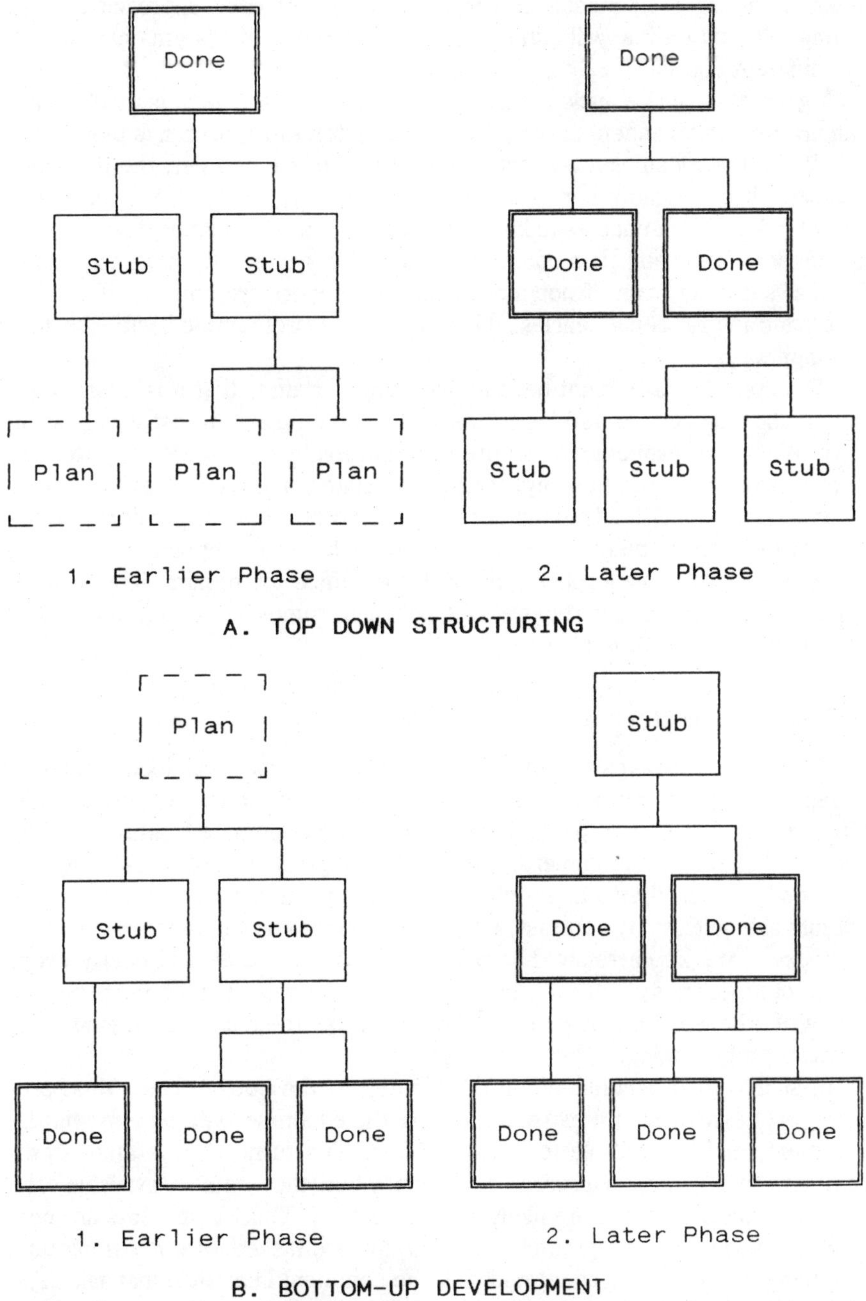


*Fig. 11-2. Top-down vs. bottom-up software development. With few exceptions, programming of major systems tends to proceed either in a top-down or bottom-up direction. Top-down programming starts with a skeleton program of the entire system and then fills in the programming in layers starting just below the top. The bottom-up style programs and tests the lowest level modules first, proceeding up the hierarchy until the top is reached.*

means of testing each module in turn. Advocates for each approach are not wanting, although a few will admit that different types of systems can benefit from different approaches.

A good case can be made for that viewpoint. When the various modules are comparatively independent of each other, the bottom-up approach is more practical. When the modules are heavily dependent on one another, the top-down approach will prove more beneficial. For example, a system that stressed complex yet independent updates to known record structures could be developed on a stand-alone basis and then consolidated into the system. By contrast, scientific analyses, and many if not most decision support systems, tend to have greater intramural dependencies. They should be programmed with the top-down approach.

Whatever the case might be, the one thing certain is that it is a mistake—often a fatal mistake—to develop a large system with plans to test it only as an entity. When this happens, the entire program might have to be rewritten. In the process of structured testing, the intermediate correction of serious errors and omissions usually leads to major revisions in other units still under development. Without these timely revisions, the errors tend to compound to the point where patchwork or boilerplate fixes will not suffice for repairs. The analogy would be the detection and removal of a malignant tumor before it metastasized to the entire organism, read system.

### 11.2.3 Documentation

Documentation takes external and internal forms. External documentation, as the name implies, consists of manuals and related documents describing how software works. In times past, these manuals were prepared entirely by the hand of other than programmers, and required a great deal of time. Programmers tend to shun them. Even when the writing of manuals is enforced, the contents age quickly. By contrast, embedded commentary demonstrates a better track record for currency. Every programming language and nearly every version of productivity software makes provision for this. The better programmers write these comment lines first, and then use them as explicit guidelines for actual programming.

In short, good documentation contributes to the bottom line. Most programs will be revised and expanded during their lifetime, yet seldom will the same personnel be available to work on them. The turnover rate among programmers in industry is severe, and even when they remain available, the details of what they coded are likely to be forgotten. Thus, comments are necessary to guide other programmers. Programmers tasked with revisions tend to be more conscientious about updating the comment lines than manuals. The consequence is that subsequent updates will be even more dependent on this internal documentation.

The value of good documentation has spurred two advances: the use of code that is closer to English and hence serves as its own commentary, and computer programs that generate external documentation and regenerate complete new editions whenever a program is revised. Section 11.7 continues the discussion on these two points.

## 11.3 STRUCTURING

In the book *Mr. Blanding Builds His Dream House*, the hero wants to add a fireplace to a downstairs room and tries to persuade the architect to modify the plans. The latter resolves the issue by warning him the resulting chimney will turn one of the bedrooms upstairs into a square donut. Similarly, the structuring of systems is the formal process of improving the internal lines of software, not only for processing efficiency but to facilitate updates and revisions to the programming itself. This structuring operates at three levels: the architecture of the system, which equates with macro configuration; modularization, which is the hierarchy of program modules and databases and what each will do; and programming structure, which concentrates on the flow—and readability—of logic within a module.

The federal tax system offers a good example of structure at all three levels. Every element in it has been computerized, although most taxpayers still complete the forms manually. System architecture would thus equate with the configuration and distribution of all IRS databases and programs. Modular structure would mean the relationship among the nearly 400 forms required to implement federal laws. The programming structure would then be the sequence of computations and readability of the forms. Figure 11-3 presents the overall picture, amplified by the discussion in the first three of the following four subsections.

### 11.3.1 Program Architecture

The conversion of logical requirements into a configuration capable of being implemented on one or more computers is called systems architecture. The details of that configuration are engineering tasks, but good engineering alone will not ensure a good design. In the IRS, the configuration, number, and distribution of databases influences mechanical efficiency as well as the ability to compare data and identify under-reporting of income. As mentioned in subsection 6.1.6, this unreported income could yield additional tax revenues in the neighborhood of $100 billion each year.

### 11.3.2 Modular Structures

Modular structuring is one of the main tasks of software engineering, which follows from the thesis that the potential for good engineering is dependent on a good design. In terms of individual tax return forms, the familiar 1040 is the main module or driver. Most all of the other forms are subordinated to it (or the equivalent for corporations) in a distinct hierarchy. The abbreviated form 1040A and the simple form 1040EZ are excerpted from this driver. The former links with only a few of the subordinate forms, the latter links with none at all.

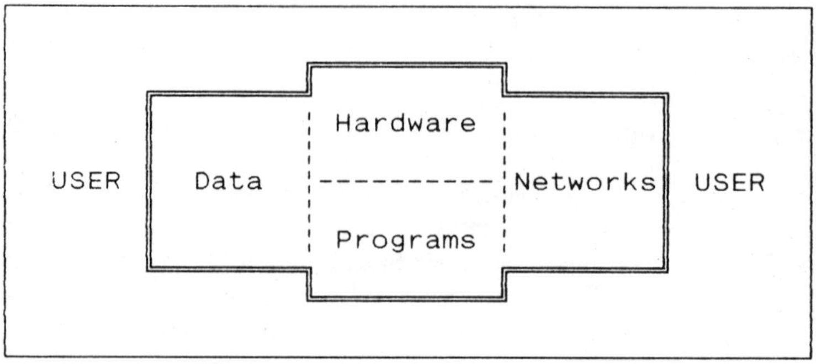


THE ARCHITECTURAL LEVEL

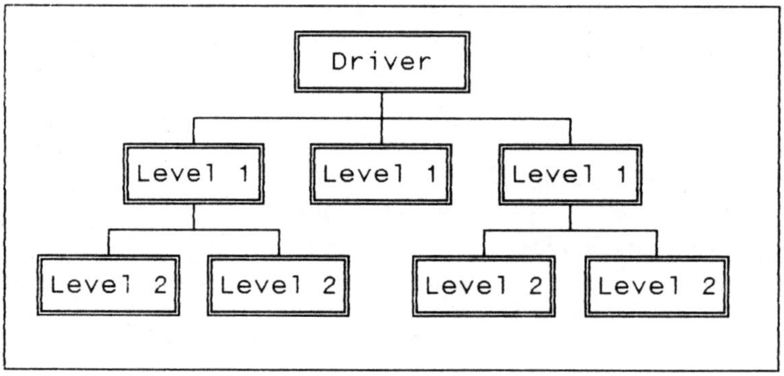


THE MODULAR LEVEL

```
IF Hours_Worked < 20
   THEN
     Pay = Hours_Worked * Rate_of_Pay * .9
   ELSE IF Hours_Worked =< 40
     Pay = Hours_Worked * Rate_of Pay
   ELSE
     Pay = Hours_Worked * Rate_of Pay
     Pay = Pay + (Hours_Worked - 40) * 1.5
END IF
```

THE PROGRAMMING LEVEL

*Fig. 11-3. The three levels of structure. Structured software operates at three levels: architectural, modular, and programming. Excellent skill at the lower levels will seldom compensate for poor practices at the upper levels.*

### 11.3.3 Programming Structure

The form 1040 is a remarkable example of structured programming. A rule of thumb in software engineering is that no module should have more than 50 lines of executable code. The 1040 appears to have 68. But the first five are used for a single input check mark and another two have been nullified (the Medicare supplementary premium), which leaves a net of 62 lines for the driver. That's not bad considering the complexity of the law applicable to individual taxpayers. Further, of the 62 lines, 12 are set to the left of the main column as "included subprograms," namely inputs for credits and payments respectively. Figure 11-4 demonstrates that the balance is 50. Further, the taxpayer always proceeds from top to bottom, except to refer back to previous entries. In the programmed versions, the use of variables negates even this minor exception.

### 11.3.4 Globals, GoTo's, and Gremlins

The three dominant sources of errors in programming appear to stem from what are known as *globals, GoTo's,* and *gremlins*. Globals are variables that can be accessed by any module in a system. GoTo's are statements in a module that direct execution to different segments of code under different conditions. Gremlins are little creatures that reside in compilers and other software that take every opportunity to make programs work in a manner other than intended by the programmer. Each has its significance for management.

**Globals.** In large systems, where the work of programming is subdivided into fine portions, keeping track of how all the modules affect each other is difficult. One module can update a global variable in a manner inimical to another module that must refer to it. All data in a database is inherently global, which can lead to conflicts and many problems. In short, this is one of those highly technical areas that is seminal enough to occasionally demand the personal attention of project managers.

**GoTo's.** GoTo's are the computer equivalent of original sin. One of the goals of structured programming is to eliminate them, at least from source code. Excessive use of GoTo's, especially if they cause execution to jump backwards in programs, are nothing but trouble. True, 99.99 percent of all programming uses loops to repeat execution of segments of code, but this is done with controlled structures that are easy to write and maintain. The real problem comes with program maintenance and minor revisions. The GoTo statement, which differs slightly in syntax among different languages, is often employed as a quick fix instead of a more fundamental reprogramming of the modules that exist, especially during testing when deadlines are usually tight. Eventually, the time saved will come back to reclaim itself with a vengeance.[1] Beware.

**Gremlins.** Gremlins do not really exist, of course, except in the minds of programmers, but that doesn't lessen the problem. The problem stems from the fact that machines, operating systems, compilers, programming language

---

[1]Every experienced programmer can recall one or more cases where the use of the GoTo statement in someone else's program proved to be a major problem. The one that this writer recalls was a 70-line module in a Defense program used worldwide, that took him, and another more senior programmer with 25 years experience in the language used, more than a week to figure out what it was doing, even after plotting every step in a micro, color-coded flowchart. It finally became clear after writing out the logic on a Moebius strip (a strip of paper twisted 180 degrees and then taped together at the ends).

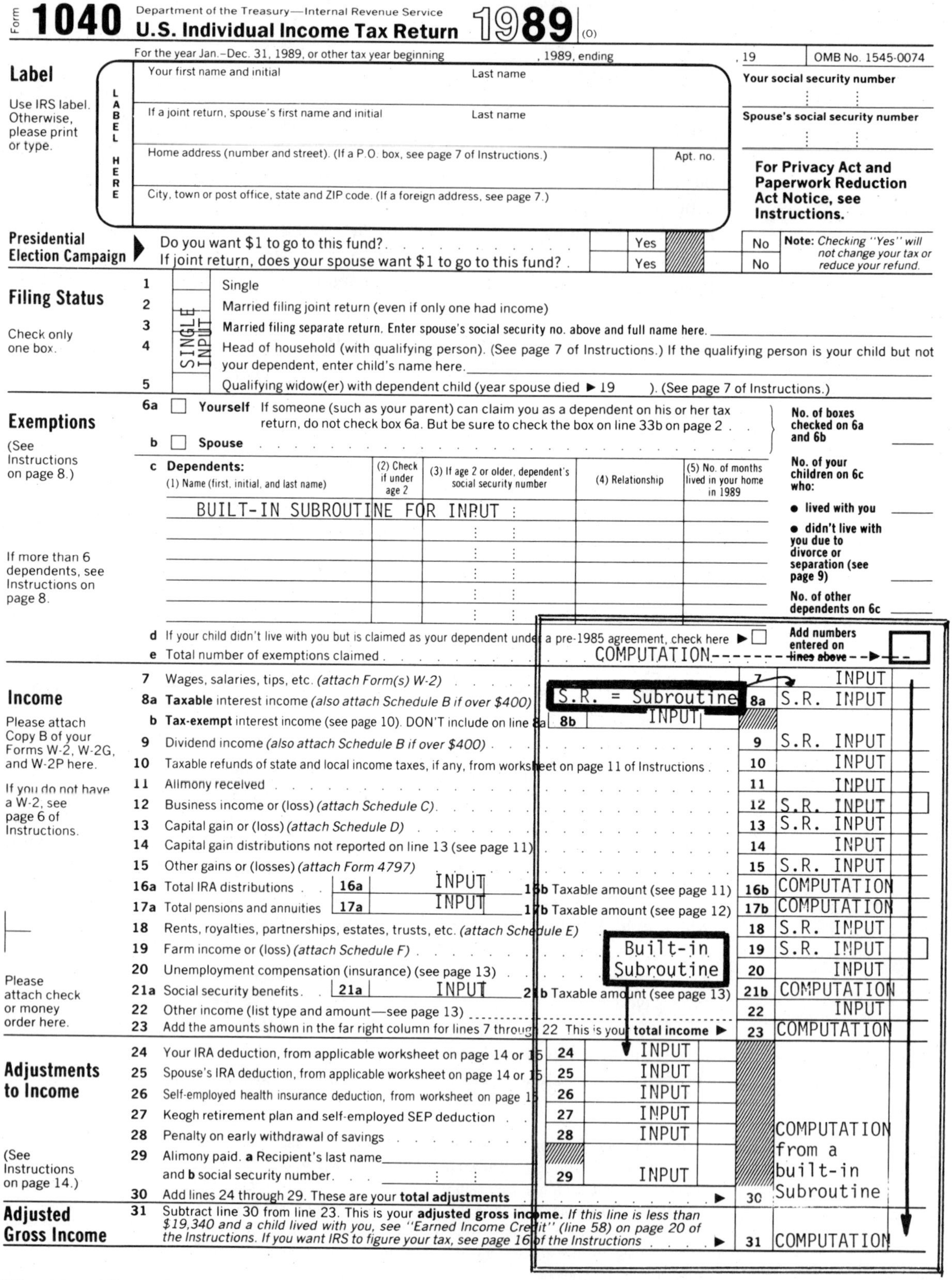

Form **1040** Department of the Treasury—Internal Revenue Service
**U.S. Individual Income Tax Return** **1989** (0)

For the year Jan.–Dec. 31, 1989, or other tax year beginning , 1989, ending , 19 | OMB No. 1545-0074

**Label**

Use IRS label. Otherwise, please print or type.

LABEL HERE

Your first name and initial | Last name | Your social security number

If a joint return, spouse's first name and initial | Last name | Spouse's social security number

Home address (number and street). (If a P.O. box, see page 7 of Instructions.) | Apt. no.

City, town or post office, state and ZIP code. (If a foreign address, see page 7.)

**For Privacy Act and Paperwork Reduction Act Notice, see Instructions.**

**Presidential Election Campaign**

Do you want $1 to go to this fund? . . . Yes | No

If joint return, does your spouse want $1 to go to this fund? . . Yes | No

**Note:** *Checking "Yes" will not change your tax or reduce your refund.*

**Filing Status**

Check only one box.

1 Single

2 Married filing joint return (even if only one had income)

3 Married filing separate return. Enter spouse's social security no. above and full name here.

4 Head of household (with qualifying person). (See page 7 of Instructions.) If the qualifying person is your child but not your dependent, enter child's name here.

5 Qualifying widow(er) with dependent child (year spouse died ▶ 19 ). (See page 7 of Instructions.)

SINGLE INPUT

**Exemptions**

(See Instructions on page 8.)

6a **Yourself** If someone (such as your parent) can claim you as a dependent on his or her tax return, do not check box 6a. But be sure to check the box on line 33b on page 2 . .

b **Spouse** . . .

**No. of boxes checked on 6a and 6b**

c **Dependents:** (1) Name (first, initial, and last name) | (2) Check if under age 2 | (3) If age 2 or older, dependent's social security number | (4) Relationship | (5) No. of months lived in your home in 1989

BUILT-IN SUBROUTINE FOR INPUT

**No. of your children on 6c who:**
● lived with you
● didn't live with you due to divorce or separation (see page 9)
**No. of other dependents on 6c**

If more than 6 dependents, see Instructions on page 8.

d If your child didn't live with you but is claimed as your dependent under a pre-1985 agreement, check here ▶

e Total number of exemptions claimed . . . COMPUTATION

**Add numbers entered on lines above** ▶

**Income**

Please attach Copy B of your Forms W-2, W-2G, and W-2P here.

If you do not have a W-2, see page 6 of Instructions.

Please attach check or money order here.

S.R. = Subroutine

7 Wages, salaries, tips, etc. *(attach Form(s) W-2)* . . . 7 INPUT

8a **Taxable** interest income *(also attach Schedule B if over $400)* . . . 8a S.R. INPUT

b **Tax-exempt** interest income (see page 10). DON'T include on line 8a | 8b INPUT

9 Dividend income *(also attach Schedule B if over $400)* . . . 9 S.R. INPUT

10 Taxable refunds of state and local income taxes, if any, from worksheet on page 11 of Instructions . . 10 INPUT

11 Alimony received . . . 11 INPUT

12 Business income or (loss) *(attach Schedule C)* . . . 12 S.R. INPUT

13 Capital gain or (loss) *(attach Schedule D)* . . . 13 S.R. INPUT

14 Capital gain distributions not reported on line 13 (see page 11) . . . 14 INPUT

15 Other gains or (losses) *(attach Form 4797)* . . . 15 S.R. INPUT

16a Total IRA distributions . . 16a INPUT | 16b Taxable amount (see page 11) 16b COMPUTATION

17a Total pensions and annuities 17a INPUT | 17b Taxable amount (see page 12) 17b COMPUTATION

18 Rents, royalties, partnerships, estates, trusts, etc. *(attach Schedule E)* . . . 18 S.R. INPUT

19 Farm income or (loss) *(attach Schedule F)* . . . 19 S.R. INPUT

Built-in Subroutine

20 Unemployment compensation (insurance) (see page 13) . . . 20 INPUT

21a Social security benefits . . 21a INPUT | 21b Taxable amount (see page 13) 21b COMPUTATION

22 Other income (list type and amount—see page 13) . . . 22 INPUT

23 Add the amounts shown in the far right column for lines 7 through 22. This is your **total income** ▶ 23 COMPUTATION

**Adjustments to Income**

(See Instructions on page 14.)

24 Your IRA deduction, from applicable worksheet on page 14 or 15 | 24 INPUT

25 Spouse's IRA deduction, from applicable worksheet on page 14 or 15 | 25 INPUT

26 Self-employed health insurance deduction, from worksheet on page 15 | 26 INPUT

27 Keogh retirement plan and self-employed SEP deduction . . | 27 INPUT

28 Penalty on early withdrawal of savings . . . | 28 INPUT

29 Alimony paid. **a** Recipient's last name and **b** social security number. . . | 29 INPUT

30 Add lines 24 through 29. These are your **total adjustments** . . . ▶ 30 COMPUTATION from a built-in Subroutine

**Adjusted Gross Income**

31 Subtract line 30 from line 23. This is your **adjusted gross income.** *If this line is less than $19,340 and a child lived with you, see "Earned Income Credit" (line 58) on page 20 of the Instructions. If you want IRS to figure your tax, see page 16 of the Instructions* . . . ▶ 31 COMPUTATION

*Fig. 11-4. The IRS Form 1040 as a model of good structure. Surprisingly, the familiar IRS form 1040 is a model of good programming structure.*

Form 1040 (1989) 

|  |  |  |  |
|---|---|---|---|
| **Tax Computation** | 32 | Amount from line 31 (adjusted gross income) | 32 DUPLICATE |
| | 33a | Check if: ☐ **You** were 65 or older ☐ Blind; ☐ **Spouse** was 65 or older ☐ Blind. Add the number of boxes checked and enter the total here ▶ 33a | INPUT from a COMPUTATION SUBROUTINE |
| | b | If someone (such as your parent) can claim you as a dependent, check here ▶ 33b ☐ | |
| | c | If you are married filing a separate return and your spouse itemizes deductions, or you are a dual-status alien, see page 16 and check here ▶ 33c ☐ | |
| | 34 | Enter the larger of: • Your **standard deduction** (from page 17 of the Instructions), **OR** • Your **itemized deductions** (from Schedule A, line 26). If you itemize, attach Schedule A and check here ▶ ☐ | 34 SUBROUTINE |
| | 35 | Subtract line 34 from line 32. Enter the result here | 35 COMPUTATION |
| | 36 | Multiply $2,000 by the total number of exemptions claimed on line 6e | 36 COMPUTATION |
| | 37 | **Taxable income.** Subtract line 36 from line 35. Enter the result (if less than zero, enter zero). **Caution:** If under age 14 and you have more than $1,000 of investment income, check here ▶ ☐ and see page 17 to see if you have to use Form 8615 to figure your tax. | 37 COMPUTATION; INPUT from a COMPUTATION |
| | 38 | Enter tax. Check if from: a ☐ Tax Table, b ☐ Tax Rate Schedules, or c ☐ Form 8615. (If any is from Form(s) 8814, enter that amount here ▶ d ______) | 38 SUBROUTINE |
| | 39 | Additional taxes (see page 18). Check if from: a ☐ Form 4970 b ☐ Form 4972 | 39 S.R. INPUT |
| | 40 | Add lines 38 and 39. Enter the total ▶ | 40 COMPUTATION |
| **Credits** (See Instructions on page 18.) | 41 | Credit for child and dependent care expenses *(attach Form 2441)* | 41 S.R. INPUT |
| | 42 | Credit for the elderly or the disabled *(attach Schedule R)* | 42 S.R. INPUT |
| | 43 | Foreign tax credit *(attach Form 1116)* | 43 S.R. INPUT |
| | 44 | General business credit. Check if from: a ☐ Form 3800 or b ☐ Form (specify) ______ | 44 S.R. INPUT |
| | 45 | Credit for prior year minimum tax *(attach Form 8801)* | 45 S.R. INPUT |
| | 46 | Add lines 41 through 45. Enter the total | 46 COMPUTATION from a built-in Subroutine |
| | 47 | Subtract line 46 from line 40. Enter the result (if less than zero, enter zero) ▶ | 47 COMPUTATION |
| **Other Taxes** (Including Advance EIC Payments) | 48 | Self-employment tax *(attach Schedule SE)* | 48 S.R. INPUT |
| | 49 | Alternative minimum tax *(attach Form 6251)* | 49 S.R. INPUT |
| | 50 | Recapture taxes (see page 18). Check if from: a ☐ Form 4255 b ☐ Form 8611 | 50 S.R. INPUT |
| | 51 | Social security tax on tip income not reported to employer *(attach Form 4137)* | 51 S.R. INPUT |
| | 52 | Tax on an IRA or a qualified retirement plan *(attach Form 5329)* | 52 S.R. INPUT |
| | 53 | Add lines 47 through 52. Enter the total ▶ | 53 COMPUTATION |
| **Medicare Premium** | 54 | Supplemental Medicare premium *(attach Form 8808)* | 54 Deleted by Act |
| | 55 | Add lines 53 and 54. This is your **total tax** and any supplemental Medicare premium ▶ | 55 of Congress |
| **Payments** (Attach Forms W-2, W-2G, and W-2P to front.) | 56 | Federal income tax withheld (if any is from Form(s) 1099, check ▶ ☐) | 56 INPUT |
| | 57 | 1989 estimated tax payments and amount applied from 1988 return | 57 INPUT |
| | 58 | Earned income credit (see page 20) | 58 INPUT |
| | 59 | Amount paid with Form 4868 (extension request) | 59 INPUT |
| | 60 | Excess social security tax and RRTA tax withheld (see page 20) | 60 INPUT |
| | 61 | Credit for Federal tax on fuels *(attach Form 4136)* | 61 S.R. INPUT |
| | 62 | Regulated investment company credit *(attach Form 2439)* | 62 S.R. INPUT |
| | 63 | Add lines 56 through 62. These are your **total payments** ▶ | 63 COMPUTATION from a built-in Subroutine |
| **Refund or Amount You Owe** | 64 | If line 63 is larger than line 55, enter amount **OVERPAID** ▶ | 64 COMPUTATION (If) |
| | 65 | Amount of line 64 to be **REFUNDED TO YOU** ▶ | 65 INPUT (If) |
| | 66 | Amount of line 64 to be **APPLIED TO YOUR 1990 ESTIMATED TAX** ▶ | 66 COMPUTATION |
| | 67 | If line 55 is larger than line 63, enter **AMOUNT YOU OWE.** Attach check or money order for full amount payable to "Internal Revenue Service." Write your social security number, daytime phone number, and "1989 Form 1040" on it | 67 COMPUTATION (If) |
| | 68 | Penalty for underpayment of estimated tax (see page 21) | 68 INPUT |

BUILT-IN SUBROUTINES

**Sign Here** (Keep a copy of this return for your records.)

Under penalties of perjury, I declare that I have examined this return and accompanying schedules and statements, and to the best of my knowledge and belief, they are true, correct, and complete. Declaration of preparer (other than taxpayer) is based on all information of which preparer has any knowledge.

| | | |
|---|---|---|
| Your signature | Date | Your occupation |
| Spouse's signature (if joint return, BOTH must sign) | Date | Spouse's occupation |

**Paid Preparer's Use Only**

| | | | |
|---|---|---|---|
| Preparer's signature | Date | Check if self-employed ☐ | Preparer's social security no. |
| Firm's name (or yours if self-employed) and address | | E.I. No. | |
| | | ZIP code | |

syntax, and productivity software that is supposed to be compatible or standardized always seems to differ in subtle ways. Thus, a programmer who inures to one setup is often unaware of these subtle differences when working in another one. What is intended is not always what is executed. When the automated navigation equipment for the F-16 prototype jet fighter was tested, the pilot discovered that it turned his plane upside down as it flew over the equator. Again, beware.

## 11.4 SYSTEMS SOFTWARE

Systems software comprises the programs that manage: the hardware components, the interfaces between that hardware and applications software, and the systems software itself. In former times, systems software was separate and distinct from applications programs and was controlled by separate instructions, often called *job control language* (JCL). Thus, every application program consisted of some front-end JCL that templated the hardware and the systems software to meet the processing requirements for itself.

The requirement for systems software will never recede, except in specialized machines that are hard-wired for a specific function. But the trend today is to automate as much system software as possible, and eliminate the dualism for the balance. One option is to incorporate the JCL instructions directly into application programming languages. A similar option duplicates or otherwise encompasses the system software in such a way that the programmer is unaware of it. A third option is to reduce the instructional requirements to some button pushing. Figure 11-5 illustrates this trend, and the following points describe the elements in more detail.

- *Operating Systems*. Operating systems do exactly what the name implies. They operate the physical system. A computer and its peripherals constitute a network of distributive processing in microcosm that must be managed. The simple action of getting a piece of information from a file and displaying it on the screen is in reality an enormously complex task when reduced to machine code.
- *Job Control Languages*. As previously implied, job control languages control the operating system, although it is usually divided into instructions which are available to programmers and instructions that can be invoked only by the individuals operating the system as an entity.
- *Protocols*. Protocols are programs which regulate and control the flow of data and instructions in a network beyond the immediate computer environment, i.e., with other computers and distant terminals. Formerly, these utilities had to be written in special systems programs, but languages such as Ada now permit insertion of protocol logic within application programs.
- *Translators and Compilers*. Translators translate code from one language into another. A compiler is a special case of a translator that reduces code into machine language. Both forms first reduce the source input to assembler language (which is one step removed from machine code).

The translator then "uncompiles" that assembler code and ascends back up into the targeted language. The compiler, by contrast, continues the descent into machine language. Technical note 8 in appendix B covers this in more detail. In combination with technical note 7 (on programming languages), the intent is to provide managers with a better understanding of the advantages and disadvantages of living with Cobol programming compared to using higher-level languages and program generators.

- *The Back End of Productivity and Proprietary Software.* All proprietary software and most productivity software must control or duplicate the functions of systems software. The degree to which this is done varies. For example, most spreadsheet packages require a separate command to save data to disk if it is to be retrieved at a later time. By contrast, most database software incorporates this feature as an automatic part of user-entered updates.

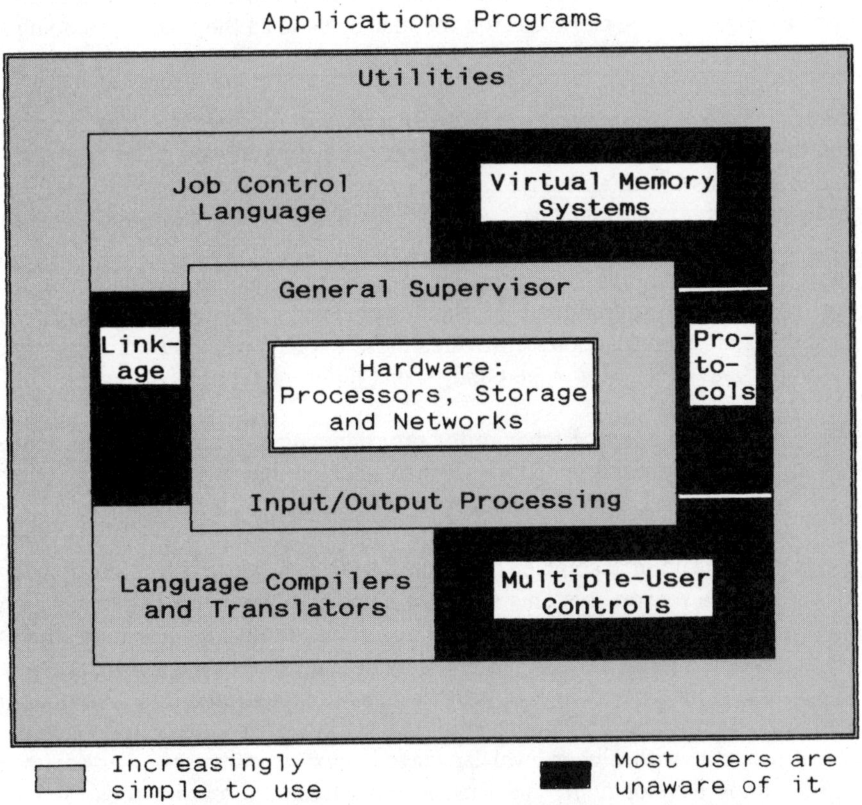


*Fig. 11-5. Systems software. At one time, the term* systems software *had a precise meaning: the software that operated the computer. Now because many software packages include their own operating software, differentiating between systems and applications software is harder. This chart depicts the present systems software environment, although it is impossible to obtain a consensus on where the dividing lines should be.*

The significance to management of this commendable trend to automate the use of systems software is that it does not solve the problem of compatibility among computers. On the contrary, it obscures compatibility. The Open Standards Interface Agreement discussed in chapter 10 will eventually eliminate the problem, but for the foreseeable future, the incompatibilities imposed by different hardware, communications equipment, and systems software will likely prove the greatest obstacle to effective integrations of systems and databases. Unfortunately, the proliferation of IBM-compatible microcomputers has created a false sense of simplicity among general managers.

## 11.5 PROGRAMMING LANGUAGES AND ALTERNATIVES

In his first book *Tales of the South Pacific*, James Michener tells about an Indonesian postal official's attempt to duplicate the modern practices of the West. He installed a variety of mail slots along a wall for: local mail, foreign surface mail, air mail, and so forth. Behind that wall, the chutes all emptied into one basket where the clerks sorted the mail by hand as they had been doing for generations. This is what happens with software.

If sufficient memory is available and there are no restrictions on processing time, *any logical requirement can be programmed in any programming language*, and for that matter in most versions of productivity software. The research to find exceptions to this axiom is legendary and futile. The reason is that the hierarchy of programming languages consist only of utilities (or micro modules) that combine two or more lower-level programming instructions. It makes for efficient programming, but the higher-level languages cannot do anything that cannot be directly programmed in the lower levels. Figure 11-6 shows this hierarchy, and technical note 7 provides more detail. Two points of significance are important: processing speed and mixing different types of software.

- *Processing Speed.* Higher-order programming languages execute slower than logic programmed directly in assembler, although C language comes close. With Cobol, the difference is dramatic, in some cases by a factor of 30 or more, which means that a major program that would take 5 minutes to run in assembler could take over 2½ hours if written in Cobol. For this reason, systems software is inevitably written either in assembler or in C. The problem is that assembler programs take more time to code by a factor of 10 to 20, and they are far more prone to errors. Fortunately, the power curve of programming demonstrates that 10 percent of most programs do 90 percent of the work. Hence, the general rule is to program with higher-level languages, next identify the over-achievers during development, and then if appropriate reprogram those units in assembler.
- *Mixing Different Types of Software.* The ability to mix different types of software in the same program is a mixed blessing. The good news is that it lends flexibility to programming requirements. The bad news is that controlling the quality of the system as an entity is difficult for project

managers. The motley collection of source codes becomes something of a Tower of Babel. After-the-fact assembler reprogramming of high-use modules is an exception. After testing in a higher-order language, they can be reprogrammed and retested in comparative isolation.

## 11.6 INTEGRATIONS

Software is reality imposed between dreams and terra firma. Attempts to integrate it sometimes turn the dreams into nightmares. It's not that software has a subconscious, but that project managers and programmers of the targeted components seldom prove to have been of the same mind. Thus, integrations go beyond mere technical linkage. The underlying logic and intent of the components must be taken into account.

**Syntheses.** Synthesizing existing software is even more difficult than synthesizing hardware. With hardware, software bridges can be developed to negotiate any compatibility gap. In theory this is also true for software, but a true synthesis might require so much bridging that the original programs are reduced to extraneous shells. A project manager might be able to salvage the logic, but a complete redesign and reprogramming will likely prove more efficient than a horde of utilities.

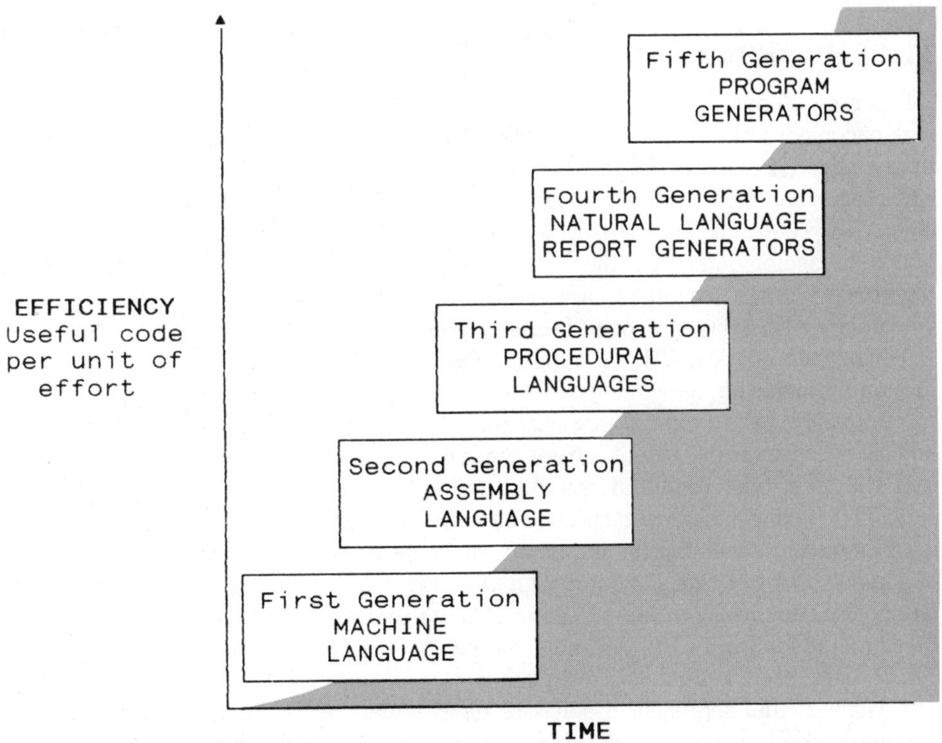


*Fig. 11-6. The hierarchy of programming languages. Because all programs eventually reduce to a handful of basic operations, and then to simple machine code, programming languages fit into a distinct hierarchy, with branches.*

**Database Integrations.** Assuming the issues of data element compatibility have been resolved, the software decisions will focus on ensuring that the database software package or packages selected can access the database as structured, and that its commands can be imbedded in the programming languages used by the organization.

**Interfaces.** Interfacing applications software is a rarity, except in the traditional and widespread practice of multiple terminals sharing the same software. Attempts to go beyond this are inherently syntheses. If that is not what is wanted, then the more practical interface is to exchange inputs and outputs and let each component in the interface do what it was intended to do. The interfacing of systems software was covered in chapter 10.

**Standardizations.** Standardization of applications software is an elusive goal. By contrast, programming languages and systems software can benefit from this approach. For example, the Department of Defense has made WordPerfect its standard word processing software, and has attempted to impose Ada as its standard programming language. Yet each application program is inherently unique, otherwise it would not be written. Beyond this example, some organizations try to unify techniques for the development, structuring, and documentation of software, which might lend some semblance of standardization, but it might also squelch ingenuity.

## 11.7 THE PROGRAMMING ENVIRONMENT

A programming environment is the collection of factors and circumstances that encompass and influence the development and testing of software. More than a hundred different models have been formalized, and undoubtedly every corporation and organization that depends heavily on computers uses some variation of one of them. The central idea of these environments is somewhat analogous to ecology, that is, the various elements and aspects should work together to create something of a symbiosis. The net result, from a negative viewpoint, is to avoid the many forms of poor software, as outlined in TABLE 11-1. They are not ANSI/IEEE standard, but their prevalence deserves consideration for inclusion.

Arguably, to the extent an environment frees the practitioners from secondary concerns is the extent it frees them to focus on the logic and algorithms that will meet user requirements, and hence the extent to which they work well. This means a maximum reliance on computer generated utilities, on standardization and compatibility, and on a management that understands the value of banking on a well thought-out design or configuration for each project. Then, within this beneficially narrowed scope of activity, the sound discipline of structured methodology at all three levels of concern—macro, modular, and micro—can be harnessed to greatest advantage.

Much of this approach to software development enlists under the rubric computer aided systems engineering (CASE). The ideal end point of CASE is to develop a gigantic hunk of expert system software that will do everything short of entering basic requirements. Until that goal is reached, if ever, the important aspect is to concentrate on translating user requirements into an efficient system, and then developing that system without any debilitating flaws.

**The Macro Level.** Although many versions of macro-level design tools are available—many of them automated—there is no substitute for a first-rate mind to translate requirements into a first-rate design or configuration. All of the supporting tools can help, however they cannot supplant.

**The Modular Level.** The modular level is where the issue of interior lines gets the most play. The macro design is the starting point but it is generally too broad a brush for direct implementation. This intermediate step is therefore indispensable. As at the macro level, many tools are available. One of the most versatile and resilient is the well-known hierarchical-input-processing-output (HIPO) chart. Figure 11-7 illustrates one of these charts pushed to its inherent limits. The versatility arises from the ability to continually rearrange these charts, and modify their content on a large table or expansive wall until the optimum modularity for the system is perceived. The deluxe version would automate the process, as hypothesized in technical note 9 in appendix B.

*Table 11-1. Software stew. Some poor programming practices have earned sobriquets drawn from cuisines. The list here is not exclusive, and many of the entries are also known by other names, not all of which are printable.*

| Nickname | Informal Description | Consequences |
|---|---|---|
| SPAGHETTI CODE | Indiscriminate use of GoTo's. *World Famous* | Difficult to maintain. |
| HAMBURGER CODE | Poor modular structure; modules too encompassing. | Very difficult to revise. |
| CHEF'S SPECIAL | New programs built from leftover modules. | Inefficient, at best. |
| SWISS CHEESE | Gaping holes in the logical processing | Fails in all but simple cases. |
| DAGWOOD BUMSTEAD | One program attempting to meet many needs. | Poor to mediocre performance. |
| COTTON CANDY | Many puffed-up displays; little substance. | Meets few, if any, requirements. |
| SALAMI CODE | It works, but you don't want to know how it was programmed. | Requires expert programmers to maintain. |

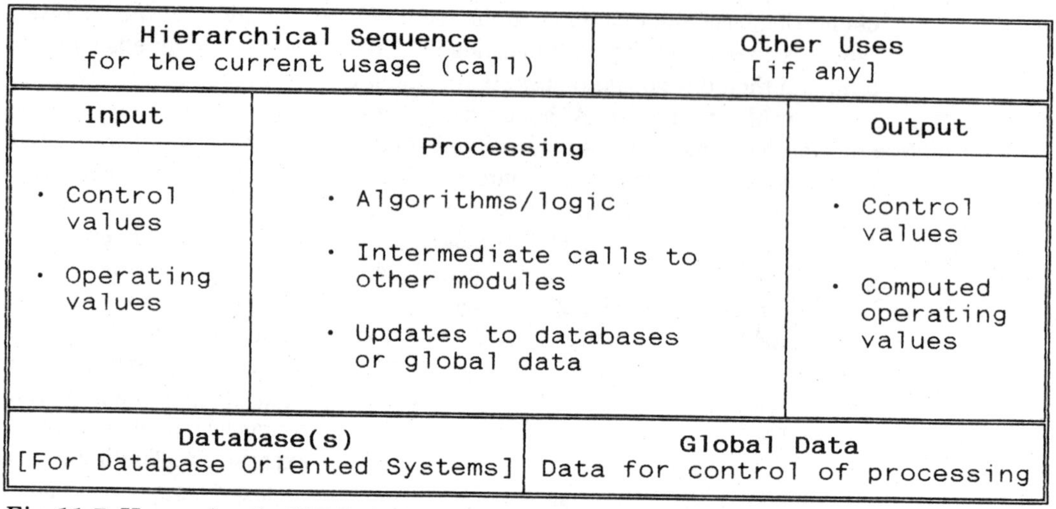


*Fig. 11-7. Harnessing the HIPO chart. HIPO is an acronym for Hierarchical-Input-Output-Organizational chart or card. One card is developed for each module in a program, to simplify the process of refining the modular structure during the design phase for a system. Unfortunately, programmers often shun the technique due its lack of detail, and systems analysts sometimes consider the cards to be a children's game. Still, the potential remains and can be harnessed by computerizing the cards on a three-dimensional spreadsheet or other form of productivity software. The input and output links can be programmed directly into the spreadsheets, and different spreadsheets displayed on different monitors in a local area network. This chart is similar to the prototyping technique shown later in chapter 17 (Fig. 17-3).*

**The Micro Level.** The ideal is to use a programming language that is self documenting. The pivotal lines of code are entered as comments that are either directly executable or that can be readily transformed line-for-line into such code. The detailed code then follows suit. The Ada programming language comes close to this ideal, combined with a standardization that really does facilitate compatibility. Unfortunately, this language is exceedingly complex and is encumbered with an academic lexicon that has scared away many if not most potential users beyond the Department of Defense. More on this in case study F in appendix A.

# 12

# Artificial Intelligence and Support Systems

*Complex problems have simple, easy-to-understand wrong answers.*

—Murphy's Law Graffiti

Artificial intelligence (AI) is probably the most overrated aspect of computer science. Paradoxically, at least one application offers the most promise for information systems. That application is the expert system, which commonly shows up as a decision support system (DSS) or its junior partner the executive information system (EIS). Both were described in section 2.4. Briefly, a DSS focuses on longer-range problems or at least on those problems with a wider range of options to explore. In contrast, an EIS lends itself to more immediate and direct what-if type questions. For the sake of simplicity, and for lack of a better term, this chapter refers to both models as *support systems*.

The checkered reputation of AI stems from the attempt to supplant human judgment with machines. Not surprisingly, this *deux ex machina* approach has been the target of ridicule for almost 300 years, and now offers fertile ground for best sellers in the computer field. Yet, after the key word *supplant* is changed to *support*, the justification for the ridicule evaporates, opening the way for a more extensive use of the technology. More than half of the Fortune 500 companies invest a total of $2 billion annually in support systems, and every projection indicates this amount will increase sharply in the next decade, perhaps by a factor of ten. Software companies continue to pump out new proprietary and productivity models (shells) at the flood level. Even IBM, never known for avant-garde marketing, has fielded a number of major products here.

This growth is a far cry from the satire that appeared in Jonathan Swift's *Gulliver's Travels*, published in 1726. In his imaginary voyage to Balnibarbi, Jonathan encounters a university where the professors inscribed different words on turnable blocks mounted on axles cranked by scribes. After each crank, the professors would write down the resulting phrases and sentences. As the phrases and sentences accumulated, they would compose chapters, which were then combined into books. Interestingly, and except for hypothetical maps, Swift chose this contraption for the only illustration in the book.

The satire continues to this day. In the Woody Allen film *Sleeper*, the hero finds himself 200 years in the future and encounters a machine that has taken the place of a confessor. Woody reveals his sins, the machine hums and buzzes, next flashes the word "absolved," and then dispenses a kewpie doll. No doubt every reader can add to the list. On the other hand, the fictional robots R2 D2 and CPO often cause film goers to wonder if these machines might really come to pass. The answer is yes and no.

The reason is that no matter how sophisticated software gets, the computer remains a robot that can do nothing except carry out explicit programmed instructions. The supposed exceptions of random choice and fuzzy logic are at root explicit algorithms that give only the appearance of independent thought. Thus, all attempts to replicate human initiative, emotions, and feelings are doomed to failure, except in the symbolic sense.

At the same time, the computer has proven itself in the realm of processing hundreds of millions of instructions per second, concurrent with accessing massive quantities of data. When this capability is linked to the logical aspects of the decision making process, it can support but not supplant human judgment. That is, it can scan, compare, relate, and link millions of pieces of information, compute potential answers or solutions—or alternatively review potential solutions if the analysis is logical—and then present the results to the user for the latter's decision. It also can do this encased in a symbolic or mechanized semihuman form. In short, the result might be an illusion, but illusions can exert enormous influence.

Most support systems operate in an interactive sequence, which creates the illusion of a conversation. The user directs the program to an increasingly sharper focus on the problem or issue at hand, which is analogous to the old 20-questions game. Here the emcee had an object in mind and revealed only that it was animal, vegetable, or mineral. The panel members could ask up to 20 questions, answerable by a simple "yes" or "no." The objective was to identify the object by the twentieth question. With today's technology, including voice recognition input, the emcee's role could be automated in its entirety. It would not replicate human judgment or initiative, but it would give that appearance.

The savant of a support system does not reside in the machine, no more so than the intelligence of an Aristotle, a da Vinci, a Newton, or a Tolstoy resides in the physical pages of their books and notes. Knowledge resides in the author's mind. Support systems, then, are the equivalent of a book programmed to flip its own pages. The clerical work of perusing indexes is mechanized. Yet because the illusion mimics human method simultaneous with oozing an obvious plasticity, many executives and information managers remain reluctant to try this path which is short sighted. No one ridicules intellectual or artistic genius just because the product of it is recorded on paper, celluloid, or canvas. The same attitude should prevail with support systems. The real danger in making the most of this technology, short of the old one of attempting to supplant human judgment, is that the program will be inadequate to meet needs and therefore a waste. A lot of effort is required to make one of these systems work well.

| PURPOSE | DESCRIPTION | ACCEPTABILITY |
|---|---|---|
| Trial/Case Scheduling | Largely a transaction-base system with what-if features added to gage the effect of re-scheduling on other cases. | Always acceptable and in practice many if not most courts already use some form of this ap-plication. |
| Legal Research | Adaptation of library reference search sys-tems, pegged to cases and legal treatises. | Usually acceptable, though some scholars believe this weakens legal scholarship that accrues from plowing through the tomes after law school. |
| Rules of Evidence* | The courtroom equiva-lent of instant replay, where a disputed use of evidence can be veri-fied before the trial begins. | The jury is still out on this one, though its use outside the court-room does not cause much stir. |
| Sentencing* | A decision support sys-tem that would provide either rules or guide-lines for sentencing in various criminal cases. | Seldom accepted except as a research tool. It would be too heuristic, and in the event would infringe on the role of the judge. |
| Judgment* | A decision support sys-tem that would be used to support difficult decisions beyond rules-of-evidence issues. | Totally unacceptable. It would be an absolute infringement on the du-ties and prerogatives of a judge. |

*WHEN IN A TRIAL PROCEEDING. THEY WOULD BE MORE ACCEPTABLE IN AN EDUCATIONAL ENVIRONMENT.

*Fig. 12-1. Application levels for support systems. Decision support systems can operate at many levels. As the level rises and attempts to supplant human judgment, the acceptability, if not the utility, of the system drops, as shown by these hypothetical examples from the legal field.*

Put another way, the idea is to push the technology right up to the threshold of human judgment and stop there without expecting to be invited in. For example, these support systems can facilitate the judicial process to the extent that they approach the bench, so to speak, but attempting to supplant the judge and jury would be a serious mistake. Figure 12-1 compares several generic examples of this, most of which have been tried in practice.

The balance of the chapter is divided into sections that discuss different forms of AI, the role of symbols, the basics of support systems, models, and implications for integrations. In order to concentrate on what seems important, the text omits the traditional laundry list of support system programs, shells, generators, and the like. In that event, the list would be out of date before the book was off the press.

## 12.1 THE FORMS OF ARTIFICIAL INTELLIGENCE

One of the main reasons artificial intelligence became a separate field of study 30 years ago was that the available hardware and software could not support the demands of its logic. That logic mandated random access to, and immediate linkage of, large arrays of data. Specialized machines and programming languages were developed to overcome the deficiencies, most notably LISP. In the absence of database technology at the time, an entire system of linkage had to be imposed within the programming language itself, which gave it an esoteric appearance.

Today's technology obviates this need, and the LISP language now compiles on ordinary hardware. This change of venue, however, has not changed the aims to which artificial intelligence is put. These aims fall into three general categories, although only the first has received anything approaching universal recognition. The first category mimics physical action, and is called *robotics*. The second concentrates on man-machine interfaces, which comes under the name *ergonomics*. The third concentrates on the thinking process, which for lack of a better term could be considered *cognimetrics*, that is, the measuring of logical thought and perception. Figure 12-2 suggest these fields often overlap in practice.

- *Robotics*. The relationship of robotics to artificial intelligence is strained, for the computer itself could be considered a robot. In practice, the term is more commonly applied to machines which substitute for human arm, hand, finger, and leg movement. Whether the robot resembles a human being is immaterial. Today, entire automobile assembly lines are run by robotics, although perhaps the best-known applications are devices to assist the handicapped.
- *Ergonomics*. This application amplifies human capability, and perhaps the best examples are the "smart" prostheses. Probably the best known of these is the computer-driven device used by the physicist Stephen W. Hawking. Other applications include receptors which react to changes in eye movements being developed for pilots of supersonic aircraft. The

time to avert many disasters is roughly equal to the time it takes to move the eye.

- *Cognimetrics*. When asked why he robbed banks, Willie Sutton replied, "that's where the money is." Cognimetrics is where the money is for information systems. As discussed in the opening chapter of this book, the potential is enormous. Most of this chapter concentrates on this field.

## 12.2 SYMBOLICS

A recent experiment at the University of Wisconsin Medical School might have set minds wondering more about artificial intelligence than all that has been developed at the Massachusetts Institute of Technology over the past 30 years.

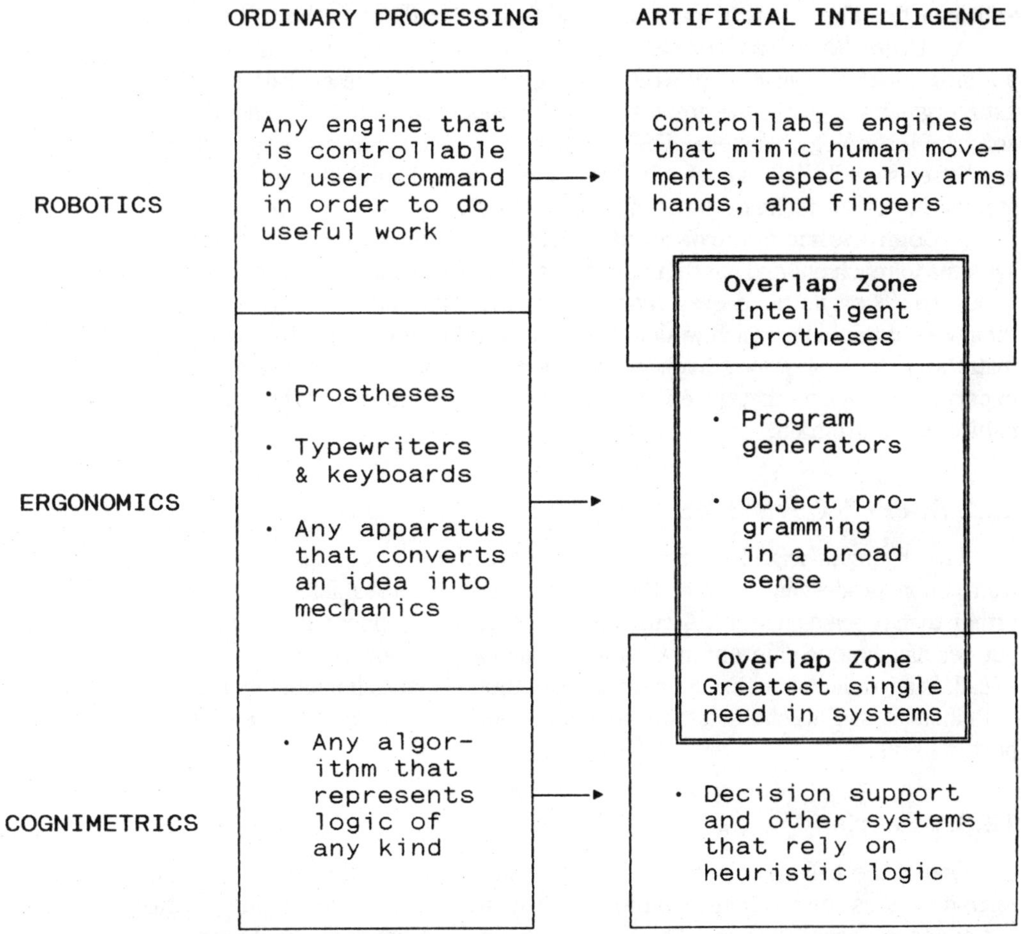


*Fig. 12-2. The categories of artificial intelligence. AI comes in three general forms, ranging from the mimicking of human physical movements to the thinking process. Notwithstanding the name, AI is always a matter of degree compared to ordinary processing, as the programming must eventually be reduced to the same simple machine steps.*

As reported in the *American Journal of Psychiatry*, Dr. Paulette Selmi divided patients suffering from mild to moderate depression into three groups. One group received standard therapy, the second no therapy and the third an interactive computer program. As expected, the patients in traditional therapy improved measurably, while those in the control group did not. As not expected, the patients in the computer program group did as well as those in the traditional group.

The power of symbols is not to be underestimated. Consider, for a moment, the effect flags have on many individuals, the gift of red roses to a loved one, or teddy bears (which derive their name from the most masculine of all the U.S. presidents) on children. This book is not the appropriate vehicle to launch into an extended discussion of symbols.

**A Robotic Environment.** The use of symbols in robotics is somewhat anticlimactic. The robot, in many of its forms, is already something of symbol.

**An Ergonomic Environment.** Although cognimetrics offers the greatest potential for the application of AI to general corporate and organizational interests, ergonomics offers the greatest opportunities to firms in the computer and software technology business. The common expression is to make the machinery "user-friendly." This does not always entail symbolism, but in limited doses it could help. See technical note 14 in appendix B.

**A Cognimetric Environment.** Businessmen do not need their support systems to reach out and pat them on the back whenever they put the results to good use. They do need even more responsive systems that edge closer to their way of thinking, which would be symbolism enough. Leave the more dramatic stuff to Hollywood. Even a cursory review of the depression-therapy experiment suggests that the effective symbolism was integral to the interactive nature of the program.

## 12.3 SUPPORT SYSTEMS

The distinguishing characteristic of support systems, compared to routine transaction processing, is that they concentrate on probabilities and trends rather than precise answers. A customer expects his telephone bill to be exact, but deciding among different models when buying a telephone, or deciding who to call, is anything but an exact process, even though a decision must be made in both instances. This characteristic seems to underwrite all of the basics of support systems.

### 12.3.1 Heuristic Logic

One of the hallmarks of most support systems is *heuristic reasoning*. This term describes the attempt to approach closer to truth or understanding without expecting exact answers. This way of thinking is often associated with profound philosophical questions, but it also applies to humdrum inquiries such as weather prediction and estimating the market potential for a new product.

The programming task for support systems is to superimpose this fuzzy thinking on a machine that feeds on exactitude. The academic name given to this approach is *symbolic processing*. It isn't all that different from the ordinary brand, no more so than statistics differs from mathematics. Inference calculations in statistics are as rigid as any equation, at least in the mechanical sense. But the input numbers, especially if the analysis is based on a sample, represent (hence the term *symbolic*) the population, and the output represents a probability or trend. Further, a support system that displays the logic used is not unusual, similar to the way a statistical report often describes the formulas or techniques employed.

### 12.3.2 Degrees

Some statistical calculations are less accurate, or less representative, of sought-after answers than others. Similarly, some support systems venture into predictive analysis further than others, and thus farther from hard data and routine logic. Certainly, the more a system attempts to preview the future, the thinner the ice becomes.

What, then, is the optimum point of analysis for a support system? The question cannot be answered, and oversimplifies the context in which support systems can be used. A set of five minisystems, on mortgage payments or what might be called the Sermon on the Amount, illustrates the point.

**Straight Mortgage Payment.** This is more or less an example of ordinary processing. Calculation of the monthly payment for the amortization of a fixed loan, at a fixed interest rate, for fixed number of years, relies on a comparatively simple, exact equation. A minor exception raises the amount to the next higher cent, and runs it through an amortization program to determine the slight reduction in the final payment. Added to the amount is the monthly fraction of the homeowner's annual insurance policy and real estate taxes at the present rate. The principal and interest payment will not change, but the escrow add-on probably will. The model cannot handle a change. What the mortgagee does is increase the monthly payment whenever the rates increase. He is not normally concerned with predicting these changes.

**Range-of-Payment Models.** This is the simplest form of support system. The user asks, "If I take out a loan for such-and-such an amount, what are the monthly payments for 15, 20, 25, and 30-year amortization schedules?" Or he might ask, "How much loan can I get for a monthly payment of so-and-so dollars?" The answers are still exact, but the user is free to change the parameters.

**Adjustable Rate Mortgage Payment Predictions.** This represents a step up in support systems logic. For a 30-year loan that can range between 9 and 15 percent (assuming only full percentage points), the total number of sequential combinations is roughly $322 \times 10^{22}$. The number is much higher if the rate can be adjusted to $^1/_4$-percentage point. Thus when the erstwhile mortgager wants to know the total of the likely payments over the life of the loan, only heuristic reasoning can provide some sort of reasonable estimate and likely variations.

**Loan Qualification.** Determining loan eligibility is in part a subjective evaluation of mortgage bankers, but formulas are commonly used. Factors such as total income, debt service, savings, credit history, and earnings potential are factored in, but the answer is seldom a precise yes or no except when the numbers clearly exceed or fall below the range of interpretation. The results perform the purely computational work for the mortgagee, and thus permit him or her to concentrate on making a judgment in each case. American Express uses a similar model to set a strawman credit limit for cardholders, plus another model to determine if it will accept, question, or reject an unusually high-dollar charge (relative to the cardholder's history of charging).

**Financial Planning.** This type of system goes far beyond mortgage payments, yet recognizes that a mortgage payment is normally the largest item in personal budgets, and the home's value is the largest asset. The user then asks, "In light of my general financial objectives, how much house should I buy and how large a down payment should I make?" Support system models at this level are exceedingly complex and the advice provided is less certain.

In principle, these five models apply equally to corporate planning. The use of the first three have nearly a direct application to borrowing, although the interpretation of the results must normally be evaluated against a wider range of factors. The loan qualification model becomes a risk assessment analysis, and somewhat parallels the way a mortgagee might view the entire portfolio of loans (providing he is not employed by a savings and loan institute). The final model becomes one for overall corporate investment strategy, and could very well be the most complex support system that a large company attempts to develop.

### 12.3.3 Impetus for Development

In general, information managers have not been the driving force behind support system development. The impetus tends to come from CEOs, internal research departments, users, consultants, universities, or just about anywhere or anyone except the shop or shopkeeper that manages information. Is this a criticism? Not at all. This shortcoming is slowly changing. In the interim at least five factors account for the problem.

**Routine Processing.** Routine or transaction-based processing remains the big-ticket item for most corporations and organizations. The information manager should and must devote the better part of his time to this arena.

**Expense and Risk.** Support systems tend to be more expensive per line of code, and take more lines of code to achieve comparable results. At the same time, the failure rates have been much higher. It is true that program generators have curtailed this expense, but competitive routine processing is also falling in price.

**Scarcity of Experience.** Only a comparative handful of data processing professionals have extensive experience in this field. Closely associated with this factor is the difficulty of working with many bona fide experts in sufficient detail to translate their acumen into programmable algorithms.

**Data Requirements.** Many support systems require extensive data that might not be readily available. Routine processing tends to apply relatively simple algorithms against repetitive units of data. Support systems, by contrast, are data hungry and might scan several thousand, perhaps several million, pieces of data before providing useful information.

**Decentralization.** Many if not most support systems tend to be specialized and lend themselves to decentralized development, often without the need for coordination with mainline systems. The coordination requirements that do exist tend to center on data access.

In fine, support systems are still on the periphery of information processing for most organizations. Yet as information systems departments and their databases grow to maturity, this situation will likely change. Case study M in appendix A expands on the vignette which introduced this part of the book and comments on another application of a complex support system.

### 12.3.4 Features or Creatures

The bottom line for support systems is whether they are used. If used, do they contribute, directly or indirectly, to marketing or production efficiency? Is the information manager providing a tool with useful features that will likely gain acceptance, or is it an algorithmic Frankenstein? The general rule, as stated, is that a support system should support rather than presume to replace users. In this vein, at least 10 characteristics enhance acceptance and utility. Few specific models attempt to achieve all 10, but even humble spreadsheet software used on a local area network is capable of this enhancement. See technical note 10 in appendix B on this point.

**Focus.** Few support systems gain acceptance unless they support corporate objectives, important projects, or genuine executive needs. A model that summarizes the financial history of a corporation for the last 20 years is of little use unless that analysis can be applied to a present or planned investment.

**Effectiveness over Efficiency.** The heuristic nature of expert systems means that effectiveness rather than efficiency is more important, which is closely associated with focus. The emphasis must be the utility of the results. Programming efficiency is of less concern.

**Mental Modelling.** Whether this means ease of use or a sophisticated mimicking of thought processes depends on the user. The idea is to have the logical processes come as close to what the user would exercise if he was analyzing the data manually, and to make that approach obvious to the user.

**On-Line Dialogue and/or Semi-Structured Approach.** This point complements mental modelling. Most manual analyses are interactive because the user proceeds in different directions depending on previous findings. The support system should follow suit.

**Type of Outputs.** The more widely accepted support systems tend to provide trend lines, probabilities, or both. A trend line is inherently probabilistic with respect to the future, which is the essence of the heuristic approach.

**Exception Reporting.** Most exception reporting is a feature of ordinary systems, but when a heuristic analysis encounters unusual "islands" of data out of whack with the balance—what statisticians call *outliers*—the results should indicate the abnormal data.

**Data Integrity.** To the extent the data used by a support system lacks logical integrity is the extent the results are questionable. This problem often arises from using copies or views of data that have become outdated or are incomplete.

**Data Access.** Ideally, a support system should permit access to data as well as to algorithms. This point can be divided into access to external data and windows to internal data. However, the problem is that as the system becomes more sophisticated, the branching that results from interactive use might need to reach into the entire corporate database, which immediately poses major security problems.

**Graphics.** Graphical displays are often the difference between visualizing and comprehending the significance of findings and being left bewildered.

**Improvement of Internal Communications.** This is an ideal, yet the improvement often helps the user if he can use the system to interact with other individuals or departments while developing a better understanding of a problem. Sometimes a telephone works just as well, but if the analysis is a group effort, then concurrent access is almost imperative.

### 12.3.5 Organizational Impacts

The effective use of using support systems also depends on a number of other factors not directly related to the technology. Three of the more noted ones are explained.

**Responsibility.** If the impetus for support systems tends to come from outside the information systems department or its equivalent, then who should be responsible for the overall development? This issue is important when managing and accessing databases.

**Organizational Hierarchy.** Someone once said that the relationship between strategy and organization is not to be underestimated. If a corporation is not structured to make effective use of these systems, or is not willing to consider a realignment of functions, then their practical utility will be more limited.

**Positions and Career Paths.** As support systems grow in importance and acceptance, especially if this occurs outside the traditional information systems departments, new careers will open up that might attract the most highly skilled individuals from those departments.

## 12.4 MODELS OF SUPPORT SYSTEMS

All forms of support systems operate on the same principles. All seek to provide or at least delimit answers to questions or problems. Yet each form is unique in one or more important aspects. As such, different models are needed for different types of problem solving. The use of a research library provides a good analogy. One person uses a library to browse and see what is new in his field of endeavor. A second will seek additional information on an issue for which they already have a good notion. A third might search for an answer for which he has only a few clues. A fourth might want to compare what others have said about such and such. A fifth can try to see where the sweep of history seems to be taking his practice. And so forth and so on.

If one analyzes how the different users of a library go about gathering information, the detailed findings will contrast sharply with the aura of benign uniformity a library outwardly displays. The routes taken by each scholar, the indexes consulted, and the branching off to other references as a result of preliminary findings will differ markedly. Support systems follow suit. For the most part, software that supports the generation of support systems programming tends to be limited to one type of search. Figure 12-3 compares a few of the better-known techniques.

- *Consequences Model.* This model is the most well known of the models and often goes by its more common name of ''what-if.'' A consequences model is the easiest to program and makes the most use of standard programming techniques and popular software.
- *Needle-in-the-Haystack Model.* This model seeks to find a specific piece of information in a large array of data. What is known is linked to related data. The program provides a list of possible further searches. The user selects one and proceeds until the answer is found or a dead end is encountered. If a dead end is found, another route is tried.
- *Optimization Models.* Optimization models analyze two or more courses of action and select or recommend the optimal. What comprises optimal equates with the criteria entered by the user or program developer. An optimization model can search for these alternatives from a large pool or it can be limited to an analysis of selected options.
- *Comparative Probability Models.* A comparative probability model is similar to an optimization model with this difference: it identifies a number of potential solutions or answers and indicates the probability that each one is correct or is likely to achieve the best results. Vehicle troubleshooting manuals tend to display this kind of reasoning. Given a set of symptoms, the mechanic is advised to check a number of items in the sequence each is more likely to be the problem.

## 12.5 CONSIDERATIONS FOR SYSTEM INTEGRATIONS

Synergistic theory holds that a sum can be greater than its parts, meaning the effect of consolidating elements might have a more significant impact or influence than the sum of effects of the elements operating separately. System integrations often seek this advantage. When separate systems are consolidated, new opportunities might present themselves far beyond what the components can offer operating independently.

| MODEL | AVAILABLE INFORMATION | WHAT IS SOUGHT |
|---|---|---|
| Optimization (Linear Programming) | A linked mass of data through which a wide variety of paths can be traced and compared in quantitative terms. | To determine the path that offers the optimal mix of advantages and disadvantages. Trip routing is a simple example. |
| Probabilities Among Alternatives | Primarily a linked set of rules by which various alternatives can be compared on a what-if basis. | Similar to the optimization model, except that there are only a few alternatives but more complex criteria. |
| Design | Construction or fabrication criteria and how that relates to various specifications. | A design that meets specifications. It may be combined with an optimization model. |
| Scheduling | A restricted and simpler version of the optimization model, due the fact the main criterion is duration of key segments. | The critical path for a project, plus the effect of compressing time required for segments of the critical path. |
| Needle-in-a-Haystack Search | Large mass of linked information, primarily deductive, that lends itself to sharper focus by way of elimination. | A specific answer in light of some clues--roughly the computer equivalent of Sherlock Holmes. |
| Open-Ended Search | Similar to the needle-in-a-haystack model except that the linkage lends itself to branching outward inductively. | Given an idea or fact, where does it or can it lead? Automated library reference systems using key words are an example. |
| Trend Line or Prediction | Arrays of quantitative data and an "inference engine" set of logical deductive algorithms. | Under such-and-such conditions or criteria, to determine the most likely outcome or trend. |

*Fig. 12-3. Variations of support systems. Support systems vary based on the inferences that must be drawn from data. General programming languages can be used to develop any model, but the process is cumbersome. Shells are much more efficient, but in general it takes a different shell to run the different forms of inference, primarily due the data linkage required.*

With support systems, the advantage accrues from an expanded database, for expanded knowledge, more than intricate algorithms, generates better answers. However, the manner in which the integration takes place might not lend itself to this goal. Thus, if the organization intends to integrate systems with these higher-level usages in mind, then the options are limited. In specific terms, this rules out the interface and the standardization, except as a means to support another model. The synthesis model also can be disregarded on the grounds that it is not necessary. After the database is integrated, integrating the entire system adds little to the operation of a support system. This situation leaves the database integration and excerpt models.

The choice between these two should be based on external factors. A database integration is much more expensive and difficult to develop than a mere excerpt. If the organization does not need it for more routine processing, trying it for a support system would be of questionable value. If it does need it, the issue is resolved automatically.

# 13

# Security Considerations

*This will surely teach me a lesson.*

—Last words of a culprit on the gallows,
Tennessee, 1915

Security aspects of data processing systems are often overlooked or at least underestimated. The aura generated by the awesome speed of many computers carries with it a mistaken notion of invincibility. Thus, when a college student wreaked havoc by inserting a virus in the seemingly secure Internet system in October 1988, the damage sent something of a shockwave among data processing professionals and senior executives.

If nature abhors a vacuum, then sophistication invites trouble. As computer-based systems are expanded or are integrated, the very interior lines that yield efficiency also facilitate destruction, probably at an exponential ratio. This relationship, shown in FIG. 13-1, isn't much different from the paralysis that results from nicking the central nervous system of an individual at a crucial point. Whether a system could grow to the point where security concerns will outweigh its value is too problematic to address here, but there is little doubt that security problems will continue to increase and demand even more attention by general managers as well as information managers.

The intent of this chapter is to heighten the awareness of the growing security problem, in order to make provisions that are appropriate without becoming paranoid or going on some form of electronic witch hunt. The sections address material damage, data and programming losses, criminal misuse, and conclude with a brief discussion on management responsibilities, risk analysis, and tradeoffs. Some common points to consider are:

**Seriousness of the Problem.** The potential for serious, perhaps fatal, loss and destruction is serious enough for senior management to make a point of minimizing the risk. The same applies to cumulative losses from less damaging incidents.

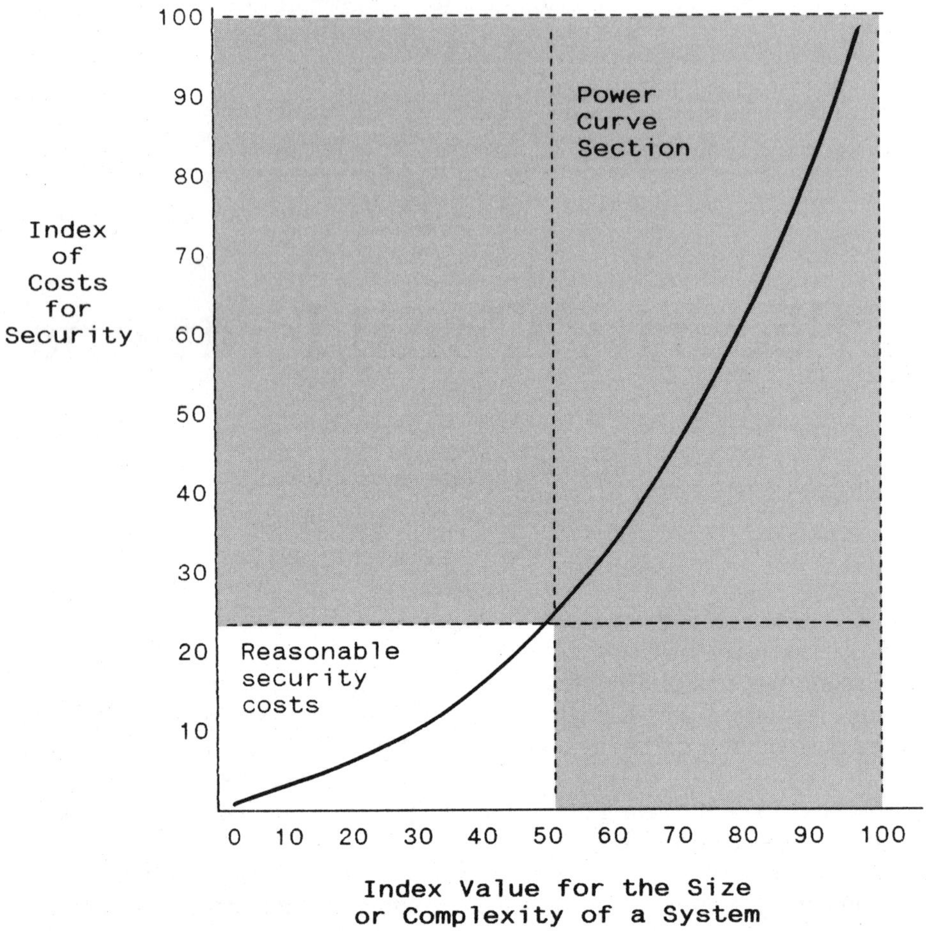


*Fig. 13-1. Security requirements vs. system size. The cost of securing systems against all forms of damage and unauthorized access tends to increase exponentially with the size of the system, especially if it involves distributive processing. Integrations, which normally increase communications, make a system even more costly to secure.*

**Sources.** Although the matter needs formal verification, most security problems, beyond banking and related firms, comes from carelessness or negligence among authorized users of systems or from failure to protect against predictable natural disasters, instead of criminal or fraudulent intent. The intense publicity given to the latter sources distorts the picture.

**Legal Aspects.** Laws and regulations affecting computer security are proliferating. Most of them are intended to improve security, but a few have the effect of increasing the problem, most notably Freedom of Information type laws.

**Inevitable Losses.** Some degree of loss or damage to all systems is inevitable. Immortality has been as elusive a goal for computers as it has been for human beings. The idea is to minimize the funeral costs.

**Situational Picture.** Although the security needs among systems vary too much for a standard approach, a generalized risk assessment methodology is almost always useful. The literature brims with these checklists.

**Frequency.** Major losses are infrequent and will not strike all organizations and systems. Minor losses are frequent and affect essentially all systems.

**Priorities.** Prevention is usually but not always a better buy than damage limitation or recovery. Absolute prevention would be too expensive and too cumbersome in most cases, that is, damage limitation and disaster recovery plans are a matter of practical necessity.

**Trade-Offs.** Effective damage limitation, where wrongful intent is the threat, requires making the risk too expensive or the access too cumbersome for all but the most determined offenders, and even at that, to force those diehards to leave clues. Where negligence is the culprit, the essence of damage limitation is early detection.

**Integrations.** Integrations seldom pose unique security problems, although they can increase the potential for damage or wrongdoing. The limited exception would be during implementation or changeover, when safeguards are often relaxed beyond what is prudent.

Figure 13-2 illustrates the relationship of most of these points to the three common sources of security problems: material damage, data and programming

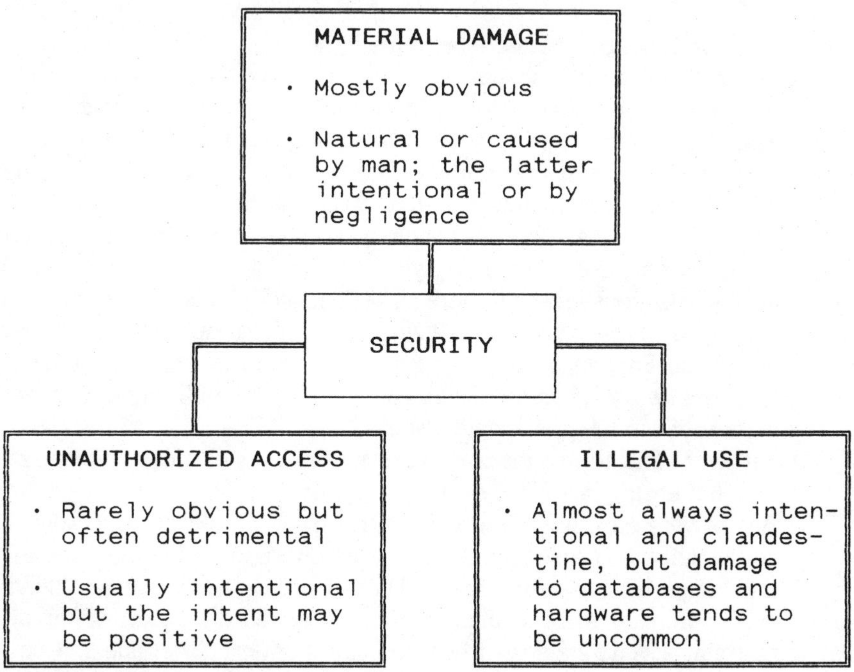


*Fig. 13-2. The three sisters of security. Like the stew concocted by the three sister witches in* Macbeth, *the problems of security merge into a singular brew from three sources: material damage or loss, unauthorized access, and illegal use. These sources inherently overlap, but each has distinctive aspects that mandate different security measures to prevent or at least minimize loss.*

losses, and criminal utilization. The third source, criminal utilization, is not entirely separate and distinct from the unauthorized access implied by the data loss source. Yet the latter can arise from negligent authorized users (or faulty programming), and the former does not necessarily denigrate existing information.

## 13.1 SECURITY AGAINST MATERIAL LOSS OR DAMAGE

Material loss or damage can affect an information system directly or indirectly. The destruction of a computer by a fire is an obvious example of a direct loss. An indirect loss, for example, would occur if a fire prevents access to a computer, even though the computer sustains no damage. The effect, albeit temporary, is the same as if the computer had been destroyed. The same is true if the computer shuts down at a crucial time from a simple overload.

Stolen or destroyed disks and other storage media present a unique problem. The means of security must be materially oriented, but the value of the material tends to be small. The real value resides in the recorded information. Put another way, storage media are rarely stolen for their material value, and when they are damaged or effectively destroyed by natural causes, the material loss is seldom of great concern. Most material losses occur under one of four well-established categories:

1) *Physical Damage or Loss*. The journals never seem to lack stories on physical damage to computer systems. An interesting case occurred at the Dallas – Fort Worth Airport on October 20, 1989. Overloaded antiquated equipment caused a 12-hour shutdown, which followed on the heals of a radar computer problem less than a week earlier that had tied up traffic for several hours. Other cases include the First Interstate Bank fire on May 4, 1988. Although the computer systems were undamaged, the employees could not get back into the building afterward. As implied, the consequences were as serious as if the computer had been destroyed. This incident was followed five days later by the Chicago Telephone Exchange fire, in which 35,000 phones (including those at O'Hare airport) affecting 4000 business, and 100,000 employees were put out of commission for several days.
2) *Sabotage*. The term sabotage raises the specter of spies and war stories, but even a cursory review of the conduct of the striking Greyhound Bus drivers early in 1990, and several mass murders—especially the social club arson case that took 87 lives on March 25, 1990—suggests that human life sometimes means little to striking or disgruntled individuals. Computer systems and networks would hardly encourage greater restraint. Even a careless driver ramming a critical power line pole could have the same effect as sabotage (although some managers are inclined to group this type of problem in the next category). Unfortunately, like the virus problem experienced with Internet, the potential risk from this source will likely be ignored in most organizations until a dramatic incidence occurs.

3) *Electrical and Electronic Disruptions*. Electrical and electronic disruptions can range from a loss of power that makes equipment temporarily inoperable to power surges of any kind that erase or otherwise destroy data on storage media, with or without concomitant damage to the media itself. A well known case involved a construction crew that grounded a lightning rod to the metal shielding of a below-ground vault. This choice was not necessarily bad, except that the vault was used to store not money but magnetic media. As the reader can well imagine, the first time lightning struck the rod, the corporation lost its entire archived database and programming.
4) *Theft*. Mini computers and their peripherals are rarely stolen, and mainframes even less so. Micros are another story. They are a favorite target of thieves for much the same reason typewriters and adding machines were objects of theft a few years back. An even more likely security risk is the theft of disks to obtain data, or the use of computers for unauthorized and illegal purposes. These are covered in subsequent subsections within this chapter.

The increasing incidence of breakdowns and disruptions has spawned firms that specialize in providing backup services. These services typically comprise alternative computer facilities where clients bring backup data in time of disaster. Drills ensure compatibility and adequate communications network access. Comdisco Disaster Recovery Services, Inc. and Sungard Recovery Services (of Sungard Data Systems, Inc.) are two of the biggest firms in this business, with more than 1500 clients between them. The cost ranges from $18,000 to $300,000 (or more) per year just for the setup. Fees for using it are additional. For example, United Stationers was able to continue business almost immediately when they discovered their system had become useless during the Chicago telephone fire.

## 13.2 DATA AND SOFTWARE SECURITY

At one time, safeguards against material loss was the primary consideration for security. Mainframes were expensive, and most data was stored on magnetic tapes that could be readily secured. That is no longer true. The main security concern today seems to be data and programming. Hardware is now comparatively inexpensive, and backup services exist. The loss of data and programming is another matter. Copies of programs might be easy to maintain in theory, but someone must make a practice of making and safely storing copies of all revisions. Maintaining backup copies of data, particularly in systems where it is continuously updated, is an even more difficult problem.

### 13.2.1 Read-Only vs. Update Action

The difference between reading and updating data is significant. Read-only means that the data cannot be changed but can be used elsewhere. At times, information managers are inclined to consider unauthorized read-only access a lesser problem than its update counterpart. Not so. The reading of proprietary information by a competitor can do more long-range damage to corporate interests than incorrect updates. The same is true for classified defense information. Unlike sensitive information falling into the wrong hands, most improper updates can be corrected.

For unauthorized updates (exclusive of malicious viruses and the like, which are covered later), the subpoints are: updating or revision of existing data, adding to existing data, and deleting existing data. For each subpoint, and for all cases of unauthorized read-only access, the question, "How much?" also should be asked. The answer will have a major bearing on risk assessment.

### 13.2.2 Categories

About 35 years ago, a college magazine published a whimsical set of cartoons depicting the eight possible combinations of wrestlers and rustlers wrestling and rustling each other: wrestlers rustling rustlers, rustlers rustling rustlers, and so forth. Something similar applies to systems, substituting the terms authorized users for wrestlers, unauthorized users for rustlers, and proper and improper access for wrestling and rustling. Figure 13-3 illustrates the more important of these combinations.

- *Unauthorized Access by Authorized Users*. In large systems, databases tend to be compartmentalized into what are called categorical databases, as discussed in subsection 5.2.5. Access to each compartment is limited to those who have a need to access it. However, without stringent controls, an authorized user can cross the boundaries, especially if views have been generated from that data.
- *Unauthorized Updates by Authorized Users*. This situation occurs either when an individual has read-only access and figures out a way to update records, or when that individual has limited update authority but a wider read-only range. Restricting the updating of programs more stringently than data is not uncommon.
- *Access by Unauthorized Users*. Unauthorized access might or might not damage corporate interests. The access could be the work of an individual filling in for a co-worker, in which case the lack of authorization is mere administrative oversight, or it could be the work of a corporate "information raider."
- *Updates by Unauthorized Users*. This access is similar to the previous category, except that when unauthorized updates go beyond administrative oversight, the intent is often malicious. However, this differs from using computer viruses. Updates are not meant to be readily detectable, whereas viruses are intended to inflict massive devastation and perforce make the organization aware of what has happened.

| USER | READ-ONLY ACCESS | UPDATE ACCESS |
|---|---|---|
| Otherwise Authorized Users | Compartmentalized databases improve security, but they restrict the knowledge base essential to drive support systems. | Limiting access for updating often increases the number of personnel required to maintain the database, and with it the quality control problems. |
| Unauthorized Users | Restricting access usually means some form of password or user identification. But the more effective barriers can make access for legitimate users cumbersome and perhaps reduce the intended use of the system. | This is a top priority security concern, as it is the source of most computer-related embezzlement and sabotage, short of destroying hardware and communications. Still, the problems with limiting read-only access apply. |

*Fig. 13-3. Access problems. The problem of minimizing unauthorized access and updates to data and software is not simple. There are many permutations and combinations, and each requires a somewhat different approach.*

### 13.2.3 Passwords and Other Access Technology

Most information systems of any size impose barriers to access, ranging from simple passwords to magnetic cards, cards with imbedded chips, machines that verify the accessor's retinal image, or requirements that two or more persons access the system concurrently, often in each other's presence. All this has become a science in its own right, with such specialties of how the codes are generated, who controls them, how frequent are the replacements, and so forth. Many books have been written on the subject. Some items to consider here are detailed next.

**Points of Diminishing Returns.** Access can be made so difficult that intended users become discouraged from using the system, or worse, begin to write down passwords because they are too long to memorize. For example, passwords of up to five random characters seldom pose any problems. Six or seven characters are borderline. Eight or more ask for trouble. Only a few individuals can easily memorize a string of eight or more random characters.

**Technology.** The technology on access barriers is increasing in sophistication and decreasing in cost, which is in keeping with the progress in computer technology itself. Yet because the stakes are also increasing, the total security costs for a system will likely continue to increase.

**Distributed Databases.** The distribution of databases and software over a network of computers greatly intensifies the security problem of controlling access. Most networks offer too many points of entry, concurrent with the number of users becoming less manageable. This problem also applies to systems that generate many secondary views of a primary database. Unauthorized updates to a primary database by way of accessing a view might be impossible in a direct sense, but read-only access can prove just as damaging to organizational interests.

### 13.2.4 Viruses and Worms

Few readers, if any, of this book have not heard of computer viruses, although the fine points of difference between them and worms might seem elusive. These intruders are typically segments of code embedded in other software or databases. After booted or retrieved into a computer's operating memory, a virus begins to copy itself and in the process overlays (and hence destroys) existing data. The alternative version activates the erase functions directly. The one thing viruses do not do is destroy material. That is, no virus can cause physical damage to a computer or its peripherals, with the possible exception of activating a built-in self-destruct program in officially classified data reservoirs.

The scope of the virus threat is a hotly contested issue. No one gainsays their existence and potential to do damage, but some service firms hype it. In preventing or at least detecting the potential for intrusion of viruses into an organization's database, they can substitute an intrusion into its wallet. On the other hand, when a virus does break through, the damage can be extensive. Furthermore, every time software is written to detect one kind of virus, another kind shows up. Therefore, and because databases are proliferating, a more permanent solution seems worth the effort.

A virus is an attack that goes for the jugular, so to speak. Protection against this form of threat might mean shielding the critical area. The computer jugular comprises the handful of subroutines in the operating system that execute commands to copy and record data and files. Thus, the only permanent way to stop viruses would be to convert these subroutines, *and added confirmation routines*, into read-only memory, or possibly to hard wire them directly into the computer board. Then, no software virus could override the instructions. Any attempt to copy or move data and programs would require a positive confirmation.

This protection would not stop viruses from being recorded in a data base, but they could not operate without confirmation by an operator or user. Moreover, any copying or related instructions that gave the slightest appearance of being repetitious or continuous would trigger a supplementary confirmation request. Further, these confirmation subroutines could match the material in a file intended for saving or copying with what was actually being executed—a variation on reliability checking. If a mismatch occurred at any point, the execution would be halted.

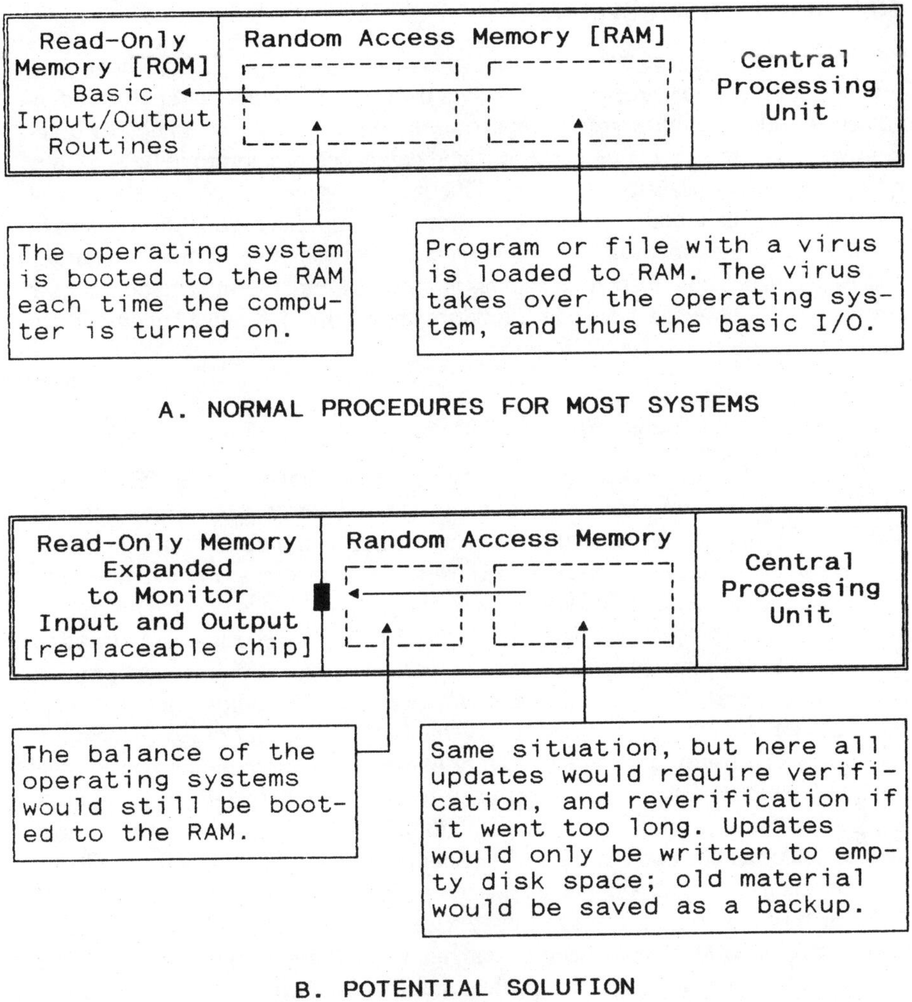


*Fig. 13-4. A permanent solution for the virus problem. The computer virus might be an insidious and many-formed invader of systems, but all of them must activate a tiny fraction of operating system software to effect damage. Securing those segments against misuse by hard wiring them into central processing units or at least read-only-memories is the only feasible permanent solution. The system might encounter minor processing delays, but the accelerating processing speeds of computers should compensate for the inconvenience.*

Figure 13-4 illustrates the general mechanics. This solution would entail a modification to existing computer boards, and to the way computer boards would be constructed in the future. Still, when data has critical importance, or where the downtime from reloading copies of destroyed software is unacceptable, the alternatives could prove even more expensive. Meanwhile, organizations faced with this threat have a bona fide concern.

### 13.2.5 Information Centers

Information centers present a special type of security problem. These centers are often set up to respond to various user requirements faster than highly structured information systems departments seem capable of doing. In practice, what happens is that new systems and databases proliferate helter-skelter, making the job of security especially difficult. The value of any one element of this dispersed data and hardware can bear no comparison with the corporate database, but the worth of the collective mass of that information is another matter. If corporate information raiding is a real threat, the information center services might have to be curtailed. Raiders know how to obtain a bigger picture by putting the bits and pieces together.

## 13.3 CRIMINAL USE OF SYSTEMS

The use of computers for criminal intent differs from other security issues. These crimes seldom result in general program or data destruction, except indirectly by delaying access to a computer when it is needed for other purposes. But criminal usage can result in severe monetary loss. For example, the California Department of Justice reports that computer-based crimes net an average of $450,000 per incident. In other cases, organized crime has turned to the use of this machinery to keep track of their activities. All this has spawned considerable legislation, of which the Computer Fraud and Abuse Act of 1986 is the most well known. The categories of this type of security problem include:

**Theft of Money.** Individuals with criminal intent often use computer systems to embezzle funds. The worst case to date was the theft of $21 million from a Wells Fargo bank in California. Other cases have involved the almost undetectable manipulation of fractions of cents, which when applied to millions of transactions can yield tens of thousands of dollars.

**Theft of Services.** The theft of services—using computers for unauthorized purposes without destroying or damaging existing information—can range from harmless electronic doodling while waiting for an interactive terminal to respond to a legitimate request, to systemic but clandestine use of equipment to run a business. Whether the business itself is legitimate or illegitimate is immaterial. The use of someone else's computer without permission constitutes theft of services.

**Theft of Software.** Making illegal copies of copyright or proprietary software is a crime in most cases, and is probably the most prevalent of all computer-related abuses. This theft ranges from occasional oversights in purely educational settings to flagrant pirating of expensive software.

**Violation of Privacy.** It's a safe bet that an average of 10,000 bytes of information is recorded on one or more databases for every adult living in the United States, and on almost every child in somewhat lesser amounts. Revealing computer-based information to parties that do not have a right to see it is a federal crime with government systems, and also with systems in a growing number of states and municipalities. The fact that the individual doing the extracting is authorized is immaterial. He or she merely becomes an ''insider.''

The most well known statutes are the *Privacy and Security Act of 1974*, and the *Right to Financial Privacy Act of 1978*.

**Malicious Access.** Malicious access is more or less defined as the intentional unauthorized access to computer-based information, even if it is read-only. Destruction of the data only compounds the offense. If the crime is done against a government database or one in which the government has a direct interest, the act is a felony and is punishable with severe penalties as specified in the *Computer Fraud and Abuse Act of 1986*.

**Use of Systems for Criminal Ends.** This final category is not really a security concern for most organizations, unless it is coupled with unauthorized access. In these situations, the ownership of computers and software is usually legitimate. That is, the use for legitimate means to illegitimate ends is seldom by itself a crime, and where it is a crime, it is seldom prosecuted. Bank robbers are rarely tried for using cars in their operations if they purchased them legitimately, even if with stolen funds from previous crimes.

## 13.4 MANAGEMENT

Fixing responsibility for security is not always a simple matter of assigning it to the information manager. Senior executives need to recognize that as soon as systems are implemented, they seldom remain under the effective control of the information manager. Security of information systems then becomes a corporate-wide responsibility. The information manager can provide a focal point and expertise, but he is seldom in a position to enforce general security.

### 13.4.1 Risk Assessment

Any workable security plan should begin with a risk assessment. Figure 13-5 portrays the four iterative steps of the process.

- *Determination of Value*. Value means the net cost of replacing losses, direct or indirect. The indirect costs of replacing data or living with the consequences of a competitor obtaining proprietary information are difficult to gauge. Yet it must be done with some reasonable degree of accuracy before major funds are invested in security measures.
- *Identification of Threats*. Threats can come from many sources. They include customers, competitors, reporters, and acts of God. Which of these sources are plausible enough for a given corporation will vary considerably, but something more precise than the vague ''national security interests'' bandied about in the Department of Defense is necessary for organizations that are concerned with a bottom line.
- *Delineation of Vulnerability*. Threats tend to materialize only to the extent of vulnerability. Vulnerability is the measure of how easy it would be for damage to occur, or alternatively how likely it would occur, without any security measures.

- *Extent of Vulnerability.* This aspect puts some numbers on the vulnerabilities and asks, "How much damage is likely to occur?" This step brings the risk assessment full circle back to determination of value, which explains why risk analysis is typically an iterative process.

### 13.4.2 Trade-off Considerations

As mentioned several times in this chapter, security measures operate at three levels: prevention, damage limitation, and disaster recovery. All three levels are superintended by what might be called the security environment, somewhat analogous to the software programming environment discussed in section 11.7.

The focal point of this environment is to decide if the security measures give the organization its money's worth of protection. Unfortunately, the answer is serpentine. If disaster strikes, and damage is minimized, the investment will appear to have been a sound one. If disaster never strikes, then as time passes, the cost of security will begin to display a patina of waste. Peace of mind is a

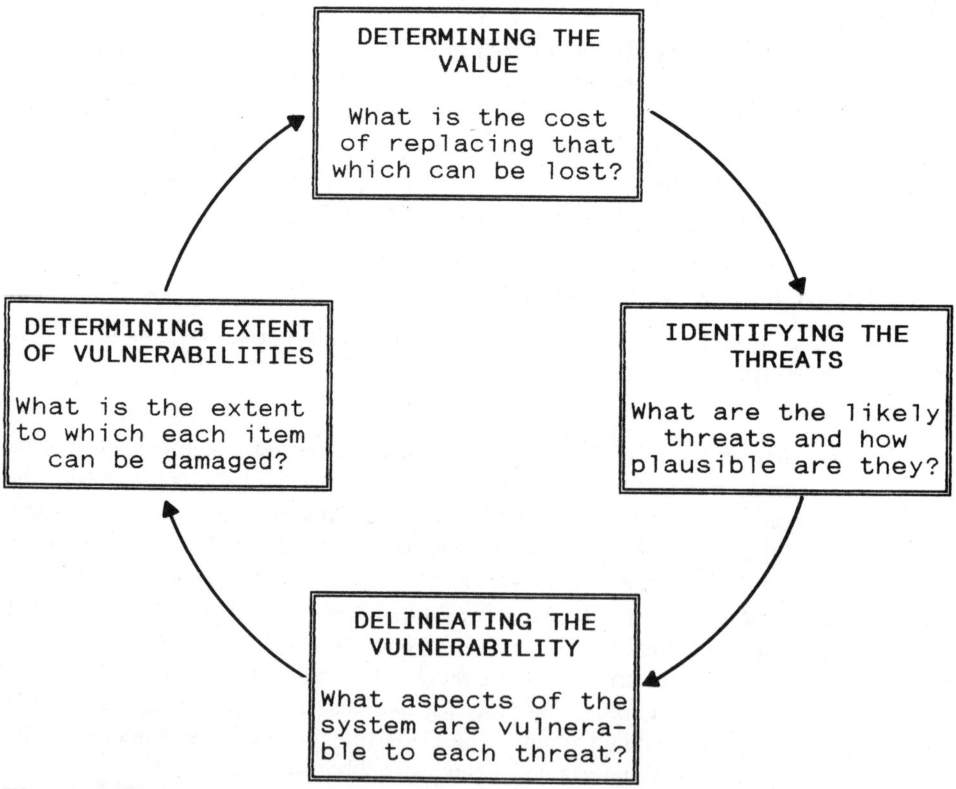


*Fig. 13-5. Risk assessment. In theory, risk assessment should be a simple process. In practice, problems arise from the complexity and interaction of the various measures needed, and determining the optimum trade-off points to avoid investment beyond the point of diminishing returns.*

fleeting attribute. Still, trade-offs must be made, and when the risk analysis is complete or updated, the funds must be dispersed among the three levels of security. The next subsections offer a review.

**Preventive Measures.** Preventive measures are any techniques employed to stop damage from occurring. The trade-off point occurs when the likely cost of damage limitation and disaster recovery will be less than the price of preventing all loss. No insurance company will ensure against absolutely all losses, simply because the price probably would equal the value of the object ensured plus the overhead costs. It just isn't practical.

**Damage Limitation.** Ounce for ounce, damage limitation appears to be the least expensive security measure. Yet it takes sophisticated early detection technology and a positive attitude on the part of supervisors and key personnel. Complacency all too easily sets in after a long period without major problems. If the organization can ensure that these qualitative standards will be maintained, more of this level of protection can safely be chosen. If not, the organization might have to invest more heavily in either preventive measures or disaster recovery.

**Disaster Recovery.** Some damage cannot be limited directly. Where there is some potential to limit damage, the possibility of more complete destruction, direct or indirect, permanent or temporary, should be considered. Bear in mind too, that although a corporation can continuously roll with the punches for ongoing minor losses, it cannot always recover from a major disaster in which no alternative plans have been set up.

### 13.4.3 Systems Design

One of the more interesting questions in the security arena is whether systems should be designed with security in mind, possibly as the dominant consideration. The answer is yes.

# 14

# Dealing with Emerging Technology

*Don't ever prophesy—unless ye know.*

—James Russell Lowell

In describing the political origins of Sparta, Plutarch says that Lycurgus inculcated his ideas with many explicit laws. One of those laws mandated that only rough hewn timbers be used for the construction of roofs. Many years later, when a successor, King Leotychides, was visiting in Corinth, he was surprised to see elegantly carved beams in the ceiling of his host's abode, and inquired how they managed to grow such fine trees in that country. Similarly, after many years of being surrounded with familiar methods of doing business, information managers are sometimes surprised at the products of emerging technology and wonder how they came to pass.

Many corporations have created special departments to analyze the significance of emerging technology, with the objective of finding ways to put it to work earlier than might occur by osmosis. The scope of these departments, of course, usually goes far beyond computers, but that does not detract from the potential contribution to the development of information systems. That potential is considerable.

"Super! Just super!" replies the hard-headed manager. "My needs are here and now. I cannot wait for all this mind-boggling technology to work its way to the marketplace, regardless of how certain the eventuality might be." True enough, but the pace of this progress is so fast that a substantial number of major improvements will be available in less than three years, and in some cases within a year. And every year after that. Taking these trend lines into account, even for here-and-now decisions, would not be a mistake in judgment.

The issue, then, is to determine out how much of this emerging technology to draw into specific projects, and into the corporate strategic information plan. To address that issue, this chapter first posits three categories of progress in technology, and discusses the predictability of each. The next section offers a brief review on the significance of the trend lines, in order to differentiate between the short- and long-range implications. The next section has a similar discussion for integrations. The concluding section then offers a profile method to gauge trade-offs between here-and-now technology and what the future seems to offer.

In perspective, however, the advice of the centuries should be recognized—namely that the introduction of new ideas is one of the most difficult aspects of management, political or technical. The expedition that first scaled

| | Description | Examples |
|---|---|---|
| Ongoing Incremental Improvements | Ongoing improvements increase the efficiency of existing technology. They are heavily reported in technical journals complete with anticipated delivery dates and prices. Bank on it. | • Increases in computer processing speed<br>• Expanded hard disk storage capacity<br>• Increased capacity for transmission lines |
| Quantum Advances | Quantum advances are reconfigurations or miniaturizations of existing technology, that often yield dramatic improvments to efficiency, sometimes bordering on the revolutionary. | • The integrated chip<br>• Productivity software<br>• The relational database structure<br>• Laptop computers |
| Revolutionary Changes | Revolutionary changes are the stuff of genius. Though only a small percentage make it past the laboratory, those that do eventually change the course of business and the lay of the market. | • The computer itself<br>• Program generators<br>• Optically-driven and biological-material computers. |

*Fig. 14-1. Categories of technological developments. Technological developments in the computer field, as in most scientific fields, come in three categories: ongoing incremental improvements, quantum advances, and revolutionary changes. The first two are certain, but details on the first are more predictable. The last is generally too uncertain for planning by information managers.*

Mount Everest offers an interesting example. The lower end of the approach was guarded by a field of giant ice boulders and bottomless chasms. The way across was by leapfrogging the placement of horizontal aluminum ladders. The Sherpas accompanying the expedition (one of whom attained the summit) didn't trust them. They preferred hemp bridges and would not cross on the ladders unless they were first intertwined with rope.

A more significant example of overlooking obvious technology was the building of the propeller-driven B-36 bomber in the late 1940s. By that time, the powering of smaller aircraft with jet engines had proven itself beyond doubt, and the extension of this technology to multi-engine planes was on the drawing board. It didn't matter. The B-36 was built anyway and then scrapped. In a similar vein, many organizations have bought large expensive computers when smaller machines were nearing the same level of capability. They paid the price for the mistake in more ways than one.

On the other hand, technology can attain capabilities well beyond needs. For example, supersonic passenger aircraft—the Concorde and the SST—have not been best sellers. The cost is exorbitant, and when the door-to-door ground times are added, the remarkable reduction in flight time loses most of its advantage. In fine, the purpose of making the most of emerging technology is to enhance the market position of the corporation, not that of the manufacturers.

## 14.1 CATEGORIES OF TECHNOLOGICAL DEVELOPMENTS

Figure 14-1 portrays three categories of technological progress: ongoing incremental improvements, quantum advances, and revolutionary change. The differences are significant in terms of how an organization should regard them.

- *Ongoing Incremental Improvements*. Incremental improvements are those that have demonstrated steady and significant advances in capacity or efficiency over many years and give no hint of ceasing. The trade magazines brim with stories on the next installments, and the items are usually in prototype form undergoing rigorous testing. Typical of these improvements are increases to computer processing speed, data storage capacity, transmission line density, and sophistication of software program generators.
- *Quantum Advances*. Active developments are usually quantum jumps to existing technology, which tend to be described in technical journals more than in trade magazines. The eventual replacement of hard-disk secondary memory with smaller and more efficient solid state memories would be an example. Most of these advances will have been tested before the onslaught of the publicity, but economic and other practical factors often intrude to throw the availability date and the price into question.
- *Revolutionary Change*. Revolutionary change is the stuff of genius, but genius is not always practical. Experimental projects might or might not

make their way to the marketplace. Still, those few that make it will revolutionize the industry. Examples, as sometimes discussed in academic journals, include biogenetic computer memories and optics-driven central processing units, such as the supercomputer in laptop size.

Besides these three categories, the accumulation of incremental improvements, or alternatively a quantum advance, can advance the configuration of interior lines to the point where the improvement has the same effect as a revolutionary change. The classic cases in point have been the integrated circuit board and the relational database structure. The parallel in the aircraft industry was the famed DC-3, a 58-year-old design still in use throughout the world. These planes are no longer built, but retrofitters that bring them up to date electronically are not hurting for business.

The implications for management differ with the category of emerging technology. In general, information managers should always take a hard look at the first category, at least consider the second, and ignore the third. Incremental improvements are as certain as death and taxes, and are predictable in terms of numbers, prices, and dates. Quantum advances are nearly as predictable, yet because pricing and availability are too often a matter of guesswork, a healthy skepticism would not be out of order. As for revolutionary change, the future is too far away to justify consideration in all but the rarest of circumstances. An example of that would be the planned use of computers to support the proposed space flights to other planets in the solar system. That project would take 20 years or more, if at all.

## 14.2 THE LONG AND THE SHORT OF IT

The opening chapter stated that the technology of computer science resembled an avalanche. Elsewhere, the suggestion was made that the miniaturization of supercomputers into laptops was more a question of "when" than "if," and that the combination of relational databases, ultradensity transmission trunk lines, the *Open Standards Interface Agreement*, and software program generators would eventually introduce a new era that would make the present one seem medieval by comparison.

The long-term significance is that all but the smallest corporations and organizations will be able to afford a system that banks every conceivable bit of information it will ever need, with the ability to access any part instantly from nearly anywhere in the world. Each software application, except those that are used to maintain the database, will stand independent and can be modified, enhanced, or expanded to meet changing requirements without the need to coordinate with other users, or with the corporate strategic information plan.

To what extent should an organization try to plan its projects to fit into that paradigm, and conversely, to what extent should it concentrate on ensuring each project works to immediate specifications? The key is the degree to which the data used by each component overlaps with other units. To the extent this is true, the long-term implications of emerging technology should be kept in mind. Eventually, the data will be merged, and therefore it behooves the information manager to simplify reaching that goal. Conversely, to the extent the databases do not overlap, the long-range implications can be ignored.

Unfortunately, the issue is not clear-cut. One of the liveliest debates in information systems is the issue of the comparative importance of algorithms vs. the extent of available data. The algorithmists seek to push the limits of support system technology, based on the assumption that most of the data required is already on hand and that a sophisticated analysis of the data can make or break a strategic information plan. The databasers advocate knowledge-based systems, a position that assumes intelligence is more dependent on information than on elegant reasoning much beyond a sequence of direct inferences.

Perhaps the resolution differs with the requirements. Many great scientific discoveries and conjectures of history have been long on reasoning and short on facts (although those that survived have been repeatedly confirmed and strengthened by relentless factual research). By contrast, improving the accuracy of earthquake and other catastrophic occurrences—or sharpening market analysis predictions—seems more dependent on data and comparatively simple relationships drawn from that data.

Not content with this, the databasers then rub salt in the wounds. They claim that the power curve phenomenon operates two ways with software. First, the cost of increasingly sophisticated programming rises at an exponential rate whereas the cost of additional data collection is often marginal (assuming the hardware technology to store it is outpacing the requirements). Second, when a case can be made for a more extensive use of programming, algorithmic shortcuts have shown remarkable accuracy.

These shortcuts are a means of carrying out the advice, "if the computer cannot be made to go faster, have the software do less work for the same answer." For example, linear programming, a mathematical technique, is often used for optimization-type decision support systems. Many applications consume hours of computer processing time. Shortcuts reduce the processing time to minutes and still provide answers within a range of accuracy suitable to the nature of the requirements, although they might require more data.

## 14.3 IMPLICATIONS FOR SYSTEMS INTEGRATIONS

The emerging technology for information systems will likely have a profound effect on integration projects, primarily as the ease with which databases can be merged increases. Figure 14-2 illustrates these trend lines.

- *Greater Emphasis on Standardization.* The impetus toward standardization is coming directly from manufacturers, and is supported by most corporations who have had to deal with the problems and high costs of

| MODEL | FACTORS | PROGNOSIS |
|---|---|---|
| Synthesis | Growing recognition that information systems are knowledge-based, and that data normally demonstrates a stronger interrelationship than outputs. | Attempts at syntheses will likely decline, or be implemented only by osmosis from a database integration. |
| Database Integrations | Many information systems share common data, but the biggest problem is accessing that data or maintaining its logical integrity. | Probably the largest growth area among the integration models. |
| Excerpt Integrations | Merged systems often cost more than the benefits and they tempt senior executives to micro manage, creating more problems than resolutions. | Strong. This model is an economical substitute for a database integration, and operates to reduce micro management. |
| Interfaces | Most attempts to use the interface model in lieu of a merger-type have failed, though straightforward exchange applications flourish. | The use of this model will probably decline except when used to transmit essential information between independent systems. |
| Standardizations | The trend towards standardization in most aspects of hardware, networks, and even software, is unmistakable. | This will facilitate all other integration models and thus encourage a much greater use of corporate-wide information systems. |

*Fig. 14-2. Emerging technology and integrations. Emerging technology is itself a form of standardization and lends itself to merger-type integrations that previously might have been infeasible.*

integrating separate systems. Put another way, standardization will be increasingly a matter of taking advantage of what comes on the market in lieu of a concerted internal effort.

- *More Specialized Use of Interfaces*. The attempts to integrate separate systems by a series of interfaces probably will decrease, on the grounds that most of them fail because of the increasing opportunities to merge databases. Concurrently, however, the trend towards manufactured standardization will simplify the interfacing of separate systems for routine passing of data and programs.

- *Decline in Direct Attempts to Synthesize*. As the ability to distribute or access a corporate database from multiple locations increases, and the relational database structure makes user programming increasingly independent of the need to coordinate applications, this form of integration should fade. However, in the limited, planning stage of considering the divergence of requirements when initially setting up the files and record structures, the integration should remain intact.

## 14.4 A TRADE-OFF PROFILE

The discussion now turns to the objective of the chapter, namely to provide a simple method to assess emerging technology in terms of embedding it in new projects and in the corporate strategy for information systems. There is a difference. The technology used in a project should be identified by the end of the design phase. By contrast, the corporate strategy might look ahead 10 years or more. Some projects will be initiated in the immediate future, others within the next few years, and still others five to seven years down the road. Further, some of these projects will likely be standalones, while others will be considered components of a larger system that require some form of linkage. Finally, the more distant the project, the more likely it will be defined in broad terms and therefore highly subject to change.

This situation suggests that the information manager should keep a map on the relationships of existing and planned systems, highlighting those points where the components will be linked or related. These points in turn should be annotated with a prognosis where the relevant technology seems headed which amounts to a profile. With this map in hand, each project can be evaluated on its own terms.

Like most profiles, it has a set of parallel scales. To the extent the evaluation of each aspect of a project veers to a higher value is the extent to which more emerging technology should be considered, especially if the unit will eventually be linked with others. Figure 14-3 illustrates this profile method in generic form. The significance of these questions follows.

- *Linkage with Other Projects*. To the extent that a project will be linked to other projects, for which the present technology imposes many incompatibilities, is the extent to which maximum consideration of emerging technology is justified.
- *Degree of Immediate Importance*. This factor is offsetting and is measured with a decreasing-value scale. Intense immediate requirements take precedence over new technology unless meeting the requirements depend on the technology.
- *Time*. Opportunities to harness emerging technology are strongly related to the time needed to implement a project, simply because predictable advances will be on the market by the time they could be used. Substituting proprietary software that is presently in the development stage might save millions, although there is some risk it will not work to specifications.

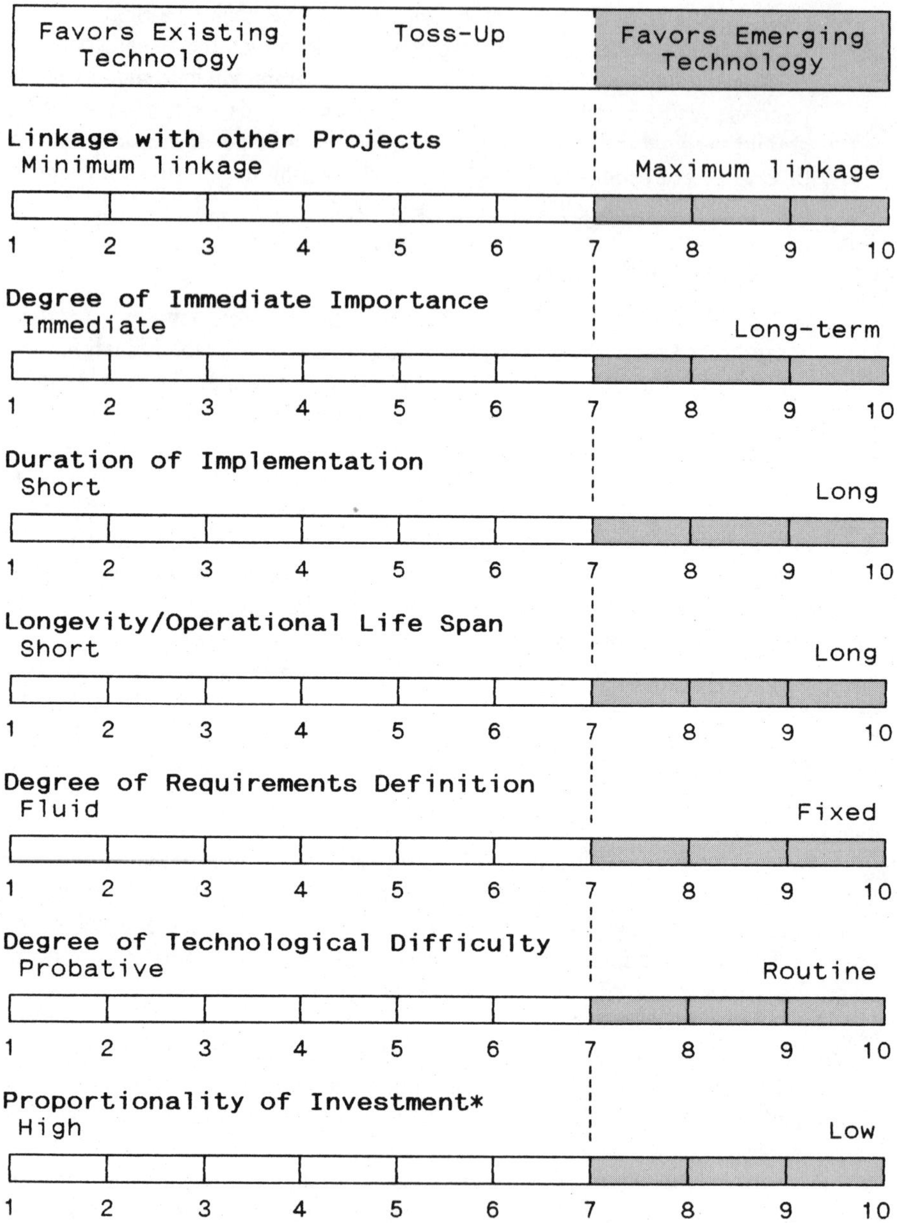


*UNDER SOME CIRCUMSTANCES, THE SCALE COULD BE REVERSED.

*Fig. 14-3. A trade-off profile for emerging technology decisions. A planning decision to incorporate emerging technology that is not yet on the marketplace depends on many factors. These factors comprise a profile. To the degree the profile curve shifts to the right is the extent to which this technology should be given serious consideration.*

- *Longevity.* A longer anticipated life span for a system also warrants consideration of using new technology. The older equipment and techniques might grow obsolete.
- *Degree of Definition.* To the extent a project evinces a fixed definition of requirements is the extent to which the application of emerging technology can be carefully evaluated.
- *Degree of Technological Difficulty.* This is also a reverse scale. To the extent a project will rely on state-of-the-art technology, or at least on technology for which the information systems department lacks experience, is the extent to which attempts to incorporate even more advanced technology could risk failure.
- *Proportionality of Investment.* The more expensive a project is, as a percentage of the systems budget, the more highly it is likely to be regarded. But whether a higher value here would justify more consideration of emerging technology, or just the opposite, depends on how the corporation operates.

The application of this profile to specific corporations and organizations will inevitably warrant the elimination or modification of some questions and the addition of new ones. Examples of additional scales include: the volatility of the corporate structure and its requirements, the degree of distributive processing involved, the likely array of hardware that will be used, and the extent of the pressures for making maximum use of hardware and other technology on hand. The important point, however, is to use the method on a comparative basis. Projects where the profiles are skewed to the right are more likely candidates for emerging technology.

How many scales should rate higher values before decisions are made in favor of considering emerging technology? The simplest approach is to weigh each scale with a value or index proportional to its perceived importance. A simple addition of the weighted scores would then yield a single number for comparison. But like any model based on heuristic analysis, the aim is only to provide some form of preliminary quantitative computations. That allows the planner to concentrate on the subjective issues. The model won't help him there.

# Part IV

# Management and Decisions

This final part of the book looks at six aspects of information systems management, and concludes with a hypothetical case study that simultaneously illustrates the use to which emerging technology and integrations can be put in the foreseeable future, and how subjective factors and ethical issues can operate to throw the efficacy of such systems into question.

The discussion begins, in chapter 15, with a look at general and personnel management considerations, with an emphasis on the dichotomy that often operates between strategic perspectives for the corporation or organization vs. the management information systems department or its equivalent. Chapter 16 continues the discussion, changing the focus to project management. Project management normally demands greater leadership than departments, and also must focus heavily on issues of risk. The two perspectives are linked by emphasizing the idea of portfolio management developed by the Harvard Graduate School of Business Administration.

Chapter 17 departs from this focus by addressing prototypes. In theory, prototypes bear stronger kinship with technology than management, but a review of the literature reveals that the technology is comparatively simple and straightforward. The problem is in the reluctance of management to use prototyping more often. The reluctance usually proves costly.

Chapter 18 looks at subjectivity and ethics in general, as they apply to information systems. Chapter 19 takes a harder look at fraud, breach of contract, and what I call *porkware*. Porkware comprises systems and wherewithal sold far in excess of user requirements. As information systems grow in scope and complexity and reach into every nook and cranny of an organization, both ethical issues and problems with contracts are likely to increase.

Chapter 20 then presents a simple decision-making model for use with the information systems, with specific applications to the phases in the gestation period of a project. This is followed by the hypothetical case study, namely that of the potential for the integration of most databases in the federal government that are used to store and use data on individuals. Because the case is hypothetical, the presentation relies on how different classes of business degree students, most of whom had spent many years in the work force, reacted to the concept.

Choosing the organization that exemplified sound management practices with respect to data processing and information systems was easy, although the selection bears an explanation. Good management should be evaluated in terms of the circumstances in which it must operate. If those circumstances present nearly insurmountable obstacles, and yet management makes the best choices and continues to turn in a remarkable performance, the recognition is well deserved. The candidate, then, is the Internal Revenue Service.

First, the disadvantageous environment in which it must operate. For starters, the tax man is easy to hate. Next, every mistake that is made, and every act of abuse that occurs—no matter how minor—will be pilloried by the general public and often by the press. Then, by law it is placed in an adversarial relationship with most citizens, and told to enforce a package of tax laws that would defy explanation by Einstein. Finally, the IRS is told it must do its work with antiquated computers and minimal staffing compared to the amount of known tax cheating.

To this must be added the bad publicity that accrued when a serious but honest mistake was made in installing a new program for entering tax returns in 1985 and the low budget that forces the agency to put clerical workers in inadequate working conditions. There also is the negative subjective influence generated by taxpayers, knowing that a sizable slice of their taxes are being used to subsidize waste and corruption, such as the Savings & Loan bailout, the recent scandal uncovered at the Department of Housing and Urban Development, the ongoing fraud and abuse in Department of Defense contracts, and so forth ad nauseam. This is not the fault of the IRS, but many taxpayers think of the federal government as a more closely woven entity than it is in practice.

In spite of these enormous problems and obstacles, the IRS has demonstrated a remarkable record in information systems. Three examples should suffice to make the point. First, the move toward automated submission of tax returns should both alleviate the working conditions of clerks and reduce the input error rate, which all too often results in unwarranted notices of additional taxes due. Second, their software uses inferential logic to determine which returns are the most likely to be fraudulent or otherwise seriously in error. In this way the system makes the best use of the limited number of auditing personnel as a means of reducing fraud and penalizing those individuals who persist in it. Third, when the agency wanted to install a new automated field auditing system at a total cost in excess of $1 billion, and the benefits from the initial phase of this project (the prototype) had not been proven, the funding for it was halted. The Information Systems Policy Board, which oversees all automation efforts within the IRS, had made the policy decision that all automation projects would first be prototyped, then benefits proved, and finally funding for implementation provided. Not many other government agencies take an honest look at return on investment.

*Fig. IV-1. The national office of the Internal Revenue Service, located on Constitution Avenue in Washington, D.C. The IRS declined to provide a photograph of the members of their Information Systems Policy Board.*

# 15

# General and Personnel Management Considerations

*Kings and bears oft worry their keepers.*

—Scottish Proverb

Herodotus, the father of recorded history, also recorded the first good-news/bad-news anecdote. His *Histories* relate that King Xerxes, after losing his bid to subdue Greece, decided to take a short cut home to Persia. He embarked on a Phoenician ship at Eion for passage across the Aegean sea, instead of marching with his troops via the Hellespont. In a severe storm midway to Persia, the ship labored heavily. Xerxes, in fear of his life, asked the captain if there was anything that could be done to lessen the danger. The captain replied the only remedy was to lighten the ship's load. Xerxes turned to his aides and implored their help in his hour of need. All 30 jumped overboard. Upon reaching safety Xerxes summoned the captain. For the sound judgment that saved his life, he would give him his gold crown, but because the remedy cost him the lives of his most trusted aides, he also would order him beheaded.

Computers and information systems also offer some good news and some bad news. The good news, as argued throughout this book, is that the potential for the strategic use of information systems has been barely tapped. The bad news is that many attempts to do so have failed. Among those that succeeded, the cost has often inspired chief executive officers, like King Xerxes, to roll some heads. An Index Group study, as reported in the Fall 1988 edition of *Information Strategy*, found that of 30 information systems evaluated, 25 failed.

In each case, poor management was the cause of the failure. Nowhere was technology to blame.

Indirectly, some blame can be laid on the technological doorstep. The record of success that most corporations and organizations have had with computers over the past 30 to 40 years is too solid to blame management alone for this new epidemic of failure. Perhaps the real culprit is the difference between the older transaction-based models vs. the newer information and decision support systems. The former begs automation; the latter sometimes defies it, although both tend to draw on the same data.

In transaction systems, processing feeds directly on data. In information systems, the answers are many permutations and combinations removed from the raw data and they need more of this processing per answer. These permutations account for the transformation of mere information into intelligence. That process can open windows of opportunity alike for businesses and nonprofit institutions. Yet under the direction of executives who might not understand or appreciate this difference, the hoped-for window becomes a mirror reflecting the inadequacies of management.

To restate the case, a workable information system, especially if it is an integration intended to draw on a necessary mass of data, is less a challenge to technology than a matter of good management. Electronic alchemy by itself will not do the job. Managers must span the gap between the perspective of a chief executive officer, and the myriad of detail required to make any automated system operational and useful.

What constitutes good management? The published attempts to answer that question fill small libraries, and perhaps there are as many schools of management as there are managers. This suggests leaving unanswerable questions to the ruminations of philosophers, and concentrate instead on the tasks of management with respect to information systems. This chapter focuses on that array with respect to general management, and the next, on project management.

## 15.1 STRATEGY VS. ORGANIZATIONAL REALITIES

First things first. *Computers do not improve market position, and they improve production efficiency only when they become a less expensive substitute for human labor*. Otherwise, computers are only a source of information, which must be put to use by management to make a difference in profits or productivity. The idea then is to get or provide information at the right time and the right place. If the informational logistics are not in place, they must be put there, and that entails change. The partner of change inevitably is risk—a Faustian bargain of sorts.

To put the matter another way, strategy departs from the norm into some degree of unknown. When strategy becomes the norm—that is, when risk is either eliminated or controlled—it changes its name to policy and procedure. Meanwhile, strategy must be willing to reach out in spite of organizational inertia.

Not that inertia is all bad. Systems are not primarily works of art. A certain amount of inertial guidance is necessary to run large departments and operate systems. As suggested in chapter 1, finding the neat balance between the two is a tough nut to crack. Figure 15-1 amplifies that introductory display. Some points to consider are:

- *Degree of Outreach*. A strategic perspective looks primarily at the marketplace, or if nonprofit, the provision of services. Looking inward to productivity is subordinate to the external outreach. On the other hand, the marketplace and consumers manifest constant change. Few information systems seem capable of reacting to these changes without major revision. Considerable effort and expense is needed to develop systems that possess this kind of resilience, but it's usually worth it.
- *Extent of Decentralization*. This is a many-faceted attribute and can refer to the dispersion of systems personnel, to other departments, to databases, or to hardware. In theory, greater decentralization of resources should improve outreach. In practice, when this happens, resources are much harder to manage and cause to work as a team.
- *Use of Technology*. Outreach concentrates on making technology work for user requirements. An introverted information systems department often looks at harnessing advances in technology as a worthy goal. The counter view is that technology can make practical tomorrow what is prohibitively expensive or time-consuming today.
- *Proportionality of Workload*. A strong outreach attitude will stress the development of new systems; the opposite will stress maintenance of existing systems. But new systems tend to complicate management, especially the ability to link them together, and a first-rate system is normally worth maintaining.
- *Trends in Integrations*. Usually, a strategic outlook will favor merger-type integrations on the simple grounds that all three models (synthesis, database integration, and excerpt integration) provide the necessary massing of data to meet the intense dietary requirements of decision support systems. When standardizations are sought, the objective is to simplify a future integration. By contrast, the day-to-day management outlook will rely on interfaces to make the maximum use of what exists, even though the rationale for standardizations tends to be cost savings. Yet many strategically important projects are self-standing, and others only require an interface. Jumping on the integration bandwagon and riding it to perdition is too easy.
- *Project-Oriented Benefit Analysis*. The use of systems to support strategic objectives should prove itself with a benefits analysis. Have the projects contributed more to profits (or to reducing cost per service rendered) than invested? As developed in chapter 4, the indirect expenses associated with return on investment calculations often make answering this type of question difficult, certainly as difficult as attempting to measure the general return on systems investments with respect to the total systems budget. The return on investment for commonly used resources is not a number that lends itself to precise subdivision.

| CRITERIA | STRATEGIC EMPHASIS | DISADVANTAGES |
|---|---|---|
| Outreach | In most cases, improvements to productivity have theoretical limits, whereas the marketplace is more open ended. | Lower costs by way of improving productivity can sometimes make a greater contribution to market share than indirect strategy. |
| Extent of Decentralization | Putting data and systems closer to users improves interior lines where they may be most needed. | Centralization of data increasingly offers major advantages, and it can still be distributed as appropriate. |
| Use of Technology | Axiomatically, requirements should always take precedence over progress in technology. | Emerging technology often provides a way of meeting requirements, that could not be met previously. |
| Proportionality | The age of information begs for innovative projects and creative use of systems. | Innovation often runs amuck, and in practice has been the source of multi-million dollar failures. |
| Trends in Integration | Mergers, if well done, almost always improve interior lines, whereas interfaces tend to denigrate them. | When requirements need only transfer of well-defined units of data, a merger is usually a serious mistake. |
| Benefit Analysis | In the absence of compelling humanitarian reasons, every project should eventually pay for itself, directly or indirectly. | As the number of projects increase, indirect benefits can outweigh the more measurable direct benefits. |

*Fig. 15-1. Strategic vs. systems perspectives: a closer look. Figure 1-2 provided a macro look at the inherent conflicts between strategic requirements and systems management. This chart expands on that figure in more detail. Emerging technology can be used to overcome some of these problems, but a concerted management effort is still needed to keep them under control.*

So what is the bottom line here? Drawing on the metaphors of other writers, how much should politically and technologically oriented leadership yield to one another? When does the creative environment degrade into chaos and the brilliant strategy degenerate into hairbrained schemes? The answer is that there isn't any answer. When one deals with the future, the future will provide answers, which is the nature of risk. All an organization can do is: size up its market and potential markets, make an honest assessment or appraisal of its resources and the way it conducts business, concentrate those resources on those few areas that offer the most promise, and balance risks in some variation of portfolio management, that is, to put itself in a position where it can absorb the losses and failures that are bound to occur.

## 15.2 GENERAL MANAGEMENT IN A PROJECT ENVIRONMENT

To continue the reasoning of the previous section, recognizing that information systems departments are large, ongoing operations that need management more than leadership is of fundamental importance. By contrast, projects tend to fail without leadership. They have sharply focused objectives and measurable outcomes, and those results involve change. Leadership finds its niche here. Yet can any one individual be equally capable in both roles? Only a few can display such characteristics. Some managers display a clear leadership style, perhaps charismatic or at least entrepreneurial in outlook. They are risk takers by nature. At the other extreme are purely administrative types, content to carry out explicit instructions preferably without having to make any difficult decisions. Between them there is an infinite variety of management styles. Yet because the nature of information systems demands a greater breadth of management outlook, a common denominator is necessary.

Perhaps the most insightful finding on this subject came out of research conducted by the Franklin Institute 25 years ago. The research focused on military leadership and management. The research was conducted by retired four-star general officers with a noted proclivity for both leadership in wartime and reflective writing and scholarship. After countless interviews and surveys of the literature, the only common element found among successful leaders and managers was their ability to digest enormous amounts of information and data, and then redirect the essence and significance of that data as intelligence or directives to be carried out. The common element among them all was essentially the same as the purpose of any information system that elevates itself above routine processing, which is in keeping with the idea that an automated information system is an integral part of a larger information system, comprising both automated and manually processed information. At one end this includes hunches played by decision makers and at the other end, dull compilations of hard data. In turn this broader information system is a component of the system that equates with an organization and its dynamics. Thus successful management of an automated system is a subset of successful organizational management. To put the matter another way, managing a system is not very different from managing an organization, including the motivation and management of employees.

In this regard, one of the more interesting studies of information systems departments was that done by Richard L. Nolan and Cyrus F. Gibson, which began in 1974. They outlined six stages of growth, ranging from initiation to maturity. The four intermediate stages were: contagion, control, integration, and data administration. The difficulties of dealing with integration lead to a better understanding of data. Working with data leads to a better understanding of corporate requirements, strategic planning, and the need to work more closely with users and other departments, which is worth bearing in mind when considering how many CEO's regard their chief information officers. And how do CEO's regard their CIO's? Sometimes very highly, but when feelings are negative, these are the complaints:

**Lack of Responsiveness.** This complaint is the most common, mostly because the CIO is too buried in the management of his department to keep the corporate goals foremost in mind. Considering the prevalence of this complaint, the situation is probably true in more instances than not, although the technical intricacy of systems and databases do not always lend themselves to this kind of flexibility.

**Poor Planning and Budgeting.** This, too, is a common complaint but not always justified. Rapidly changing requirements and the onslaught of progress in technology, combined with the long lead times required to develop most systems, offer extenuating circumstances.

**Excessive Optimism.** This complaint is subjective and hard to pin down, except for delivery dates and claims of compatibility. The number of times when delivery in advance of deadlines occurs, or where the products are more compatible than planned, are just too rare to fight the issue in the court of management opinion.

**Inability to Handle Peak Loads.** This problem is often prevalent, and stems from the lack of testing for peak loads. Most tests are oriented toward logical processing and compatibility. The resolution of problems under those criteria can prove almost oppressive. When that work is completed, the motivation for further testing often will have waned.

**Poor Control Over Distributed Data.** The complaint is usually warranted, but the problem, as drawn out in chapters 5 and 10, is inherent in any attempt to distribute data and still maintain control over it as an entity. Arguably, this problem is the single most difficult for any system that is used in multiple locations.

**Poor Documentation.** This problem is nearly a universal failing among both information managers and programmers. The advent of program generators and database oriented systems will go a long way to reducing the intensity of this problem. In the interim, the problem takes the personal attention of the boss to rectify.

**Excessive Personnel Turnover.** Generally true, but as long as the demand exceeds the supply and highly skilled individuals of necessity often must work on the bottom rungs, the problem will continue.

Offsetting these complaints is the tendency of CEO's, as mentioned in another chapter, suddenly and frequently to change the bidding, and then hold CIO's accountable without the necessary responsibility, authority, or control over resources external to the information systems shop to get the job done. Ultimately, the individual who calls the shots must accept the credit or blame for failure. In short, if the CIO, or his equivalent, is competent, the responsibility lies with CEO to make the proper use of that competence. This responsibility requires a greater understanding of systems technology than most CEO's seem willing to learn. In return, the CIO needs to appreciate more fully the burden that only his boss can carry in practical terms, which often translates to resilient databases.

## 15.3 COMMITTEES, TECHNICAL ADVISORS, AND GURUS

The difficulties of dovetailing strategic outreach with the grind of technology usually lead to reliance on one of three adjunct human resources: the steering committee, the formal technical advisor, and the informal "guru." The steering committee is generally intended to compensate for an information manager that leans toward the technical side of issues. The other two resources support a more corporate-oriented manager. The steering committee is also common for project management, as covered in the next chapter.

**Steering Committees.** A discontented manager once concluded the only things steering committees could steer were their cars on the way to work, providing no two members rode in the same car. The criticism might be valid in some circumstances, but in general steering committees are valuable resources and a means of high level quality control. They do not work well when they try to supervise the day-to-day work of the information manager. Sometimes their success depends on how well that information manager draws out and reconciles the inevitable differences among the members.

**Technical Advisors.** Drawing on a child's tale, when technical advisors are good, they are usually very good, and when they are bad, they are horrid. Because the position by definition excludes formal responsibility, it is sometimes used to put an incompetent but well-liked individual out of harm's way. In practice, effective technical advisors assume unique roles dependent on personality and opportunity. At one extreme, he may advise only when asked; in another, he will operate as an active quality control overseer and take initiative in spite of any lack of authority, which can sometimes lead to abuse.[1]

**Gurus.** The guru is an informal variation of a technical advisor, with an extraordinary depth of technical knowledge or an exceptional organizational ability, perhaps augmented with an insatiable appetite for complex and intricate problems. A guru can occupy any position in an organization, but in contrast to most formal advisor positions, he is not officially recognized in that role. Few information systems departments are without them.

---

[1]As such, some technical advisors quickly wear out their welcome. No less a figure than Sir Isaac Newton fell prey to this trap. According to Daniel Boorstin's *The Discoverers*, Newton's work elevated him to the lifetime presidency of the renown Royal Society. In a day when most scientific publications consisted of copies of letters distributed to members through such societies, the president was in a position to hype his reputation and denigrate that of others, especially those that might compete for recognition in the same field. Newton was guilty of this abuse on many occasions, but his reputation was so overwhelming that no one could do anything about it. A parallel case in recent times was the long and abusive tenure of the late Admiral Hyman Rickover within the Department of the Navy.

## 15.4 PERSONNEL MANAGEMENT

The literature on the benefits of treating personnel with respect, and as an indispensable element of a corporation or organization, is fulsome. Yet not all employees are equal in capability or in the potential to reach a high level of capability. Further, specialties in data processing and systems display a greater divergence of skills and attributes than perhaps any other technical endeavor. Making the most of this pool of human resources takes some creative thinking and some realistic limits on expectations. Demanding too much variety of work from any one individual or even expecting co-workers to work out differences with each other is unrealistic. That duty is the job of managers. Technically oriented managers who eschew this responsibility—and the profession has its share—are not managers.

### 15.4.1 Skill Areas in Data Processing

Most books, charts, and job description manuals organize skills by related tasks, but a few stress orientations. Figure 15-2 illustrates this different viewpoint. The two viewpoints are not poles apart, but after employees are hired, how they work together is probably more a function of these orientations than specific skills. When a manager wants to get the most from his personnel, he should at least consider them and how they work or do not work very well in concert.

- *Orientation Toward Hardware and Communications.* These are the electronic mechanics, and are the least concerned with user requirements except to the extent they can be reduced to numbers. In general, they tend to work apart from the other skill areas.
- *Orientation Toward Programming and Software.* By definition, this group includes the programmers and that breed of systems analysts whose primary focus is the modular structure of systems. In development work, this group is where the largest slice of the dollar is spent.
- *Orientation Toward Data and Information.* As information systems increasingly veer toward database structure, and those databases increase in size and scope, these positions gain increasing importance. The orientation, however, has two distinct subsets: one gravitates to systems analysis in terms of the structure and scope of the database, the other leans to database administration and maintenance. These two sub-orientations are different in practice, and seldom interchangeable.
- *Orientation Toward Procedures.* These are the system auditors and the systems-architecture brand of systems analysts. They ensure quality control, or alternatively, that a user requirement can be reduced to a workable system. The good ones are scarce.
- *Orientation Toward People.* This trait is the hallmark of information resource managers (who often staff information centers), of user representatives, and of those systems analysts who work primarily with users. This people-orientation is often stronger than that found in the better managers. But by the same token, charging them with wide

responsibility could be a mistake. For better or worse, a hardnosed approach is needed, no matter how outwardly amicable, to see a difficult task through to completion.

These orientations explain the inherent difficulty of nailing down the job descriptions for systems analysts and software engineers. As previously outlined, different incumbents of the former demonstrated three different orientations. The combination of all three in one individual is rare. With the software engineer, the situation is worse. In theory, that job should encompass all five orientations, except possibly the one toward people. In practice, they tend to specialize in a combination of the hardware, programming, and the development side of data structures. Alternatively, software engineers become proceduralists with a wide technical perspective.

| Orientation or Proclivity | Typical Skill Areas | Orientation ranges for: Systems Analysts | Software Engineers |
|---|---|---|---|
| **Hardware** | • Systems operator<br>• Systems architect | | Secondary |
| **Software** | • Programmer or coder<br>• Software designer | Secondary | Primary |
| **Data** | • Database administrator<br>• Information specialist | Secondary | Secondary |
| **Procedures** | • Support system analyst<br>• Technical manager | Primary | Secondary |
| **People** | • User representative<br>• General supervisor | Secondary | |

*Fig. 15-2. Skill orientations in data processing. The usual categorization of job skills might be inadequate for management. Consideration of the five orientations could be more helpful: hardware, software, data, procedures, and people. Most MIS departments and every major project can benefit by a complementary mix of these orientations.*

### 15.4.2 The Distribution of Relative Competence

The distribution of ability in most fields adheres to a normal curve, which means that for any skill area, an individual near the high end consistently produces or achieves more than an individual in the middle. Concurrently, an individual near the lower end consistently produces less than his or her peers in the middle. Thus the normal distribution of individual skill and talent yields yet another case of the power curve for productivity and work accomplishment. Figure 15-3 represents the normal distribution curve and its effect on various skill levels. The slope of the power curve effect increases sharply with respect to the skill level at issue.

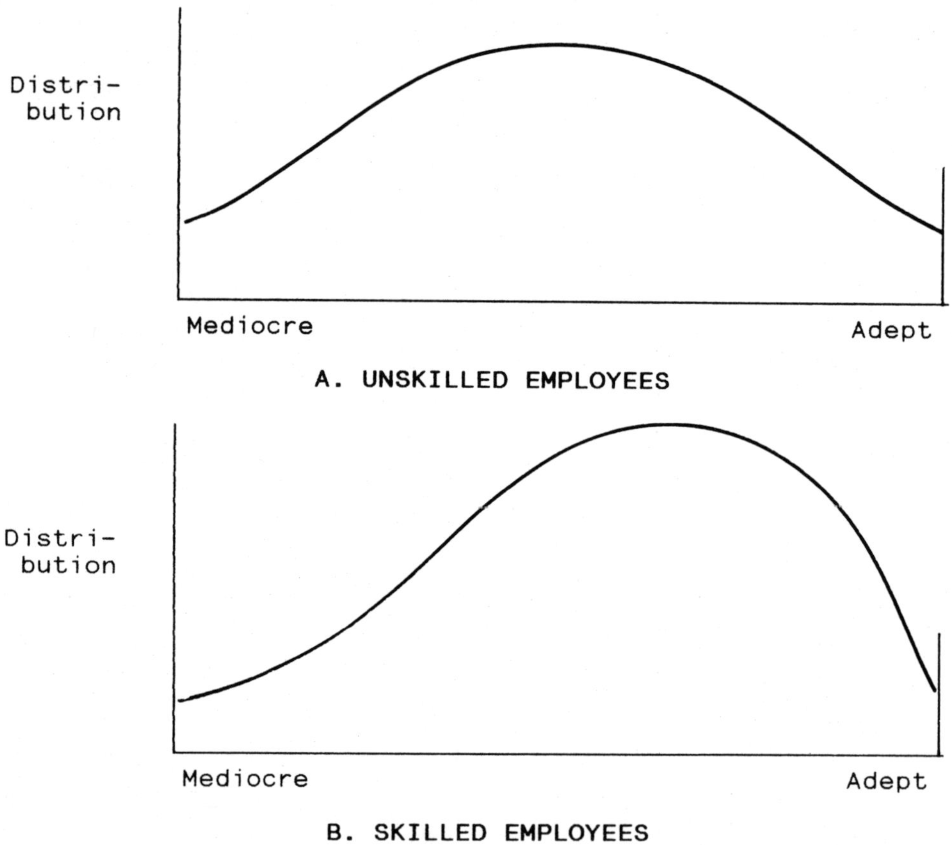


*Fig. 15-3. Distribution of technical competence. Similar to most other human attributes, technical competence among individuals seems to adhere to a normal distribution, with the bulk crowding the mean. The few at the extremes evince exceptional competence and mediocrity, respectively. As skill levels increase, the lower end of the curve tends to shrink and the upper end stretches out, probably because mediocrity works as a barrier to enter the field. As shown in Fig. 15-4, this is of major significance to information managers.*

The research on this phenomenon is extensive both in quantity and in the fields of endeavor studied. One survey indicated that a mere 3 percent of scientists and researchers accounted for 50 percent of published articles in their fields, and 10 percent of those could claim 90 percent of the literature. This result does not mean that the large balance of individuals don't accomplish anything. Far from it, but the data suggests that the value of their work is nowhere near on a par with the top producers.

### 15.4.3 Routine vs. Highly Skilled Work

In work that requires few skills, exceptional personnel have limited opportunities to prove high productivity. Besides, the few that try are often labelled *rate busters* by their peers. Similarly, marginally qualified personnel have limited opportunities to slough off and get away with it. To use a simple example, laborers hired by movers to load and unload furniture seldom vary much from the mathematical norm. The slow ones don't get rehired, and the potentially fast ones avoid showing that talent. Thus, for obvious reasons, there are practical limits to just how fast the best workers can exceed the norm. The furniture is heavy and often takes two people to move it.

The same is not true of highly skilled work. Individuals at the high end consistently outperform the norm, and those at the low end consistently fall short. An application to data processing can be demonstrated by reference to one of the simpler and more reliable measures of productivity—is the average number of lines of tested source code (programming) produced per person per day. Depending on the study consulted, this average is between 8 and 12 lines. The key word is *average*. The best programmers have been known to reach averages of 20, 30, and sometimes 40 lines per day. If the high end programmers are writing 30 or more lines of code per day, and the industry average hovers around 10 lines, then the low enders are writing close to zero or less. True, they are writing some code, but if it doesn't test correctly, it cannot be counted. When a more skilled programmer must rewrite bad code, time is taken from his or her productivity, and hence the effective contribution of these marginal personnel can be less than zero. More code can often be produced with fewer people by excluding the marginally qualified. Figure 15-4, which is an application of FIG. 15-3, illustrates this point.

On the other hand, exceptionally qualified personnel can be a mixed blessing. When Henry Luce, the founder and editor of *Time* magazine, visited the Philippines shortly before the outbreak of World War II, he had a long talk with General Douglas MacArthur. Afterward, he wondered aloud if the famed general was the world's greatest strategist or the world's greatest egotist, and concluded that he was probably both. Some exceptionally qualified personnel in the computer field provide interesting parallels. Another problem is that many personnel prefer to work alone. When required to work in close concert with others, their remarkable productivity often goes up in smoke.

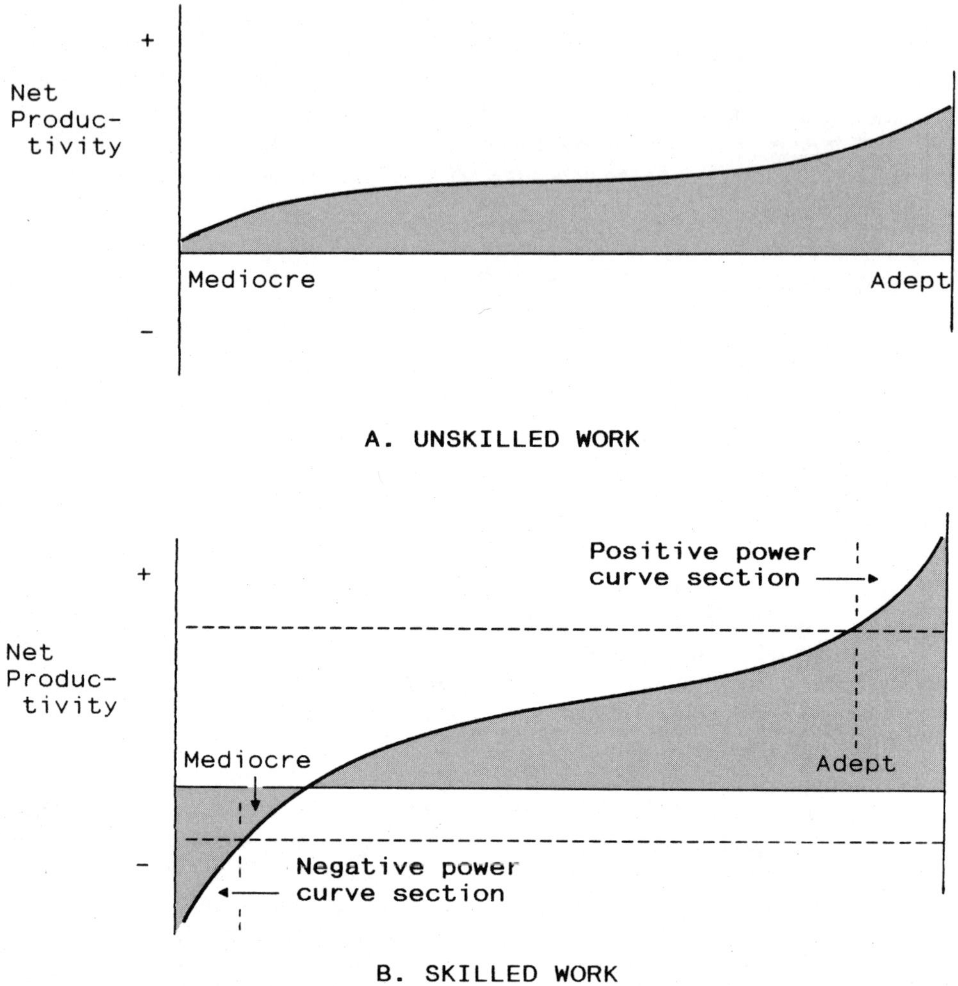


*Fig. 15-4. The effect of marginal personnel in skilled areas. As the skill level under consideration increases, the few highly competent individuals tend to outperform their peers significantly. Conversely, the few at the mediocre end perform badly. Some of them introduce so many errors, that whatever few contributions they make are more than negated by the time it takes competent personnel to correct the errors.*

### 15.4.4 Compensating Management Techniques

Because the use of computer-based information systems continues to grow each year, the demand for skilled professionals likely will continue to exceed the demand for the foreseeable future. Accordingly, the problem of marginally-qualified personnel will continue to exist if not grow. Some of them will improve with training and experience, some will not. Measures should be taken to keep the error rates from detracting from general productivity. These measures usually comprise an emphasis on orthodox practices, although the price is often to stifle the initiative of the hard chargers.

**Documentation on Progress.** This documentation is not the same thing as programming documentation. It is much more of a means of controlling progress and development, and is probably the most common systems management technique. For the federal government, at least, it is *de rigueur*. The documentation on the documentation requirements itself runs several thousand pages under various directives. The chief advantage is that a permanent audit trail of sorts is established. The chief disadvantage is the considerable, sometimes enormous, time and effort needed to keep this instant history up to date. At worse, documentation degenerates into another edition of ''management by objectives,'' where the exercise itself often becomes the objective.

**Maximum Supervision.** Maximum supervision means intense personal review of each employee's work. The chief advantage is that errors are caught before they can lead to extensive damage. The chief disadvantage is that it discourages good supervisors who quickly grow tired of ceaseless checking of irksome detail.

**Frequent and Extensive Testing.** It goes without saying that every aspect of every system should be thoroughly tested before it is used and few, if any, managers downplay the importance of testing in theory. Therefore, this approach is normally the best. Performance remains the primary objective. The only disadvantage is that changes to the system during development are more difficult to implement. Each requires a massive change to the testing environment.

### 15.4.5 Upgrading Skills

Beyond doubt, computer technology continues to advance markedly each year, and some would say every month. Hence, the academic preparation of even the best personnel becomes dated in a short time. Some upgrade their skills by constant study, or participation in various computer societies, or working with new hardware and software on their own computers. Still, on the job experience seems the best and most common means of upgrading skills. Unfortunately, few organizations offer a sufficient range of work assignments for across-the-board skill improvement, which exacerbates the high rate of personnel turnover. The benefits of reducing this turnover might be worth what it takes to make employees feel that their professional growth is an important factor in management decisions.

## 15.5 SPECIAL PROBLEMS WITH INFORMATION CENTERS

The information center is a great idea that gets out of hand more than any other place in the management of information systems. The ostensible purpose is an outreach to potential users of automated information, especially those who do not depend on a centralized corporate database. What often happens in practice is that the center becomes a conduit for the interchange of the frustrations that develop between the information systems department and the rest of the organization.

**Backlog.** The demands of users are often high in comparison to the capabilities of the center. The result is that a backlog quickly builds up, and both parties grow dissatisfied.

**Naivete on the Part of Users.** Users do not always appreciate the work that is needed to develop a good system, or that this work load usually increases at an exponential rate with respect to the complexity of the requirements. This reinforces the previous problem.

**Lack of Documentation.** If poor documentation is the rule within organized information systems departments, it is positively abysmal in this arena. Users are even less appreciative than programmers on the need for successors to work with their systems.

**Lack of Standardization.** This is a very common problem. Each system is developed with respect to the needs of each user. Standardization is usually a secondary consideration. But when the time comes to integrate these systems, more work might be necessary than redoing the entire system from scratch.

**Unusual Staffing Requirements.** These shops require personnel who have a wide range of orientations, from people to hardware, as well as some degree of teaching ability. Further, this area is not always considered the prime path to personal advancement.

Summing up on this point, information centers are a worthwhile practice for large corporations and organizations, but the inherent pitfalls are not to be underestimated. More significantly, they are not a substitute for the more fundamental problem of aligning corporate strategy and objectives with the work and outlook of the information systems department.

# 16

# Risk and Project Management

*If human progress had been merely a matter of leadership, we should be in Utopia today.*

—Thomas B. Reed

Risk is the complement of probability. If a project has a high probability of success, it has low risk. If the probability is low, it is a high risk project. The significance of that logic applies to information systems more than it seems. A manager cannot increase the probability of success directly. He can only do that by decreasing risk, or where the risk is too great, killing the project before it consumes any more resources. For that reason, this chapter focuses on risk. Throttle the risks, including the risks inherent in depending on decidedly poor managers, and most projects will take care of themselves.

Risk is a problem that the Roman Empire struggled with for almost 1200 years, and in all that time never quite understood it. Under the umbrella of a well-defined strategic plan, the Romans pursued many interesting projects: Greece, the Levant, Egypt, Carthage, Spain, Germany, France, and Britain among others. In the end, all was for naught. The failure has been attributed to everything from the lead content in water pitchers to the tradition of dictatorship established by Caesar Augustus, although he himself rarely abused his power.

Undoubtedly, the ultimate collapse was the result of the collective effect of many of these causes, but the one that seems to have the strongest relevance for information managers is detailed in Paul Kennedy's thesis in *The Rise and Fall of the Great Powers*, namely *overextension*.[1]

---

[1]This book begins with the year 1500, so it does not address the Roman Empire directly. Yet most of the histories on the famed empire have implied the same point.

Overextension is the expenditure of resources for objectives beyond the reach of a nation—or an organization—to sustain them. This ambition mortgages the future to attempt to pay the unaffordable bill. The debt being unaffordable, the bill collectors eventually foreclose on the organization. The quality of the leadership and management might forestall the decisive moment but cannot prevent it.

If there is a common theme with the kinds of risk inherent in the development and management of information systems, it would be the tendency to push resources beyond their known capabilities. This might appear as an underestimation of the difficulties of the requirements, or as an overestimation of the capabilities of resources, or in any other form that seeks to impose influence without sufficient clout to ensure and sustain success. Bear this in mind when taking on any major project.

## 16.1 THE TYPES OF RISK

Risk comes in many forms, both direct and indirect.[2] For information systems, direct risks are those that operate to defeat a project before it becomes operational, although sometimes the futility is not recognized until several months or even years afterward. Indirect risks are those generated by the success of a system after it becomes operational. For example, the system might invite competition that eventually reduces market share to below presystem levels. As such, this type of risk is sometimes called a case of winning the battle but losing the war.

Direct risks can be further subdivided into those that are inherent in the situation, and those that are attributable to poor management practices. The two are not poles apart. Dealing with system-inherent risks is a management responsibility, and most management practices this side of Nirvana have inherent shortcomings.

### 16.1.1 Direct Management-Type Risks

Direct management-type risks are shortcomings in management personnel and project leaders that operate with all projects. That is, the failures are likely to be repeated from system to system until the individuals change their ways. Figure 16-1 illustrates these risks and their relationships.

- *Indiscriminate Judgment.* This might be the single most common source of failure: the acceptance of a broad-brush plan to automate a require-

[2] I am indebted to the excellent text *Corporate Information Systems Management*, written by Professors James I. Cash, Jr., F. Warren McFarlan, James L. McKenney, and Michael R. Vitale, at the Harvard Graduate School of Business Administration. This text brings out the subject of risk better than any other, although what appears in this chapter is my own work and is not intended as a draw on their reputation. Their book was also the single best source of cases described in the Comparative Case Studies in appendix A.

ment without thinking through the difficulties or underestimating the investment required. The best project manager in the world cannot compensate for objectives that are beyond the realm of possibility. Even when the situation is not this dark, the product will seldom compare favorably with the aspirations.

- *Overkill*. Some tasks don't need automation, and others might be too loosely defined at the moment to benefit from a system. Subsection 16.2.2 provides a case in point.
- *Insufficient Resiliency*. Until the overwhelming bulk of the details that go into a system are nailed down tight, the management of the resources invested in the project should be resilient enough to absorb the vicissitudes of cabbages and kings, meaning the predictable discoveries of logical rot in the development work and the changing wants of the powers that be.
- *Overreliance on Consultants*. Consultants make their money up front, and seldom have to live with their failures. They should be chosen with far more care than, say, a specific brand of hardware.
- *Cost Overruns*. Cost overruns can kill a project. Even when they don't, the additional funds are usually carved from the hide of other projects. As explained in chapter 3, major cost overruns, except for after-the-fact changes to requirements, are clear evidence of bad planning management.

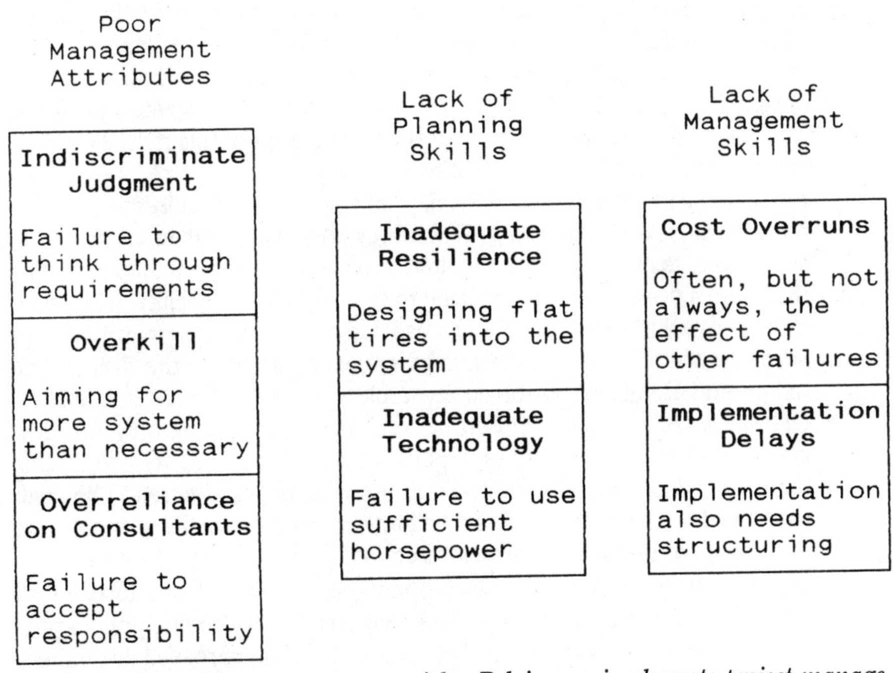


*Fig. 16-1. Direct management-type risks. Relying on inadequate project management adds to the risk of failure of any project. Sometimes these risks are acceptable; at other times they are not acceptable. But they should always be recognized.*

- *Delays*. Systems can, and usually do, take more time to develop and implement than planned. Delays can turn users against the project and perhaps against the information manager. As soon as his reputation is damaged in this way, he might find reversing the tide extremely difficult.
- *Technical Performance*. Few systems fully live up to their billing. To the extent they do not, they might be regarded as failures. When a system is unused or underused, then no matter how well it works in the technical sense, the project will often be regarded as a failure.

### 16.1.2 Direct System-Inherent Risks

System-inherent risks are those that come from circumstances beyond the control of the information manager, but they recur with sufficient frequency among different projects that managers should be leery. Figure 16-2 illustrates some of these risks.

- *Resistance to Change*. Resistance to change in most endeavors has been noted by historians, psychologists, and social analysts for millenniums. Information systems are no exception, and the literature on this issue is increasing. Although some of the literature is couched in socialistic tones, the facts suggest that passive resistance to change can defeat a system more effectively than taking an ax to a mainframe (which has happened). Unfortunately, the risk of failure from this cause is difficult to gauge in advance.
- *Changing Circumstances and Requirements*. This is inevitable in perhaps 90 percent of all projects, and a distinct possibility in the balance. Sometimes the future pace of change can be interpolated from changes during design work, or for that matter from the record of completed projects. Still, there is no foolproof way to predict the extent of this risk. This difficulty, incidentally, is one motivation for the development of large corporate databases. They are easily adapted to changing requirements.
- *Uncertainties with Emerging Technology*. As discussed in chapter 14, some aspects of emerging technology are predictable enough to schedule them into a project, but that applies to technological capability. The applications to which this technology can be put is another matter. It's a happy problem if the corporate information strategist is the first to see the potential, but will not be so favorable if a competitor sees it first.
- *Overdependence on Limited Sources of Data*. This applies only to a few systems. Here, the system is dependent on sources of data over which the organization has little control and few alternative sources. The analogy would be the definition of a small town, namely that there is only one gas station to provide the wrong directions.
- *Incompatibility*. In theory, management should be able to foresee all technical and logical incompatibilities that could serve to denigrate a proposed system. As discussed in chapter 10, this is an unreasonable expectation. There are just too many sources of incompatibility, and manufacturer's statements to the contrary must be taken with a grain of salt.

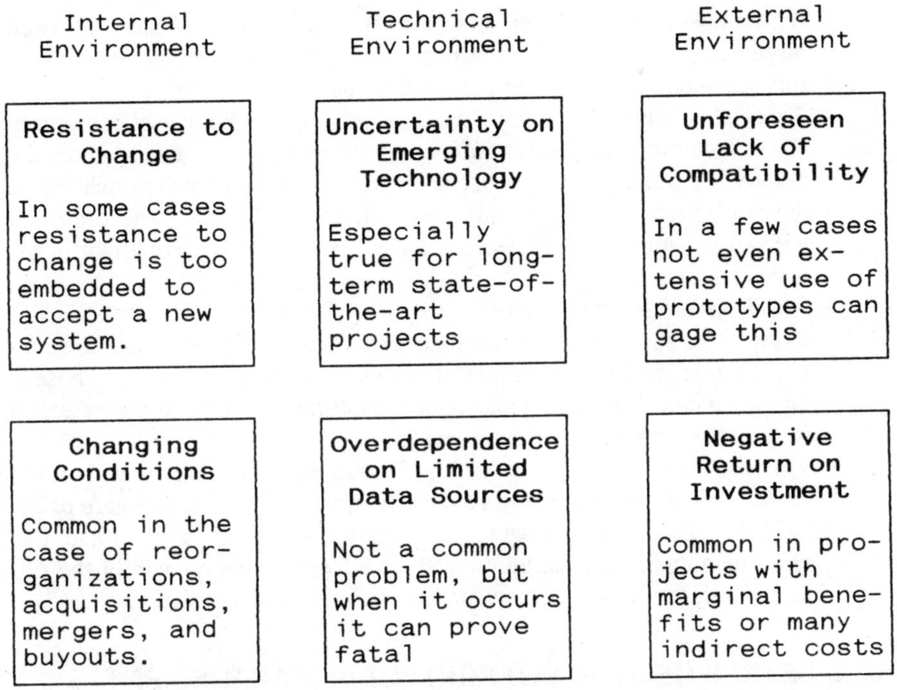


*Fig. 16-2. Direct inherent-type risks. Project risks, beyond inadequate management, are either direct or indirect. Direct risks are part and parcel of the project. Indirect risks, by contrast, are problems which come from the success of a system. It is difficult to gauge indirect risks in advance, but direct risks should be carefully considered before embarking on any project.*

- *Negative Return on Investment.* When systems lose money, the reasons are usually traceable to other risks of failure. That is, the negative return on investment is the conclusive evidence that the risks were not successfully negotiated. Yet in some cases, the anticipated return on investment might be too indirect to predict with any accuracy, or it might be marginal from the start. The difference between a $2 million system that returns 1/2 percent on investment, compared to one that loses that amount, might only be $20,000. Still the former will be considered a marginal success; the other, a drain.

### 16.1.3 Indirect Risks

Besides the direct risks described in the preceding subsection, projects sometimes encounter one or more of four indirect risks. These are difficult to predict, but they do occur.

- *Insatiability.* After a decision is made to employ computer technology to support a strategic objective, the effect can commit the company to use it more extensively than planned. Competitors can follow suit and negate the competitive edge gained, which therefore seems to demand even more systems to maintain the pace. The hardware manufacturers love this situation, but it can get old for the information manager.

- *Thresholds*. This is related to the previous item. The use of computers can reduce production costs sufficiently for other companies to enter the market. A variation on this occurs when a company invests millions to develop programs, only to find competitors paraphrasing the program, without violating any laws. Software can be protected by copyright, basic logic cannot.
- *The Regulation Mill*. Systems that simplify access to data also invite abuse. The abuse engenders public dissatisfaction, which leads to regulations to protect the consumer. These laws usually increase the cost of operating if not developing information systems, perhaps to the extent of negating the return on investment.
- *The Watershed Effect*. When too much systems technology is laid on the customer's doorstep, perhaps in an attempt to win a greater share of the market, the customers might find a way to turn the tables and use it to play one supplier against another. This effect is a microcosm of the pitfalls in balance-of-power machinations in international relations.

## 16.2 LEVELS OF RISK AND PORTFOLIO MANAGEMENT

After the nature and diversity of risk is recognized—and the argument accepted that risk management should be a prime objective of project management—the next step is to place as much of a quantitative handle on the risk as possible. Because most information shops have many projects on the drawing board or in development concurrently, the general management task becomes onc of prudent management of the set, or what the Harvard Graduate School of Business Administration calls *portfolio management*.

### 16.2.1 Levels

Subsection 2.5.3 outlined five degrees or levels of risk, ranging from negligible to insurmountable. Negligible risk means that project success is almost certain. On the other hand, insurmountable risk means that failure is inevitable. The three levels between—moderate, calculated, and precipitous—is where managers earn their pay. Figure 16-3 displays these five levels with examples.

- *Moderate Risk*. Most projects of any scope pose at least a moderate risk, primarily from the risk of poor management. System-inherent risks are few. Thus with solid management, the general risk of failure can be reduced to a negligible level, which is not always feasible. No organization ever laid claim to flawless management practice in every aspect of its work.
- *Calculated Risk*. A calculated risk means that while there is a better chance of success, the potential for failure is definitive. This means that

the system poses an inherent risk of failure, but at a level where good management practices can carry the day most of the time. In a portfolio of calculated risks, almost certainly some of them will fail, even if the ghost of Herman Hollerith were at the helm. Still, the better information managers will keep that number down.

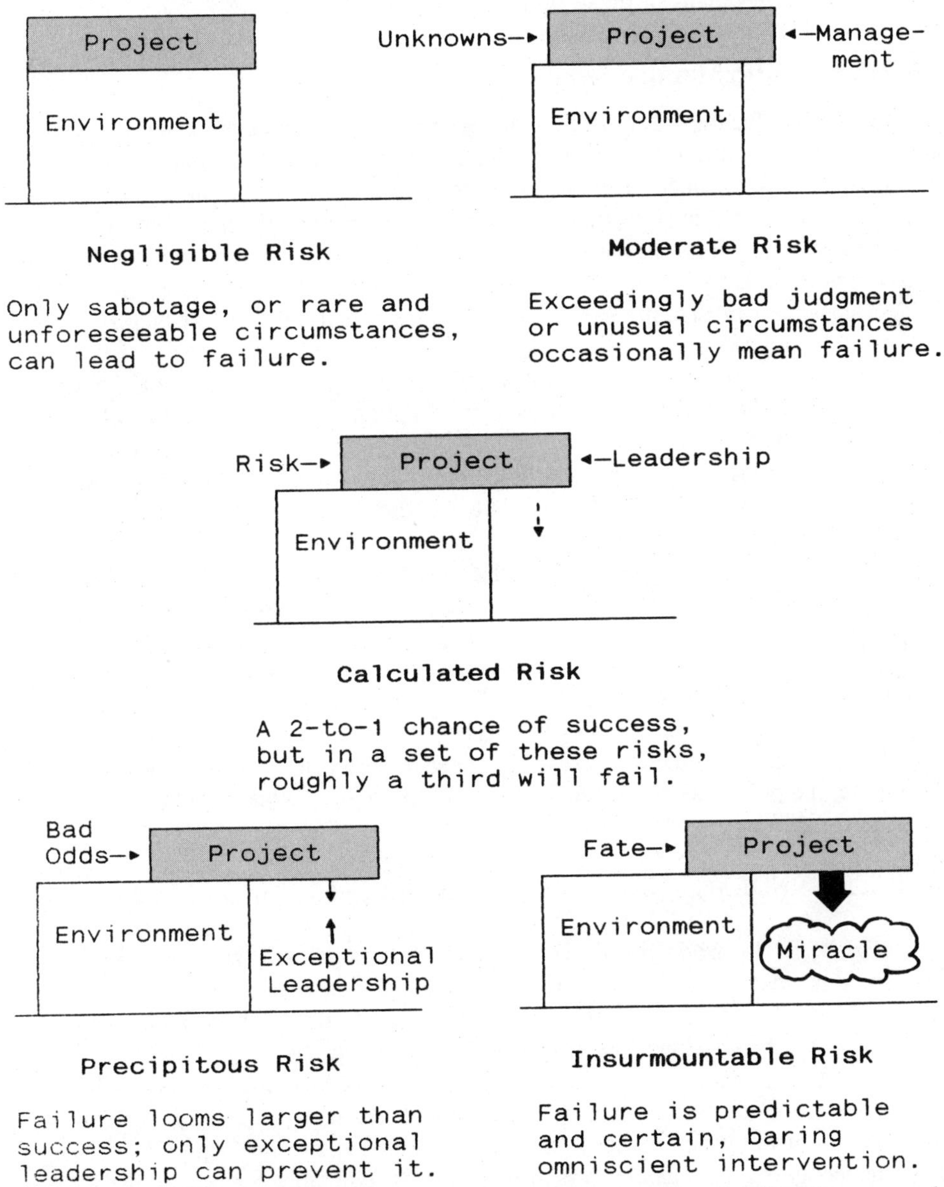


*Fig. 16-3. Levels of risk. Although risk, as an application of probability theory, can be measured in percentiles, it is more practical to think of it by levels: negligible, moderate, calculated, precipitous, and insurmountable. Understanding calculated vs. precipitous risk is the most important aspect for information managers.*

- *Precipitous Risk*. Precipitous risk means that there is a greater chance of failure than success. The inherent risks are obvious, and the only possibility of reversing these odds is to staff the project with an exceptional leader-manager. Even then, no organization can hope to succeed in more than half the projects entailing this level of risk. In short, no portfolio can tolerate too many of these projects.

### 16.2.2 Portfolio Management

Investment Strategy 101 teaches the essence of portfolio management: put an earning edge on the mix of investments so that there is little chance of being wiped out, a solid chance of obtaining a steady return on investment, and an outside chance of making a fortune. In terms of information systems, this translates into ensuring little chance of departmental failure, earning a solid reputation for systems that really work, and leaving the door open for the potential for an occasional spectacular success. Figure 16-4 presents a rudimentary picture of this portfolio approach.

Is there a simple formula to figure out what would be a good mix of risks in a systems portfolio? Not really. Heuristic reasoning does not lend itself to formulas, but the latter can be used to generate some rough ideas. The first task is to select the criterion for evaluation. Is it: dollar investment, return on investment, perceived strategic value, irrespective of the dollar figures (perhaps due to indirect benefits), or survival?

Whatever the criterion is, the simplest mathematical model is to assume that negligible risk is no risk at all; that moderate risk leaves a 90 percent chance of success; calculated risks offer a 65 percent success rate; and precipitous risks give a 35 percent chance of success. Insurmountable risk, by definition has a zero chance of success. Next, the sum of planned projects and those in development are assigned an arbitrary index value of 100 points, and the level of risk for each is assigned. Then, depending on the criterion or criteria for evaluation, the points are proportioned among the projects, which leads directly to a simple formula for predicting the rate of success.

$$\text{RATE} = \text{INDEX}_{NR} + \text{INDEX}_{MR}*.90 + \text{INDEX}_{CR}*.65 + \text{INDEX}_{PR}*.35$$

$\text{INDEX}_{NR}$ is the proportional share of the 100 index points assigned to negligible risk projects, $\text{INDEX}_{MR}$ is the proportional share for moderate risk projects, $\text{INDEX}_{CR}$ is the proportional share for calculated risk projects, and $\text{INDEX}_{PR}$ is the proportional share for precipitous risk projects.

TABLE 16-1 provides some examples of using this formula. However, the reader is cautioned that this is a vast oversimplification, is a good example of when not to attempt automation, except possibly with a simple spreadsheet. The knowledge experts can be put to work, and predictably they can develop algorithms that require the input of at least 20 parameters per project. Next, values have to be factored for the stage of development for each project. Then,

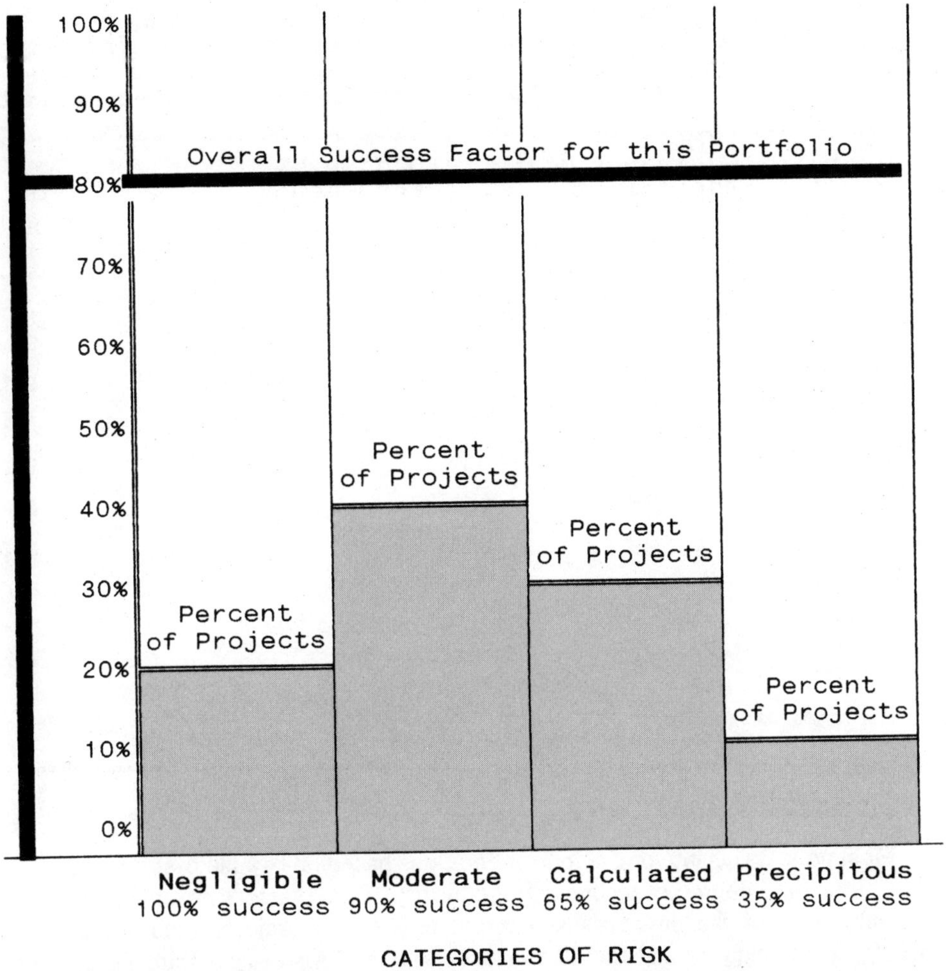


*Fig. 16-4. Portfolio approach to risk management. Similar to balancing risks in an investment portfolio, risks with systems projects should also be balanced. As information managers push MIS technology to new limits, the risks increase, making portfolio management even more important.*

a simple criterion is abandoned in favor of a complex calculation that takes five or six criteria into account. Then the program would produce a number that was within 3 percentage points of the calculation made with the simple formula, complete with a warning that the result was considered to have an error range of plus or minus five points.

## 16.3 PROJECT ORIENTATIONS AND SETTINGS

Before the idea of risk management can be put to work, the types of projects first need to be categorized.

*Table 16-1. Risk portfolio calculations. With arbitrary percentiles assigned to various risk levels, calculation of various portfolios provides an overall risk level. An information manager would want to think twice before dropping below the 75 percent level, and twice more before rolling the dice at any level below that.*

| Distribution of Risks with Respect to Criteria Selected by Management | | | | Portfolio Success Factor |
|---|---|---|---|---|
| Negligible | Moderate | Calculated | Precipitous | [Maximum = 100] |
| 90% | 10% | --- | --- | 99.0 |
| 80% | 10% | 10% | --- | 95.5 |
| 70% | 20% | 10% | --- | 94.5 |
| 60% | 25% | 15% | --- | 92.3 |
| 50% | 30% | 15% | 5% | 88.5 |
| 40% | 30% | 20% | 10% | 83.5 |
| 30% | 30% | 30% | 10% | 80.0 |
| 20% | 40% | 30% | 10% | 79.0 |
| 10% | 40% | 30% | 20% | 72.5 |
| --- | 50% | 30% | 20% | 71.5 |

### 16.3.1 The Four Orientations.

Most projects fall into one of four orientations based on two factors: degree of definition, and degree of technological difficulty. These factors are more-or-less subgroups of the direct risks inherent in systems projects (subsection 16.1.2). Some analysts add the size or scope of the project as a third factor because risk increases with size, all other things being equal.

**Degree of Definition.** A high or fixed degree of definition means that requirements are well defined in terms of what data is required and how that data is to be processed to generate equally well-defined outputs, which is common with transaction-based systems. Degree of definition is not common with many decision support systems, which can be said to have low or fluid definition. A fluid definition means that the present method of meeting requirements involves hunches, intuition, or judgment calls. To the extent that these practices are unavoidable, the logic of the automation must lean toward a heuristic model (subsection 12.1.3), which might or might not work in practice.

**Degree of Technology Difficulty.** The degree of technological difficulty does not refer to the number of computers and other items to be used, but to the extent emerging technology must be used or proven technology must be applied in ways that have not been tested before. The use of multiple-processor computers would constitute the use of emerging technology for many organiza-

| Degree of Technology Required | Degree of Definition of Requirements: FIXED | Degree of Definition of Requirements: FLUID |
|---|---|---|
| ROUTINE | Conceptually simple projects that permit explicit scheduling and accurate cost estimates. They rarely exceed a moderate level of risk. | Probably the most common orientation for information systems. And though the technology is routine, the lack of definition imposes considerable risk of failure. |
| PROBATIVE | Systems here have long standing requirements that older technology could not sustain. As such, the risks are calculated. Many projects will succeed; but some will fail. | Projects in this catgory are sometimes described as "heroic." The potential for strategic gain is high, but the risk of failure outweighs the chance of success. |

*Source:* Derived from material in James I. Cash, Jr., *et al.*, *Corporate Information Systems Management* (Homewood, Illinois: Irwin, 1988), 433.

*Fig. 16-5. Four orientations of projects. Most projects are shaped by two key parameters: degree of definition and degree of technological difficulty. The combination of these two factors provides four polemic orientations, although the size of the project will often affect the significance of one orientation or another.*

tions, as it requires new programming techniques in return for obtaining supercomputer processing speed at a comparatively low cost.

Figure 16-5 illustrates the four orientations generated by these two factors, admitting that some projects occupy a middle ground on one or both of those factors.

- *Fixed Definition + Routine Technology.* These are the conceptually simple projects that lend themselves to explicit scheduling and a minimum need to coordinate with users. They rarely entail risks greater than the moderate level, and often lend themselves to implementation with proprietary software.
- *Fixed Definition + Probative Technology.* Projects with this orientation are not common, and those that occur have a tendency to place too much emphasis on using a high degree of technology to gain a measure of efficiency. Whatever the case might be, probative technology usually carries with it at least a calculated risk.
- *Fluid Definition + Routine Technology.* This might be the most common orientation for information systems, other than those that emphasize

transactions. Yet the risks are nearly as strong as those in the fixed definition/probative technology orientation. Although technology might give the appearance of awesome difficulties, at least it is a matter of discovering how to make technology work. When it comes to working with users who do not fully understand what they want, the route of discovery keeps changing course.

- *Fluid Definition – Probative Technology.* Projects in this orientation are inherently precipitous and sometimes insurmountable. Only the potential for a high return on investment warrants these projects, and then only if the investment itself does not consume too much of the systems dollar.

### 16.3.2 Settings

System projects occur in at least eight different settings, and in general, each setting affects the level of risk, sometimes lowering it, sometimes increasing it.

**A New System.** The discussion on risks to this point has presumed a new system, and therefore it offers the baseline for comparing other settings.

**System Enhancement.** In general, the risk level should not change. Inserting an enhancement on an existing system often poses difficult logical or compatibility problems, but this is offset by the narrower focus of the project.

**System Expansion.** An expansion extends a proven aspect of a system, and is therefore well defined and only rarely involves probative technology. If the risk exceeds moderate, then either the project involves more than an expansion, or unusual factors have been introduced.

**System Replacement.** In theory, a replacement system should present a lower level of risk than a new system. The experience gained with the old system should be a major asset, combined with the fact that most of the new features will have been suggested by definitive inadequacies and thus also be well defined.

**Synthesis or Database Integration.** A synthesis is normally one of the most difficult kinds of projects to manage (as described in section 1.7). Database integrations are less of a risk only to the extent that the work can concentrate on the database. All things considered, finding one of these merger-type integrations posing anything less than a calculated risk is rare.

**Excerpt Integration.** An excerpt integration is probably the simplest possible project and it lends itself to prototyping. The risk, if any, is that after copies of the data are merged, the intended programming will not work, especially if it requires extensive heuristic logic. In a word, the mechanics of this merger rarely pose a serious risk, but the results might prove disappointing.

**Interface Integration.** If the interface is a straightforward exchange or transmission of data, any risk can be carefully gauged with a prototype trial. If the interface attempts to operate as a synthesis, the level of risk is precipitous at best.

**Standardization.** These risks run the gamut. The level of risk in any given situation is largely a function of the extent of the differences between the existing units or aspects and the standardized replacement. Replacing an array of microcomputers that were already compatible, with a standard model from one manufacturer, seldom poses any risk. Demanding that every program in a large organization be written in one programming language is another matter.

## 16.4 LEADERSHIP IN A MANAGEMENT ENVIRONMENT

There are two positions in corporations that need definitive leadership and management skill. One is the CEO or his equivalent. The other is a project manager. The second is often more difficult than the first, due to an inherent lack of control over resources. Yet for information systems, the cumulative results of their work are the main contributor to the successful strategic use of informational resources. In short, if there is any one thing an information manager can do to improve his standing in court, it is to pick good project managers and then make a special effort to support them.

### 16.4.1 The Nature of the Problem

The management of a project differs markedly from the management of an information systems department. The former is evaluated in terms of definitive, measurable criteria. For example, does the system meet requirements, and if not, by how much does it miss the mark? The latter, by contrast, is an ongoing operation that is line-management oriented. More to the point, the head of that department seldom works as project manager. Instead, individuals are commonly assigned to this task, often without the necessary training or experience of working with users.

If the information systems department is organized—and continually reorganized—by project lines, the practice should not hurt projects. But when the department is structured along more traditional lines aligned with job descriptions, project management often suffers. In this environment, the projects often become unwelcome step children, whose existence tends to get in the way of ongoing management tasks. Some CIO's have solved this problem by a structure similar to the matrix of line departments and product managers. Unfortunately that model interfaces two kinds of ongoing management. A project usually requires more intense, personal leadership than does an established product.

Other information managers try the user-orientation approach, with different departments aligned with different divisions of the corporation or organization. Unless these departments concentrate on one major project at a time, the conflicts between ongoing line management and project leadership will continue to surface.

### 16.4.2 The Kitchen-Cabinet Structure

One way to bypass the line-management vs. project-management conflict is to adapt the kitchen cabinet structure on an ad hoc basis, which means assigning a mix of specific skills to each project, part time or full time. A team of this

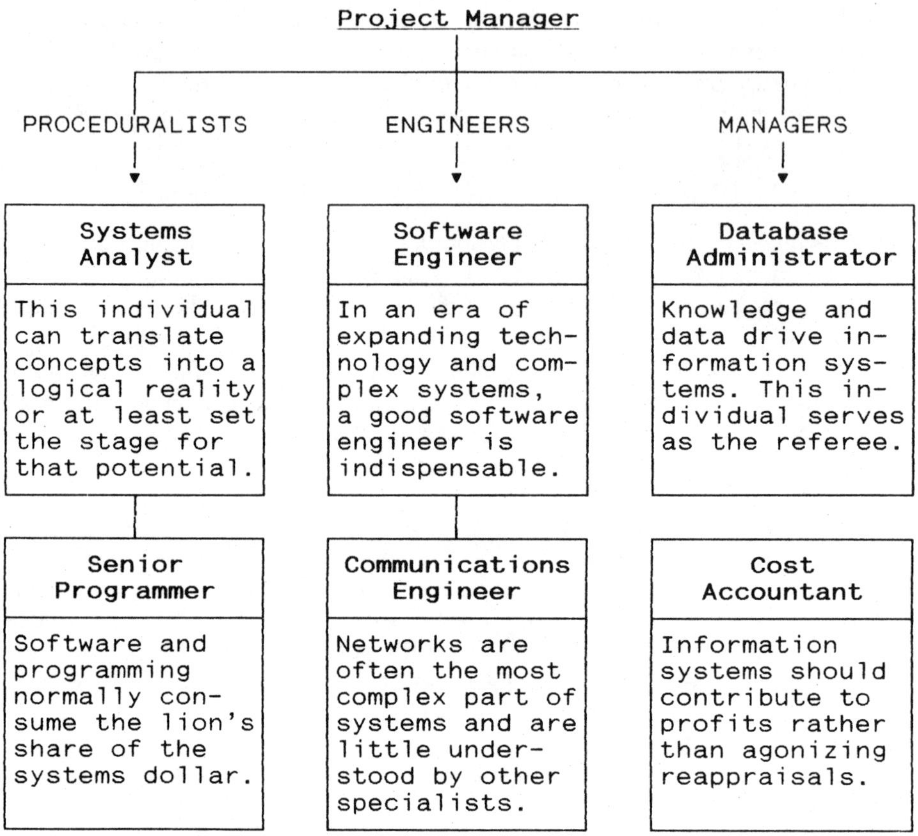


*Fig. 16-6. Kitchen cabinets for project management. The complexity of information system projects demands both leadership and technical management. These skills do not always mix well in the same individual. Because leadership is something of an indispensable element in high-risk projects, the project manager must often rely on a team of experts. Although these experts need not report directly to the project manager, failing to consult with them frequently would be a mistake.*

caliber can handle the major problems that are likely to crop up in any project. Figure 16-6 portrays this team.

- *Systems Analyst.* This term is becoming passé, replaced by software engineers, systems architects, configuration managers, and the like. Unfortunately, these newer skills have grown too technical in many cases to be effective in the give-and-take of the negotiations between potential users and the reality of systems. Sometimes the manager himself can and does take on this role by default, at least at the macro level.
- *Software Engineer.* This is the individual who, if he or she is good and the design is within technical reach, can turn aspirations into reality, especially those that involve probative technological aspirations. The best of them avoid the need for a separate specialist in hardware.

- *Communications/Network Specialist.* A manager must rely on this specialist in a system or integration that requires a complex network, though he or she is probably more of an electronics engineer than a software logician.
- *Senior Programmer/Database Design Specialist.* In theory, a good software engineer is also a good programmer, but database design has become a specialty in its own right, and a complex program often requires its own software architect for logical and integrated flow. Further, circumstances can force the software engineer to concentrate on the mechanical configuration of the system and its testing.
- *Database Administrator (DBA).* In theory, the database design specialist also can serve as the DBA, but the former should be a superb technician. This administrator, for reasons mentioned in section 4.7, should be the most persevering, resilient mid-level manager money can hire. Further, the database design structure is a one-time task, the management of it is a career. The DBA often continues with the system after it becomes operational.
- *A Really Good Cost Accountant.* The development costs of the largest systems can exceed $5 billion. That fact suffices for commentary here.

A recent survey published in *Information Systems Management* (Spring 1988) found that management information systems (MIS) departments in the bottom half of the Fortune 1000 industrial companies averaged 50 employees. A reasonable interpolation of these findings would suggest that 95 percent of the largest 5,000 companies of all types in the United States have MIS departments with at least 10 employees.

Presuming then, that in the smaller companies within this range, some personnel will have multiple skills workable for smaller systems, and further presuming that these top 5,000 organizations (plus all major governmental and other nonprofit agencies) account for 93 percent or more of the total information systems dollar spent in the country, the projected key staff is within the reach of most readers of this book. For small organizations, the skills can at least be obtained part time or by contract.

An interesting question is whether this kitchen cabinet approach would be worthwhile for the information manager with respect to developing a strategic information plan for the entire organization, or at least working out the details set forth in objectives laid down by the CEO or a steering committee. If the units of this strategy will be strongly linked, the answer is yes. But if the components will remain more or less independent, then it probably would be a waste of time, except perhaps as an internal review board.

### 16.4.3 Some Attributes of Good Project Managers

The literature on what comprises good project management is extensive. Some of the common attributes noted are:

**Ability to Live with Ambiguity.** A good system might operate like clockwork, but that is not true of project managers. Constant change and dealing with ambiguities until all details can be resolved is a way of life for all but fixed definition/routine technology projects.

**A Sense of Commitment (and Deadlines).** Notwithstanding the ambiguity, a sense of meeting deadlines is imperative, even if they are missed. Deadlines take a commitment and drive that might not always sit well with the personnel assigned to work on the project.

**Orientation to Planning and Problem Solving.** At the beginning of a project, the majority of a project manager's time will be spent on planning, but changes rapidly until about 90 percent of his time is spent on tracking and problem solving. These attributes do not always occur in the same person.

**Ability to Gain Commitment from Users.** He has little or no control over them, yet must gain their support and commitment before the inevitable changes to requirements lay waste to the project.

**Keeping Superiors Informed.** Communications with superiors is a lot tougher job than it sounds, even when the individual does not suffer from what is called *skilled incompetence*—the ability to cover up shortcomings and failures. Timely reporting of major and potentially major problems is sometimes the only thing that can salvage a project with inherent risks.

## 16.5 CONTRACT VS. IN-HOUSE APPROACHES

The vast majority of systems are developed by some combination of in-house resources and contracts, even if the latter comprises only manufacturer support and maintenance of hardware. But any attempt to gain a consensus on when and where to rely on contractors for a more substantial part of the work is doomed, even when the answers are rendered in abstract terms. One information manager has nothing but kind words to say for his contractors, another has only language that is unfit to print. Compounding this problem is the variable potential for relying on contracts at the different stages of systems development and operation.

About all that can be said with any chance for wide acceptance is to start with in-house resources, and then make exceptions for the contractual alternative to the extent the latter offers sufficient advantages to offset the generally higher cost and the loss of control the organization will likely experience. That advice, plus $.60, will buy a cup of coffee.

Still, one point can be discussed in more detail, and that is the purchase of a computer service firm to implement and perhaps operate a system. This has been tried on a few occasions with mixed results. The most notable example was the purchase of Electronic Data Systems by General Motors. The largest manufacturing company in the United States spent $700 million to get rid of H. Ross Perot when the company recognized that he did not fit into the way they did business there.

An outright purchase of a service firm comes packaged with major conflicts and inefficiencies. For example, if the firm is purchased for expanding the in-house staff, not all the personnel and other assets will prove ideally suited to the organization's needs. If the purchase is intended to expand corporate business, then work on an internal system will conflict with the primary business of selling new services.

If the service firm was acquired as an adjunct of a major merger, it could be put to work on a system as a project of opportunity to make use of the assets. That sounds good on paper, but systems are expensive propositions and should not be developed unless they are clearly necessary. And if they are necessary, waiting for an opportunistic acquisition is hardly the best approach to implementation. To this result must be added a question: what is to be done with the acquired assets after the project is completed?

In short, the acquisition of a service firm to develop one or more systems, as an alternative to a contract arrangement, is normally a serious mistake, and therefore should be considered only as a court of last resort.

## 16.6 APPLIED PRINCIPLES OF INFORMATION MANAGEMENT

One set of principles per book is sometimes one set too much. Two sets would be intolerable. To avoid that problem, the principles developed in section 2.2 can be applied with minor rewording to the management of systems themselves. Figure 16-7 outlines these applications.

- *Objective*. The principle of the objective for information systems is to, ''direct the information resources toward objectives that will make a significant improvement in the implementation of policy, at an acceptable cost.'' The rewording for management of a system itself would be, ''direct the resources of the organization to implement and manage a system as it was intended to operate.'' That is, the system itself is the objective, and the word ''resources'' is stripped of its adjective ''informational.'' This brings personnel to center stage.
- *Configuration*. The information systems principle here suggests ''configuring the elements of a system . . . to facilitate attaining the objectives of the system without undue risk of compromising information to the detriment of those objectives.'' The rewording would be, ''configure and schedule the organizational resources to facilitate the implementation or management of system without undue risk of depleting those resources beyond what is essential.'' The rewording here is self-explanatory, but the intent can be more difficult to put into practice than configuring the system itself.
- *Initiative*. The information systems wording is, ''ensure that a system provides a sufficient and timely view of information to make a significant difference in the conduct of business, the share of the marketplace gained, or the provision of services.'' The colloquial equivalent would be, ''to stay on top of things.'' The application to systems management therefore would be, ''take whatever initiative is necessary to ensure that the intended system is implemented.'' The point is, most if not all systems will encounter unanticipated hurdles, either from flaws in the

design, inadequate resources, competing and perhaps higher priority demands for the same resources, or from any one of many other sources of management difficulty. When this happens, the successful manager takes whatever initiative is required to see the project through, if it is at all possible to do so, and without violating laws or introducing unethical practices.

- *Resiliency.* The systems wording is, "organize and direct the application of resources to effect a resilient superiority of information sufficient to prevail in the marketplace or in the provision of services." A useful rewording for management would be, "manage organization resources in such a manner as to keep an implementation on track or an existing system operating in spite of inevitable difficulties and obstacles that will be encountered." This rewording nearly alloys the principles of configuration and initiative as applied to systems management, and a good case can be made for substituting a single but expanded version of the princi-

<table>
<tr><td colspan="2">

PRINCIPLES RELATED TO PURPOSE AND STYLE

OBJECTIVE. Direct the resources of the organization to implement and manage a system as it was intended to operate.

SIMPLICITY. Manage and direct resources with the simplest possible orientation and directives.

</td></tr>
<tr><td>

PRINCIPLES RELATED TO INTEGRATION AND INTERIOR LINES

CONFIGURATION. Configure and schedule the organizational resources to facilitate the implementation or management of the system without undue risk of depleting resources beyond what is essential.

RESILIENCY. Manage organizational resources in such manner as to keep an implementation on track or an existing system operating in spite of inevitable difficulties and obstacles that will be encountered.

</td><td>

PRINCIPLES RELATED TO MANAGEMENT AND LEADERSHIP

RESPONSIBILITY. In the planning, development, or operations management of any system. fix general responsibility on one individual, and vest him or her with sufficient control over the necessary resources to effect the objectives. *No change.*

INITIATIVE. Take whatever initiative is necessary to ensure that the intended system is implemented.

</td></tr>
</table>

*Fig. 16-7. Applied principles of project management. An organization is itself a system, of which automated systems are inner systems. Therefore, the strategic principles for information systems also can be adapted to project management. This chart compares the original and the reworded versions.*

ple of resiliency. But there is a difference. Configuration applies to arrangement and scheduling, resiliency applies to sufficient resources to take up the slack.

- *Simplicity.* The systems wording is, ''design systems with the simplest possible configuration and directives for use.'' Applied to management, the principle would say, ''manage and direct resources with the simplest possible organization and directives.'' Simplicity and interior lines are nearly synonymous. To the extent management imposes artificial boundaries on its resources is the extent to which the team effort will lack the resilience to deal successfully with changing requirements and other risks.
- *Responsibility.* The sixth principle requires no rewording. It already addresses management, ''in the development, implementation, or the management of any system, fix general responsibility on one individual, and vest him or her with sufficient control over the necessary resources to effect the objectives.'' The argument can be made that given this principle, the first five are superfluous for management purposes. Perhaps so, but responsibility does not necessarily encompass management skill.

# 17

# Prototypes

*I fear explanations explanatory of things explained.*

—Abraham Lincoln

Almost every manufacturer builds a prototype of a new product before putting it into production. Further, the introduction of a new product is usually preceded by a market test in representative areas. Yet for reasons that are not always clear, many system developers assume they are exempt from this step. Department of Defense Directive 5000.29 and Standard 2167 go to the point of discouraging prototypes by insisting on complete specifications for systems before any work is done (although an amendment to the standard provides some relief).

Perhaps the reason for this reluctance stems from the belief that extensive documentation, structured programming, and thorough testing obviate the need. Or perhaps it comes from an attitude that prototyping for an automated system is impractical, i.e., the only satisfactory prototype for a system is the system itself. This view concedes that testing should be concurrent with the development of modules, but that's about it.

The results of many projects suggest otherwise. What often happens during development is that major changes put the design and test plans into disarray. Some of these changes are the result of insights gained during the detailed work of development, others from a realization of inadequate design, and still others from changing requirements. As deadlines cannot be postponed indefinitely, compromises are made and the project suffers. In many cases, building and using a rudimentary prototype to gain those insights before investing in the whole nine yards would have been less expensive in time and money.

The rationale goes back to the argument posited in chapter 3, namely that the development of most systems adheres to a power curve. Normally, a handful of parameters will suggest if not dictate the appropriate design and structure for a system. A prototype can be built around those parameters and tested, although experimentation might be a more accurate word. Moreover, established techniques can cut the prototyping work to a small fraction of the cost of a full-scale system. Even this cost could be offset by savings generated by early identification of many problems and errors. Finally, some but not all prototypes can be used as a framework for the intended system.

So where is the appropriate place to discuss prototyping; with management subjects, or with technology and wherewithal? Stephen J. Andriole, in the *Handbook of Decision Support Systems*, answered the question in the simplest of terms: prototypes are a state of mind. He went on to explain that the reluctance to take this road lacked fundamental rationale, except perhaps in the earliest days of computer technology. In that era, just about everything was a prototype.

To expand on this point of view, if software testing begins with an attitude, prototyping should be a way of life with systems because prototyping precedes the testing part of development. Further, while testing is socially acceptable, if not *de rigueur*, prototyping is something of a social sin and often considered beneath the dignity of professionals. A commitment is needed to reverse this course of events. Ingenuity is also necessary to gain insight with a minimum of expense and effort. That is why prototyping appears in this part of the book. One caveat: a prototype is not always necessary or appropriate. This situation occurs in at least three instances:

1) *Productivity Software*. Adapting proven productivity software to meet requirements in a parallel environment needs no prototype. Good analysis is important to pick the right package and a good warranty to cover the unforeseen glitches.
2) *Small Projects*. Although any new system can in theory benefit from a prototype, the smaller the project is, the fewer the details and the fewer the number of individuals that will be involved. Small projects increase the ability to foresee some problems, and decrease the difficulties of dealing with the balance. At a certain point, in size not time, proceeding directly with development makes more sense.
3) *Program Generators*. The use of program generators can obviate the need for prototyping because development is reduced to a minimum. Put another way, the first crack at development can be considered as the prototype, which can then be refined with subsequent passes.

## 17.1 PURPOSE AND APPROACHES

The usual purpose of a prototype is to test—before development—any aspect of a system, if the feasibility is in question. The occasional alternative is to test several known feasible options to decide what offers the most advantages in practice. As prototyping aims only at what might prove infeasible, there is seldom any need to check on the balance. This situation lends itself to a variety of approaches. Figure 17-1 illustrates some of them:

| APPROACH | DESCRIPTION | APPLICABILITY |
|---|---|---|
| Logical versus Technical Focus | This approach focuses only on the algorithmic or on the technical aspects of a project. The former can include database structures. | Useful when the logical and technical aspects are comparatively independent, especially when the feasibility of only one is at issue. |
| Cross-Section | Combines logical and technical aspects but only on a cross-section of the project. | Excellent for testing interfaces between stations or accessing a specified database. |
| Phase Prototype | Starts with the core of a project and expands to dependent features in phases. Similar to top-down structuring. | A good means of testing a complex concept when the relationship with or among the dependent modules is not clear. |
| Microcosm | Tests an entire system in microcosm, relying extensively on simulation, such as a spreadsheet model. | An economical means of testing a complex system or project in order to uncover major flaws. |

*Fig. 17-1. Approaches to Prototypes. The term* prototype *connotes a model of a manufactured product for testing prior to mass production. This interpretation would restrict prototypes for systems software and other software products that are intended for wide distribution. Still, whenever the feasibility of any aspect of any system is in question, one or more prototype techniques are available to test it. This chart shows some of the available approaches.*

- *Logical vs. Technical Prototypes*. A logical prototype focuses only on logical or algorithmic processing, which can include the structure of the database. A technical prototype addresses primarily the capabilities and capacities of hardware and communications networks, and possibly systems software, under the anticipated operating conditions for the intended system. For example, a support system will normally succeed or fail based on its logic. By contrast, a communications network tends to depend more on the quality, and quantity, of its technical capabilities.
- *Cross-Section Prototype*. A cross-section prototype covers a slice of a system, to include both logical and technical aspects. A good example would be the exchange of software between systems. The communications must be able to transmit the software, which must then meet the recipient's requirements.
- *Phased Prototype*. A phased prototype uses a sequence of increasingly detailed tests, with the design of later phases depending on the results of

the earlier. The logic closely follows interactive support systems, and in some cases the latter could be developed for the express purpose of prototyping specific applications.

- *Microcosm Prototype*. A microcosm prototype mimics an entire system, but may rely on simulation techniques and only a small sample of the anticipated load. This is not the same thing as top-down structured testing. Here the entire system is tested in microcosm, although some writers might substitute the term *pilot*.

Irrespective of the approach, prototyping is not development. The aim, as with support systems, is effectiveness not efficiency. To carry this line of reasoning one step further, prototyping could be considered a special case of support system technology. The decision maker seeks trends and probabilities for success. When the intended system is too ambiguous or too broad to develop a prototype with reasonable expense and effort, then perhaps the wisest course of action would be to scrap the project altogether. Development is not the place for research.

## 17.2 ORIENTATIONS

Most prototypes gravitate to one of four orientations based on two factors. The first factor is ***degree-of-simulation***. The second factor is ***degree-of-load***. Simulation means the extent to which the mechanics, but not the intent, of the prototype veer from those that will be used in the intended system. Load means the extent or percentage of anticipated data and traffic that will be tested. Figure 17-2 depicts these four orientations. In a sense, the sampling size could be considered a special case of simulation, but there is a major difference. The sample load can be increased, whereas a simulation cannot readily be brought closer to the actual system.

Now what is meant by simulation is modelling, and modelling has degrees. For example, the physiology of a human cell can be simulated by a mathematical model, programmed on a computer, and then manipulated to test the effects of external factors, which are themselves simulated by other mathematical models. A lesser simulation would use animals whose physiology, with respect to the item at issue, resembled human tissue. When humans are used, the simulation is eliminated, although the sampling size might not pass muster.

Similarly, various aspects of systems can be simulated by models, as described in section 17.3. Irrespective of the application, be it medicine, systems, or whatever, increased simulation runs the risk of failing to address all the factors that affect outcomes in the targeted operation. That is, prototype results tend to be rosier than justified.

Loading, or sampling, also has degrees, although what constitutes a low or high sample is relative to the aspect being tested. Statistical theory holds that when samples are truly objective and comprise a random slice of the population at issue, a glimmer of what is happening begins to come into focus with a mere 30 trials. At 300, the predictions offer 95 percent reliability; at 1600, the 99 percent level is reached.

| Degree of Load \ Degree of Simulation | LOW | HIGH |
|---|---|---|
| HIGH | Low Simulation High Load<br>The purpose here is usually to test peak loading under conditions where the simulation is not likely to suppress compounding errors. | High Simulation High Load<br>This orientation comes closest to the actual system, and yields the most accurate findings. It is also the most costly form of prototype. |
| LOW | Low Simulation Low Load<br>This is useful for testing logic in combination with hardware, data storage mediums, and network communications. | High Simulation Low Load<br>This orientation is furthest from the intended system, and is limited to testing record structures, algorithms, and other logical aspects. |

*Fig. 17-2. Four orientations for prototypes. Prototypes rarely duplicate an entire system. Some form or degree of modelling is almost always employed. The two key parameters of modelling are degree-of-simulation and degree-of-load. These two factors yield four orientations for prototypes. Interpretation of prototype results should take the orientation used into consideration.*

Unfortunately, this ideal doesn't apply to all experimentation. For example, if a cause-and-effect relationship is likely to occur only once in 10,000 trials, then either a much larger sample is needed, or the problem must be intensified artificially so that it occurs more frequently. The latter, incidentally, is a common practice in experiments with suspected carcinogens. Similarly, when the possible outcomes in a system number in the thousands, the test load for a prototype should be larger just to qualify for minimum acceptability. When the feasibility issue is the effect of overloading, the test loading should be higher than the anticipated traffic. With these caveats in mind, the four orientations can be considered in more detail:

- *Low Load - Minimum Simulation.* This orientation closely resembles the project but relies on sampling. It works well for transaction-type systems when there is little need to simulate the algorithms, and most of the processing falls into a few predictable categories.

- *Low Load - High Simulation*. For obvious reasons, this is the riskiest orientation. Still, it is often useful in phased prototypes for complex systems or merger-type integrations. If failure is encountered at this level, the project almost certainly will prove to be a debacle.
- *High Load - Minimum Simulation*. In contrast to the previous orientation, this one presents the least risk. However, it differs from development in that only the aspect at issue is tested. This approach is particularly useful in communications. The prototype can focus on what is likely to prove the heaviest traffic between established stations.
- *High Load - High Simulation*. This approach is handy when testing for peak loading is imperative, but fielding the intended system on a trial basis would be prohibitively expensive. A good example would be a prototype for distributive processing, and is the basis for the proposed model described in technical note 6 in appendix B.

## 17.3 TECHNIQUES

The extent to which high simulation and low loading can be tolerated in a prototype is the extent to which ingenuity and shortcuts are available. A few possibilities are explained.

**Bare Bones.** This technique almost parallels the front end of top-down programming. The entire system is thrown together in skeleton form, with the object of identifying glaring errors. You would be surprised to see how much of a system can be put together in a short time if the general structure is emphasized and the processing details overlooked at first. Then, as problems begin to surface, short programs are written and tested. Overall, this technique is sloppy and probably the antithesis of a good system. Yet it is the way first-rate minds work when wrestling with a complex problem. The practitioners of this technique can figure out if they are on the right road or not in a short time.

**The LAN Spreadsheet.** This technique uses 3-dimensional spreadsheet software on a local area network. The former permits multiple spreadsheets to be accessed and linked to each other. The latter simulates distributive processing and networks. Figure 17-3 illustrates this approach. As described in technical note 10 of appendix B, the spreadsheet is a handy microcosm of the entire software development environment. This technique merely puts that attribute to work.

**Microcomputer DBMS.** This is a variation on the spreadsheet option, with or without a LAN. It simulates a mainframe or minicomputer system on micros by way of low loading and maximum use of database management software to create and modify the database structure.

## 17.4 ORGANIZATIONAL OPTIONS

Prototyping need not always be done in the information systems shop. At least four other options are worth considering, some more so than others.

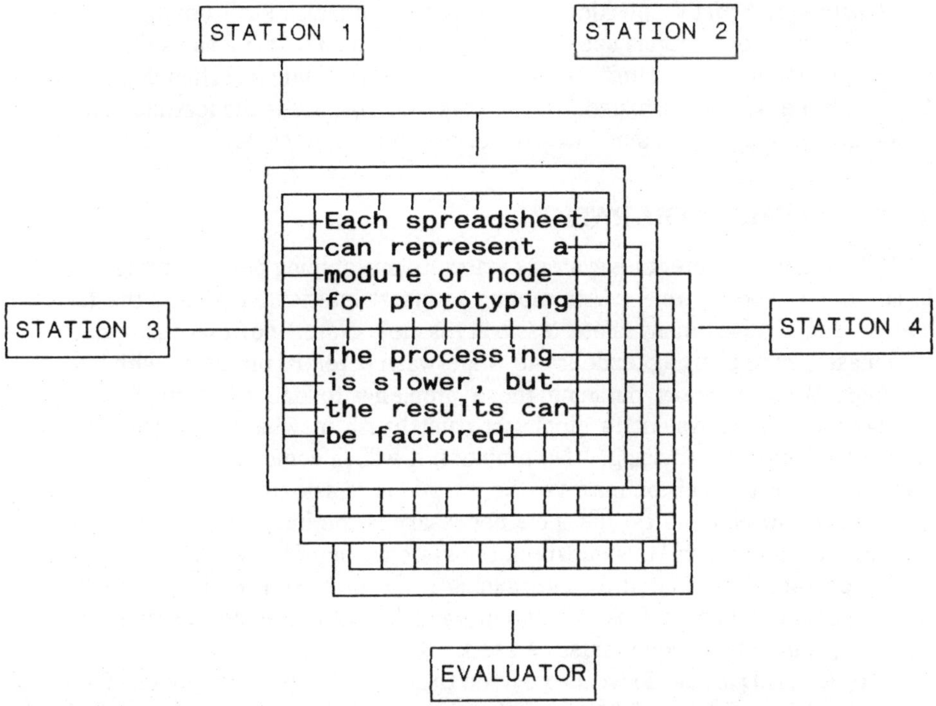


*Fig. 17-3. The spreadsheet as a prototype technique. The spreadsheet is probably the simplest and the least expensive means to prototype a system, especially if the so-called three-dimensional models loaded in a network are used. Spreadsheets offer instant programming and equally instant display of results, plus what-if processing to determine how the item being tested in the prototype will operate under different parameters.*

**Information Centers.** The usual intent of an information center is to decentralize control over information systems resources, and to increase sensitivity to user requirements, which takes priority. If there is any slack, the personnel in these departments might be a good source for whipping up a prototype. The attitude in these shops is to provide or help provide maximum results with a minimum of development, and is the essence of prototype mechanics.

**Research and Development Departments.** The idea of using a semi-independent department that prides itself on objectivity might be the ideal place for prototypes, if the personnel are skilled in systems development and do not have higher priorities.

**Emerging Technology Department.** The use of an emerging technology department to prototype a project is often tempting and usually a mistake. The orientation of these departments is to find ways of applying new technology to know requirements instead of scientific modelling. Yet, an exception might be made when the feasibility issues are on the mechanical side, especially if the prototype can focus on comparing older and newer technologies.

**Contract.** Strictly speaking, this is not an organizational option. Yet in practice, many corporations use contractors on such an ongoing basis that they become members of the family, so to speak, while retaining a certain degree of independence. Using a firm under these conditions bypasses the learning-curve problem that a more "distant" contractor would need to climb.

## 17.5 SYSTEMS INTEGRATION

The attempt to integrate systems warrants prototyping perhaps more than in any other type of project. Attempting to insert interior lines after the fact almost always raises many acute feasibility issues. Note, too, that many decision makers have a strong tendency to white-wash potential problems with integrations. Bring a report outlining these problems to one of them, and his reaction will be equivalent to dipping a paint brush in white-out, stroking it across the page, and advising, "No problem, it will all come out in the wash." For less optimistic decision makers, the questions to ask are:

**Degree of Necessity.** Just how necessary is the integration? If a prototype is needed to answer this question, the system cannot be very necessary. A prototype should be limited to determining if the proposed method to implement the integration is feasible. If not, and because the necessity hasn't changed, some other model must be used.

**Logical Intricacy.** To what extent do the components fail on points of logical and database integrity? The complexities themselves often make analysis impractical without some form of prototype.

**Technical Intricacy.** What is the extent of the technical intricacy of the proposed integration? This question is often difficult to assess without a prototype. In general, unless the targeted systems themselves can be modified, extensive transition and translation software and perhaps hardware are likely to be required, even where the underlying logic of the separate systems meshes flawlessly.

**Operating Effectiveness.** Will it work under design specifications? The incompatibilities described in chapter 10 will usually denigrate the performance of any intended integration.

**Effort.** How much work is necessary to make the system perform to specifications? No matter how difficult the integration might be, in theory at least it can be made to work. In practice, the integration could entail the complete rebuilding of the targeted components.

**Cost Effectiveness.** Will the result be cost effective, both in the objective and subjective senses? The objective sense means the return on investment. The subjective sense means the lost opportunities that might have otherwise accrued from replacing antiquated systems with newer versions.

Consideration of these questions lends some insight to the way prototyping can be profitably used with respect to different models of integration.

**Syntheses.** A complete synthesis of existing systems is so prone to failure that a phased prototype is usually warranted. Relying initially on high simulation and low loading, no matter how skimpy, will likely reveal major problems and disconnects. If not, more detailed prototypes on specific aspects of the project will be in order. It takes a devil's advocate approach.

**Database Integrations.** A database integration poses nearly the same risk of failure as a synthesis, but a prototype can perforce focus on just the database structure. One or more of the shortcut techniques described in section 17.4 can be used in combination with phased prototyping, which makes for an inexpensive test.

**Excerpt Integrations.** This is the easiest to prototype. The work entails only the use of sample copies of the planned data arrayed in a desktop computer with DBMS software.

**Interfaces.** To some extent, this prototyping must proceed piecemeal. Those paths or exchanges of data or outputs presumed to be the most error prone need to be tested on a cross-section basis. If no major disconnects or other problems surface, the chances of a successful project are good.

**Standardizations.** Prototypes of standardizations are the simplest if not the easiest by trying the intended hardware, software, or other item on three or four elements that show the greatest divergence. If the polemics adapt to the standardization, then all is well and good. If not, the problem becomes one of determining the exceptions that will have to be made, or alternatively, the cost of forcing compliance. As discussed in case study F in appendix A, the implementation of Ada as the standard programming language for the Department of Defense glossed over this type of prototyping. Although the technical prototyping was exhaustive, it was a mistake.

## 17.6 EVALUATION OF PROTOTYPE RESULTS

As stated, prototypes tend to generate results more favorable than will likely occur with the full project. Any degree of simulation and less-than-full loading inherently poses risks of inaccurate findings, not to mention the tendency of many project managers to interpret findings in the best possible light. This situation is not entirely unrelated to the fact that couples who cohabit before marriage have a higher divorce rate than those who don't.

**When the Results Seem Adequate.** Proceed with caution, unless the prototype was low simulation and high load and it passed with flying colors. In that case, proceed with even more caution. The test probably missed something.

**Unanticipated Benefits.** Prototypes sometimes reveal unanticipated benefits or new ideas for meeting requirements, which is a happy problem, but still a problem. An engineer at the Minnesota Mining & Manufacturing Company (3-M) worked several years to persuade his superiors to market a failed adhesive by way of those now ubiquitous post-a-note pads. Fortunately, when a prototype precedes development, the sunk costs are low and the opportunities to change course are at a maximum.

**Dealing with Apparent Failure.** When a good prototype suggests the intended system will fail or fall far short of expectations, the decision maker has the same slate of alternatives that are available after the preliminary analysis.

He also could benefit from considering the outcome of the original prototype. The great flood depicted in the Old Testament—subsequently confirmed by archaeological research—was inflicted on the human race because the latter did not live up to specifications. Afterward, the Creator had second thoughts. Glossing over the problem with the spectrum of the rainbow, He let the human race continue its generation and conduct. Nothing in the intervening 4,000 years suggests that human nature has improved substantially. Thus a manager who proceeds with a project after the prototype fails is in very good Company indeed. But it doesn't mean the system will work any better.

# 18

# Subjectivity and Ethics

*As far as the laws of mathematics refer*
*to reality, they are not certain;*
*and as far as they are certain,*
*they do not refer to reality.*

—Albert Einstein

Computers and systems operate only by objective rules. Individuals and corporations do not. Thus when management faces up to a major systems decision, there is bound to be a collision of sorts. That is, computers fundamentally cannot tolerate subjectivity, while good managers thrive on it. On the other hand, the reason good managers thrive on subjectivity is that they can make good decisions in spite of the conflicts.

These conflicts come in two forms. The first form lends itself to quantified alternatives, but the results are not always comparable. This comprises *subjective* factors. The second form, which might be considered as *ethics* or *ethical issues*, involves primarily qualitative issues that defy meaningful quantification. However, the conflict that generates an ethical issue can itself be quantified. For example, a decision to reduce personnel by substituting computers, especially in areas where jobs are hard to come by, is considered by some executives to be an ethical issue, yet the number of employees affected is by definition a quantity.

Sometimes ethical considerations override subjective or other numerical arguments. Often the decision is based on numbers, which might depend on whether a manager tries to live by absolute standards or by trying, "to do the greatest good for the greatest number." In short, the relationship between subjectivity and ethics is difficult. Figure 18-1 tries to illustrate the paradigm, but the inherent nature of the subject matter defies a pure objective analysis.

**Subjective Issues without Ethical Overtones**
Quantitative aspects dominate

- Deciding on priorities for marketing versus productivity.
- Determining the extent to which a system should be decentralized.

**Subjective Issues with Ethical Considerations**
Quantitative factors contend with ethics

- Using computers to monitor work performance of employees in detail.
- Creating large, necessary databases that will nevertheless be abused, especially on privacy issues.

**Subjective Issues where Ethics Dominate**
Quantitative factors are secondary

- Using a decision support system to replace subjective judgment, such as determining who receives medical treatment when it is rationed.
- For corporations that give personnel high priority (such as IBM), deciding on a new efficient system if that system means the layoff of employees

*Fig. 18-1. Subjectivity vs. ethics. Ethical issues are inherently subjective, but not all subjective issues have ethical overtones. The relationship is complex, but the point for information managers is that most subjective issues have quantitative factors, similar to heuristic logic in support systems. Those numbers often suggest a resolution. The same is seldom true in ethical issues, although the numbers here cannot always be ignored.*

Subjective factors permeate most management decisions, and ethical issues intrude on many of them. These factors and issues must be addressed. The advantages and disadvantages of each alternative should be determined and weighed first with respect to quantities, and then with respect to the qualitative aspects. To ignore the numbers is to make the final decision all the more difficult, even when the quantitative aspects eventually decide the issue.

Drawing on a case from another field, if funds for medical treatment are limited, should they be invested in liver transplants or in pre- and post-natal care for indigent mothers? Given the high infant death rate among the poor and the low cost of this care, at least compared to the extremely high cost of transplants, the numbers would tend to favor the maternal requirement. But if transplants cost the same as the maternal care, then the decision would be much harder to make, especially if one presumes that age should not be a factor.

This issue is not abstract. Great Britain, for example, has found that because of limited resources, it has had to curtail medical services to the elderly in favor of the young. Thus an older person in need of kidney dialysis will often be rejected in favor of a younger person with the same dysfunction. In the United States, where such practical limitations have never sat well, the resolution of the problem will be more difficult. An even more difficult situation will arise if computer-based systems are used to decide, or at least set the boundaries of, who receives and who does not receive treatment.

The focus of this chapter is on the more immediate subjective factors and ethical issues affecting the use of computers. These problems have increased as applications expand from transaction-based models into information and decision support systems. They might not involve the dramatic life-and-death issues in medicine, but they still operate.

## 18.1 SUBJECTIVE FACTORS

Subjectivity operates on at least three levels with respect to systems: the technical level, the managerial or organizational level, and the strategic level. The lower levels more readily lend themselves to quantification, but the need for those numbers can stem from a strategic objective. Conversely, the quantitative measurement of subjective factors can affect strategic posture. Between these polemics exists management, which in a fundamental sense exists only to put lower-level resources to work to meet strategic objectives. Figure 18-2 attempts to illustrate these relationships.

- *The Technical Level.* Most subjective factors at the technical level equate with trade-off decisions. For example, the amount of data to include in a system is often debatable, particularly with respect to anticipated but loosely defined future enhancements and extensions. In theory, these decisions should be dictated by strategic or at least by managerial perspectives, but those views are often too broad to be useful as guidelines for this level of detail.
- *The Managerial Level.* Probably the most perennial subjective management issue is to determine the best organization to get the most out of resources. The parallel for information systems would be the configuration and distribution of data processing resources and databases. This level presents the highest number of options and the least ability to measure the effect of a particular configuration on results. Perhaps this is why the middle management arena is one in continual turmoil.
- *The Strategic Level.* This level is concerned with an optimum mix of information systems to gain market position and to improve productivity, both by direct and indirect means. The subjectivity is intense, but at least the options are fewer and the results can be evaluated with a little more objectivity than the effect of configurations.

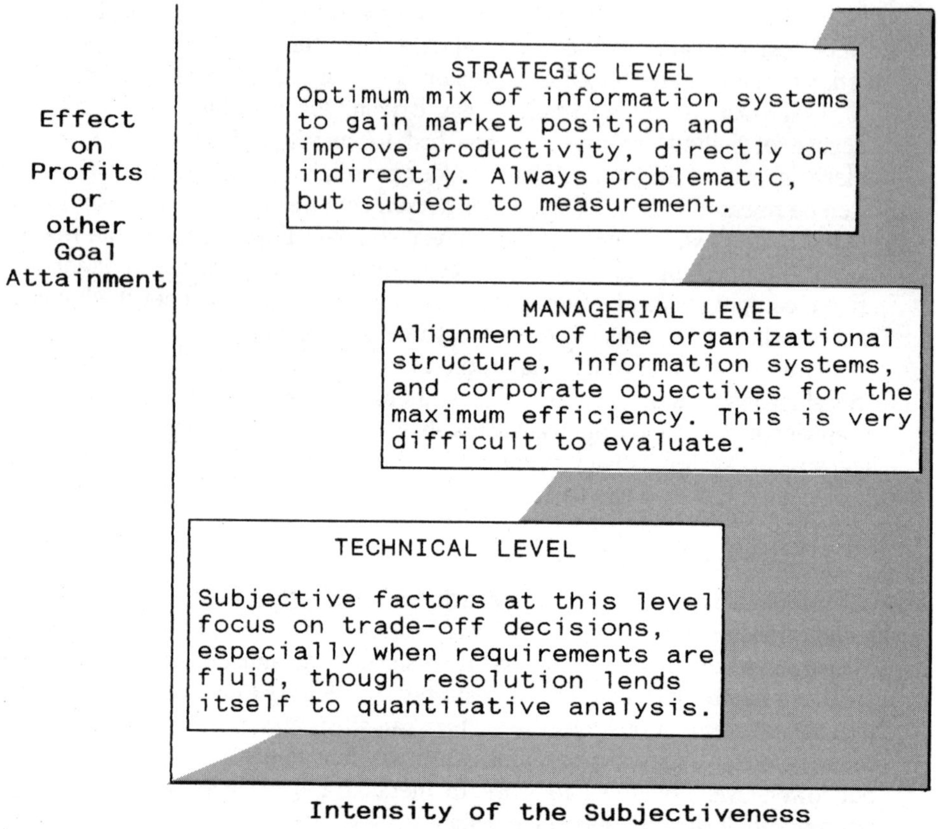


*Fig. 18-2. Levels of subjectivity. Subjectivity operates at all levels in systems: the technical level, the organizational or management level, and the strategic level. Factors at one level tend to affect factors at other levels.*

The existence of this spectrum of factors accounts for the heuristic approach to the structure of decision support systems, as discussed in subsection 12.3.1. When computer-based models are themselves used to support decisions for other applications of information systems, the system performs the quantitative computations and predefined logical comparisons. The results are then displayed to the manager, who must then wrestle with the balance of the subjective considerations. See technical note 8 in appendix B for an example.

## 18.2 SUBJECTIVE FACTORS AS A FUNCTION OF TIME

The subjectivity of some issues can increase or decrease from the perspective of time, or more accurately with respect to the normal phases or steps of systems design, development, and operation.

**As an Impetus for a System.** History is replete with examples of individual perseverance, against all advice to the contrary, that succeeds in developing a product of notable merit. However, for every success along these lines, there are probably between 10 and 100 failures. Computer systems follow suit, at least for those where there is no clear cut, indisputable requirement. The impetus for the airline reservation systems was no act of genius. It was the customers beating down the door. But many of the case studies provided at the end of the book evince considerable ingenuity and perhaps a measure of that elusive genius. The interesting point is that while quantifying this kind of subjectivity is impossible, the exercise of it usually takes numbers and magnitudes into account, be it sales, dollars, time, breakdown-and-repair rates, number of fliers mailed, advertising space purchased, or whatever.

**During Planning and Design.** One great mistake in systems planning and design is to presume one is creating something. The creativity ends with the conception of the idea. The emphasis should be on discovering the details of the logical relationships among the required data and outputs, and then to uncover the handful of good options for implementing that logic, although the latter might involve some technical creativity. As such, the primary subjective issues make the best trade-off decisions when faced with the need to compromise.

**During Development.** During development, subjective trade-off decisions continue, although usually at a lower level of detail. The more significant instances come with recognition of problems that were not foreseen, of which the most difficult are compromises with requirements or operating specifications.

**During Operations.** Probably the more significant subjective factors here arise when the use of the system suggests methods of improving it or adding features. These suggestions pour in continuously, yet there are severe limits to which major systems can be revised to meet every whim. On the other hand, maintaining or upgrading a system is essential. Deciding where to draw the line is inherently subjective.

## 18.3 ETHICAL ISSUES

No one has ever developed a definition of ethics that satisfies the majority of readers. To some, ethics connote only standards of personal conduct. To others, including Aristotle and Spinoza, ethics has a broad enough sweep to encompass law, morals, and psychology. It is a fascinating debate, but one that is far beyond the scope of this book.

What can be done is to attempt to view ethical issues as a hierarchy of four levels. Whether the reader wishes to consider each level as an ethical matter is immaterial. Problems exist at each level, irrespective of what they are called. The first level would be criminal conduct. That is, to the extent conduct is felonious, it is unquestionably unethical, except perhaps in some civil disobedience cases (including one discussed later in this section). As conduct veers from the criminal level, the proportionality of ethical issues increases until at the extreme the issue is entirely one of ethics.

These four levels, then, are: felonious conduct, abuse of authority or position, the use of improper means for legitimate ends, and quandary ethics. Figure 18-3 portrays these four levels in terms of the proportionality of criminal vs. ethical content.

In a system, these polemics would be manifested at one end by outright fraud in the provision of goods and services, and manifested at the other end by the need to decide between two claims on services in the face of limited resources, where the group that is left out will be at a predictable disadvantage. Or, in the situation previously mentioned, where computer technology is used to reduce the number of employees in a locale where other jobs are not available.

Now as theoretical as this might sound, it is essential to address the growing ethical issues in computer science. In the early days, the major issue was the conflict between computerized procedures and loss of jobs. That issue materialized in a different form: educating and training the work force to adapt to the more demanding requirements of an increasingly knowledge-oriented work force. But that is not the only issue now.

One well known issue concerns the monitoring of employee performance through computers, a common practice in the communications industry and

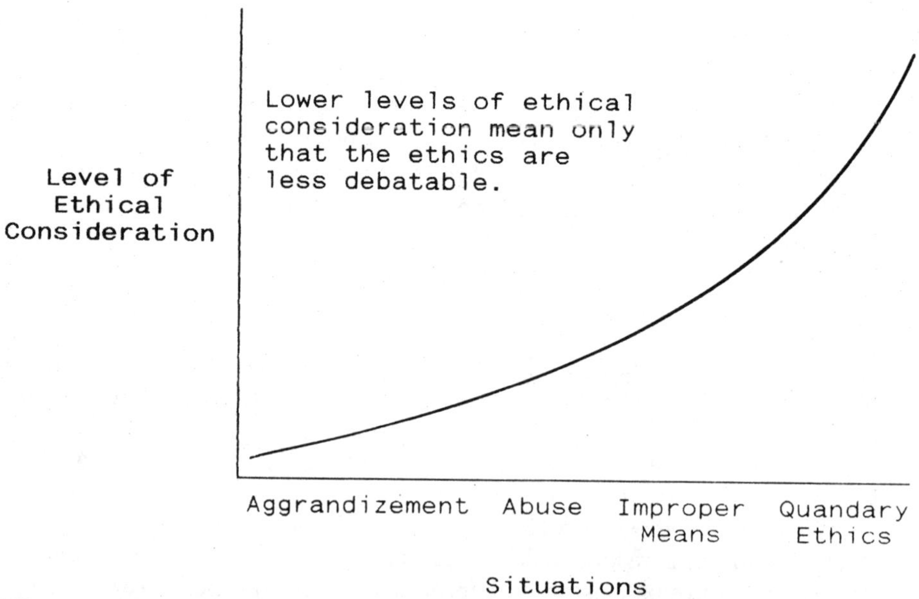


*Fig. 18-3. The spectrum of ethical issues. Most ethical issues fall into a spectrum of four categories: aggrandizement, abuse, improper means to a legitimate end, and quandary ethics. The ethical issues become more complex as the conduct involved becomes less opprobrious. With information systems expanding beyond routine processing, these ethical issues rise in significance.*

many other jobs where the bulk of the employees' work is conducted by telephone. If the employees agree to this condition of work, the ethical issue would be less serious than when personnel have no say in the matter. Another case is the intrusion of the government and corporations into private lives by way of massive databases, not the least of which is associated with credit ratings. As stated, these issues can be categorized under four headings.

**Felonious Conduct.** Felonious conduct means either the use of computer systems to support illegal activities, or the theft of computer time or services to support any kind of activity. The degree to which the conduct extends can vary from negligible to operations that net millions of dollars, but the ethical issue is usually easy to resolve. The conduct is inherently wrong and usually subjects the practitioner to both criminal and civil proceedings. The next chapter examines this at greater length.

**Abuse of Authority and Resources.** The next level of conflict edges away from outright criminal behavior toward abuse. In practical terms, this abuse usually means creating systems for personal influence or gain in the absence of requirements, just short of conduct that would be actionable in court. The next chapter also covers this topic at greater length under the nickname *porkware*.

**Improper Means to Legitimate Ends.** This is the familiar ends-justifying-the-means debate, and is perhaps the oldest conflict in the history of civilization. Public events repeatedly resurrect the conflict on a much larger scale than generated by issues with which most information managers contend, such as the Iran-Contra scandal. Perhaps the most common application to information systems—and it is far more common in government than business—is the invasion of privacy for the sake of larger goals.

**Quandary Ethics.** Quandary ethics mean the necessity to make decisions from a slate of options, all of which have disadvantages and perhaps destructive consequences. Far and away, the best-known case of this in this century was the decision to use the atomic bomb on Japan to bring World War II to a close. The best-known applications in the information systems—if the number of widely sold books is any indicator—is the use of computers in the field of artificial intelligence and especially with decision support systems. Should some doctors be replaced by technicians armed with medical diagnostic systems? Should middle managers be replaced by executive information systems at the fingertips of more senior executives? The latter process has already started.

A fascinating case in computer ethics occurred on June 2, 1987. Katya Komisaruk (who had earned an MBA degree from the University of California at Berkeley) broke into an unmanned building belonging to the Air Force and for two hours, using a hammer, crowbar, and other tools, methodically destroyed an IBM 3031 computer she mistakenly thought was programmed to launch a first-strike nuclear attack by the United States on the Soviet Union. She made no attempt to conceal her role and promptly earned a five-year sentence in federal prison. Released on parole after three years, she was simultaneously accepted at Harvard, Stanford, and the University of California law schools, all of whom knew her background.

Now at what level of ethical conflict should her conduct be considered? Was it the equivalent of felonious conduct, abuse of computer systems, an ends-justifying-the-means act of civil disobedience, or a matter of quandary ethics? A federal court veered to the conservative interpretation, three well-known universities went in the opposite direction. Not many convicted felons are accepted at Harvard Law School, especially those on parole. And how effective was the protest? This might be an unusual and dramatic case, and it might not have a direct bearing on the typical conflicts faced by information managers. Yet the point remains: ethical conflicts are not always easy to categorize much less resolve.

## 18.4 SOURCES OF ETHICAL STANDARDS

Perhaps the most difficult factor to deal with in ethical issues is that of different, valid ethical perspectives. What is ethical from one perspective might be at strong odds with another perspective. Many of these differences stem from differing sources of ethics.

**Business Ethics.** Business ethics concern those issues that relate to the conduct of business, which seems to change from generation to generation. Or more accurately it cycles between higher and lower standards. This source of ethics is rarely reduced to writing in explicit terms, but often operates as a kind of common law that goes beyond the courtroom. When the canons are published, they tend to overlap with the next category.

**Professional Ethics.** For personnel in the systems field, the Association of Computing Machinery (ACM) has promulgated a widely accepted set of ethical standards. These canons are discussed in the next section.

**Personal Ethics.** Personal ethics, as the name implies, are those standards that an individual develops for his or her conduct. They might or might not coincide with business or professional ethics, and they might be stronger or weaker than those canons. When they don't agree, the conflicts can create much difficulty for information managers in the personnel management arena.

## 18.5 THE ACM CODE OF PROFESSIONAL CONDUCT

The ACM Code of Professional Conduct contains five canons that respectively address integrity, competence, personal responsibility, professional responsibility, and human welfare. As abstract and impractical as the last canon might seem, it is by far the most explicit in its considerations. The human welfare canon is probably more explicit than any other code of professional ethics written since Hippocrates develop his famed oath for practitioners of medicine.

**Integrity.** Integrity is defined to mean warning others when speaking beyond the sphere of one's expertise, or indicating on who's behalf any partisan statements are made, and to act faithfully on behalf of employers and clients.

**Competence.** The six considerations closely parallel those for integrity and stress: not using credentials to misrepresent one's competence, striving to develop first-class work, and improving one's competence.

**Responsibility.** This canon has only one consideration and that is to accept only assignments for which there is a reasonable expectation of meeting the specifications.

**Conduct.** The three considerations here tend to reinforce the previous three canons in terms of special obligations imposed by ACM membership, for example, to avoid using the membership as a means of misrepresenting one's competence.

**Human Welfare.** This canon starts off with a general admonition to keep the health, privacy, and general welfare of the public in mind in the performance of work. It goes on to emphasize privacy with five explicit provisos, namely: to minimize data collected, to limit authorized access to data, to provide proper security for that data, to determine an appropriate retention period of the data, and to ensure proper disposal of the data.

With this level of explicit detail, this last canon could be considered as a form of knowledge environmentalism. But if the industry feels this strongly about masses of data maintained in a system, at a time when massed data is the essence of most effective integrations beyond transaction interfaces, and when technology is opening the doors for even larger databases, human welfare is worth considering. The issue is the centerpiece of the hypothetical case study presented in chapter 21.

# 19

# Fraud, Breach of Contract, and Porkware

*Our greatest error is that we suppose mankind more honest than they are.*

—Alexander Hamilton

An informal maxim among some security firms is that 25 percent of an organization's employees are honest, another 25 percent dishonest, and the balance honest except when opportunities for misappropriation arise and they think they can get away with it. Just how accurate this depressing picture is with respect to information system contracts is speculation, and whatever the facts are, the increasing number of court cases decided against vendors could reduce the rate of incidence. Still, fraud, breach of contract, marginal performance, and the hawking of more goods and services than required—what this book calls *porkware*—are problems that cannot be ignored.

When these problems are ignored, the corporation or organization inevitably suffers loss. Accordingly, the emphasis should be on prevention, even more so than security. Some losses are inevitable and therefore a security plan should include damage limitation and disaster recovery as well as preventive measures. The former includes insurance, but with rare exceptions, insurance against fraud and breach of promise is not available, and the equivalent of performance bonds is seldom practical. As for warranties, some of them are not worth the paper on which they are written.

True, a defrauded company can sue in civil court and seek damages, but that is not the same thing as collecting on an insurance policy. Winning in court is an uphill battle. Even when a case is decided favorably, the compensatory damages will seldom cover indirect losses, which might be significant. With few exceptions, only punitive damages can compensate for indirect losses, but to obtain compensation requires proof of wanton intent, which is not easy to do. If the vendor goes bankrupt, the award could be meaningless. In short, the courts are instruments of justice, not instrumentalities of insurance.

This chapter tries to make that point indelibly clear. It starts by discussing the matrix of courts and conduct, which is followed by sections on fraud, breach of conduct, marginal performance, and porkware. The concluding section addresses management responsibilities.

## 19.1 HIERARCHY

After a corporation has been short changed on goods and services delivered, the focus of corrective action is compensation. The focus of the courts, including the court of public opinion, is justice and retribution. These two aims overlap, yet in terms of cash, the power curve is sharp. Only at the upper end do they coincide, and sometimes even that equivalency operates only in theory. This paradigm stems from the forms of justice vs. the degree of conduct. Figure 19-1 illustrates the matrix. The three levels of retribution are familiar to every reader:

- *Criminal Law*. Criminal law pits the state against an individual or a corporation, which is considered a person for legal purposes. The criterion is the degree to which the conduct offends the citizens of the state collectively. Compensation for victims is rare and secondary, although there is a slight movement in that direction.
- *Civil Law*. Civil law is divided into two main areas: tort and contracts. Roughly speaking, tort law is criminal law applied to the benefit of victims. Contract law, by contrast, drops below the threshold criterion for criminal behavior and works primarily as an arbitrator between formerly consenting parties. The problems are not considered directly offensive to the state. If they were, the jails would turn into urban centers.
- *The Court of Public Opinion*. The court of public opinion really exists and it is called the media at the high end, and reputation at the low end. Public opinion covers the gamut of conduct, but when the courts render justice, it merely reports that. When justice is not or cannot be rendered, it tries to compensate. Poor performance is labelled and publicized for what it is, and as a result the defendant might suffer a loss of business. In extreme cases, public opinion has been known to force an issue back into the courts. In other cases, public opinion is the impetus for legislation to open the courts to subsequent cases.

The other axis of the matrix has five categories, although many incidents of conduct stretch across two or more of them.

**Criminal Conduct.** Criminal conduct is conduct that is felonious, or in minor cases, a misdemeanor. It ranges from murder to a speeding ticket.

| | Criminal Conduct | Business Fraud | Breach of Contract | Marginal Performance | Porkware |
|---|---|---|---|---|---|
| Criminal Law | Felony or misdemeanor prosecution. The state is more offended than the victim. | Rarely prosecuted except when the government itself has been defrauded. | Not applicable | | |
| Civil Law | TORT LAW | | CONTRACT LAW | Rarely applicable | |
| | Victims can, in theory, sue for damages concurrently. | When loss is sustained by individual parties, rather than the state, civil law takes the place of criminal law. | | | |
| Court of Public Opinion | Other than a reportorial role, the press becomes active only when the system of justice fails to work, usually in a general sense but on occasion for specific cases. | | | Contractors often suffer a loss of reputation. | Opinion can turn against clients for their lack of judgment. |

*Fig. 19-1. The matrix of performance failures. The conduct axis of the conduct-justice matrix ranges from intentional destruction to mild puffery. The justice axis has three levels: criminal, civil, and the court of public opinion, the effect of which is usually underestimated. Problems and failures with contract work in information systems tends to fall into one of the blocks created by this matrix.*

Although every crime has a victim somewhere, the law presumes the conduct is more offensive to citizens as an entity than to that victim, and proceeds accordingly. Sentences range from capital punishment to a $1 fine.

**Business Fraud.** Fraud is actionable in both criminal and civil court. In practice, when committed against the state or the government, it is tried in criminal court. When committed against an individual or a corporation, it is tried in civil court. The emphasis is on compensation, and even when tried in criminal court, fines in addition to, or in lieu of other punishments, is common. As in felony cases, there are degrees of fraud that influence the extent of punishment or damages awarded. On the civil side, awards have ranged from millions of dollars to one penny.

**Breach of Contract.** A breach of contract is the first instance of conduct where for all practical purposes, criminal law no longer applies. A contract is normally an agreement between two persons; one who provides goods or services in return for some form of consideration from the other. Assuming the agreement itself is legal, the law presumes both parties were competent to make that agreement, and therefore if one party does not live up to the agreement, the remedy is between parties. It does not seek direct retribution to assuage the state. A breach of contract can be full or partial, and it can involve goods or services (or both). As discussed in section 19.3, the latter point is of great significance to information managers.

**Marginal Performance.** Marginal performance is a breach of contract that is too poorly defined to sustain a court case in practice, but the implications are just as significant. If the system doesn't work well enough to meet requirements, the loss, except the salvage value, will be total.

**Porkware.** Porkware is hardware, software, communications, or any other element of a computer system that is sold, installed, or developed by the provider knowingly in excess of requirements, but to which the user has agreed. Unless fraudulent misrepresentation can be proved—and that is difficult to prove—there is no recourse. On the contrary, even though the expense can drive the company bankrupt, the law recognizes this as the fulfillment of an agreement. Even opinion begins to operate against the supposed victim that says, ''This is your fault for buying that bill of goods.''

Figure 19-2 illustrates the effect of this matrix in terms of compensation. The shortfall is intentional. As implied, both the law courts and the court of public opinion assume that management has responsibilities and that failure to exercise those responsibilities is contributory negligence. The system-wide recognition of this doctrine is the general shortfall in compensation for most cases. The right recognition occurs when a defendant (in a civil case) makes a point of the plaintiff's failure to live up to his side of the bargain. If he succeeds, the damages will be reduced.

## 19.2 FRAUD

The word *fraud* is commonly used both legally and informally. Legally, the law prefers explicit definitions. Informally, the descriptions have too broad a range to provide any utility, which suggests that the use of the word be limited to its legal connotation, although this does not restrict the usage only to cases that go to court.

**Definition.** Quoting a legal opinion rendered in a Minnesota case, *Black's Law Dictionary* defines fraud as, ''an intentional perversion of truth for the purpose of inducing another in reliance upon it to part with some valuable thing belonging to him or to surrender a legal right; a false representation of a matter of fact, whether by words or by conduct, by false or misleading allegations, or by concealment of that which should have been disclosed, which deceives and is intended to deceive another so that he shall act upon it to his legal injury.''

**Degrees of Fraud.** The intentional nature of fraud does not allow for many degrees, except in the measure of damages. However, the courts recognize that fraud can be intentional or constructive. Intentional fraud means exactly what it says—the defendant intended to defraud. Constructive fraud is conduct by the defendant that operates with the same effect of intentional misrepresentation, and is vaguely analogous to gross or wanton negligence. If nei-

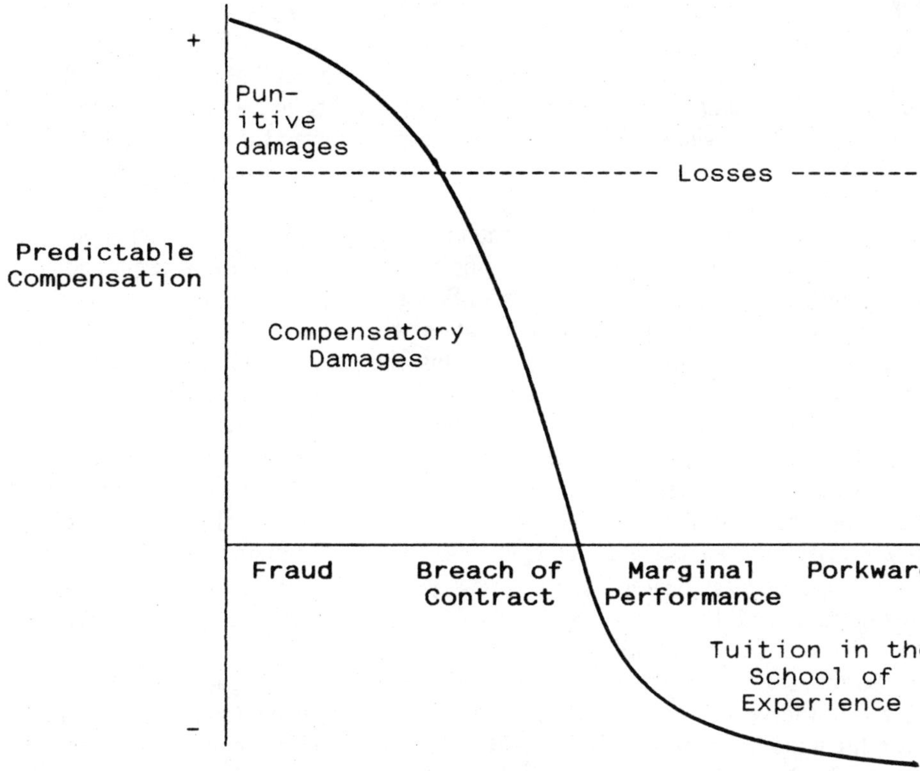


*Fig. 19-2. Compensation vs. losses. Compensation awarded for failed or poor performance in contracts seldom equals the sum of the direct and indirect losses sustained. That is, a court of law is not an insurance company. The way to avoid these losses is to avoid the circumstances that lead to them. In all but a few cases, this is within the ability of good management.*

ther is within the range of the available evidence, then the plaintiff must lower his sights to a breach of contract suit.

**Extent of Damages.** Fraud is the most severe form of civil offense among those that do not involve physical injury. A finding for the plaintiff will assuredly be accompanied by an award of compensatory damages. However, compensatory damages are a mixture of more than 30 kinds of damages recognized by the courts, not counting punitive damages. As a result, and irrespective of the amount asked for by the plaintiff, the amount of damages actually awarded is too difficult to predict. Then, if the conduct of the defendant has been particularly wanton, the court might add punitive damages. Punitive damages are intended to punish the defendant, not to compensate the plaintiff, but in practice the only difference is that sometimes the money comes in a different envelope.

For information systems, the most serious case of fraud to date was *Glovatorium vs. NCR Corporation*. In 1982 a Federal Appeals Court upheld a lower court finding that NCR had willfully and maliciously defrauded Glovatorium for a computer system that never worked. The compensatory damages were

$285,000 and the punitive damages were $2,073,000. Before that time, some vendors believed that civil law did not fully extend to the selling of computer products and services, perhaps on the mistaken assumption that they were still experimental and inherently subject to failure or inability to be produced even after a contract was signed. The Glovatorium case resolved the matter in decisive terms. Additionally, the court of public opinion turned strongly against NCR, and they lost a major share of the market.

The last point to note here is that fraud can take many forms and can apply to goods and services that exceed specifications, as well as to systems and components that are absolutely worthless. Some examples are given next.

**Pricing.** Fraudulent pricing is a situation where goods and services are delivered under the terms of an agreement, but the pricing itself exceeds what would otherwise have been charged under the conditions of the agreement. If the contract states only a flat price, then irrespective of how fair or unfair that price might be in ethical terms, and if the goods are delivered as promised, there is no fraud, no case, and no recourse. But many contracts, especially those negotiated with the government, are based in part on actual costs or have some provision for adjusting the compensation because of unanticipated costs. When these costs are misrepresented in excess of actual costs, the act constitutes fraud, even if the product works like the proverbial charm and eventually makes millions for the plaintiff.

**Goods.** With goods, the dividing line between fraud and breach of contract is fuzzy. If the vender delivers an empty steel box and claims that it is a computer, the fraud is obvious. But if he delivers nothing at all, it would be a breach of contract. Between these extremes, the proof of fraud depends on the extent to which the plaintiff relied on information provided by the defendant. Thus if part of the contract calls for testing, and the vender certifies this has been done, but hasn't, then to the extent goods do not measure up to specifications, an allegation of fraud will likely be sustained.

**Services.** Similar to goods, a vendor or contractor can agree to provide services, falsely state they were performed, and cause the plaintiff to rely on that statement to his detriment. The most common case would be maintenance services. Negligent work, however, would not constitute fraud unless it was so grossly negligent that the contractor knew it was useless. Incidentally, the example of testing in the previous point is not a service, but part of the manufacturing process for a good.

**Staff Qualifications.** This occurs when a contractor misrepresents the qualifications of his personnel, and the plaintiff relies on those statements to his detriment. Qualifications are relevant when the focus is proving the services were fraudulent, less relevant when the focus is on goods, and irrelevant when the allegation concerns the billing (unless the compensation was a variable as a function of the skill levels employed).

Summing up these points, at least in terms of significance for information managers, an allegation of fraud will likely provide higher compensatory damages and is the only practical route to obtaining punitive damages in all but a few situations. Yet fraud is much harder to prove than breach of contract. If the case fails, the plaintiff looks bad and it might affect his potential to collect on the lesser allegation of breach of contract.

## 19.3 BREACH OF CONTRACT

Quoting from an opinion rendered in a Maryland case, *Black's Law Dictionary* offers a simple definition of breach of contract, "failure, without legal excuse, to perform any promise which forms the whole or part of a contract." As such, breach of contract cases do not focus on intent. Instead, the court asks three questions: what did the defendant agree or promise to deliver, what did he actually deliver (and when if time is an issue), and what is the difference? The difference is the breach. The breach can be either in goods or services (or both), and it can be absolute or partial. A late delivery is equivalent to no delivery at all, unless there is a provision in the contract for late deliveries in return for reduced compensation.

A good is a movable item that is clearly identified in a contract and can be physically identified and inventoried. By contrast, a service is something that is performed. A computer is a good. Maintaining the computer is a service, including all parts replaced. Coaxial cables are goods; transmitting messages is a service. But what is software? Is it a good or a service? The answer is that it is whatever the contract defines it to be, except possibly for the nominal value of the medium on which it is delivered.

In situations where there is room for debate, vendors prefer contracts that specify services, while corporations should insist on a maximum specification for goods because proving shortcomings—breaches—in a service is harder than for a good. Processing efficiency is a fuzzy idea compared to data storage capacity. Further, services lend themselves to descriptions that come under the legally-safe concept of *puffery*. More to the point, vendors prefer to bundle hardware and other goods with services so that every element in the package must be evaluated in terms of criteria applied to services.

All this is related to the issue of explicit vs. implied promises. Contract law is notorious—perhaps that is a poor choice of words—for interpreting contracts exactly as they are written. The more interesting cases have involved software. The vendors delivered object code (code that can be executed directly on the computer) but not source code (which enables the holder to modify the program more easily). The courts have consistently held that without an explicit promise to deliver the source code, the object code by itself was sufficient to fulfill the promise to deliver programming.

A related problem occurs with the use of subjective adjectives in contracts, such as "adequate user manuals," "movable computers," "efficient disk storage," or "heavy traffic loads." Because the definition of these adjectives is a judgment call, the defendant has more leeway to defend the quality of the goods and services delivered. Explicit descriptions for the four examples here might take a paragraph and include precise numbers, but would be a wise investment of effort.

One last point. The law recognizes contributory negligence. When an organization runs into legal problems, the courts generally consider, and the counsel for the defense will assuredly focus on, any contributory actions on the part of the plaintiff. The maxim is, "come into court with clean hands," which means the plaintiff must have fulfilled his part of the bargain and made payments when scheduled, unless there is clear legal cause for withholding them. Other problems arise when the plaintiff has established a record of acceptance for goods and services previously delivered and then upgrades the criterion for acceptance without the contract specifying differences.

## 19.4 WARRANTIES AND MARGINAL PERFORMANCE

Marginal performance occurs when the quality of the goods and services is insufficient to meet intended requirements, but the magnitude of the deficiency is insufficient to warrant a court case, or at best will likely result in only nominal damages. The supposed remedy is to insist on a good warranty, but this misjudges the intent of that feature. The legal effect of a warranty is that it extends the time the plaintiff has to examine the goods or the effect of the services delivered. If flaws occur or are discovered during that time, then he has recourse. If the defendant fails to make good on the problem, the action is called breach of warranty instead of breach of contract.

Yet, what is the utility of a warranty that is worded no more tightly than the provisions of the underlying contract? The courts are inclined to interpret warranties as strictly as contracts. True, implied warranties and statutory provisions often have the effect of making warranties more explicit than the written word, but without these, claimants often discover that the statute of justice is not only blindfolded but is wearing ear plugs too. Only the vendor's risk of losing reputation can lead to free repairs. Scrupulous vendors keep this in mind. Unscrupulous operators will not. Their object is to defraud, even if they are careful enough to disguise the crime in ways that make proof in court difficult.

The last point to mention here is the use of performance bonds. A performance bond, like a bail bond, is an indemnity contract, which for all practical purposes is an insurance policy. The corporation purchases, or requires the vender to purchase, a de facto policy that says in the event of failure to perform, the third party will pay compensation. Unfortunately, these contracts are intended primarily for money handlers or for service contracts, like house cleaning services where the individuals doing the work are in a position to do damage or misappropriate property. Except in these well-defined cases, performance bonds are hard to come by and are also impractical. The underwriting costs tend to be high, which means that contracting with a more expensive but more reliable vendor would be cheaper.

## 19.5 PORKWARE

As defined in the introduction, porkware is computer and software capability sold or leased beyond the capacity needed, but which the corporation or organization agrees to buy. In the absence of fraud, which would have led the plaintiff to believe the additional capacity was necessary, and providing the goods and services are delivered as promised, the buyer has no recourse. Even if the costs drive the company bankrupt, the laws says, ''You made your bed, now lie in it.'' To repeat what was said earlier, the courtroom is not an insurance company. Even if it were, no insurance company would agree to indemnify the consequences of bad management decisions.

Porkware is especially prevalent in government, universities, and other nonprofit institutions where cost accountability is a matter of politics more than practicality. Grady Booch, in *Software Engineering with Ada*, stated that more than 90 percent of the software developed for the Department of Defense went unused. This situation was a strong motivation for developing a standard programming language.

## 19.6 MANAGEMENT RESPONSIBILITIES

The prevention of contract and porkware problems requires a 4-tier approach: to create an environment that minimizes the opportunity for fraud, breach of contract, and other shortfalls; to identify and evaluate the quality of potential vendors and service firms; to negotiate contracts carefully so that they don't favor the vendor at the expense of the organization; and to track the performance of working contracts carefully to avoid giving the appearance of accepting poor workmanship.

Prevention of these problems is easier said than done. In some cases, a corporation might come to depend on a supplier and therefore not think of questioning his practices each time. Even if fraud occurs on a minor scale, finding a substitute supplier might be difficult. Or an organization might succumb to the foot-in-the-door approach, which is a variation of the sweetheart contract used by labor unions to organize a company. That is, the contractor might realize that a system will cost more than an organization anticipates, yet nevertheless agrees to a loss leader contract for a first phase. This practice is common with firms doing business with the government. Thus the ground rules are simple:

**Know What Is Needed.** Porkware, like many kinds of insurance, is not bought, it is sold. When requirements are well defined and contracts are explicit, the selling of porkware is less likely to occur.

**Avoid Marginal Suppliers.** Corporations are not normally in the welfare business. The attempt to save front-end money by using marginal suppliers is usually a bad investment.

**Write Explicit Contracts.** The burden of proof in a court case is on the plaintiff. The lack of explicit provisions always works to the advantage of the defendant. An explicit contract is likely to motivate the vendor to live up to his side of the bargain.

**Specify Goods Instead of Services Whenever Possible.** Shortcomings in goods are easier to prove than shortcomings in services.

**Insist on Explicit Warranties.** Again, the burden of proof is on the plaintiff, and a lack of explicit wording accrues to the advantage of the plaintiff.

**Keep Books.** This is a variation on quality control. The performance and quality of goods delivered should be monitored and all deviations carefully noted.

The above provisions put the contractor or vendor in a potential adversarial relationship with the corporation. They might not be necessary—and might even be detrimental in the political order of things—when a long-term relationship has developed and both parties trust each other. But if this is not so, these provisions are the only insurance policy available on the market, and the cost is very low.

# 20

# Decision Making

*We never deceived ourselves.*

—John D. Rockefeller, explaining the success of Standard Oil

At an ecumenical conference, ambassadors of several denominations were struggling to arrive at a common understanding of baptism. Unfortunately, technological incompatibilities held up the sought-after integration of opinion. One theologian argued that partial immersion was necessary to wash away sins, another argued that sprinkling would suffice, providing the water was first blessed, still another said that total immersion was the answer, but that blessing the water was unnecessary, especially if it was a river.

After many fruitless hours of debate, they turned to the Quaker representative, who had been silent until that moment, and asked him how the Brethren had resolved the issue. He pondered this for a moment, and then replied, "Well, our predecessors did wrestle mightily with this issue many generations ago. They prayed for understanding on how the physical water could wash away the spiritual propensity to wrongdoing. Yet after many days, the Spirit did not move them any closer to comprehending the mystery. So we decided to just dry clean 'em."

Similarly, decision making in information systems development appears to need a type of ecumenical outlook. Subjective and ethical factors should be reconciled with the objective decision on physical matters such as hardware, communications lines, storage media, and the programming that puts them to work. To simplify that type of "washing," chapter 19 emphasized the need to quantify the subjective factors to minimize the discontinuities as much as possible. Yet it also advised that these quantified factors would continue to provide the decision maker with trouble.

The attempt to resolve all relevant ethical and subjective issues when making an objective decision is somewhat like the benign executioner who wanted to dispatch his charge, "just a little bit." It doesn't work. A decision maker must live with the ethical and subjective consequences of his or her decision. A good decision can minimize the fallout, but it cannot eliminate it.

For business decisions, the dry cleaning approach is the only workable solution. That is, even if ten million conflicting nuances are competing for the decision maker's attention, the computer could care less. It will either be used or not used. If used, it will be used in a certain way within certain limits. The subjective and ethical factors might affect the decision and should be cited in the decision papers, but in the final analysis, the decision must be objective and within range of implementation using physical and informational resources.

This necessity lends itself to a straightforward approach. For starters, making decisions by definition requires a choice to be made among alternatives, burden or no burden. The key is leverage. Archimedes was reputed to have said if he could stand at the right place he could move the earth with a simple lever. So too, an information manager can relieve part of the psychological burden of decision making by leveraging his approach to decisions. He or she needs to find or develop the pattern of interior lines that logically tie together the requirements, facts, and options surrounding the pending decision. Without this preparation, the decision might not only be a poor one, it could affect operations beyond its intended scope.

This means relying on some form of model for decision making, with which textbooks overflow. Some are tomes; others advocate the pyramid or newspaper-article structure, which starts with a brief executive summary and then proceeds with layers of increasing detail. Still others suggest the one-page approach, which the Army seems to be the strongest proponent. A century ago, the Army developed a version of this approach called a *staff study*, and later offered a modification called a *decision paper*. Variations of both have been adapted by so many companies and in so many forms (often by way of former officers migrating to industry) that it is difficult to recognize the source.

The essence of this model is to reduce the description of the pending-decision environment to five or six paragraphs (on one page), adding appendices if necessary to carry detail on the points made. The unwritten assumption of this approach is that if the individual who prepares the description cannot compress it to this length, he does not understand the situation. If he does understand the situation, he has not wrestled with it long enough to bring matters into a sufficiently sharp focus to aid the decision maker. Or if he has gained that focus, he still has not recognized which factors or assumptions are the dominant ones—the ones that shape the power curve of influence.

This method forces the interior lines of the logic of the situation to the surface, letting most decisions take one of three forms. Figure 20-1 outlines the relationships of the three forms, suggesting the following points:

- *Menu*. This situation offers the decision maker a choice of options or alternatives. For example, option A, option B, or option C. Occasionally, one or more of the options can have suboptions, but they are moot until a decision is made to go that route (a second decision paper can be prepared for these subsequent options).

- *Yea-or-Nay.* This decision means to proceed or to stop. If the decision to proceed has caveats, it is really two decisions: the first one is a yea-or-nay on proceeding, the second is a menu-type selection of an alternative route. A decision not to proceed (or to stop an existing project) also can require a second decision, namely the same menu approach for choosing among alternatives. In those cases where the availability of options is itself a factor in the first decision, then the situation needs only one menu-type decision, that is, to continue, to substitute option #1, or to substitute option #2.
- *Postponement.* This interim decision is a variation on the yea-or-nay model, where for one reason or other the decision must be postponed. The key word is *postponed.* It is not *pigeonholed.* The parties recognize that a decision must eventually be made, but also that there are substantive reasons for delay. The options, such as they are, consist of identifying one or more justifiable reasons for the delay, combined with a proposed target date for the decision.

| | Description | Preparation |
|---|---|---|
| Menu Decision | A choice among known options or alternatives must be made. | Advantages and disadvantages of each option should be listed and compared on critical points of difference. |
| Yea-or-Nay Decision | This decision has only two options. When a NAY decision is followed by other options, those options are part of a second decision. But if they are linked to the first, a menu situation exists. | As simple as a yea-or-nay decision is, the difficulty is knowing when (and when not) the alternatives are part of the yea-or-nay. |
| Postponement Decision | Although this is a special case of a yea-or-nay decision, it includes an estimate of the length of the postponement. | A decision to postpone should be a positive decision. It is not an occasion for waffling. |

*Fig. 20-1. Basic decision formats. The striking thing about most decisions for information systems is that they evince only a few patterns. When a pattern in practice appears to be more complex, either the supposed decision is really a sequence of related decisions or the analysis is still groping with the definition of the problem or issue.*

All three forms presume the decision maker is prepared to make a decision. None of them fit the individual who for any reason seems incapable of making a decision when the circumstances call for it. The only practical approach in these situations—when a decision is imperative—is to water down the options to a degree sufficient to make the waffle digestible. It might be short-sighted. It might fail. It might (and usually does) open the door to unaccountable woes. But there is little else that can be done. Working in any organized environment has always been hazardous to maintaining sanity.

The balance of this chapter suggests a systemic approach to decision making along the simplest possible lines. It first outlines a generic decision paper format. Next it applies that format to the three major decisions in the implementation of a system: the planning decision, the development decision, and the operational decision. Then the chapter reviews variations for phased systems, integrations, and a few unusual situations.

**OPTIONAL BACKGROUND PARAGRAPH.** Useful when the decision maker is not grounded in the situation that underwrites the project. Three or four sentences should be enough. Use an appendix if more text is appropriate. When this paragraph is used, it should lead directly to the statement of the issue or requirement, as if the latter were a part of the background.

**STATEMENT OF THE ISSUE OR REQUIREMENT.** If this cannot be stated in one sentence or question, the situation is not yet understood with sufficient clarity to make a good decision.

**ASSUMPTIONS AND FACTORS.** This section should list no more than five or six factors that bear on the decision. They operate as determinants for making a choice among the options.

**OPTIONS.** List the two or three most feasible options. All others should have been discarded by this point.

**ANALYSIS.** Given the statement of the issue (or requirement) and the factors, which option is best?

**RECOMMENDED DECISION.** A terse wrapup.

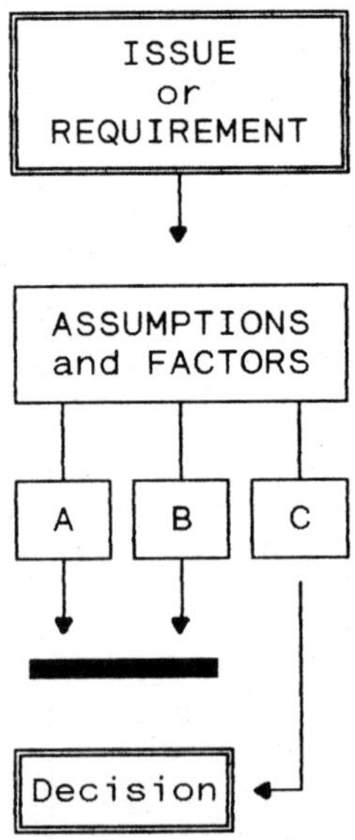


*Fig. 20-2. A generic decision paper format. The generic decision format depicted here is based on techniques that have been in use in government, the military, and business for more than a century. The key is to bring the critical issues and alternatives into focus in a very short space, with relevant detail consigned to appendices. The inherent complexity of information systems does not obviate the need for this focus. On the contrary, it might be the only way to grasp the interior lines of the project.*

## 20.1 A GENERIC DECISION-PAPER FORMAT

The generic decision paper reduces to five brief sections: a statement of the issue or requirement to be decided, the factors and assumptions bearing on the pending decision, a list of the options, an analysis, and the recommended decision. A brief paragraph describing the background would be an optional insert at the front end, and dissenting opinions can be appended. Figure 20-2 illustrates this model.

- *Optional Background Paragraph*. This paragraph is essential only to the extent the decision maker, or others who will review the paper, are not familiar enough with the situation to proceed directly to the issue. When this paragraph is included, it should lead directly to the next item, so much so that an English teacher would suggest that the latter be made the last sentence of the former. The background paragraph is kept separate only for emphasis.
- *Statement of the Issue or Requirement*. The issue or requirement is stated in one sentence. The recommended course of action must resolve this issue or meet the requirement. When one sentence will not suffice, it's a safe bet the writer hasn't done his homework. Further, breaking the problem into subproblems might be appropriate for academic and research papers, but not here. Bear in mind that the recommended course of action must be singular at its root, and therefore the issue or requirement it addresses also must be singular in nature.
- *Assumptions and Factors*. This paragraph lists no more than five or six factors or assumptions (or both) bearing on the issue or requirement. Anything beyond this amount should be grouped into larger categories, with details relegated to appendices. An assumption differs from a factor only in that the former must take a stab at something in the absence of facts, whereas the latter is more or less factual. An anticipated market share is an assumption; the cost of purchasing certain critical equipment is factual, although the price two years from today would be an assumption. In general, the only reason for differentiating assumptions and factors is to make the uncertainty of the former explicit.
- *Options*. This paragraph lists the two or three—possibly four—feasible alternatives for resolving the issue or meeting the requirement. In the case of a straight yea-or-nay decision, this paragraph can be dropped. The alternatives would be understood.
- *Analysis*. This paragraph summarizes the advantages and disadvantages of the options, with reference to the assumptions and factors. The analysis should conclude with an explicit statement why one option is better than the others, although some managers prefer a separate conclusion paragraph or a rationale added to the recommendation paragraph.
- *Recommended Decision*. If the conclusion is not explicit in the analysis, it should be included here, or else the contents of this paragraph consist of a cryptic resolution of the issue or indication of the option to be employed.

- *Optional Reclama Paragraph.* The key personnel that contribute to a decision paper are rarely in complete agreement, although there is a tendency to pave over opposing viewpoints for the sake of a presented united front, which might be all right for operational decisions. But at this stage, these dissenting opinions should be listed (on a second sheet of paper if necessary) to give the decision maker a fair opportunity to review them.

## 20.2 THE PLANNING DECISION

As discussed in chapter 3, the planning decision is a commitment to invest a moderate amount of organizational resources and funds to investigate or evaluate the potential for using automated methods to meet an informational requirement, or alternatively to replace or integrate existing systems. This decision is somewhat analogous to a grand jury hearing, which based on an abbreviated show of evidence, decides whether that evidence is sufficient to proceed with a formal trial.

As such, the planning decision paper is the culmination of informal analysis and discussions with users. In turn it becomes the beginning of a systematic approach to meeting requirements. If the fuzziness still prevails after the paper is written, the only appropriate decision is a postponement. All issues do not have to be resolved at this point, but those issues must be identified with at least one feasible approach to meeting the requirements if the issues can be resolved favorably.

**Background.** A background paragraph is normally justified for a planning decision paper. If nothing else, it will describe briefly the situation that appears to lend itself to automation.

**Statement of the Issue.** The statement of the issue can take one of three forms. The first is a problem-type question that asks if automating the requirement is feasible. The second presumes that the requirement can or must be automated by asking which option should be used. The third version is an issue-type situation that typically mandates a prototype to determine if automation is feasible.

**Assumptions and Factors.** In a planning decision, factors often take the form of general specifications, and almost always require an appendix. Other factors include the magnitudes of the required data and outputs. The assumption should take the form of a preliminary calculation of anticipated return on investment.

**Options.** As implied, the statement of the problem dictates the scope of the alternatives. This listing merely makes that list explicit.

**Analysis.** The analysis is not a prelude to the planning work. It is a comparative analysis of the options or alternatives listed in the preceding paragraph, although sometimes a sharp analysis will suggest that the list of options be revised before the paper is presented for action.

**Recommendation and Reclamas.** To the extent the proposed system addresses unknowns or poorly defined requirements, is the extent to which *reclamas*, or dissenting opinions, should surface. If none are listed, the individual who makes the decision should keep sending the paper back until these dissenting opinions show up.

As implied, the writing of this paper marks the change from exploration or reconnaissance to a definitive if preliminary approach to meeting a bona fide requirement. Reducing risk at this point is not as important as understanding it, or if the risk isn't clear, determine its extent before development. Because there are often many loose ends at this point in a system, the distillation of the essential points to one page is nearly imperative. If this goal cannot be reached, the analysis hasn't been distilled enough.

## 20.3 THE DEVELOPMENT DECISION

The development decision is the key decision. After a project is accelerated to this level of motion, stopping the process is nearly impossible, short of insurmountable problems uncovered during development. Even at that, some reduced-scale vestige of the project will fight for survival irrespective of any lack of utility. The idea is to put that kind of resiliency into the system itself, not the organizational steamroller.

Some information managers will argue that this is an exaggeration, and perhaps it is. Yet the record of system failures suggests that self-deception is not a problem that can be safely ignored. Consider the fateful launch of the Challenger space shuttle in January 1985, as discussed in the Public Broadcasting System program on public policy narrated by Bill Moyers. If deception can lead to a decision to risk the lives of seven astronauts unnecessarily, it follows that organizations can and do go ahead with systems in the face of mounting evidence that the risk of failure or waste is unacceptable. For this reason, the decision paper should be as tightly and as cogently reasoned as humanly possible. Points to note follow.

**Statement of the Issue or Requirement.** If the results of the planning work are questionable, the development decision paper will likely be a yea-or-nay type to proceed or not with development. If favorable without the need to consider options, the paper will be largely a formality to commit sufficient resources to the project, or possibly a last minute review of the bidding to find out if other projects have gained higher priority. If favorable, but with the need to consider options explored during the planning work, the decision will be a menu type.

**Assumptions and Factors.** For the most part, the assumptions and factors should be a restatement of those in the planning decision, as revised by the planning work. Any new factors uncovered or assumptions made during that phase should be highlighted. As these little surprises are all but certain to occur, the decision maker who does not see them in the decision paper would be a fool to sign off on it.

**Alternatives and Analysis.** If there are options to consider, and the factors do not adequately point to one as better than the others, then the planning work was inadequate. Development is not the place for exploration. Instead, the decision paper should be a postponement until the necessary information is obtained.

**Reclamas and the Weight of the Decision.** Unless the project demonstrates well-defined requirements and makes few demands on technology, the decision maker would be well advised to seek out dissenting opinions, even more so than with the planning decision paper. If the decision commits the organization to a long and expensive project, the decision maker puts his or her reputation on the line. As the majority position will likely gloss over some major difficulties, consideration of those reclamas might be the only means of averting a debacle.

## 20.4 THE OPERATIONAL DECISION

If insurmountable problems surface during development, then before that work draws to a close, a decision must be made to stop work or find an alternative. The approach and paper for the operational decision will closely resemble the environment of a planning decision. If not, it will tend to comprise a sequence of decisions to accommodate practical issues that arose during development that could not be fully resolved at the time, but which were peripheral to the technical aspects of the system.

**An Issue and Its Factors.** The point to note is that the word is *issue,* not *requirement*. The requirements should have been ironed out during development. The contention is on the inability of the system as developed to meet a requirement, but for which there are alternatives.

**Options and Analysis.** The options should have been identified during development in sufficient detail to permit a decision without further development or prototyping. A typical example would be to expand or reduce the number of stations in a network for reasons that have little to do with the technical ability of the system to meet requirements, such as availability of personnel.

## 20.5 PHASED SYSTEMS

The planning-development-implementation sequence is an oversimplification in cases where a major system is developed by phases. Some factors to consider are:

**Sequential Independent Phases.** For the most part, independent phases can be treated as separate projects, with the proviso that assumptions in earlier phases often become factors applied to later phases.

**Sequential Dependent Phases.** The problem here is that the earlier phases might work well but not the later phases. Perhaps the best approach would be to insist on a more comprehensive planning phase with prototypes. Then, as each phase comes on-line, additional prototyping might be essential to obtain a sharper view on the feasibility of subsequent phases.

**Overlapping Phases.** This factor is probably the most difficult type of project for which to prepare decision papers, at least past the planning phase. The problem is that new work is being done before the predecessors have proven themselves, an intellectual polygamy of sorts. Unless the general risk of failure is low, the best decision is to avoid this approach. Losing control is too easy, and that can push a calculated risk to a precipitous level.

## 20.6 DECISIONS FOR SYSTEMS INTEGRATIONS

In terms of the three key decisions, systems integrations are the same as any project. The problem, as discussed in section 16.3, is that most integrations inherently pose a greater risk of failure than systems with the same requirements. With this in mind, the following variations of the decision process, especially with respect to the planning decision, might prove useful.

**Merger-Type Integrations.** Except the excerpt model, merger-type integrations offer the highest potential return on investment and the greatest degree of risk, which is not too much different from other types of investment. Accordingly, the planning decision paper should be couched in terms of issues. For example, to determine the feasibility of merging the targeted systems without denigrating existing functions. Prototyping in some form is indispensable.

**Interfaces.** When the interface is limited to well-defined passing of data or software between nodes or stations, the planning decision would best be supported by a sharply focused prototype test. If that works, development and operations will normally be synonymous. When the interface is an attempt to substitute for a merger-type integration, the decision process is even simpler. Don't do it.

**Standardizations.** Although standardizations in practice occupy the entire range of computer technology and information systems, perhaps the wisest approach is to prepare the planning decision paper in research terms, or even a series of research terms. These issues, for example, might ask: what present elements or components differ widely from the proposed standard, or to what extent can exceptions be made without degrading the intent of the standardization? These issues could substitute for the list of options. The analysis should precede the list and lead to it.

## 20.7 OTHER DECISIONS

Most decisions on complex issues and those with far reaching implications can benefit from a straightforward analytical approach, but not all of them can use the planning-development-operations sequence. Among these exceptions are:

**Termination of Systems.** Most terminations of systems are tied in with a replacement or with another system that meets requirements as part of a larger package. These decisions should have been thought through in the planning phase, but often they are not. When the older system has functions that the replacement cannot handle, a separate termination decision becomes imperative. Inevitably, the decision paper will present three options: to downscale, to develop a new, smaller system to meet the residual requirements, or to add the requirements to the intended replacement.

**Major System Enhancements.** The problem with a major system enhancement is deciding whether the enhancement is essentially a new project or an extended maintenance task. Given the way each organization defines the two, and the way funding is allocated, this decision itself must be dealt with, however briefly, as a separate issue. In the process, the planners are likely to uncover different ways of meeting requirements or improving efficiency.

**Major Systems Extensions.** An extension differs from an enhancement in that the emphasis is on extending what exists to new locations and is therefore a communications or network issue. On the other hand, development is seldom necessary. The planning decision usually focuses on the feasibility of the extension. If that turns out successful, the next step is the formal installation decision. Installation is tantamount to operating.

# 21

# A Hypothetical Case: Efficiency vs. Ethics

*The road to hell is paved with good intentions.*

—Proverb

One major implication of this book has been that the technology of computer science and information systems appears to have a theoretical end, at least for the purposes of corporate or organization strategy. Beyond that point, efficiency could be improved, data expanded, and analysis refined without involving any fundamental change to the setup. That end is a macro system where a network of computers operates as if it were a single unit.

In a macro system, the database is physically centralized to ensure maximum logical integrity and completeness, yet is ''distributed'' to any location or individual who needs it by way of high-speed trunk line access cables. Updates are entered as close to the point of origin as possible, but again with direct trunk line access to the central database. Further, additional data can be added and maintained at local stations without affecting the main database. These expanded records would consist of access to the common data plus regional information. Finally, the database system could generate any excerpt or view of its data prerequisite to meeting new requirements.

As for hardware, accelerating increases to computer processing speed and simultaneous access to expanding data storage media could process any conceivable number of transactions and inquiries in sufficient time to meet requirements, providing the logic necessary to arrive at that answer, or at least to narrow and compare the alternatives, is known. Then, too, software development environments would have progressed to the point where senior analysts and programmers could concentrate on algorithm development and testing, without coordinating efforts with other users.

True, this prognosis might seem on the rosy side, but even if it takes 40 years, note that almost 50 years have passed since the arrival of *ENIAC*, during which time the capabilities of that machine, which filled a large room, have been reduced to a credit-card-size object with a thousand times the capability. On the other hand, as stressed in chapters 13 and 19, and also in the ACM *Code of Professional Conduct*, the security problems to prevent or at least curtail abuse increase exponentially. The purpose of this chapter is to provide a major example of where emerging technology seems to be leading the development of information systems, especially in terms of integration, and to suggest the extent of the problems with technology.

A hypothetical integration of well-known existing systems is described, and the four searching questions are posed. In practice, this exercise was developed initially in abbreviated form for use in a classroom setting by the author, but it can be easily replicated in any other classroom or discussion group. First, the system.

## 21.1 THE HYPOTHETICAL CASE

The case centers on the federal government, which is probably the world's largest user of computer systems. Among the biggest agency users are: the Social Security Administration, the Internal Revenue Service, the Department of Defense, the Federal Bureau of Investigation, the Immigration and Naturalization Service, the various public health agencies, and the Bureau of the Census. Essentially every citizen of the United States and every legal alien residing in the United States has his or her name and other data recorded on one or more of the databases maintained by these agencies.

The hypothetical proposal is to merge these databases into a singular system, with all common data maintained in one central location. All agencies would have access to the common data, to which they would add their unique requirements on their computers. The agency responsible for the common database also would add its unique requirements to its computers, although access by user agencies to this additional data would be restricted.

The theoretical goals would be:

**Elimination of Duplicated Data.** This goal is inherent in the hypothetical integration.

**Improved Database Integrity.** This goal is the inevitable benefit of eliminating overlapping but separate databases.

**Reduced Costs.** A singular system would be presumed to save costs, both by eliminating the duplicated data and the indirect costs of reconciling differences.

**Increased Tax Revenues.** The singular database, in theory, would enable the IRS to better track tax cheats and to locate individuals who are known to owe taxes in specific amounts. The estimated dollar amount, as mentioned in chapter 5, is $100 billion per year, plus a one-time backlog of $85 billion. The system also might be used (in conjunction with other databases) to reduce fraud in the Medicare system, which is believed to exceed $10 billion per year, plus another $15 billion in inflated charges.

**Facilitate Management of Government Programs.** As demands begin to outpace the supply of tax dollars, the management of the available funds could be weighed against requirements gleaned from the common database, a sort of decision support system on a grand scale.

**Facilitate Research.** This goal would include tracking medical problems, epidemics, and for the matter, the census.

## 21.2 SYSTEM STRUCTURE

The structure of the hypothetical system is a straightforward application of the emerging technological developments described in other parts of this book:

**The Database Structure.** Figure 21-1 presents a graphical representation of the integrated database under the euphemism of a National Registry. The common data would be maintained in one macro-system database, probably at the Social Security Administration. All agencies would tap into that database for that information, and add additional data that was unique to their operation.

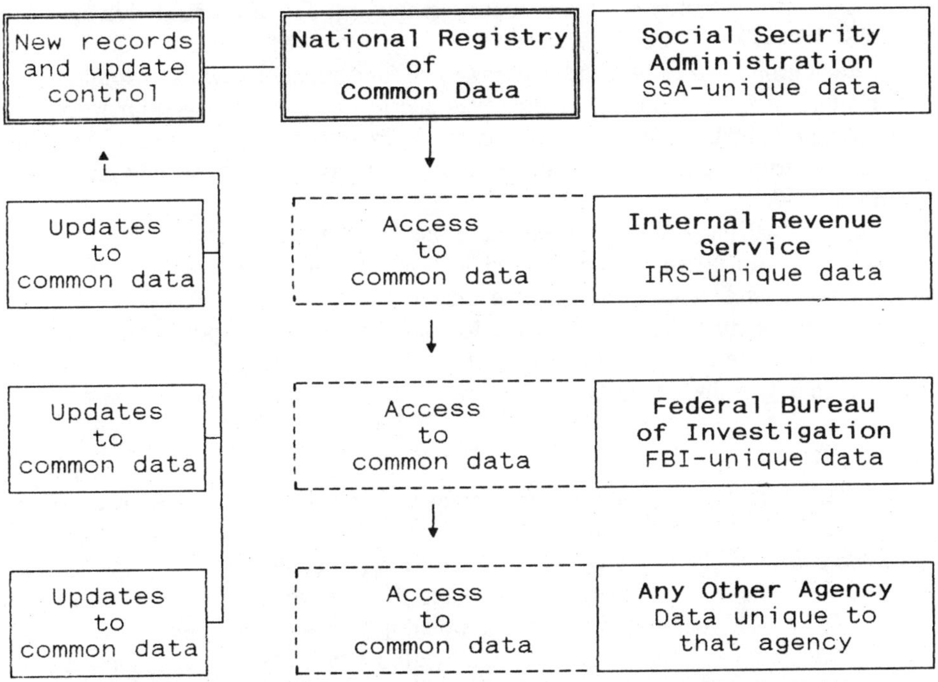


*Fig. 21-1. Database structure for a hypothetical National Registry. This chart illustrates a possible version for the hypothesized integration of existing databases among a number of federal government systems. It is a strict hierarchical distributive system, with the Social Security Administration driving the key and all common data fields, and each agency adding fields required for its obligations. Mutual accessibility of this specialized data would be subject to major restrictions.*

In all but a few special cases, any data that was not unique to one agency would reside in the common database.

**The Macro System.** The hypothetical design of the macro system follows directly from the design of the database illustrated in FIG. 21-2. Note that the number of trunk lines—lines of communications that can pass data with nearly the same density as computer hardware—would be comparatively few, and that if an agency were itself decentralized into several locations, each would be linked with the common database. Whether each agency chose to link its own regional computers with the similar macro system is left open to the decision of that agency.

**Adjunct Users.** Figure 21-2 includes provision for adjunct users of the common database, primarily: secondary federal agencies that use the data for research more than operations, state and local governments, certain nonprofit agencies, and possibly commercial agencies, who would pay a fee for access to information for which they already had a right to maintain.

## 21.3 THE QUESTIONS

The students participating in this exercise were in a business degree program, and for the most part were presently employed. The class ranged in age from 25 to 55. Classes were divided into study groups averaging four students each. Each group had to present answers to all four questions within a total of ten minutes. An equal amount of time was allotted to questions and answers after each presentation. At the conclusion of the presentations, the class met as a class to attempt some sort of resolution. To encourage candor, the only grade given was an A.

The original purpose of the exercise was to motivate students to think through both the potential and the implications of computer systems when pushed to the limit. It was not objective research.

Yet on issues that combine ethical factors and long-term perspectives, opinion is about the only source of facts that exist. The surprising thing about the presentations was the consistency of the responses. The four questions asked were:

1) *Technical.* Is the hypothesized system technically feasible, now or at a future but foreseeable time?
2) *Legality.* Would it be legal in the constitutional sense?
3) *Practicality.* Could the system be made to operate? If so would it fulfill the intended objectives, and if so, would it be cost effective?
4) *Ethical.* Even if the system operated with marvelous efficiency, would it be ethical, given the greatly increased opportunities for abuse and invasion of privacy?

After the presentations, the class was asked if they thought the government would eventually attempt to field this hypothetical system.

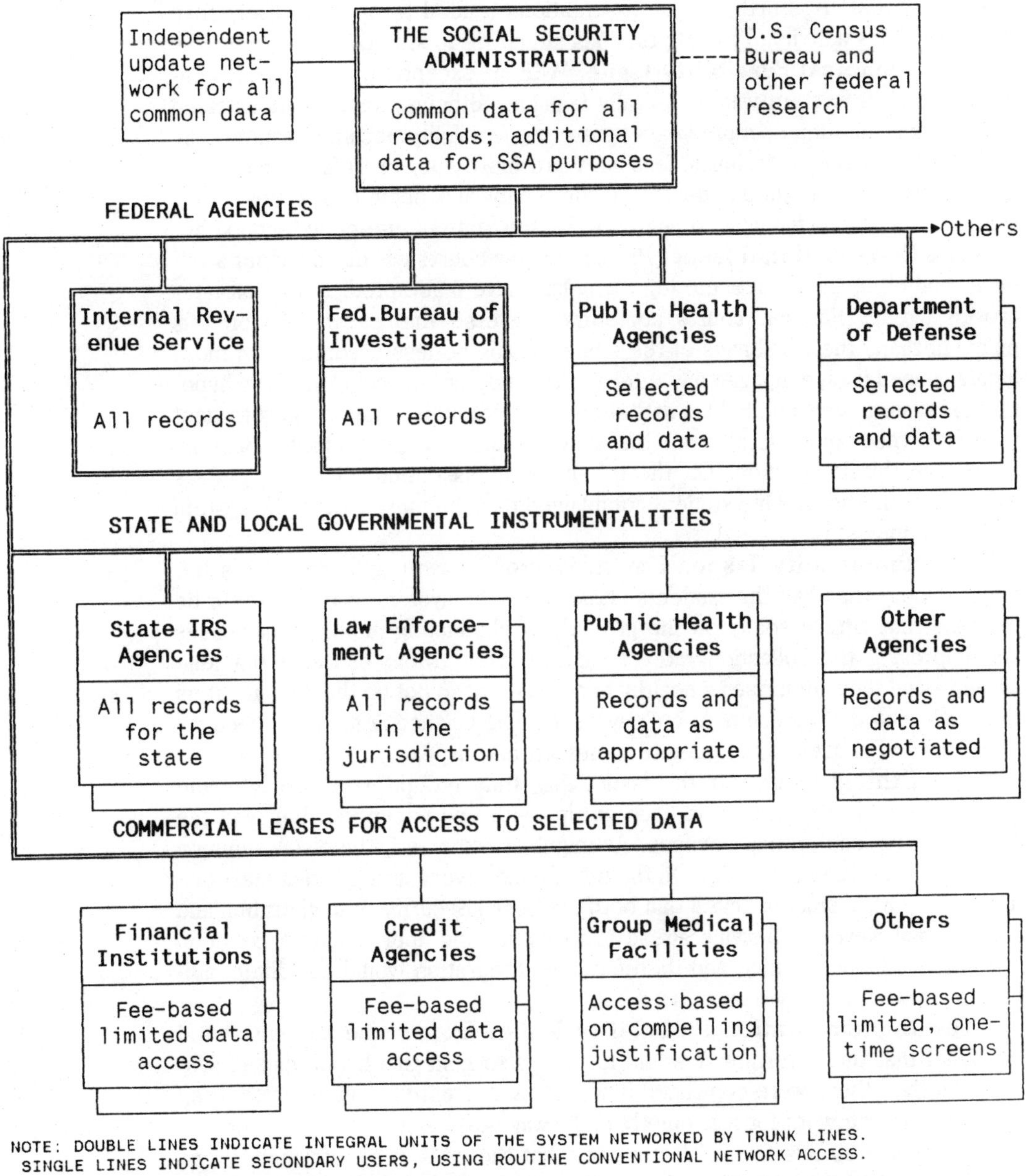


*Fig. 21-2. Network structure for a hypothetical National Registry. The communications network for the hypothesized database integration is not unusual, except for extreme-high-density trunk lines that permit satellite users to access the common database without making copies of it.*

## 21.4 PRESENTATIONS

Nearly all the student groups presented roughly the same answers. Dissenting opinions did occur, but rarely did the majority opinion of any study group differ from the others, neither in the same class nor in comparison with other class presentations. Further, the presentations tended to be more lively than any other class activity. Type-B personas all but disappeared.

**The Technical Feasibility Issue.** Without exception, every group concluded that the system was technically feasible, although some demonstrated that it might take ten or more years before the feasibility became economically feasible. Questions of technical feasibility are more subject to facts than opinion, but the textbook in use belabored the technical aspects of systems. They drew their opinions for what appeared to be the state of emerging technology.

**The Constitutional Issue.** Predicting how courts will decide is not a science, and often the most acute legal scholars have made predictions that later proved wrong. Further, courts sometimes reverse themselves. So on this point, perhaps the consensus of the students was no less accurate than more highly trained legal minds. At any rate, all the study groups concluded the hypothetical system would be held constitutional, primarily because the government already owned and operated all the systems and databases that would be merged in this integration. On the other hand, dissenting minority opinions were often emotional. One student complained that the mere idea of the system was a communist plot!

**The Practicality Issue.** The study groups were split on this issue. Slightly more than half the students argued that the system would prove to be practical, but almost solely on the grounds of eliminating duplicate databases and improving the collection rate of income taxes. Most of those that disagreed—and they comprised a healthy minority—did so not on the design but on the track record of government-built systems. The balance argued that security problems and abuses would operate to defeat the purpose.

**The Ethical Issue.** On this issue, the study groups were nearly unanimous. The majority position in each group, with one exception, believed the system would lead to major abuses. As might be expected, the discussions on this issue were the most lively. On the other hand, every group had at least one dissenter. These students cited that both the Social Security Administration and the Internal Revenue Service already had something approaching a common database on most citizens, and therefore the integration would not differ radically from what already exists.

**The Implementation Probability Issue.** Exactly one student stated his belief that the government would never try to field this hypothesized system. All the others were convinced it would be attempted, some conjecturing that the planning work for it is quietly underway now.

So what is all this saying? It is saying that the pen—read information systems—is finally becoming as mighty as the sword of competition. But the wisdom to employ it to the benefit of strategic objectives resideth not in the computer. On the contrary, it is an onus imposed on the shoulders of every senior executive. And it isn't going to get any lighter.

# Appendix A

# Comparative Case Studies

*The truth shall set you free,*
*but first it will make you miserable.*

—James A. Garfield

The literature on information systems describes thousands of cases, and several hundred of the accounts are written in great detail. Further, because every reported system offers its own unique aspects, selecting a representative sample is problematic. The solution applied here was to choose approximately 40 cases that could be grouped under 15 headings, corresponding roughly with major points discussed in the text. In this way, comparisons within or between sections provide a better perspective on the range of successes and problems with different kinds of projects and information systems.

The descriptions of each case are not extensive. On the contrary, the intent is to focus on three points: a strategic fit or its lack, good or inadequate management, and interior lines. Technological detail is kept to a minimum, except in three instances. These three exceptions involve ongoing processes that because of their significance should be followed closely by general and information managers. They are: the centralization vs. decentralization issue (section I), faster single-unit chips vs. multiple-array chips (section K), and the use of decision support systems applied to securities trading (section M).

## A. A SENSE OF STRATEGY

Although many companies and organizations exhibit a general sense of strategy applied to information systems, two in particular seem to stand out: the Chrysler Corporation and the USAA insurance company. These companies were featured in the introductions to parts I and II, respectively, and USAA is also discussed in section I (on the centralization vs. decentralization issue). Many other companies have done equally well, among them: Otis Elevator (a subsidiary of United Technologies Corporation), the Health Care Products Division of the 3M Corporation, and the Pillsbury Company. In each case the utilization of information systems became a precision instrument in the hands of managers who knew what was needed and what they were doing.

The first, Otis Elevator North American Operations, had an easier task than Chrysler.[1] Their operation is much smaller and each edition of its product line stays in one place. As a result, management could concentrate effort on one issue: namely to improve customer satisfaction. The result was the OTISLINE system. Before installation of this system, the best that could be done was to react promptly to service calls and inquiries. The problem with that approach was that even under the best of circumstances, the average time from the call until repairs were completed was two to three days. Meanwhile, the building managers seethed.

The strategy chosen was, "to head the dissatisfaction off at the pass," which meant predicting the occurrence of major problems instead of waiting for them to develop. Usually, the necessary information can be inferred from an increase in service calls or, alternatively, from comments made by service personnel after repair and maintenance calls. This management-by-exception approach was successful, and no small accomplishment. The typical district office for Otis (there are 11 in North America) received an average of 4,300 calls every weekday, which required a sophisticated database and a fast-response system.

This setup permitted a greater emphasis on preventive maintenance, and it freed Otis to be more responsive to unexpected calls. In turn, the extensive OTISLINE database set the stage to support additional objectives with only marginal increases to the data. This increase included a program to identify prospects for new installations, and the ability to calculate accurate cost estimates on sales visits. The next steps are to install computers in elevators that will monitor performance and transmit data whenever the sensors indicate major problems are brewing, and perhaps to link the emergency telephones located in elevators directly with the district offices, which have personnel on duty 24 hours a day, 7 days a week.

In general, OTISLINE is a remarkable system serving many purposes. Its one pitfall—common in most hierarchical or hub designs—was the tendency to centralize control at company headquarters. In this case, as the number of service calls per installation reached certain threshold levels, higher levels of management were informed. These individuals in turn became involved in the day-to-day operations of the regional offices, much to the irritation of the regional managers. But when Bob Smith, the Executive Vice President and Chief Operating Officer of Otis Elevator learned of this practice, he put a stop to it.

---

[1]James I. Cash, *et al.*, *Corporate Information Systems Management*, 2nd Edition, 146–162.

Thus the lesson is simple. Strategy might originate in the minds of a few senior executives, but its implementation must be the work of personnel at lower levels. The interior lines of a strategic information system should extend to these personnel as a matter of support, not as a leash. The top management at Otis Elevator understood this.

Turning next to the Health Care Products division of the 3M Corporation, the situation changes from a customer-driven need to be responsive to a corporate need for more competitiveness.[2] The precipitating problem for 3M was a heavy reliance on sales rebates. The backlog of these rebates had passed $13 million, and many of their customers had become unhappy campers. Something had to be done.

The Rebate/Sales Reporting System was created to meet that need. Although it was essentially a transaction-based system, it was so well designed that it became the centerpiece of a more comprehensive strategic information system. Like OTISLINE, the system had an extensive database and an even stronger user orientation. From the design phase forward, the system was under the control of the National Accounts manager and various users. Data processing professionals were respected, and made valued members of the development team. Their advice was avidly sought, but they worked in an environment that was unmistakably under the control of the users.

Notwithstanding the pressure to get something up and running quickly, these managers took the time to analyze their requirements and the data flow essential to meet those requirements. With this information, they gradually developed a database and system on paper, from which inexpensive prototypes or models were then used to test unclear aspects. In turn, the system was built quickly, with very few changes. In time the users realized that by adding a few more data elements, the system could respond to a wider array of requirements. They were on the happy part of the power curve. It now supports the entire marketing program.

Is this strategy by osmosis? Did top management presume that the company's personnel inherently or instinctively knew what was required, and simply opened doors to put that knowledge to work? The answer seems to be yes. The marketing strategy was already in place, but the processing of information had been too inefficient. The users knew what was needed, but did not have sufficient technical background to devise a system on their initiative. Teamed with the necessary expertise, that obstacle was overcome and morale went up in the process. The difficult compromises between a sense of strategy and the hard realities of computers were negotiated successfully and creatively. It is difficult to expect more than this.

The Pillsbury Company offers a third viewpoint.[3] The environment was too diverse to apply the 3M approach directly. Instead, the company opted to hire

---

[2]Kenneth A. Kozar and John M. Mahlum, "A User Generated Information System: An Innovative Development Approach," *MIS Quarterly*, July 1987, 163–173.

[3]David A. Ludlum, "MBA's Recipe for Success Has Dough Raising at Pillsbury MIS," *Computerworld*, October 13, 1986, 1,6.

an individual with a general management orientation and sufficient technical expertise to serve as an information strategist. The individual chosen was John Hammitt, who reported directly to Pillsbury's executive vice president and chief financial officer, Roger Headrick. Hammitt designed a systems architecture that looked to the proverbial bottom line as the ultimate criterion, and then redesigned the systems pieces to make a good fit.

This case personified the informational strategy in one key individual, who could keep the door wide open to requirements. In turn, he relied on project managers who understood general management responsibilities more than technology. He made the presumption that most of the technology needed had become commonplace and that it was the management orientation that would make or break the setup. He was right.

## B. SHARPLY FOCUSED OBJECTIVES

The principle of the objective for information systems, formulated in chapter 2, states, "direct information resources toward objectives that will make a significant improvement in the implementation of policy, at an acceptable cost." Some companies have put that idea to work in more ways than one. The two cases described here suggest how: American Hospital Supply Corporation (AHSC) and American Express. The first took a more direct approach than the latter, and between these polemics, literally hundreds of other companies have applied the principle to one degree or other.

The essence of the AHSC approach was to substitute full-time computer terminals in hospitals with salesmen that rode circuit and a passive order processing department.[4] Hospitals, depending on their size, can stock between 10,000 and 40,000 different items, with reorders ranging up to 60,000 per year. The administrative cost of each order can be as high as $25, sometimes higher, which means the paperwork alone can exceed $1.5 million for the largest hospitals. Further, some orders fall between the cracks or experience unacceptable delays. Finally, within a hospital, orders can originate in ten or more departments, adding to the delays and errors before they even get to the mail box.

Still, the intrusion of a computer terminal in hospital purchasing offices gave the appearance of a grubby hand reaching into the till of mostly nonprofit organizations. So what AHSC did was to contract with hospitals to be a major supplier, in return for the cost efficiencies and prompt service the system could offer. Appropriately, the system was named ASAP—Analytic Systems Automatic Purchasing.

In time, ASAP went through several growth stages. The original model was little more than an automated telephone service. Next it became a network that provided on-line communications for all parties. Then it linked hospital and AHSC computers, and even translated hospital stock numbers to the control designation used by AHSC (and vice versa).

---

[4]James I. Cash, *et al.*, *Corporate Information Systems Management*, 2nd Edition, 217–234.

With this setup, prearranged order times gave way to around-the-clock ordering, be it for normal resupply or on an emergency basis. As ASAP continues to grow in sophistication, the company and the hospitals reap the benefits. In fine, the extension of the interior lines had cut through the red tape, the delays, the errors, and the confusion in nearly a literal sense, and in turn yielded more efficiency than the most optimistic estimates in the early phases.

American Express, by contrast, did not have the same opportunity. It could not place a computer in the customer's company or home. To improve profitability, the aim had to settle for persuading the cardholder to make additional purchases with the card. In general, the only way to do this was by advertising. That route is notoriously inefficient, and the return on investment is difficult to evaluate. Further, when cardholders are inundated with too many flyers, the additional material could have a negative effect.

Enter Lynn Whitton, vice president of marketing research.[5] Before she tackled the problem, the practice at American Express had been to flood their cardholders with special offers, or suggestions to upgrade from the green to the gold-colored card (or from that to the platinum one). Whitton suggested that a computer-driven analysis of cardholder charge patterns would suggest which customers would more likely respond to specific advertising campaigns. It worked. With few exceptions, the number of positive responses increased with fewer mailings—a fascinating case of increasing the market share while lowering production costs with the same system.

Still, selling the idea to management was not easy. Several years of patient but persevering salesmanship were needed to win the approval of her bosses. Fortunately, she did not make the mistake of trying to let the computer make all the decisions. Instead, the system was a decision support model. It provided precise information that enabled managers to concentrate on key decisions instead of wading through reams of printout data.

A final point to consider here is the debate between knowledge-driven vs. algorithm-heavy models. Whitton was on the side of knowledge-driven models. She advised that many corporations have hidden resources in their databases that are ripe for harvest with the application of comparatively basic statistical inference techniques. That is, the interior lines are latent in the database, and only need to be focused to reach deeper into the marketplace. This finding parallels the assumption of many management consulting firms that 80 percent or so of the information needed for any assignment is already resident in the client's firm, but not in a readily accessible form.

## C. MERGER-TYPE INTEGRATIONS

A synthesis is a database integration plus a major, coordinated overhaul of programming to meet a strategic objective. By contrast, a database integration by itself is the strategic objective. Programming revisions are normally limited

---

[5]Bob Christman, ''American Express Improves Its Aim,'' *Arizona Daily Star*, March 15, 1989.

to fit changes to the file and record structures. From another perspective, a synthesis could be thought of as a new way of doing business, whereas a database integration stresses improving efficiency. The merged database might open the door for new opportunities, but that is rarely the original intent.

The two cases here show the difference. The first, the Joint Operations, Planning & Execution System (JOPES) under the aegis of the Organization of the Joint Chiefs of Staff (OJCS), Department of Defense, was intended as a decision support system for the entire defense posture of the United States. The second, the Computer Service System (CSS) developed by British Telecom in Great Britain, had a more humble objective. It aimed at eliminating intolerable problems in a disjointed network system that could no longer handle the traffic, although the requirements of users did not change in any fundamental sense. They wanted to continue calling whom they wanted to call.

First, JOPES. The growing complexity of DoD and its increasing emphasis on technology and heavy, maintenance-hungry equipment and weapons has made the management of defense plans into something of an administrative nightmare. JOPES was conceived as the answer to that problem.[6] It would integrate approximately 80 separate systems—especially those that covered personnel, operations, and logistics—as a means of supporting top-level defense planning and control.

No one could argue with the concept. The problem was the condition of the systems. Most of them were periodic batch-processing transaction systems with limited databases. Many of the databases were recorded only on reels of tape, and much of the data was questionable. A few of these systems did not even exist, except as a plan. Worse, the separate services made little headway agreeing on a standard data element dictionary, and DoD did not have the authority to impose one. Still worse, the compatibility among most of the targeted systems became something of a standing joke.

So the approach taken was to gloss over these "minor technological difficulties" and proceed with the project. One firm was hired to manage the project, others to develop it, and a third—a semi-captive DoD nonprofit contractor—was hired to resolve any differences. In addition to this menagerie, the Worldwide Military Command & Communications System (WWMCCS)—on which JOPES would run—was about to undergo a total overhaul. That overhaul would require a major rewrite of many systems that JOPES was to encompass, although in a direction different than JOPES would require. Further, OJCS had little control over the Defense Communications Agency, which had responsibility for WWMCCS. Gilbert and Sullivan, were they alive today, would have had a field day with this kind of decision making.

The lesson to be learned, of course, is that integrations work only when the logical and the technical interior lines are available or at least are within range of being inserted. For JOPES, just the opposite was true, and it is highly questionable if high-level command decisions need to wrestle with that level of

---

[6] "Know-How Versus Know-When in Systems Integration," *Information Strategy*, Winter 1990, 22–26.

detail. A much simpler excerpt-type integration might have been a better solution.

Now compare JOPES with the British Telecom project CSS.[7] The existing telephone network was a centrally-managed government communications monopoly, yet one that relied on six or more main computer units that were not compatible. Responding to the expanding but largely routine problems of the districts was no longer possible. CSS changed all this. A single unified system replaced the six incompatible ones, and 29 service districts were created with a genuine role in the decision making.

As might be expected, ambition got the better of the districts. The objectives of CSS were expanded to grandiose proportions, without thinking through the technical requirements to support it. As a result, the system initially failed. However, when the objectives were scaled back to the original specifications, where everybody understood the simple interior lines of the networks, the difficulties subsided to manageable dimensions. Under those conditions, CSS passed.

## D. AN EXCERPT INTEGRATION

Case studies on excerpt integrations are somewhat rare. This model is usually an adjunct of a larger project rather than a system in its own right. Yet at least one company recognized that potential: the familiar McDonald's.[8] The name of their system is the Integrated Services Digital Network (ISDN). This system extracts key data from the computers in each restaurant and transmits it to company headquarters. In the process, the computer equipment in each restaurant is being upgraded for local use.

The advantages are obvious. Summary data on sales of products can be stored and compared over a period of time, which is useful for gauging trends, evaluating various promotions, and understanding regional preferences—a more significant management problem than appears. Store managers are freed from the task of sending in summary reports and then being asked to explain them. Instead, data is drawn from the points of sale, i.e., the cash registers. The system also serves as a telecommunications network, so that executives can call and compare notes drawn from a common database. In that sense it goes beyond an excerpt model of integration. Still, the main idea held. The system is used primarily to extract data from the stores rather than to integrate all of them in some sort of grandiose strategic scheme.

## E. INTERFACE INTEGRATIONS

The fate of attempts at interface integrations ranges from brilliant success to dismal failure. The unquestionable successes include the airline reservations systems and electronic banking. Other successful projects are often touted as interfaces, but many of them are really new programs that involve a major net-

[7] *Datamation*, October 15, 1988, 37.

[8] Richard Layne and Cassimir J. Medford, "McDonald's Serves Up Global ISDN Strategy," *InformationWEEK*, February 15, 1988, 36–37.

work. The integration or interfacing was built into these programs from the beginning.

An interface integration is a project that imposes communication linkage between systems that were not designed with linkage in mind. Thus the focus of an interface is or should be on the transmission of data or programs from one system to another as is necessary. When the project goes beyond that level—in the direction of a merger-type integration—the task becomes one of imposing a form of logical uniformity over system managers who might not see the benefits.

Perhaps the classic example of this is the Army's 15-year attempt to interface its pay and personnel systems. It began in 1975 with a project known as COPPER.[9] COPPER is an acronym for COmbined Pay and PERsonnel system. It didn't go anywhere. The finance side of the house relied on a number of different data elements, and many elements that were the same had a different range of legal values. Further, the pay system—known as JUMPS (Joint Uniform Military Pay System)—required extensive audit trails and higher standards. The personnel system—known as SIDPERS (Single Installation/Division PERsonnel System)—did not have any such requirements.

The second attempt was an end run. When SIDPERS was extended to the Reserve components, it was given a charter to serve also as the input for JUMPS. The theory was that if one end of the interface could be built into the project from the beginning, the other end would take care of itself. That is, the planners could make a point of ensuring the finance side of the house was satisfied. Unfortunately, they never did accept those strictures. JUMPS backed out of the project, and SIDPERS, for the reserve components, was further diluted to a rehash of what already existed.

The third attempt was known as VIABLE. This was a major project with a projected cost of more than $600 million. Electronic Data Systems Corporation (EDS) won the bid as the primary contractor. The design selected was that of major regional processing centers instead of one at every station, or conversely a single administrative center. But the finance processing was already centralized, and used installations only as input stations. As such, the design placed new obstacles in the already confusing interior lines. Moreover, emerging technology was not taken into account, especially on network efficiencies.

As might be expected, VIABLE was scrapped after several years. It was replaced by a more ambitious plan by the Army to integrate almost all its systems, somewhat along the lines of the JOPES project described in section C.

## F. STANDARDIZATIONS

The literature on standardizations is feast or famine. The small projects are seldom reported. By contrast, the few large ones have so much significance that

[9]This source is the experience of the author. The history of this series of projects deserves a fuller account by a more impartial analyst, because the intent of the concept and its potential savings were genuinely worthwhile and presented no real technical obstacles. The failure was that of management, but perhaps it would have taken a rare form of leadership to overcome the inherent risks.

one or more periodicals begin to concentrate on describing the progress and to serve as a forum for new ideas. Among the latter are the Open Standards Interface Agreement and the Department of Defense project to impose the Ada programming language on all or at least most of its systems.

The open standards agreement has the greater significance for corporations, but Ada garners the lion's share of the publicity. Although its adoption within the Department of Defense is moving along, the best that can be said for organizations beyond the DOD is that they gave Ada a few compliments. This situation deserves more scrutiny. When a standardization can be imposed only by fiat, something is missing. On this point, Frederick P. Brooks, Jr. made an insightful observation, namely that the Ada philosophy was more of an advance than its syntax.[10]

Ada is a case of a project that vastly outgrew its original intent, but unfortunately was saddled with technical specifications that did not permit it to accommodate this wider perspective. Specifically, Ada was intended only for embedded systems in military equipment and weapons, similar in application to, but much more complex than, the computers installed in cars today. The language specifications were written with the operating environment of this equipment in mind, which could range in speeds up to 18,000 miles per hour. That environment required maximum processing efficiency and exact answers—just the opposite of decision support systems, where applicability is more important than efficiency, and a heuristic approach supplants rigid processing logic.

Still, the designers of Ada did a commendable job with elevating the standards of structured programming and modularity to new heights. Other features included the ability to write protocols within applications programs, and a maximum emphasis on what is called *object programming*. As discussed in section 1.5, this term has become a catchall for a variety of techniques that convert machine-oriented programming syntax and procedures to application-oriented terms. The designers believed that the standardization would not only solve a wide range of compatibility problems, but that it would vastly improve the software environment where complex requirements must be reduced to logical steps.

The problem was ergonomic. The Ada syntax is overbearing and does not take high-level program generators into account. It introduced a truly neat set of interior lines and then made them too narrow and inflexible to traverse with ease. True, some program generators have been developed that produce Ada source code, but that is a tail-wagging-the-dog situation. Program generators are their own source code. Compilation from that level should proceed directly to machine code without a middle-man language visible to the programmer.

## G. AMBITION AND INCOMPETENCE VS. REQUIREMENTS

The old saw that erring is human but that it takes a computer to really make a mess of things stems from the latter's ability to process information infinitely

---

[10]Frederick P. Brooks, Jr., "No Silver Bullet: Essence and Accidents of Software Engineering," *Computer*, April 1987, 10–19.

faster (well, almost) than the human mind. If it is programmed incorrectly, and an organization and their customers and clients come to depend on it, the errors will become intolerable. Because of that truism, many projects vie for the honor of being the worst case. Four are described here. The first three evince incompetence in different forms: Bankamerica Corporation, the New Jersey Division of Motor Vehicles, and Blue Cross/Blue Shield of Wisconsin.[11] The fourth case suggests that ambitious thinking, even when it is based on bona fide requirements, can do a system in, in this case, the U.S. Government Patent Office.[12]

The Bankamerica case was the most serious. Estimates of losses stemming from several failed systems have been as high as $5 billion over a seven year period, although most of it was in the form of lost business. Bankamerica slipped in assets from first place to twenty-ninth among all banks worldwide. Many information systems had to be scuttled in their entirety, including the Masternet system designed for the employee benefits and trust services department. Fortunately, that one only cost a mere $80 million.

The New Jersey case was noted for the problems it generated, mainly that a million drivers were unable to register their cars or had them registered incorrectly. An investigation after the fact indicated that Price Waterhouse, the primary contractor, had "professionally misjudged" the implementation. The culprit was the most common one. The plan was poorly defined and ambitious, and it used an inappropriate programming language. The resulting loss was $6.5 million, and many observers would be willing to substitute the term incompetence for "professional misjudgment."

Still, the New Jersey case was peanuts compared to the Blue Cross/Blue Shield case in Wisconsin. This was a $200 million project to replace seven ancient systems and three outdated databases with one setup. Electronic Data Systems Corporation (EDS) was the primary contractor. The system as implemented worked only in the sense of driving a car over a cliff. It will hit bottom. So did Blue Cross. Many claims were either overpaid or not paid at all. The company lost $28 million in 1985 and close to that in 1986 from overpayments. Further, 22,000 subscribers left Blue Cross and went with other carriers. Finally, the system invented the town of None, Wisconsin.

The Patent Office situation was more benign. The requirement was to automate the processing of 126,000 patent applications every year. Each application had to be checked against an average of 1600 pages of related patents, for a total of 200 million page comparisons each year. A budget of $300 million was established and a 2500-page request-for-proposal written. The project got off to a good start. But within a year, the Patent Office upgraded the objectives from paper handling to improving the quality of the patent search itself—a change from routine search-and-find operations to a heuristic decision support model. That ambition cost the taxpayers an additional $160 million with nothing to show

---

[11] Glenn Rifkin and Mitch Betts, "Strategic Systems Plans Gone Awry," *Computerworld*, March 14, 1988, 1,104–105.

[12] *Datamation*, November 1, 1988, 122.

for it. The project was scaled back to its original scope and is now operational, albeit several years behind schedule.

## H. DATABASE AND INPUT TECHNOLOGY

The core of an information system is its database. If the interior lines into and out of that database are in good shape, the opportunities to make use of it for strategic purposes are almost limitless. If they are entangled, the attempt to restore the simplicity beyond the database is an uphill proposition. As developed in part II of the text, the relational database structure provides the cleanest interior lines for environments with divergent requirements, and the trend to semi-automated input improves both the quantity and the quality of the data. Firms manufacturing relational database management packages are perhaps the fastest growing segment of the computer business.

Two cases make the point on streamlining input. First, colleges and universities are increasingly switching to automated registration.[13] For example, the Georgia Institute of Technology offers the Apply by Computer (ABC) system, and the University of Richmond has fielded its copyrighted Computerized Application Process (CAP). CAP is more sophisticated. It is not just a matter of getting on a telephone and pushing buttons in response to an interactive system. Prospective students fill out their registration requests on a computer and then turn in the disk (and fees) to the college, which gives students time to plan their schedule carefully. In turn, the college can process the massed input for both transaction-type processing and automated rescheduling of classes to accommodate more student preferences.

An entirely different input system is used at West Point Pepperell, headquartered in Atlanta, Georgia.[14] The problem was having personnel on the assembly line. Personnel loading pallets enter data into the system for quality control and inventory purposes. The option of a keyboard was absurd, so a voice recognition system was substituted. The information on defects is transmitted to a central database, where programs immediately price each roll or production unit based on the manufactured quality. In the carpet business, less-than-perfect material is unavoidable, but the right price means good business.

Turning to the database structure itself, one of best cases involved a corporation that recognized its need for a singular system to replace several hierarchical data structures. This corporation was the New York branch of the international banking firm of Credit Lyonnais, headquartered in Paris.[15]

The objectives included quick access to customer information, the ability to dig deep into the data for detail when necessary, and conversely to survey the data collectively for general management. The relational database design filled

---

[13]Kenan Woods, *PC/Computing*, November 1989, 64.

[14]Thais Mazur and Ives Brant, "The PC Hear and Now," *PC World*, November 1986, 226–228.

[15]Scott Humphrey, *Computers in Banking*, January 1988.

the bill. True, it took more programming to compensate for the hierarchical linkage of the old databases, but that task was considered insignificant compared to the benefits.

## I. CENTRALIZED VS. DECENTRALIZED DATABASES

The issue of centralized vs. decentralized databases is probably the most far reaching of all technical information system issues. Centralization favors top management, decentralization favors field managers. The great advantage of centralization is the maximum use of interior lines, but it also encourages top management to immerse themselves in detail and decision making for field operations. See section A (OTISLINE) for an example. See also technical note 6 in appendix B.

The case summarized here is USAA, which was featured in the introduction to Part II. The USAA database is almost totally centralized at the headquarters in San Antonio, including a complete backup installation.[16] But as the company continues to expand, operations are being decentralized. In 1988, 30 percent of the employees were in field offices, and most of them were involved in claims processing. By 1990, that percentage increased to 40 percent, and is expected to reach 50 percent by 1992.

Decentralization has two levels. The higher level concerns the advantages and disadvantages of relocating a major slice of the personnel and functions, beyond claims processing, presently at San Antonio. The second issue is the distribution of the database itself. One option would be to distribute it to the regional centers and then transfer records as necessary. A second option would be to do the processing at the regional centers, and then transmit the updated records for primary storage at San Antonio. The third option would be to leave things the way they are, and merely access the central database from the regional centers.

These two levels of consideration are not independent. The present setup works close to perfection, with new features added each year. The attempt to distribute it might or might not prove advantageous. Further, emerging technology makes the retained-centralization option more feasible. Finally, if that option proves the best, the question must be asked if regional processing centers would still offer greater efficiency.

USAA will not make a decision before all the details have been thought through and a prototype tested exhaustively. The company has avoided serious mistakes for more than 55 years, and they are not inclined to risk that reputation. Their subsidiary federal savings bank (FDIC insured) is one of the largest in the country and is rated the safest of all such banks after just seven years of operation. But that is not the point. The point is for other corporations who are considering decentralizing their databases to follow the decision making at

---

[16]Robert F. McDermott, "Bringing Your Association to You," *Aide Magazine*, April 1990, 3. Other sources include unpublished material sent to the author by USAA, and subsequent telephone conversations.

USAA. In so many words, it is entirely possible to decentralize operations and still maintain the database in one location for reasons of technical efficiency—the cleanest interior lines.

## J. NETWORKS

Probably the largest number of published case studies in information systems involve large-scale networks. The capability for worldwide stations to communicate with each other fascinates analysts, and many of these systems work with startling efficiency. The reason might be that network technology has been progressing for at least 90 years. The replacement of telephones and related equipment with computers is minor in the larger scheme of things. Restated, the technology exists to meet essentially any network requirement, although this does not necessarily mean the information system itself will meet specifications. On the contrary, excessive networking can denigrate control over data and hence affect the accuracy of computer generated reports.

The standard text at the Harvard Graduate School of Business Administration offers not one but five cases involving networks. The two that focus on that aspect of the business deserve special attention.[17] The worldwide network, called GEONET, of Manufacturers Hanover Corporation might be the most complex system in existence, although not in terms of the number of terminals. The success of GEONET has been attributed to a careful analysis of the subsets, such as specialized networks, vender interfaces, and internal design and management. As far as possible, each unit is configured and managed separately, and interfaced with the others as appropriate.

This hierarchy of interior lines is more than significant, and is vaguely analogous to the logic of the reduced instruction set chip discussed in the next section and in technical note 2 of appendix B. The bulk of the traffic was compartmentalized, which is where Manufacturers Hanover concentrated its effort. These subnets worked well and could be finally tuned to specialized requirements. The macro interfacing was secondary, and the work there could focus on the comparatively routine task of transmitting information between two or more stations.

The second Harvard case study involved IBM's European headquarters and focused on their office automation system PROFS. This system was developed in conjunction with the consolidation of eight centers into one building located in Paris, linked to many terminals throughout Europe. Unlike Manufacturers Hanover, each separate module ran well. The discontinuities and incompatibilities among them created the problem. The replacement setup concentrated on overcoming these interface problems, and added direct linkage to IBM headquarters at Armonk, New York. Incidentally, this project had the earmarks of all five models of integration.

In an era where office automation systems seldom live up to their promise,

---

[17]James I. Cash, *et al.*, *Corporate Information Systems Management*, 2nd Edition, 163–199, 515–531.

this one seems to exceed it. The credit is due the extensive analysis and prototyping before any serious development work began. Perhaps it would have been too embarrassing for IBM to have a marginal computer system on the front line of sales, but this one is a model of clean interior lines bridging many functions efficiently. Moreover, it is easy to learn.

Another case of extraordinary success is COINS, the Commercial Online Information Network System of the Canadian Imperial Bank of Commerce.[18] This system has 10,000 (no exaggeration) minicomputers linked to two IBM mainframes at the Toronto headquarters. Approximately 8,000 of the terminals are used as intelligent workstations, and the remaining 2,000 serve primarily as controllers, all spread out over 1,500 branches across Canada. Normally, this many nodes in a network would become a mathematical impossibility to control and still be useful. But by sticking to straightforward hierarchical or hub design, and pushing as much processing as possible down into the workstations, traffic with the headquarters has been kept at a minimum. As the interior lines reach inward to the core, the traffic has to be minimized to avoid an overload.

The last case here is that of TRW International Distributive Services.[19] The problem was managing orders worldwide in most of the 24 time zones. The aim was to reduce the processing time for an order from an average of 3 days to 3 minutes, improve the accuracy of the data in the process, and cut costs. The challenge was fascinating because the program logic had to take precedence over dazzling network technology, and still dazzle. So TRW relied on an existing network, namely General Electric's Mark II data network system. With that decision, they could concentrate on the transaction-type programming requirements. This case creatively merged two well-worn pieces of technology.

## K. HARDWARE

The thrust of hardware technology is to improve the interior lines of system architecture, which means hardwiring as much of the logic as possible, increasing the lines in the bus, compressing the size of the chip, and so forth. This improvement is described in more detail in technical note 2 in appendix B. Yet, as the introduction of the reduced-instruction-set chip suggests, the headlong approach to technology can be a mistake. The hardwiring of too many logic circuits passed the point of diminishing returns on the power curve. Designers calculated that by returning the bulk of them to firmware status would improve efficiency, and they were right.

A more complex issue has now arisen: the multiple processor array chip vs. the continued traditional single-processor chip technology. The reason is that the multiple-array processor can increase computer processing speed by a factor of 100 or more in one step at only a marginal cost. In practical terms, this

---

[18]John Helliwell, "Pioneering a Unique PC Network on a Grand Scale," *PC Week*, November 11, 1986, 55–58.

[19]Winn L. Rosch, "Firm Has Parts for Global Network," *PC Week*, February 3, 1987, C/5.

means putting a mainframe in a micro at a cost that is closer to the micro, or alternatively, substituting one mainframe for a bank of 20 or more behemoths.

The drawback is that special programming is required to ensure that instructions are not executed out of sequence. In repetitive processing, the task is simple. A block of records is accessed, and each logical record in the block is processed simultaneously, one per chip. For slightly more complex programs, read-ahead utilities can check the code for inputs and other steps that can be executed in part before they are needed. Still, the software environment necessary to make the most use of these multiple array processors is far from a completed science. And until it is, the case or issue could become virulent. Some subissues that need to be addressed are:

**Requirements.** How many systems need this kind of processing speed? How many of them are repetitive transaction-type systems, and how many involve more complex logic, and to what extent?

**Software and Programming Environment.** To what extent would special programming techniques be required to make the most use of multiple-array processors, and what are the practical limits of simultaneous processing as a function of different types of algorithms?

**Data Access.** To what extent can multiple array processors built into smaller size computers mimic the data access capabilities of mainframes, especially in cases where other than physical blocks of repetitive logical records are accessed?

**Pricing.** What are the marginal costs for shifting to multiple array processing and what is the likely return on investment?

These are not easy questions to answer, but until they are addressed systemically, the value of the multiple array processor will only be divined by long experience.

## L. USE OF SOFTWARE

The ideal in software development is to eliminate as much original programming as possible. To this end, companies are switching more and more to program language generators, database management systems and other productivity packages, and to buying proprietary software when it is available and fills the bill. The cases here are not dramatic, but the savings are.

The first and simplest of the five cases included here is the product management and municipal leasing department at Citicorp, Inc.[20] The requirement was to facilitate the selling of capital equipment and financing agreements to investors. A potential investor might have several million dollars to invest, but also might have restrictive stipulations. A simple application of dBASE III+ solved the problem in almost every situation, and the department could then analyze the impact of the financing arrangements on the total portfolio. All this could be produced in one session on a microcomputer and yield one report, the

[20]Joanne Kelleher, "Data Bases: Why They're Finally Usable," *Personal Computing*, October 1986, 85.

ultimate in interior lines in programming for management information purposes.

The Romano Bros. Beverage Co. offers another good example.[21] The requirement was to examine selected samples of sales history in detail. Formerly, each request took from one to three weeks to meet, and many fell by the wayside. When the backlog became intolerable, Romano Bros. switched to a database management system with SQL (Structured Query Language). This technique reduces complex programming requirements to comparatively simple interactive commands, and cuts the time required for programming from days to hours. Many managers learned to use SQL themselves. Within a half year, the backlog cleared up, and the answers the managers were getting were more comprehensive and accurate than under the old methods.

GTE Midwestern Telephone Operations faced a similar situation.[22] The breakup of AT&T and deregulation forced the players to become more competitive in a changing market, GTE among them. The programming requirements were fewer, but they had greater implications. What was wanted, therefore, was a shortcut to programming that would serve as a prototyping tool. They chose a software package called RAMIS from On-Line Software. One example of the programs developed was that of showing customers what could be saved by flat rate vs. usage billing. Software to put that kind of information on phone bills is a major undertaking. With RAMIS, they could substitute one or two lines of instruction for what would have been 50 to 100 lines of Cobol.

San Diego Gas and Electric Company took a different approach. Most of the requirements of the 2500 different company users did not require access to a centralized database, or high tech programming.[23] Instead, an information center was set up and staffed with 12 personnel. Users were provided with, and taught to use, various productivity software packages, including those that could access the main databases on the company mainframes when necessary—about 20 percent of the time for this company. The others operate on a standalone basis with limited data requirements. The combination of simplicity and not having to negotiate with the MIS department filled many needs.

The last case in this set is Pacific Northwest Bell.[24] This problem was slightly different, that of reducing complex requirements to coding, not so much for speed as accuracy. They relied on a software package called Excelerator (developed by Index Technology Corp.). This package simplified the reduction of requirements to pseudo language so that MIS-department programmers and coders could start from there. The shop was still Cobol oriented and the programs had to mesh. So in effect the use of the software inserted cleaner interior lines between users and programmers.

---

[21] Joseph W. Schmitt, "SQL Pays Off in Real Dollars," *Computerworld*, October 27, 1986, 19–20.

[22] "Integral Prototyping Tool," *Infosystems*, February 1987, 21–22.

[23] Michael Sullivan-Trainor, "Utility's Info Center Frees DP Staff for Sophisticated Projects," *Computerworld*, August 11, 1986, 55.

[24] Stan Kolodziej, "Working in Harmony," *Computerworld*, February 19, 1986, 19–20.

## M. EXPERT SYSTEM TECHNOLOGY

Expert system technology in the form of decision support systems is the difference between accumulations of data and putting that data to work. These support systems, called inference machines, can be simple or sophisticated, but they take the drudgery out of analysis and let the manager focus on the problem. The use of these systems at the DuPont company was highlighted in the introduction to part III, and many other companies offer hundreds of other examples. Yet there are two ongoing projects of enormous significance that rate the careful attention of information managers who might doubt that support systems technology has much to offer, or conversely, who might think that it is without its fair share of problems. These cases are securities and investment trading, and econometrics.

The case has been made that Wall Street trading relies on programs that were designed in the 1960s. As a result, not even the extensive use of high speed computers can handle today's loads, especially on heavy trading days and with international trading becoming a larger factor.[25] A more efficient system is needed, which by itself is not an earth-shaking requirement. The significance comes into play with automated buy-sell decision support systems operated by pension funds and other major investors.

If October 19, 1987 was to repeat itself, and the stock market had a system that could handle the traffic, would the market collapse? At the present time, there are safeguards that close the market in such cases, but would those safeguards continue if the replacement system could handle the transactions? Even if the safeguards remain, would the enforced cooling-off periods be able to stop a determination to sell too much stock, and perhaps usher in another edition of the Great Depression? If so, could the standby controls be tightened further in a form of martial law imposed on the securities and investment business?

The other side of this issue asks if the algorithms in the buy-sell support systems can be revised or controlled? Would users voluntarily improve them to prevent an application of catastrophe theory on Wall Street, or could the government regulate their use? These are not simple questions, and there are no simple answers. The point made here is only that the issues are worth following.

The econometrics case has even greater significance. The research on this has been funded by the National Science Foundation and the Federal Reserve Bank of Minneapolis. The goal is to create a better computer model of the United States and world economies. Assuming this can be done, can or should the federal government use the model neo-Keynes to regulate the economy? And should the control go beyond interest rates, rate of taxation, and spending? If it is done, will the inevitable pork barrel and other political interests make enough exceptions to denigrate the effectiveness of the model and perhaps make the economy worse? To repeat, the issues here are serious and plausible enough to give cause for reflection.

---

[25]Frederick E. Matteson, "What October 19 Almost Showed Us," *Information Strategy*, Fall 1988, 4–8.

## N. MANAGEMENT

Good management is the basis for good systems, and vice versa. Therefore, it may be a mistake to provide cases on management that are not related to a specific type of systems project. Yet the literature often provides cases where good management seems the focus, irrespective of the MIS context. The textbook used at the Harvard Graduate School of Business Administration is an example in point.[26] The three cases that seem worth mentioning here are: Frontier Airlines (before it was absorbed in a buyout), Mishawaka Industries, and Hercules Incorporated. In each case, one key player made the difference between a solid use of information systems to further strategic objectives and mere routine usage. The first two are summarized here. The third—on Hercules Incorporated—should be read in full. It is an interesting case of a chief executive officer, Alexander Giacco, with considerable vision on how information systems should work without fully anchoring that vision to practical realities.

The history of the development of information systems at Frontier Airlines offers a fascinating tale, for this regional airline underwent three radical changes concurrently. First, deregulation forced the company to become more competitive. Second, the management information objectives changed completely (not entirely attributable to deregulation). Third, the era of the mini and later the microcomputer began to supplant the mainframe, when a decision was made to cut back on MIS because too many managers were managing printouts instead of operations.

The key player to sort through all this was Lowell R. Shirley, whose former background had been as an aerospace engineer. His pivotal decision was to scrap their reservations system and tie in with the Apollo system run by United (although that later resulted in a major court case against United, in which Frontier won). Instead, MIS would be concentrated on financial and customer data. A second decision was made to back away from mainframes and distributed processing by way of decentralized minicomputers (the IBM series 38 computers). A third decision was to permit micros, but standardize them and control their use to prevent excessive decentralization. A fourth decision also was made to stretch out an existing policy that every system or program had to show a positive return on investment within 18 months. Fifth, by becoming an early user of a database-driven system, he cut program development time in half. Sixth, he used the database to underwrite some early decision support systems to analyze competitor's fares.

None of these decisions were radical or even startling. The emerging technology that was incorporated was no longer emerging by the time it was purchased. Shirley just kept in mind what the strategy of the company was, and then put his information resources to work to support it—with an essentially unbroken record of good judgment, high initiative, and taking personal responsibility for success or failure, which is a tough combination to beat.

---

[26]James I. Cash, *et al.*, *Corporate Information Systems Management*, 2nd Edition, 24–40, 57–69, 365–371.

At Mishawaka Industries, Inc., a highly diversified company ranging from pharmaceuticals to heavy machinery, the problems were not nearly as radical as those faced by Frontier Airlines, but internally the organizational structure and the antipathy of many if not most managers toward MIS all but doomed it to payroll processing and the like. Into this inferno was cast Gary Templeton, who had been manager of corporate systems planning before taking over the job.

Recognizing that the problem was management-oriented, Templeton studied the situation in more detail and then wrote a remarkable two page memo that almost literally redrew the interior lines of information and data flow for the entire organization. That is, he believed that the flow of information was the basis for understanding how the company did operate and how it should operate. The establishment of regional computing centers and standardization of equipment and programming environments were really a means to an end to realign the company, although after that was done he put those machines to work.

## O. LOCAL POTPOURRI

The author lives in Tucson, Arizona, and while writing this book over a period of seven months, four local cases involving failures or serious problems with information systems and an integration arose.[27] Three of them made front-page news in the morning paper. Although the fourth never surfaced beyond personnel knowledge, the institution behind it managed to make headlines with an even bigger fiasco.

The first case involved the county's new financial management system. The extent of the problems it caused can be gauged by an out-of-state rental car agency's refusal to accept the county credit card of the sheriff because they knew they wouldn't be paid. So what was intended as a management information system could not even handle basic transactions.

Further, the problems were close to inexcusable. First, financial transaction systems have been in existence for decades and have been reduced to a science. Second, the system was installed, and the old one discarded, before the former was tested. Third, county officials blamed the advice given by a consultant, notwithstanding a very large MIS department, headed by an individual selected from over 80 candidates.

The second case centered on a computer setup shared by the Pima County Sheriff's Department and the Tucson Police Department. The joint system saved money and kept information on criminal suspects readily accessible to both departments. Then both departments decided to go their separate ways. Each bought a new system more expensive than the singular one it replaced, and they were not really compatible. Smaller police departments that had formerly tied in with the single setup then had to decide which of the two new systems to link with, and then buy the necessary equipment. The lesson is plain.

---

[27] *Arizona Daily Star*, September 30, 1989, B1 – B2; February 9, 1990, A1 – A2; March 24, 1990, A1 – A2; and other issues.

In the final analysis, a commitment is needed by management more than technology to make an integration work.

The third case involved an excellent example of indirect failure. That is, a system that worked marvelously well but nonetheless created more problems than it solved. This case was an automated property assessment model. The theory was that if a program could be developed to evaluate property for tax assessment purposes more objectively, it would stop the constant bickering and appeals. Unfortunately, that is not what happened. Before the system was implemented, a board ruled on appeals, and for the most part its decisions were considered as final. But after the computer model took over, it started a cottage industry among lawyers challenging the algorithm in court on behalf of various clients who wanted their property taxes reduced. They have been winning more cases than not.

The fourth case occurred at the College of Medicine of the University of Arizona. A high-end minicomputer was bought, complete with expensive software, programming, and a growing staff to meet information needs that could have been accommodated by a few microcomputers and inexpensive database management software packages, probably at 1/10 the cost of what is being spent. The evidence surfaced when it was learned that although the new minicomputer was located in the medical center, nobody could communicate with it. Instead, all traffic had to be transmitted to the computer center on the main campus and back to various micros, which then operated at capacities less than if they had direct access to data.

This situation was not publicized, but the College of Medicine announced it would be adding 300 beds to its teaching hospital. (Arizona had let its hospital requirements certification process lapse.) But because Tucson already had 300 excess hospital beds, the announcement raised a major furor. In less than a month, the University offered that there had been a misunderstanding and only 100 beds would be built. The furor did not die down. Further announcements offered that these would be specialty beds and that some of their general medical-surgical patient load would be diverted to other hospitals. Few people believed that. Then the Medical Society of Pima County (Tucson is in Pima County) formally expressed opposition to the expansion. Perhaps, as a compromise, the College of Medicine could use its excess computer capacity for electronic simulation of the extra beds. Stay tuned.

# Appendix B
# Technical Notes

*Science is a first-rate piece of furniture*
*for a man's upper chamber, if he has common sense on the ground floor.*

—Oliver Wendell Holmes

This appendix provides detailed explanations or descriptions of some technical aspects of computers and systems technology. The criterion for inclusion was the comparative significance to management in terms of the points made in this book.

## Note 1
## INTERIOR LINES, ARRANGEMENTS, AND ENTROPY

As explained in the text, *interior lines* for information systems means the ability to shift data and programming resources quickly and without hindrance from one place to another to meet changing requirements. *Critical arrangement* describes a particular pattern or compression of interior lines that yields a remarkable—at times radical—improvement to efficiency. The combined phenomena are considered an application of *entropy*.

The intent of this note is to show, beyond the brief survey in chapter 1, that these concepts permeate the physical and social sciences, and underwrite some well-known everyday expressions and mechanical devices. Among the former are: "matters coming to a head," "the straw that broke the camel's back," and "lining up one's ducks." Among the latter are several brands of shop machines that offer five or more major power tools in one unit by merely shifting the position of some components.

The most brilliant display of interior lines occurs with the diamond. The crystallographic alignment of the carbon atoms permits maximum refraction, and diamonds are said to be flawed when there is any misalignment in the structure that detracts from the remarkable display. Perhaps the most startling display of interior lines occurs in the only two locations on earth where one can see "moonbows." At Cumberland Falls, Kentucky, and at Victoria Falls between Zimbabwe and Zambia, the submicroscopic carbon crystals in the mists cooperate with the light from a full moon to generate brilliant rainbows in the middle of the night.

From the perspective of scientific analysis, the first serious commentary on interior lines appeared in the nineteenth century. The renowned physicist James Clerk Maxwell, in his small volume *Matter and Motion*, described the phenomenon at some length, although he admitted he could not account for it. That accounting came 60 years later with the advent of nuclear reactions. But meanwhile, the theory of interior lines had its greatest audience in psychoanalysis. A key technique to this form of therapy is *associationism*, in which the patient is encouraged to freely associate anything that comes into his or her consciousness. The object of this kind of therapy is to increase self-understanding by recognizing the linkage underwriting one's seemingly random thoughts.

True, emotions play a stronger role than logic (as always), but this does not deny the effectiveness of establishing these mental interior lines of understanding. As for critical arrangement, Karl Menninger, in *Theory of Psychoanalytic Technique*, noted that the emotional regression process, which is part and parcel of the therapy, usually goes on for several years until it suddenly reverses itself in a moment that resembles a crisis. Patients who do not carry their therapy to this point—the expression is "flight into health"—seldom attain the full benefit. Within the scope of his discussion, Menninger reminds his readers that the same phenomenon is observed in physical medicine, namely that most acute illnesses reach a point at which they take a sudden turn for the better or for the worse.

The second most popular use for the interior lines argument has been in military tactics; for example, the advantage the Union forces gained at the battle of Gettysburg by concentrating their defense around the high ground on Seminary Ridge, which thus enabled them to prevail over a much larger Confederate force.

An even more dramatic example, popularized in a film circa 1964, was the defense of a small compound at Rorke's Drift (a ford) during the Zulu wars in South Africa in 1879. A contingent of 80 British soldiers, 35 of whom were in a hospital-patient status, held off six charges from a force of more than 5,000 Zulu warriors. The courage was unmistakable; eleven Victoria Crosses—the British equivalent of the Medal of Honor—were awarded afterward. Yet what made that courage succeed against otherwise impossible odds was the ability of the defenders to shift resources instantly to thwart each charge.

A variation on this theme was the construction of the *autobahn* system in Germany before World War II. The intent was to facilitate the shifting of military resources in case the country would have to fight on several fronts simultaneously, which is exactly what happened.

Still, the idea of interior lines remained undefined until the discovery of nuclear power, critical mass, and chain reactions forced the issue. However, the term *critical mass* is a misnomer. The popular conception is that the chain reaction occurs only when sufficient radioactive material is massed. This is true, but how much mass is dependent on arrangement. The more accurate expression, therefore, would be *critical arrangement*. A nuclear reaction can be sustained under any of four arrangements: by imploding, that is, compressing a given mass; by increasing the mass without compression; by removing incompatible material from an otherwise fixed mass and configuration of nuclear material; or substituting a more volatile isotope for part of the mass without changing that mass or its configuration. Figure B-1 compares these four arrangements, although the objective is not to provide a primer on nuclear power.

The recognition of this phenomenon led many scientists to consider the wider implications, and about 20 years later, they developed the subscience of *catastrophe theory*, on which there is an excellent introduction by E.C. Zeeman in the April 1976 issue of *Scientific American*. The author concluded that the reason for the long delay was that the process defied mathematical analysis in all but a few special cases. Yet when topology—which emphasizes comparative arrangements instead of quantities—was applied to the problem, headway was made. What remains is to link analysis with entropy.

This book suggested that *entropy* was the measure of the availability of energy. In terms of certain equations in thermodynamics, this definition is accurate. In a larger sense, entropy is regarded as the measure of disorder in the universe. That is, in a system of any size, either more energy escapes than is introduced, or the arrangement of the available energy loses its efficiency or ability to do work. This definition is the Second Law of Thermodynamics. Fortunately, the Third Law says that under certain conditions the process is reversed. A person who is dying can give birth to a healthy child.

Interestingly, Marilyn vos Savant, the columnist in *Parade* magazine, was once asked if there was any physical law in the universe she would like to see revised. She demurred as the laws were too interrelated to fiddle with just one of them, even if it were possible. Yet she went on to say that if an exception could be made, it would be to reverse the law of entropy. That was a very sharp piece of thinking, for while energy can neither be created or destroyed (except in the limited sense of conversion between mass and energy), systems can be rearranged to restore their previous level of efficiency. The strength of a weakened permanent magnet (as differentiated from an electromagnet) can be restored by a few strokes with another magnet. The result is a 100-fold return on investment, so to speak. The energy used to restore the magnetism is insignificant compared to the energy restored. Restored, not created.

A more practical case of reversing entropy occurs with heat pumps. A heat pump, in its heating mode, transfers the energy available in the outside air to heat the air inside a building. Under mild winter conditions, the magnitude of the energy transferred is greater than the energy expended to move it. The key word here is *transfer*. Energy is not being created, it is being transferred from where it is of less use to where it can be of more use. From this perspective, entropy can be considered a function of arrangement. Improve the arrangement, by transfer, restoration, or any other technique, and the return on investment could be significant. Figure B-2 attempts to illustrate the rationale of this process.

| | SOURCE OF CHANGES TO INTERIOR LINES<br>Mass | <br>Configuration | <br>Material |
|---|---|---|---|
| A. IMPLOSION 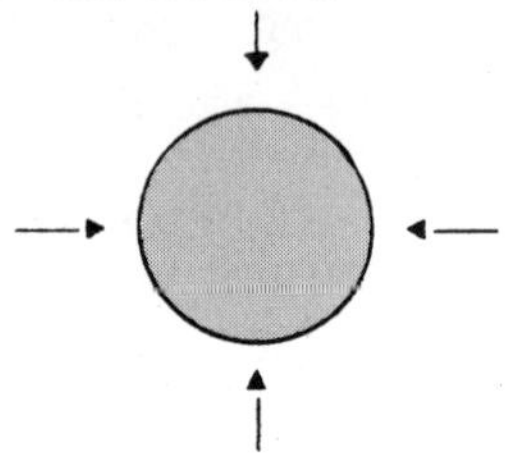 | No change, but the mass must be sufficient to sustain a chain reaction after compression | None proportionally, but the compression changes the density | No change |
| B. GUN TYPE 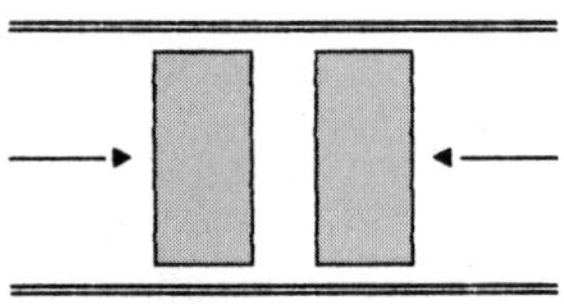 | Increased | Indirect only by way of joining two existing configurations | No change |
| C. CONTROLLED 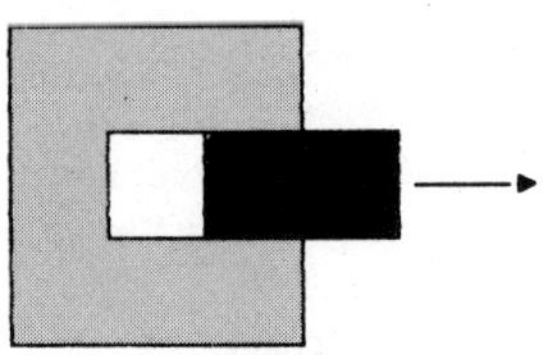 | Reduced by removal of a material that otherwise absorbs sufficient neutrons to prevent a chain reaction | None to the radioactive mass | Removal of neutron-absorbing medium |
| D. SUBSTITUTION* 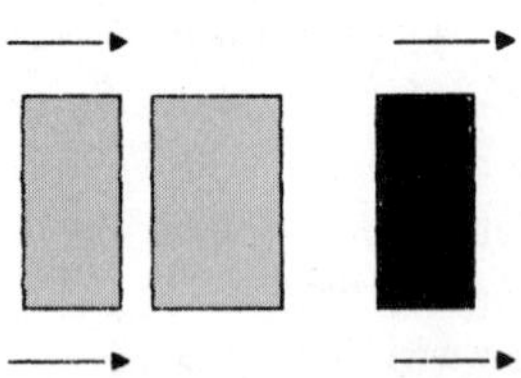 | Beyond slight change of isotope mass, it will vary depending on the isotope substituted | No change necessary except if the substituted mass is larger or smaller | Some or all of the mass is changed to a more radioactive subtance |

*THEORETICALLY POSSIBLE BUT IMPRACTICAL EXCEPT AS A MATTER OF DESIGN

*Fig. B-1. Critical mass vs. critical arrangement. The popular belief is that a nuclear reaction will occur when the accumulation of radioactive material reaches critical mass, which is misleading. Arrangement is the more critical factor. Different arrangements require different masses. The lesson applies to computer systems.*

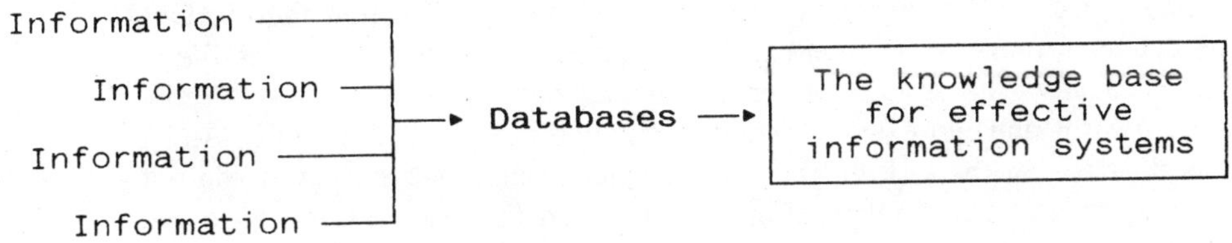


1. If energy can be considered as a measure of the exchange of momentum, then intelligence could be considered as the exchange or linkage of information. Thus the first step in an information system is to ensure that enough relevant information is gathered—the knowledge base of a system—and maintained in a database.

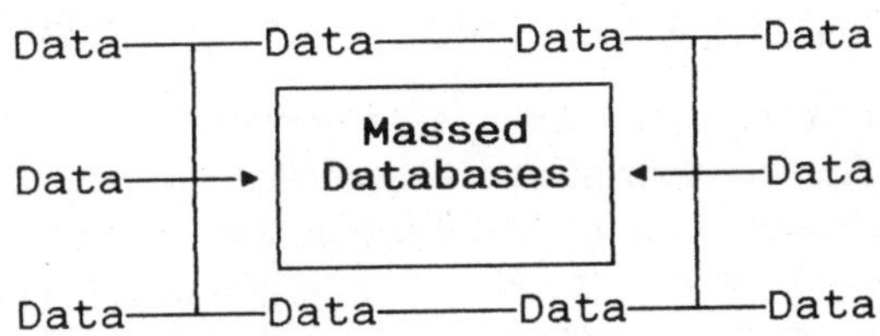


2. Once the information is gathered, it next must be linked with efficiency—that is, the value of the intelligence gained should exceed the cost of producing it, analogous to the cost of transferring energy in an unusable form to a usable form at a cost less than the value of the energy itself. This means centralizing the data in one location, or at least the capability of obtaining copies in one location.

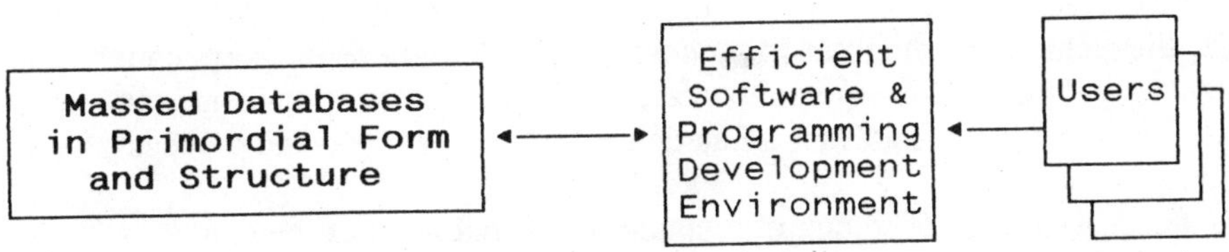


3. Then this theoretical efficiency must be made usable in different forms for different purposes—a high degree of fungibility. Thus if the data is stored in its most primordial form, then views can be generated to meet diverse requirements. Moreover, programming should be reduced to pure algorithms and logic—automating as much of the housekeeping code as possible—so that personnel without extensive training in software can use the system directly.

*Fig. B-2. Entropy and interior lines. If entropy is a function of arrangement, and arrangements depend on clean interior lines of communication or interaction for efficiency, then the crucial design criterion for any information system is to provide and maintain the simplest possible set of those lines.*

The concept of entropy has been extended into information theory. One book confuses readers; a second with the same information enlightens them. Why? Because of the way the material is arranged and the choice of the "connecting" words and expressions, readers can understand text differently. And if this is the case for the written word, it is inconceivable that entropy would not also apply to automated information systems. On the contrary, because the automation extends the storage and use of information in a direction back toward physics, automation seems to apply all the more sharply. The available energy of an information system resides in the arrangement of its interior lines, or as energy was defined in the first edition of the *Encyclopaedia Britannica* (1768–1771), "a term of Greek origin, signifying the power, virtue, or efficacy of a thing."

## Note 2
## SYSTEMS ARCHITECTURE AND PROCESSING CAPABILITY

The potential to increase computer processing speeds far beyond the already awesome capabilities has four points of significance for management: the ability to run complex analyses on a while-you-wait basis, the capacity to increase the size of databases with no increase to access times, the capability to increase the number of concurrent users in the same system, and the chance to reduce costs by way of miniaturization, or to put more processing power in smaller, lower-priced units. This discussion tries to explain the enormity of the potential, and that few trade-off considerations operate to put a damper on it.

This potential is tillable in all three categories of technological progress (as described in section 14.1): incremental, quantum advances, and revolutionary change. The incremental advancements are inherent in the nature of the chip. The central measure of computer capacity is how many instructions it can execute per second. The next most prevalent measure is access time to data stored in secondary media. Most other measures are functions of these two. For example, the ability of a computer to process multiple programs or users concurrently is largely a measure of just how fast it can swap information in and out of primary memory, which in turn is a function of both access time and processing speed.

The fortunate aspect of computer architecture is that most of the elements lend themselves to cumulative improvement. Thus if the operating efficiency of two elements is doubled, the effect on the entire system is to quadruple the cumulative efficiency. If six elements are improved ten-fold each, then the cumulative effect begins to approach one million. An improvement of that magnitude means that what formerly took 11 days to process will now take less than one second.

However, a few trade-offs are forced on system architects. The most common example is the number of lines in the bus vs. the size of the chip. Processing speed can be increased by increasing the number of parallel lines in the bus and reducing the size of the chip (the central processing unit). Yet to some extent, the smaller a chip is made, the fewer the lines the bus can have. Further, the more signals that are processed in a given space, the greater the heat

Incremental Improvements

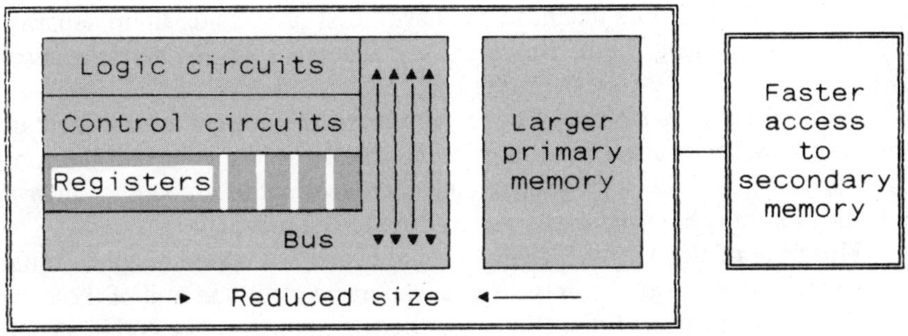


| Quantum Advances | Revolutionary Change |
|---|---|
| · Reduced instruction set | · Optical architecture |
| · Multiple/array processors | · Biogenetic materials |

*Fig. B-3. Elements of computer capacity and efficiency. Many elements of a computer contribute to its capacity and efficiency. Some are mutually reinforcing, and most lend themselves to further improvement without detracting from other elements. For this reason, computers will continue to increase in capacity and decrease in size and price in the foreseeable future.*

from resistance. In the microscopic world of the chip, that heat is significant.

Fortunately, new technologies find ways of bypassing these limitations, sometimes by making the lines in the bus even smaller, or supercooling the chip to reduce the resistance, which is common in supercomputers. Thus in the long run, the cumulative effect of the improvements continues to mount unabated. Figure B-3 illustrates the relationship of some incremental-level elements of a chip that lend themselves to this progress.

**The Bus.** Roughly speaking, the bus is the wiring harness that routes information among the components of a computer. It comprises the micro equivalent of a parallel printer cable, one line for each bit of information that can be processed simultaneously. The earliest computers processed only one bit at a time. Today, all but the cheapest computers have at least an 8-bit bus. Among microcomputers, the 16-bit bus is essentially standard and is about to be supplanted by 32-bit buses. Buses with 64-bit paths have been on the market for more than a year, and discussion of the 128-bit bus is beginning to surface in the trade journals.

**The Computational Logic Unit.** All computations and instructions can be broken down to a handful of logical steps, each of which can be executed by a small circuit designed to replicate that logic electronically. The problem becomes that of the software necessary to break the problem down to its most fundamental steps, which takes time. Logic units are designed with more and more complex circuits to process the instructions directly, or at least with less parsing. Because hard-wired processing is from 10 to 100 times faster than software parsing, processing speed can be vastly increased. The most common example of this technology is the coprocessor. This chip supplements the main chip in a computer and crunches numbers (other than pure integers) directly instead of having the software embedded in main chip—called *firmware*—to parse the number into its mantissa and base, next processing them separately, and then recombining them. However, see the point on *Reduced Instruction Chips*.

**Control and Switching Logic.** Similar to the computational logic unit, processing efficiency also can be improved by hard-wiring as much of the control logic as possible, with a corresponding decrease in the amount of firmware embedded in the chip (firmware) required to do the job.

**The Size of the Chip.** Signals travel at nearly the speed of light—roughly 186,000 miles per second. Thus a signal can move from one end of the chip to the other in a very short time. But when the computer is processing millions of instructions per second, these infinitesimally small travel times accumulate. The smaller the chip, the faster it will operate.

**The Registers.** Registers are memory sites on the central processing unit itself. Access time to these locations is 10 to 100 times faster than for primary memory. The increase in speed comes from both the proximity and the fact that the chip is wired to read these registers directly instead of interpreting what is in them (in most cases). The number of registers is limited, because above a certain number, the computer cannot handle them efficiently. Incidentally, the reason assembler and C language programming is so fast is that the programmer can control these registers directly and thus reduce the amount of data fetched from primary memory.

**Operating or Primary Memory.** Operating memory, when booted, stores the operating system, and as much of the application program or programs and its files that it can hold. All other instructions must be stored in secondary memory and *paged* or *cached* into the operating memory as necessary. Therefore, most complex programs benefit from having large operating memories available. For multiple concurrent users, large memories are indispensable. Without them, each user would have to be paged in from secondary memory for his split-second shot at the CPU.

**Access to Storage.** Access to secondary storage takes roughly ten times what it takes to obtain data from the primary memory, presuming that the secondary storage is on-line. The faster this process works, the faster programs will execute, when they require this access.

In the arena of quantum changes, at least three developments offer major improvements to processing speed, most of them with a significantly larger return on investment than the incremental improvements:

1) *Arrayed Processors*. Arrayed processors place two or more processing units in parallel in the same computer. Vaguely analogous to increasing the number of lines in the bus, this structure permits more than one instruction to be executed simultaneously. Working models now include a thousand or more chips in one unit. Understandably, these processors require special software techniques to keep any part of the logic from being executed before prerequisite computations can be made, but the

bottom line is that processing speeds can be increased by a factor of 100 or more.

2) *Reduced Instruction Chips*. As discussed in case study K in appendix A, system architects discovered that the addition of too many hard-wired circuits to execute instructions directly reduced processing speed. The power curve of usage indicated that only a small fraction of the instructions accounted for the bulk of the processing. Therefore, by eliminating the least used circuits, the chip size was reduced and processing speed increased.
3) *Three-Dimensional Chips*. The potential exists to manufacturer chips in layers or tiers and thus vastly increase the efficiency of the interior lines, although the research and development costs are steep.

The discussion now turns to the revolutionary changes, of which there are least three:

1) *Optical Processors*. Analogous to the storage density of optical disks compared to magnetic disks, central processing units that rely on light or optical signals instead of electronic pulses would be far smaller in size, generate very little heat, and would increase the efficiency of incremental changes by a factor of ten or more. The new IBM Series 390 mainframes have initiated this.
2) *Biogenetic Components*. This research tries to replicate the processing and memory circuits of the brain, using organic materials. However, it might not be as efficient or cost-effective as the optical model.
3) *DNA-level Computers*. This field of study is at the edge of research—the use of organic material to grow biogenetic components as needed.

## Note 3
## DATA STORAGE MEDIA

Similar to advancements in computer processing speed, progress in data storage proves that more data can be stored in less space, with faster access times, at lower costs. More data formerly considered of secondary importance can be stored on-line, which not only enhances the potential increased database processing in lieu of batch processing, but provides more opportunities for decision support systems. This brief note explains why, and parallels the discussion on computers in the previous note. The main components of this emerging technology are:

**Size.** Reduction in size offers two distinct advantages: It reduces the amount of time needed for a physical access mechanism to reach a sector, or it can access more data in the same time. Further, smaller units can be placed closer to the computer, which reduces the amount of time to transmit data to primary memory. The time saved for one transmission is insignificant. For millions of accesses, it is significant.

**Access Mechanisms.** The efficiency of the access mechanisms is steadily improving, which results in major reductions in access time.

**Caching.** This technique adds a controller in the computer, vaguely analogous to registers in the central processing unit. It enables more efficient data access. Among other things, the computer can read ahead in the instructions and store information in the cache as if it were a holding area. With a little programming, records or instructions that are accessed frequently can be stored in the cache area.

**Solid State Memories.** This quantum advance eliminates the access mechanism altogether and substitutes a storage medium that resembles primary memory more than it does traditional disks. They are not as fast as primary memory because the information on them must be kept after the power is turned off. But they are much faster than traditional disks. A good analogy would be this: primary memory is equivalent to human consciousness. Traditional secondary memory is the equivalent of material stored in a file cabinet. Solid state memory would be similar to information written on a blackboard.

These developments, when combined with the relational database and larger primary memories, have the effect of improving computer processing speeds by yet another factor of ten or more.

## Note 4
## INPUT TECHNIQUES

The trend in input technology is to eliminate unnecessary clerical processing. The key word is *unnecessary*. Most data in an information system first exists in the mind of an individual or is inherent in something that is done. The ideal—for purpose of discussion—is for the computer and its storage media to operate as if it were an observer and a note taker. This ideal is not going to happen, but the effect can be achieved in part by way of input techniques that record the information at the time it first becomes apparent, with little additional effort.

The uniform product code (UPC) is a good example. In theory, the next step will eliminate the checkout counter. That is, as the item is placed in the cart, the UPC or some future equivalent will be added to the bill (or subtracted if the item were subsequently put back on the shelf before leaving the store). In practice, this approach probably will be too impractical. Either it might encourage shoplifting, or to avoid that problem, turn the store into something of a miniature police state. For many old people, talking with the clerk at the checkout counter is one of the few social contacts they have left. This is not a joke in any sense of the word.

The effect of applying interior lines to input technology is to eliminate or reduce hindrances in the electronic, or optical, recording of data. The following examples are a small sample of what already exists in some systems, and probably deserves scathing reviews for short changing the state of the art.

**Scanners.** Page scanners record a page of information as an image. Access to that page is done by recalling the image and reading it on a terminal or on a printed version of it. The page can be transmitted anywhere in the world almost instantly. The FAX machine is the best known example, but is mostly an input-transmission-output system. The effect is to insert a computer system between two or more terminals.

**Direct Digital Readers.** The older form of this technology is the best-known. Examples include marking sense forms, magnetic ink, and optically readable type-fonts. The problem was that either the user had to record the information in a special form or use specialized equipment. The trend now is to read the information directly as it is normally recorded. Thus an electronic sheet is substituted for paper. As an individual writes on the electronic sheet, the image is converted directly to digital data. That is, each character or digit is recorded separately, which allows the information to be used in programming and support systems, not just transmitted and read. More advance technology eliminates the reading part and instead recognizes and translates the voice. At the far edge are receptors that can interpret eye movements or even brain waves.

**Digitizers.** A digitizer combines the above two techniques. It records an image and converts that image into information. Computer aided design, known as CAD, has harnessed this technique for more than 15 years. A stylus is drawn across an object or blueprint, and the information is immediately converted into a digit value for dimensioning purposes. More advanced versions take a sheet of writing and convert that to digital information. Handwriting ambiguities are overcome by interactive programming that learns to interpret penmanship.

The economics of using these techniques are obvious. They cut labor costs, and for the most part improve the accuracy of the data. The unfortunate side effect of this trend might be to increase unemployment. Earlier fears of computers and robots doing this have not materialized, but eventually they might.

## Note 5
## PRINTERS & CONTROLLING HARDCOPY OUTPUT

Two trends dominate the technology of printing. The first is to reduce the amount required, the second is to use laser printers for the balance. Printed material by its very nature eliminates the opportunity to use the processing power of the computer. Storing and retrieving data from a computer is simpler than storing and wading through closets of printouts. As data access technology improves, this alternative becomes economical. Someone has said that the written material maintained in the Library of Congress could be stored in optical format in one room, with instant access to it by thousands of users concurrently.

On the other hand, when hardcopy is appropriate, the efficiency of the laser printer is hard to beat. These printers tend to be more expensive than dot-matrix models for personal computer setups, but they are less expensive than the large mechanical models that print entire lines and sometimes entire pages in what gives the appearance of single impact. A laser printer can do specialized work that formerly took several different printers (except multiple-color printing in one pass).

The reason a laser printer works so well is once again the harnessing of interior lines. The image of the page is kept in electronic memory until the last possible moment when it is projected on the page, usually by a line scanning method analogous to the way a television picture tube operates. Different parts of the image can be reformatted into different fonts instantly. Further, because the laser printer has fewer moving parts, it seldom jams, and it requires less maintenance.

The significance for management is this: First, the expression that "paper is cheap" is no longer true. Reduction of hardcopy by relying on information technology and networked systems is cheaper, both in terms of direct costs, and in the indirect sense of eliminating the costs that accrue from storing hardcopy. Second, when printing is required, laser printers should be considered as the best choice unless there are compelling reasons to use another method.

## Note 6
## DISTRIBUTIVE PROCESSING ANALYSIS MODEL

Distribution of data sacrifices control for convenience, except in the limited circumstance where the data is centralized and only copies are distributed, or conversely, distant users access the central location. Although this star or hub model is not always practical, it provides a standard with which to compare more practical alternatives. The processing would follow these steps:

1) *Application of the Standard*. Given the number of stations and the traffic, the program would first calculate what is needed to apply the standard single-hub arrangement to meet those requirements.
2) *Point-of-Origin Application*. The next step would be to calculate the workload if all data were entered and maintained at stations closest to the point of origin, or where usage is more intense than input, at stations where it is accessed the most. This step sets the end of the curve started with the first calculation. The object is then to plot that curve and find the low point.
3) *Linear Programming or Optimization*. The third step would figure out the cost and difficulties of using distributive processing intermediately between the two end points. Actually, there would be two curves: one for costs, and another for operating efficiency.

When separate stations use entirely different databases, and the utility of massed data is essentially zero, the point of diminishing returns will be reached when the analysis goes one step beyond the point-of-origin solution. The curve will climb toward the hub model. But where the data is common to all systems and the central use of that data is of primary importance to senior management, then the curve will likely continue downward until it reaches the hub model. Figure B-4 illustrates some possible curves.

This process sounds simple, but it is not to be underestimated. Some items to consider are compatibility, capital and operating costs, existing stations, peak loading, and the likelihood of changing requirements. In all, the system would be a sophisticated decision support system. Further, because its use would be

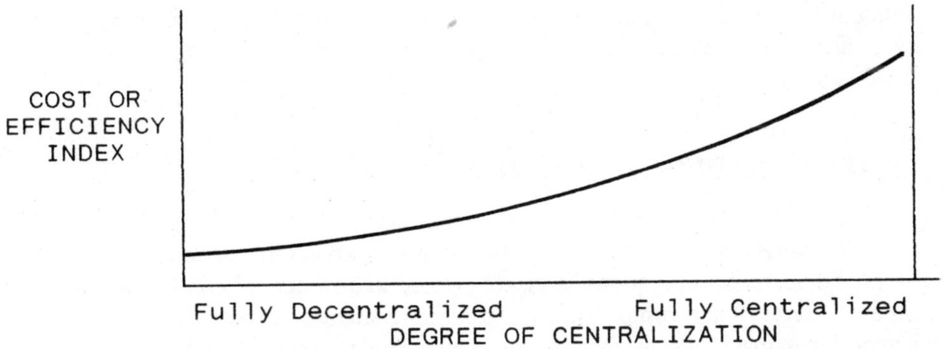


A. System with Maximum Decentralization of Data and Usage

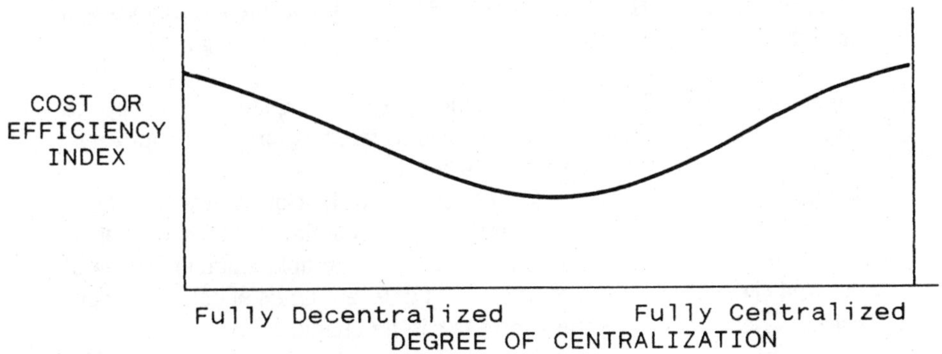


B. System with Mixed Centralization and Decentralization

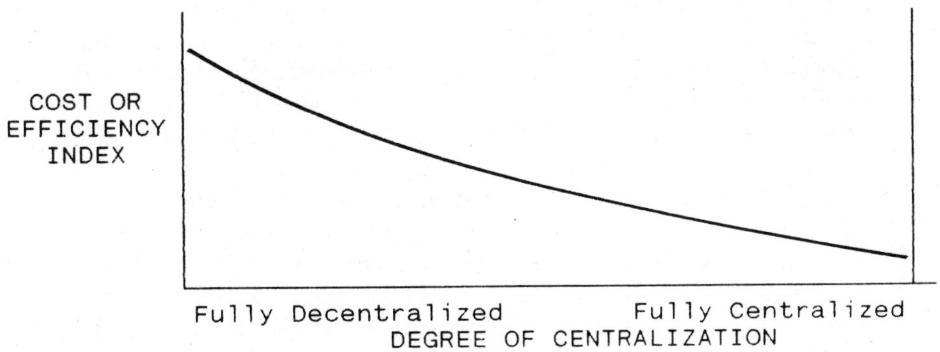


C. System with Maximum Centralization of Data and Usage

*Fig. B-4. Distributive processing optimization curves. The polemics of distributive processing range from complete centralization with access-only by other stations, to complete parsing of all data and programs to separate stations linked as required. Many options between these polemics are available, and each has its own cost and measure of efficiency. These points comprise a curve, the shape of which will vary with the situation. The optimum point is the lowest one.*

infrequent for any one corporation or organization, encouraging a university or service firm to develop just one system and then charging a consulting fee for its use would be more efficient.

## Note 7
## ELEMENTS OF PROGRAMMING

Most programming breaks down to combinations and permutations of only six simple operations. Figure B-5 depicts these operations in relational terms. Understanding these operations leads to better knowledge of compilers and translators (note 8) and comparative programming languages (note 9). The significance for management is that this perspective can provide a better understanding on the issues like: replacing Cobol programming with higher-order languages, seeking to impose a singular programming language on an entire organization (e.g., Ada, in the Department of Defense), and the advantages and disadvantages of translating existing programs into a standard language.

- *Input and Output*. These two operations are self-explanatory, except to add that the instruction also must include information (called an *argument*) to specify from where or to where.
- *Variables*. A variable is the informational equivalent of a bin with a name or label on it. A program stores information in a bin, and then uses it by referring to the name of the bin. These bins can hold singular pieces of data, an array of related data, or a mix of different kinds of data. They are called variables because the contents can be changed.
- *Operations: Adding and Subtracting*. There are two forms of adding. The first is the familiar kind in arithmetic. The second is to string two or more expressions together such as appending a paragraph to a letter. The appending form carries the technical name of *concatenation*. If quantities or expressions can be added, they also can be subtracted. Further, multiplication is repeated addition, and division is repeated subtraction (this is how early computers performed these operations). Finally, integral calculus is a simultaneous addition of multiplications. Differential calculus is a simultaneous mix of subtraction and division.
- *The IF Test*. When used in combination with the Jump statement, the IF statement gives programming great power. The IF test compares two quantities or variables by some criterion. If the criterion is met, the program will do a particular set of statements. If it fails, it will do another set (which might be nothing at all). These tests are simple: if A = B, *or* if A > B, *or* if A is not equal to B. Several tests can be combined in one test statement, but the computer checks one at a time.
- *The Jump or GoTo Statement*. Probably the most famous Jump statement in the world appears in the board game *Monopoly*. If the user lands on a certain block, or draws a certain card, he is told to go directly to jail (and not to pass GO or collect $200). That is, the normal sequence of progressing around the blocks is interrupted by a leapfrog move to another part of the game board, read *program*.

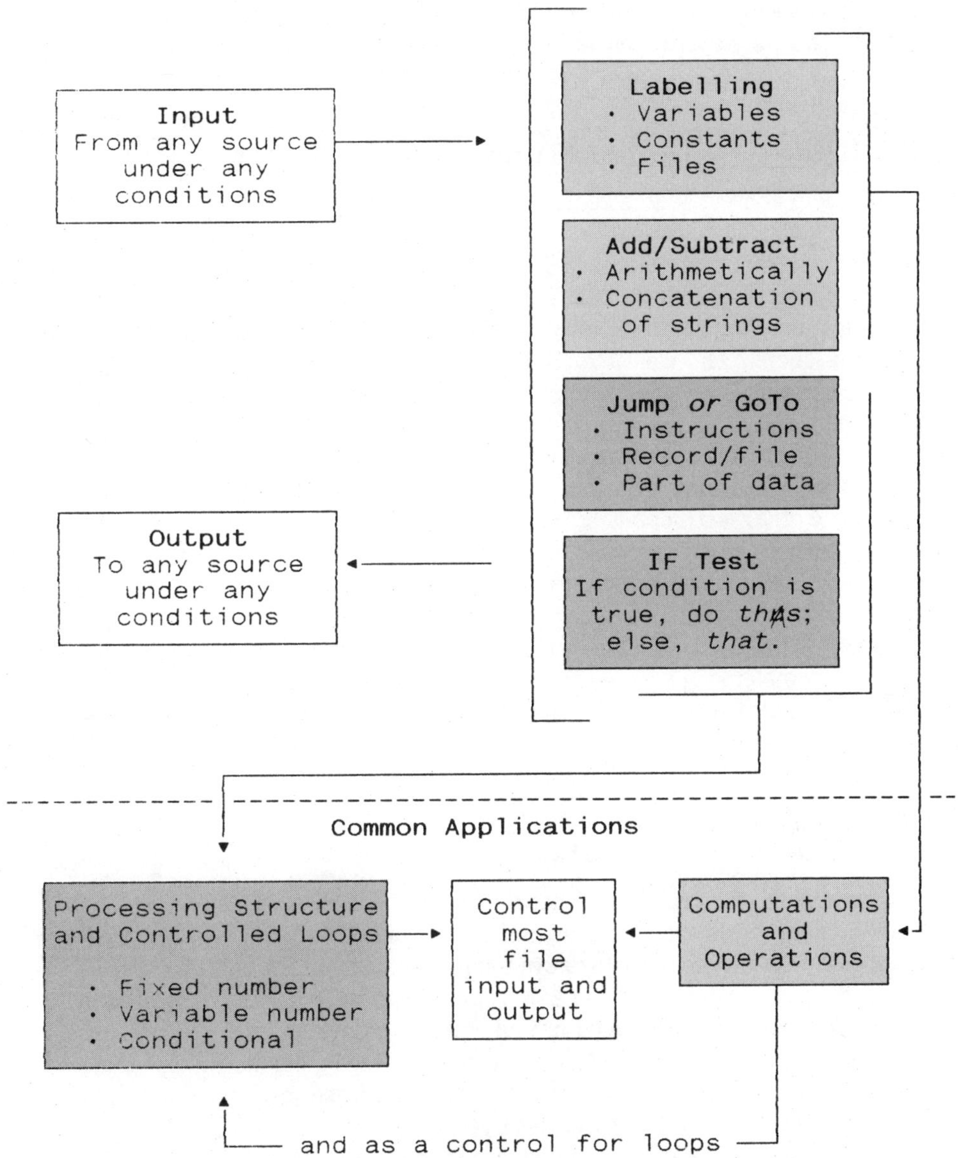


*Fig. B-5. The six elements of programming. Essentially all programming reduces to permutations and combinations of six simple operations. Understanding these operations offers a perspective to gauge the advantages and disadvantages of higher-level languages.*

Structured programming has sought to eliminate the GoTo statement, but this needs to be understood in perspective. The Jump operation is indispensable in 99.99 percent of programs, but it can be misused to the point where reading the programs becomes a chore. Structured programming seeks to eliminate the abuse by substituting elegant programming statements that use the GoTo statement implicitly. The compiler (note 8) then parses the instructions into simple instruction steps that include the necessary GoTo or Jump statements.

## Note 8
## COMPILERS AND TRANSLATORS

Compilers convert source code, or whatever instruction a user enters, into machine language that a computer can execute. A translator, in effect, combines a compiler and what might be called an *uncompiler*. That is, a translator reduces source code into something that is close to assembler language and then rewrites it in another language, which is similar to what happens in spoken language translations. The translator reads or hears something in one language. Next, the meaning is reduced to more fundamental ideas. Then those ideas are recast in another language. Word-for-word translation is either impossible or leads to major problems, and has been a rich source of many anecdotes.

A compiler operates with four steps. The first (*lexer*) step converts the variables and other instructions to common symbols and lists them in tables for management purposes. The second (*parser*) step breaks complex statements into sequences of simple instructions. The third (*optimizer*) step rearranges the instructions for improved processing efficiency, for example, to make better use of registers. The fourth (variously named) step then converts these instructions into assembler language, which is normally a one-for-one swap. This product is then reduced to machine code by a separate assembler. Figure B-6 illustrates the above sequence.

## Note 9
## PROGRAMMING LANGUAGES

Management often asks why there must be more than one standard programming language. In theory this is entirely possible. In theory, it is also possible for every country to drop its native tongue and take up English. Any logical requirement can be programmed in any programming language and translated to any other language. Thus it would not take much to develop an *Esperanto* language for programmers. In fact, this language already exists and is called *assembler*. But because assembler is too intricate to use for direct programming, higher-level languages are necessary.

Each language offers different practical advantages to simplify different programming requirements. Fortran lends itself to scientific programming, Cobol is for record processing, and so forth. Figure B-7 illustrates some of these comparative advantages.

The issues for management then become threefold: Would it be practical to create a single language that can compromise among the various advantages of separate languages, or possibly to offer variations where appropriate? That failing, would translating programs into a standard language be worthwhile? If that alternative is impractical, can standard program generators be developed that will produce source code in these separate languages?

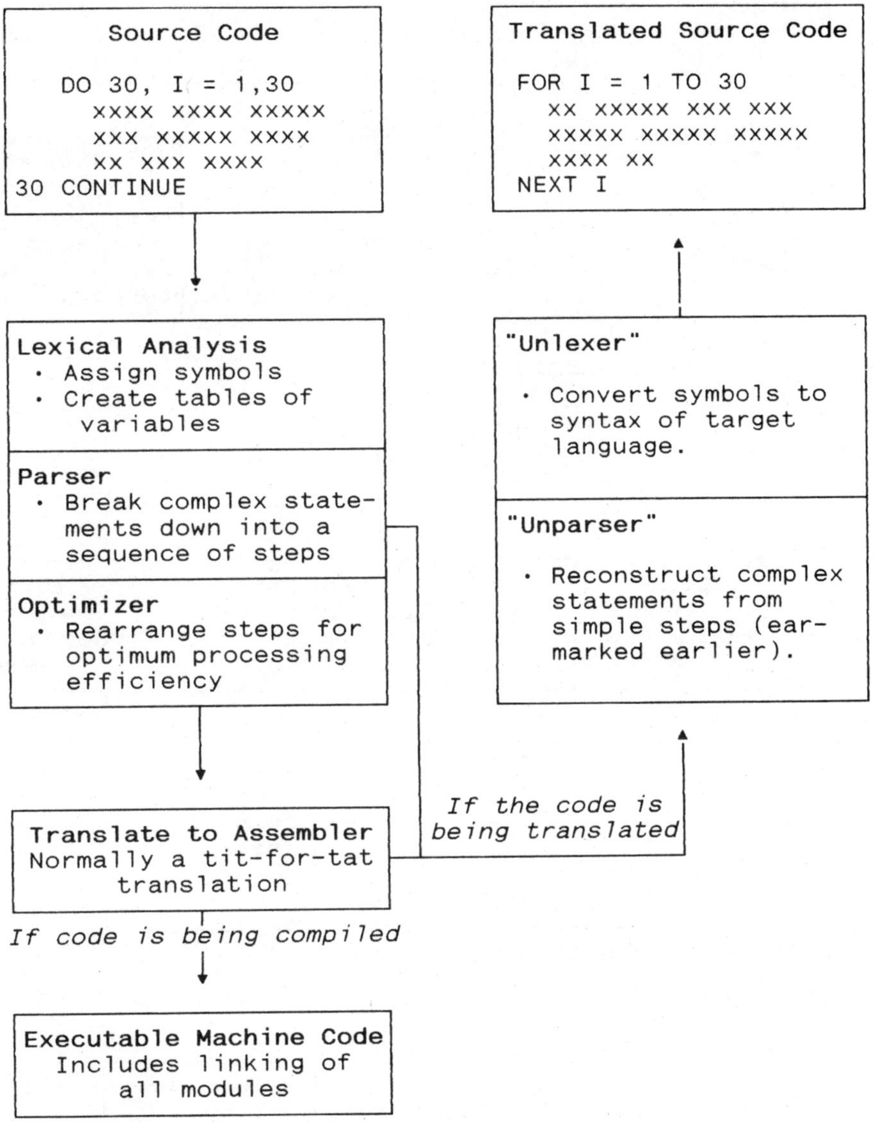


*Fig. B-6. Compilers and translators. A translator converts source code written in one language into another. A compiler translates source code into machine language and is therefore a special case of a translator. The significance to management is understanding the advantages and disadvantages of translating existing programs into other languages for the sake of either standardization or ease of maintenance and revision.*

The answer to all three questions is negative. The attempt of the Department of Defense to force the use of Ada for all its systems has succeeded to a significant degree by way of fiat. But many programs are exempt, and few organizations outside DoD have adapted it. The C language has gained enormous popularity, but it is cryptic and has not made much headway against the 70 bil-

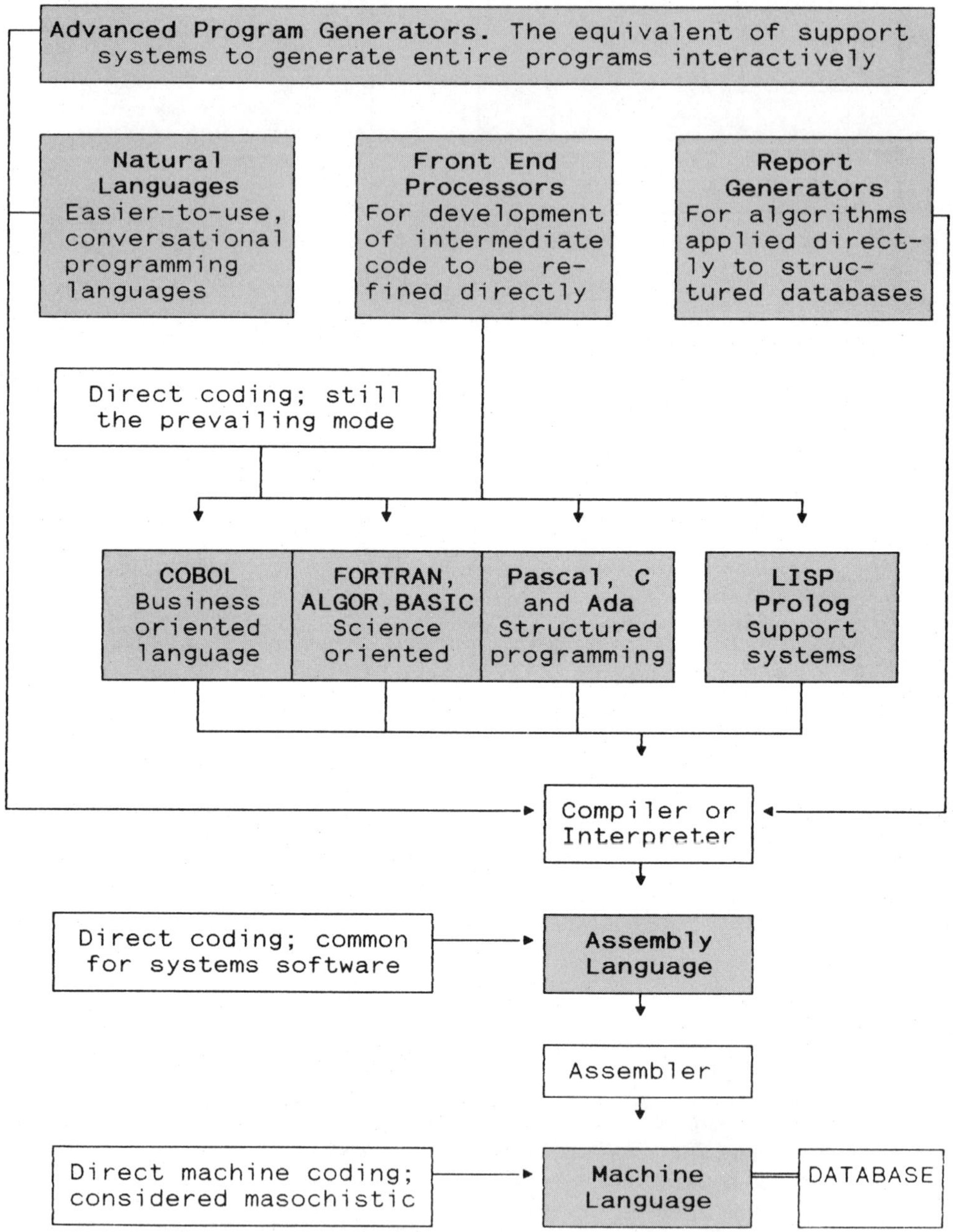


*Fig. B-7. Relationships among programming languages. The expression* programming languages *is misleading. It implies that they are all variations on a common theme, which is true in theory, but not in the practical sense. Some are intended for general programming, others primarily for database access and utilization, still others for expert systems. To date, no single language has been developed that will meet all these needs.*

lion lines of Cobol programming still in use. QuickBASIC (and its professional-level counterpart) probably comes closest to a compromise language, and it offers several options for programming. Although it is popular with amateurs, its use in the corporate world is limited. In short, there is little reason to believe that any attempt to develop a universal language would succeed.

The alternative of translating programs into a standard language also would fail. After translation the language would be difficult to maintain. If a universal language is impractical, creating a back-up standard would be even more impractical, which leaves the alternative of program generators. These are already used extensively, but programs written with them can be compiled directly into machine code. Other versions are in effect pseudo code for Cobol and other languages. With Cobol, maintenance is usually done directly with the source code produced by the generator.

In short, the Tower of Babel that exists among programming languages is likely to remain a fixture of the systems landscape in the foreseeable future, and it is not without its advantages. Instead of continuing the Quixotic endeavor, therefore, management can concentrate on more practical measures: the use of program generators designed for specific purposes; the use of prototyping, structured programming, better documentation, and extensive testing; and above all relational databases with standard data element dictionaries. With these measures, the programming language problem should stay at the subcritical level.

## Note 10
## THE SPECIAL CASE OF THE SPREADSHEET

The spreadsheet is a popular piece of software, and various surveys show that one brand (Lotus 1-2-3) is the most popular software package on the market. True, this statistic is slightly misleading. The collective sales of word processors outweigh the corresponding sales of all spreadsheets, yet it still seems unusual that something so specialized as a spreadsheet can give word processing a run for its money. What is the secret?

The "secret," such as it is, is that the spreadsheet simplifies programming. All six elements of programming (note 7) are visible at the same time in a form of graphical display (not to be confused with the generation of graphs from spreadsheet data). In a sense, a spreadsheet can be used as the equivalent of a flowchart that is also the program. Branching logic—IF tests and GoTo's—are immediately visible and organized. Figure B-8 portrays this utility. A spreadsheet will lend itself to prototyping complex logic.

- *Input and Output*. For spreadsheets, input and output are divided into internal and external forms. *Internal input* is where the user directly enters the data into a cell, although for the sake of neatness, it can be entered in one cell and then read by another cell in the same spreadsheet. *Internal output* is where a cell displays the results of a computation based on a formula that is written in that cell. That is, the user makes a one-time entry of a formula or miniature program in a cell and the software displays the results. *External input* is by reference to cells of other spreadsheets. *External output* comprises routine printing or graphs.

- **Interactive Input.** Direct entry of data into a cell.
- **Processing Input.** Function or reference in cell that obtains data from another cell or spreadsheet.
- **Instant Output.** The display of the cell with a formula or a function in it.
- **Display Output.** Graphs and printouts.

| | 1 | 2 | 3 | 4 |
|---|---|---|---|---|
| A | LOAN | $50,000 | | |
| B | RATE | 10% | | |
| C | YEARS | 30 | 25 | 20 |
| D | | | | |
| E | PAYMENT | $439.79 | $454.36 | $482.52 |
| F | Exceeds 30% of Disposable Income? | | | |
| G | | No | No | Yes |

- **Variables.** The cell is the variable, e.g. A1 or G4.
- **Operations.** Entered as a formula/function in a cell. *The cell displays the results, not the formula.*
- **IF-Test.** Entered as a function: (@IF(test,do,else do)
- **Jump/GoTo.** Difficult to use. Data is obtained from another cell rather than being "sent" to another cell. To shift control to other cells requires the use of advanced program commands.

*Fig. B-8. The spreadsheet as a microsystem. The original intent of spreadsheet software was to adapt the advantages of word processors to financial sheets. Unwittingly, the geometry of a display was combined with the algebra of programming, paralleling the contribution of analytical geometry for mathematics developed by Descartes several centuries ago. The upshot of this software is a fundamental tool for systems development. Slow processing speed is a delimiting factor, but that is immaterial for design work and prototyping logical arrangements.*

- *Variables*. The cell is the variable, or colloquially speaking, the bin into which data is put. If the entry is a formula or function, then the value will change when the values in the referenced cells change. If not--except by way of elaborate programs—it can only be changed by the user making a new entry.
- *Operations*. These are formulas or functions that are written into a cell, and consist of three types: simple computations that reference cell labels, functions that are programmed in the software and inserted by their respective names, and functions that primarily fetch data from other spreadsheets or tables in another part of the spreadsheet.
- *IF Tests*. In most spreadsheets the IF statement is nearly identical with those used in ordinary programming. The problem is the lack of elegant structures to bypass the infamous GoTo statement. On the other hand, the GoTo in most spreadsheets operates in reverse.
- *GoTo Statements*. In older versions of spreadsheets, any jumping had to be accomplished by bringing the mountain to Mohammed, so to speak. Instead of the logic branching to other cells, the data from other cells had to be brought to the cell where the IF test resided. This was clumsy, and sometimes impossible, for all but simple logic. This difficulty was overcome by adding a form of programming language to the spreadsheet software, although it remains an intricate programming task. The need is for an IF statement/junction (other than a programming command) that directs one cell when the test is true, and update in (optionally) elsewhere when it isn't.

The utility of spreadsheet software is further enhanced by the ability to insert a visible relational database, and many users have built practical systems directly this way. For those who prefer a separate database management package, utilities are available to link the two. Thus, as a summary, spreadsheet software makes interior lines more visible. Further, the inclination to avoid giant-sized printouts serves as a motivation to make those lines as tight and as efficient as possible.

## Note 11
## DATA ELEMENT CODING

When independent databases are integrated, the most likely form of intractable incompatibility will be differences in the definition of equivalent data elements, or the closely related problem of identical definitions with different breakdowns of legal range of values. Even something as mundane as the respective fields for "name" can cause heated debates. Is the field singular or divided into subfields? Will an initial suffice for the middle name, and should it have a period to differentiate it from middle names that consist of one letter (Harry S Truman being the most well known case)? Or what about the hyphen in hyphenated names? Should a blank be interpreted as a hyphen or are there cases where the blank is appropriate and does not represent a hyphen? These are not facetious examples. For example, the Social Security Administration did not add the hyphen to its database until 1988, and then only under public pressure.

Compromise rarely works. Usually the only practical solution is to apply the greatest range of legal values for any one system to all systems. Yet even that fails when different systems use different ranges of values. Yet neither can be said to have the wider range or the strictest criteria. The only practical solution is to develop an even more detailed set of values that will encompass both sets, analogous to the mathematical concept of the lowest common denominator. Figure B-9 shows a simple application of this technique.

This solution is not without its problems, as it could increase the number of input coding errors. This problem can be overcome by software routines that convert any specific input to the required code, using interactive prompting for more information if necessary. Revised codes, for the most part, would require revisions to programs that relied on the former range of codes. Still, if the integration is imperative or at least comes packaged with obvious advantages, this approach might be necessary. Further, the integration does not ask any user to compromise on the standards that the targeted systems were originally designed to meet. All that will happen, beyond a one-time revision to some programs, is that the inputs will be stored with a greater degree of refinement, and much of that will be computer generated.

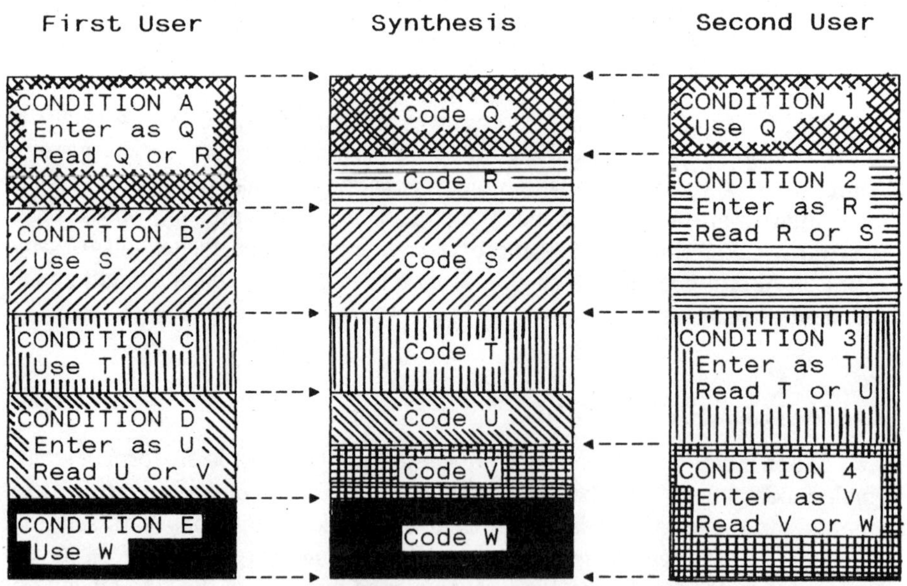


*Fig. B-9. Data element coding for integrations. A difficult problem in integrations is reconciling differences between data element definitions and legal range of values. This problem might give the appearance of minutia, yet it has been the death of more then one attempt at integration, wasting millions of dollars in the process. The discontinuities often can be resolved by refining the range of values. This refined set would accommodate different users without denigration to their respective requirements, yet permit the integration to proceed.*

## Note 12
## NORMALIZATION IN A RELATIONAL DATABASE

Normalization in a relational database is a measure of the absence of entangling relationships among the records and data elements. The theory is that the fewer the relationships, the cleaner the interior lines between users and the database. The practical effect is that different users can access the same database for entirely different requirements without coordination with other users. Restated, a high degree of normalization offers resiliency.

Figure B-10 portrays the five levels of normalization. Each level starts with the criteria of the preceding level, and then adds new restrictions. Of the five levels, maximum digestibility seems to occur at the third level. The fourth and fifth levels are aggravating to work with, but they offer major advantages in some circumstances by eliminating ambiguity in return for creating additional fields, or worse, additional files. In very large systems, a trade-off analysis is imperative before using these higher degrees.

- *First (Format) Level.* This level simply means that every record must have the same number of fields.
- *Second (The-Key-as-an-Entity) Level.* In this level, all data must relate to the key field as an entity. If the key field is "name," then an informational field cannot describe what a part of the name means, for example, the full spelling of a middle initial. Either put the full spelling in the key field or don't include it.
- *Third (Informational Field Independence) Level.* No informational field can contain information that is dependent on the value of another informational field. Thus, the current age of an employee cannot be entered in the same record as the date of birth (nor need it be, except possibly in a generated view). On the other hand, this does not eliminate the potential for compatibility checks. For example, date of birth and date of employment are not logically related in an absolute sense, but when they are too close, an input error is probable.
- *Fourth and Fifth Levels.* These levels refer to problems when working with variables that have multiple relationships, and usually require additional fields or multiple files. Figure B-10 shows one example of the former.

## Note 13
## INDEXING TECHNIQUES

As databases expand in size and database processing replaces batch processing, the problem becomes that of locating a specific record as quickly as possible. Sequential searches have always been impractical. Some form of logical shortcut is necessary that reduces access time to 1 percent or less, preferably much less of the time necessary for a sequential search. Many techniques are available. The three most popular are: the index method, the binary search, and the hashing technique. Any two or all three can be combined, although usually in a sequence of different techniques at different steps in the search.

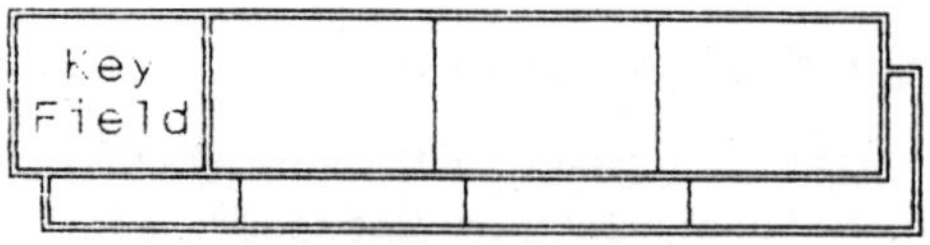


FIRST FORM

Every record in a file must have the same number of fields, implicitly used for the same purpose. The value in the key field must be unique and not null. No restrictions on other fields.

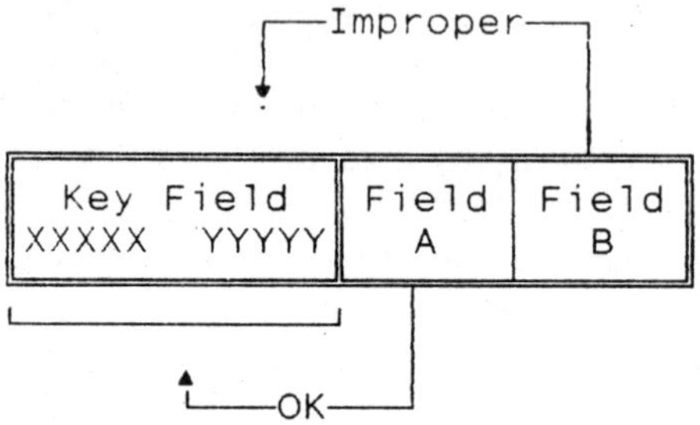


SECOND FORM

A nonkey field must describe the key field in its entirety. This applies only to composite key fields. When this is logically necessary, restructure the database with two or more files and use programming to link relationships.

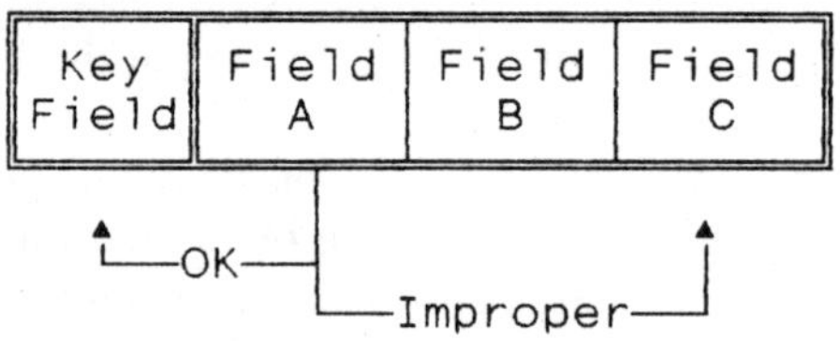


THIRD FORM

A value of a nonkey field cannot depend on the value in another nonkey field, though this does not bar compatibility checking. Again, when this situation is logically necessary, use separate files and let the programming do the linking.

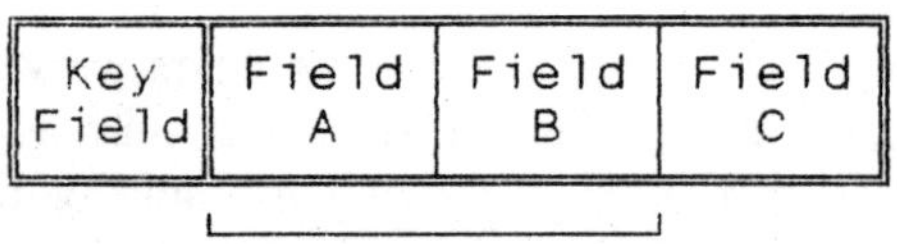


Avoid fields that have two or more legitimate values for the same record at the same time.

FOURTH & FIFTH FORMS

These forms restrict underlying relationships among the nonkey fields for the sake of reducing ambiguity. Solutions include separate records, or separate fields for each potential value of each field. These forms are impractical for some databases.

*Fig. B-10. Degrees of normalization in relational databases. The value of a relational database structure increases with improvements to the simplicity of its interior lines. These improvements go by the name* degrees of normalization, *which is the degree to which the structure approaches a theoretical ideal. The ideal (fifth) form normally requires a greater breakdown among files, but the trade-off is that ambiguity is eliminated.*

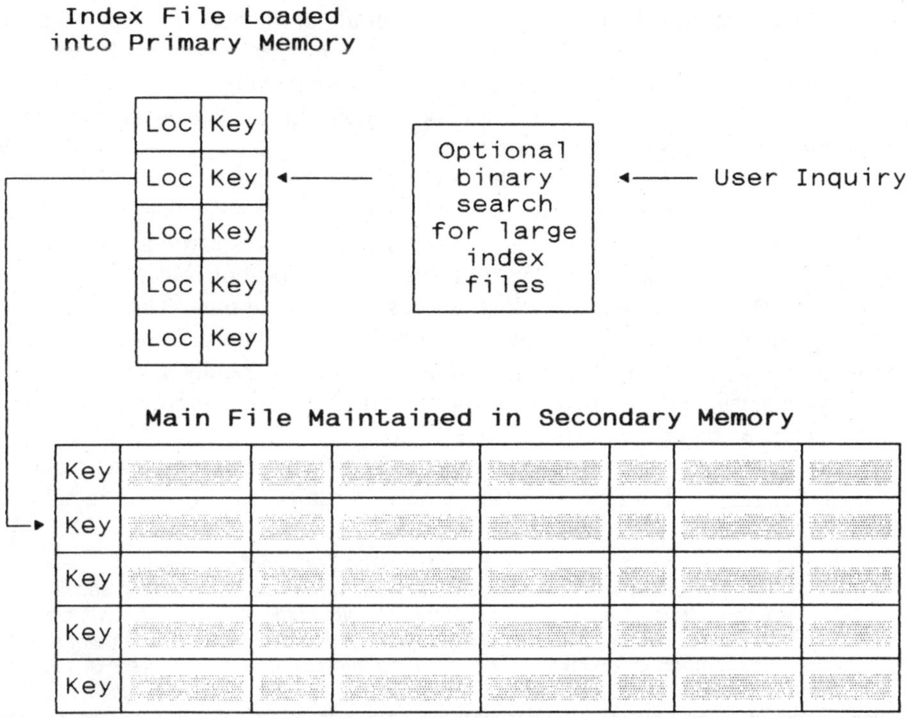


*Fig. B-11. The index method of direct access. The index method parallels the logic of an index in the back of a book. A book index lists the key terms and the pages where those terms can be found. The user quickly scans through this index and then uses the location data, or pointer, to proceed immediately to where the relevant information is stored. The computer automates this process the same way.*

**The Index Method.** In its simplest form, the index method is a computer parallel to the index in the back of a book. The key fields of the file are entered in a secondary table with the storage location of the full record, as shown in FIG. B-11. When a record is needed, the program searches the index record sequentially (which is often maintained in main memory during program execution) until it finds the record, and then goes to the storage location. In more advanced forms, the index record itself is searched by the binary method (described next). This method is similar to using a mental index with a book index. A reader searches for the first letter of the word he is looking for, and then further brackets his search until he finds the key word.

**The Binary Search.** If the records can be stored in a definite alphanumeric sequence, the binary search is the fastest and simplest approach. Although the logic is irrefutable, it never ceases to amaze observers. Briefly, the search goes to a predesignated number that is roughly in the middle of the file. If the value of the key is lower, the pointer is placed in the middle of the lower half. If higher, the value goes to the middle of the upper half. The search keeps eliminating half the balance—like the half-life of radioactive decay—until the record is found. TABLE B-1 provides some data on how this done. Because the mathematics are identical with compound interest, huge increases to the size of the database require only a few more trials. In practice, sophisticated algorithms make this process even faster.

**The Hashing Technique.** This aptly named technique uses a formula that computes a value based on information contained in the key field, and then uses that number as the storage location for that record, displayed in FIG. B-12. Inevitably, more than one record will be stored in each location, but a computer can and usually does access a block of records at the same time. The potential problem is that one bin can overflow while others remain empty. To prevent this problem, the logic of the hash must be thought through carefully. Even at that, some means will be required to accommodate an occasional overflow, such as a point that leads to a secondary location.

The significance to management is that as knowledge-based systems proliferate and as the need to generate many views of a database increases, the need

*Table B-1. The binary method of direct access. The binary method requires that all records be sequenced in some alphanumeric sequence. This method permits finding any record, with only 30 trials, from a file containing 1 billion records. Each move cuts the remaining pile in half. This method is the inverse of compound interest at an interest rate of 100 percent per microsecond. The table indicates the number of trials required for different size files.*

| Number of records in the file | Maximum accesses to find any record | Time required for a sequential search at one millisecond each | | | |
|---|---|---|---|---|---|
| | | Days | Hours | Minutes | Seconds |
| 10 | 4 | | | | 0.01 |
| 100 | 7 | | | | 0.1 |
| 500 | 9 | | | | 0.5 |
| 1,000 | 10 | | | | 1 |
| 5,000 | 13 | | | | 5 |
| 10,000 | 14 | | | | 10 |
| 50,000 | 16 | | | | 50 |
| 100,000 | 17 | | | 1 | 40 |
| 250,000 | 18 | | | 4 | 10 |
| 500,000 | 19 | | | 8 | 20 |
| 1,000,000 | 20 | | | 16 | 40 |
| 2,000,000 | 21 | | | 33 | 20 |
| 5,000,000 | 23 | | 1 | 23 | 20 |
| 10,000,000 | 24 | | 2 | 46 | 40 |
| 50,000,000 | 26 | | 13 | 53 | 20 |
| 100,000,000 | 27 | 1 | 3 | 46 | 40 |
| 250,000,000 | 28 | 2 | 21 | 26 | 40 |
| 500,000,000 | 29 | 5 | 18 | 53 | 20 |
| 1,000,000,000 | 30* | 11 | 13 | 46 | 40 |

*EQUAL TO .03 SECONDS AT 1 MILLISECOND PER ACCESS

```
123-45-6789
   |
   |--> • Peg the location to a segment of the
   |      number, such as the last four or five
   |      digits: in this case 6789 or 56789
   |
   |--> • If the number segments were unevenly
          distributed, a computation could be
          used, e.g., the sum of the digits
          or a more complex formula.
```

**A. Some Alternatives with the Social Security Number**

```
SMITH......
   |
   |--> • Using a segment is normally impractical
   |      because names have different numbers
   |      of characters. Also, letter patterns
   |      are not always randomly distributed.
   |
   |--> • For variable-length character data, a
          computation is normally used. Each
          letter has a numerical value (A = 65,
          B = 66, C = 67, and so forth). One
          method would be the sum of the values
          of the first three letters, sometimes
          multiplied by a factor to compensate
          for the letters in the first half of
          the alphabet occurring more frequently:

ABD... 65 + 66 + 68 = 199; Hash = 199 * .9 = 179
STR... 83 + 84 + 82 = 249; Hash = 249
```

**B. Some Alternatives with a Last-Name Field**

*Fig. B-12. Direct access by hashing. The hashing technique for direct access consists of computing a numerical value from values contained in the key or access field. This computed value is the location of the record. In theory, this is the simplest and fastest method of direct access, but in practice an uneven distribution of records among storage locations can detract from that efficiency.*

for efficient direct-access methods will become more critical. Although direct-access methods can be overdone, this is one area that even general managers might wish to assure themselves that the technical professionals give these methods a high priority.

## Note 14
## OVERCOMING THE ERGONOMIC GAP

If ergonomics is the weak point in computer technology, then investment here might offer greater marketing opportunities for hardware, networks, and software in both national and international markets. Notwithstanding the brilliance of computer technology, it is often clumsy to use, to link, and to program. Figure B-13 illustrates the extent of the problem in terms of a work station.

The object of this brief discussion is to indicate how some of these problems might be overcome, although a cooperative venture is required among some leading manufacturers of hardware and software. The current agreement between the WordPerfect Corporation and the Lotus Development Corporation

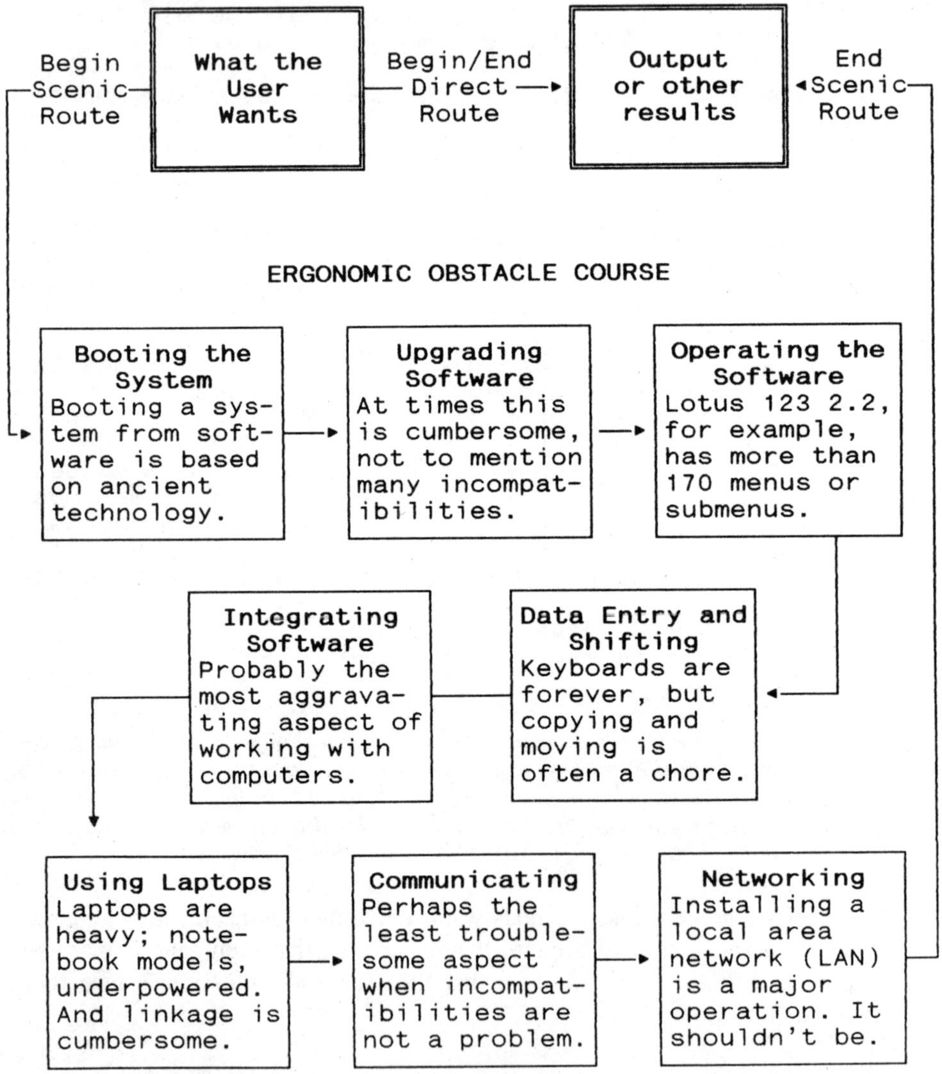


*Fig. B-13. The ergonomic obstacle course. Notwithstanding the magnificent record of advances in computer technology, man-machine interfaces—*ergonomics*—have been largely ignored except in the specialized fields like prostheses and high-speed immediate-reaction environments. The obstacle course which confronts the ordinary user is another matter.*

to produce integrated software is the precedent. At the same time, the failure of the proposed consortium among six hardware manufacturers, to produce a more competitive memory chip, should be kept in mind.

The emphasis in the proposed specifications is a practical integration in the broadest sense of the word, with the intent to simplify the use of computers and software for the user. Figure B-14 provides a schematic of the setup. The technology is focused on those points where the user and the machine must interact. A brief description of the key features follows:

**Modularity.** All components would be modular. The user would be able to install any setup by plugging modules together with minimum difficulty.

**Mini-Micro Integration.** The work station could be purchased as a single unit or as a unit in a network supported by a minicomputer. In the former case, the computer module would plug into the work station. In the latter case, the work station would plug into the mini via trunk line cable units. A possible alternative would be to create software only for each work station, and use the mini (or some equivalent) only for the storage of user created files and databases. In that setup, the central control point would be just another work station, albeit with certain software controls over the database.

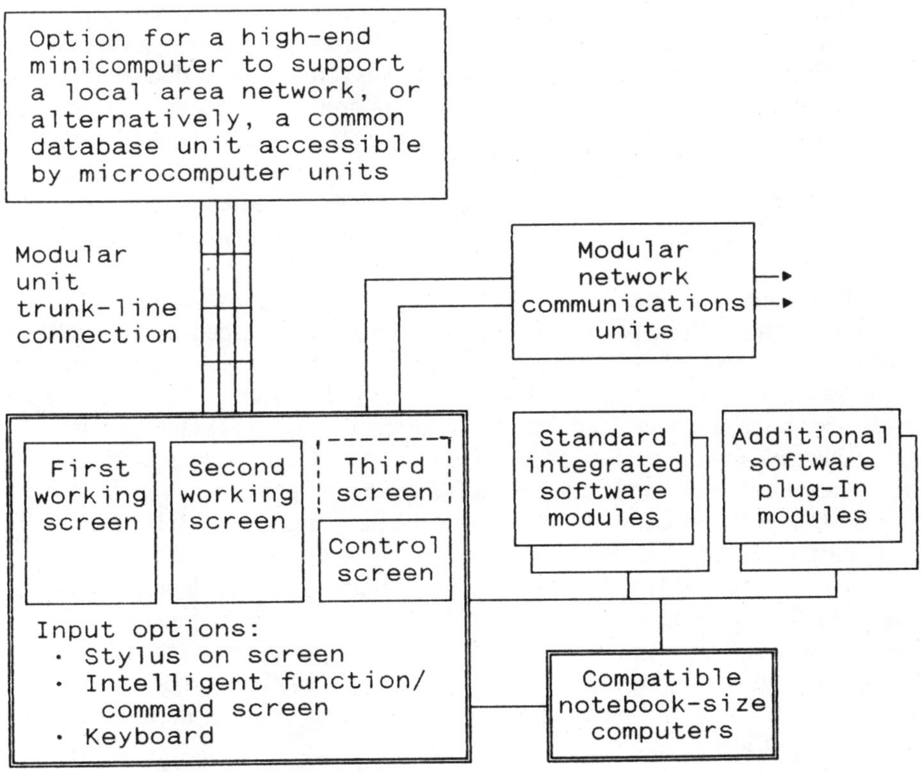


*Fig. B-14. A proposed approach. This proposal is simply an integration of proven technologies to reduce the ergonomic obstacle course between man and machine in most applications.*

**Trunk Line Cable Units.** These units would be approximately ten feet long, except for right-angle connectors and one-foot extenders. Each would have a relay circuit at one end to ensure reliable parallel transmission of data in densities approaching those within a computer. The power line would be part of the units, and might not need shielding if the transmission lines were fiberoptics. The idea is to give the user the ability to instantly install a macro system in any configuration.

**Wide-Area Networks.** A wide variety of plug-in modules with necessary modems and utility software should be made available to connect the system with other systems that are not directly compatible.

**Compatible Laptop or Notebook Computers.** The setup would include the option for compatible laptops or notebook computers, with the ability to connect them with a cable and read user developed files directly in either direction. The software would also be identical in a logical sense, but it would be available only in separate modules. The laptops themselves would also be modular, with the capability of changing screens, disk drives, and so forth. None of this involves a hint of new technology; it would be a matter of reconfiguration only.

**The Work Station Screens.** The work station itself would eliminate the traditional monitor. Instead, it would consist of two (with the option of three) solid-state screens capable of display and input from using a mouse-type stylus. Thus if there was a spreadsheet displayed on one screen, and a document on another, the user would merely trace the stylus around the portion that was wanted, click a button, move the stylus over to the other screen, position it, and then click the button again. The images on the screens could be instantly magnified, compressed, or shifted by slide-type switches located on edges of each screen. A long list of similar features can be produced without much imagination.

**Traditional Keyboard.** A slide-out keyboard would be available for traditional text entry, but the present function keys would be replaced with a small, touch-sensitive rectangular screen. Functions that could not readily be incorporated with sliding switches and an "intelligent" stylus would be displayed as a cascading series of menus. The display of context-sensitive help information or other guidelines would be automatic (unless turned off), probably in a window on the screen other than the one to which the function pertains.

**Software Modules.** All software would be packaged in read-only modules that plug into the system. However, to preclude abuse of licensing agreements, the modules intended for the mini, the work stations, and the laptops would each be a different configuration. Further, and with one exception, no computer would be able to access or read the software modules in another computer. The exception would be the modules for the mini, which could be read by the work stations. Purchase of these modules could have a variable price, depending on the number of work stations.

**Standard Software.** The five main units of the software would be a word processor, a spreadsheet, a database management package, a sophisticated graphics package, and desktop publishing. All would be developed for instant relatability and transfer of files or segments between any two units.

**Additional Software Modules.** There is no limit to the number and variety of productivity and proprietary software modules. The extent to which they were compatible with the standard package or with each other would be a decision for the manufacturer.

**Providing for Future Enhancements.** Modularity is intended for ease of installation and for updating technology. The latter is more difficult, as advances in technology sooner or later will go beyond ability of the setup to accept. For this reason, the modularity should be thought through carefully. In this way the eventual obsolescence will be later rather than sooner—like the old reliable axe that has had its head replaced twice and the handle three times.

**Pricing.** These setups would be more expensive than work stations in use today. But with the accelerating computing capabilities of microcomputers, eliminating the expense of the minicomputer might be feasible for local area networks, except as a means of storing common data and files. Further, for most corporations and other organizations, the hardware bill is a small fraction of the systems budget. The advantages gained should outweigh the increase in capital investment.

The unfortunate aspect of these proposed specifications is that they lack imagination, and imagination seems to be what motivates advances in technology. To overcome that deficiency, a few additional features might be considered:

**Three-Dimensional Holographic Images.** The technology to project a three-dimensional image in space has been available for at least ten years. The best-known application is displayed in the computer center at Epcot Center in Disney World, Orlando, Florida. The application would be to project files as images. However, except for some graphs and CAD software, the three-dimension effect would be used to view different parts of a database, spreadsheet, or pages of related documents.

**Interfacing with the Image.** The ability to interface with the holographic image—analogous to the use of an "intelligent" stylus—would be a valuable addition to a system.

**Program Generators.** This idea is an extension of the potential to use so-called three-dimensional spreadsheets for prototypes. In combination with program and expert-system generators, the effect of the program could be visualized as an entity, as well as permitting different users to test and operate different portions concurrently.

The totality of the above specifications, both ordinary and advanced, is a tall order. Very few companies in the United States would be in a position to invest in it. Moreover, some of the ideas might run afoul of antitrust legislation. To minimize the chance of this happening, several precautions should be taken:

**Hardware.** It is difficult to imagine any company in the United States, other than IBM, that could take on a project of this magnitude. IBM already invests $6 billion a year in research and development. Further, the basic specifications, for the most part, stress configurations of existing technology, instead of the more avant-garde stuff that IBM tends to avoid. Finally, IBM sales have been declining steadily for several years now (though this trend seems to be abating). The company really does need to bite into something new. On the other hand, opening the gates should be of interest for any other company that might want to compete for the balance of these setups. There would be no formal consortium. By the same token, the project would not be undertaken unless it appeared that other companies were more than interested in pursuing their share of the work.

**Communications & Networks.** AT&T would be a good bet, especially if they could see their way clear to disengaging from the largely futile squabble with the IBM-Microsoft team on the matter of operating systems. Perhaps the ideal would be for IBM to concentrate on the hardware, while Microsoft teamed up with AT&T to work on the network components and the necessary systems software. As it is, the relationship between IBM and Microsoft gives hint of having grown a little testy of late.

**Standard Software.** The agreement between the WordPerfect Corporation and the Lotus Development Corporation would be a good starting point. If Ashton Tate, which markets dBASE IV, could not be persuaded to join the agreement, then either another firm could be considered, or what would be more likely, the database software already produced by the WordPerfect Corporation could be brought to bear. But the difficulties of coming to agreement in this arena should not be underestimated. The intended parnership between Lotus Development Corporation and Novell took a nosedive before it got off the runway.

**Additional Software.** The marketplace for competitive software is fierce, and one of the surest ways of avoiding antitrust problems would be to provide free assistance (and seek no license fees) from any competitor who considered developing compatible software modules. Carried to the ultimate, all of the primary manufacturers could make a point of not producing any additional software for the general setup.

Summing up, the whole show is intended to extend the interior lines of information systems into the hands of users.

# Appendix C

# Atlas of Interior Lines for Systems

*Concentration is the secret of strength*
*in politics, in war, in trade, in short*
*in the management of all human affairs.*

—R. W. Emerson

Flowcharts and schematics are ubiquitous in computer science and information systems, but an atlas is lacking. This appendix does not supply that lack, yet it does illustrate the role of interior lines from the inmost recesses of a chip to the strategic use of information systems. The seven charts cover the following items:

1) *Overview*. Figure C-1 is an overview on the relationships and hierarchy of the main components of information systems.
2) *The Hardware Setup*. Figure C-2 covers the concept of interior lines applied to computers and peripherals. The emphasis is on the ability of the mechanics to react to user requirements.
3) *Networks and Distributive Processing*. Figure C-3 illustrates transmissions (and their incompatibilities), networks, and distributive processing. The interior lines here are obvious.
4) *Database Structure*. Figure C-4 covers database structures, which are the logical basis for interior lines of information systems.
5) *Database Access*. Efficient access, both for updates and utilization, makes the interior lines of the database structure extend almost to the user, as shown in FIG. C-5. Software intervenes.
6) *Software*. Figure C-6 indicates that software is still the key for turning the mass of information into useful intelligence.
7) *The User Environment*. Figure C-7 suggests that the interior lines of a system should extend to the grasp of users.

## OVERVIEW

### Interior Lines

In any system, the interior lines run in many directions, and there is seldom any one obvious best design. Still, the lines between users and hardware, and the return trip, should be the most direct for the majority of users most of the time.

**Problems.** Existing, piecemeal systems do not always lend themselves to strategic purposes beyond the profits to be made from efficient routine transaction-type processing. They rarely adapt to integration, except perhaps for a few critical interfaces.

Network and communications capabilities lag the processing speed of computers. The consequence is to concentrate too much thinking on hardware and to rely excessively on communications and interfaces to overcome the deficit.

**Power Curves and Trade-Off Considerations.** Replacing existing systems or integrating them with a more expensive merger-type model usually provides handsome returns on the greater investment. However, there comes a point when separate systems are too different to warrant any further attempts at linkage no matter how worthy the strategic goals.

The most far-reaching strategic decisions will likely remain the province of a few senior decision makers, drawing on extensive experience and perhaps intuition. The development of effective information systems to support that level of decision, beyond providing useful data in response to queries, might be asking too much.

### Significance and Implications

The potential for effective information systems has hardly been tapped, but the pitfalls are deeper and perhaps more insidious than commonly presumed.

### Dominant Principle of Information Strategy

**Responsibility.** The intracacies of modern information systems will usually overwhelm any approach except when an individual sets his mind to make a difference.

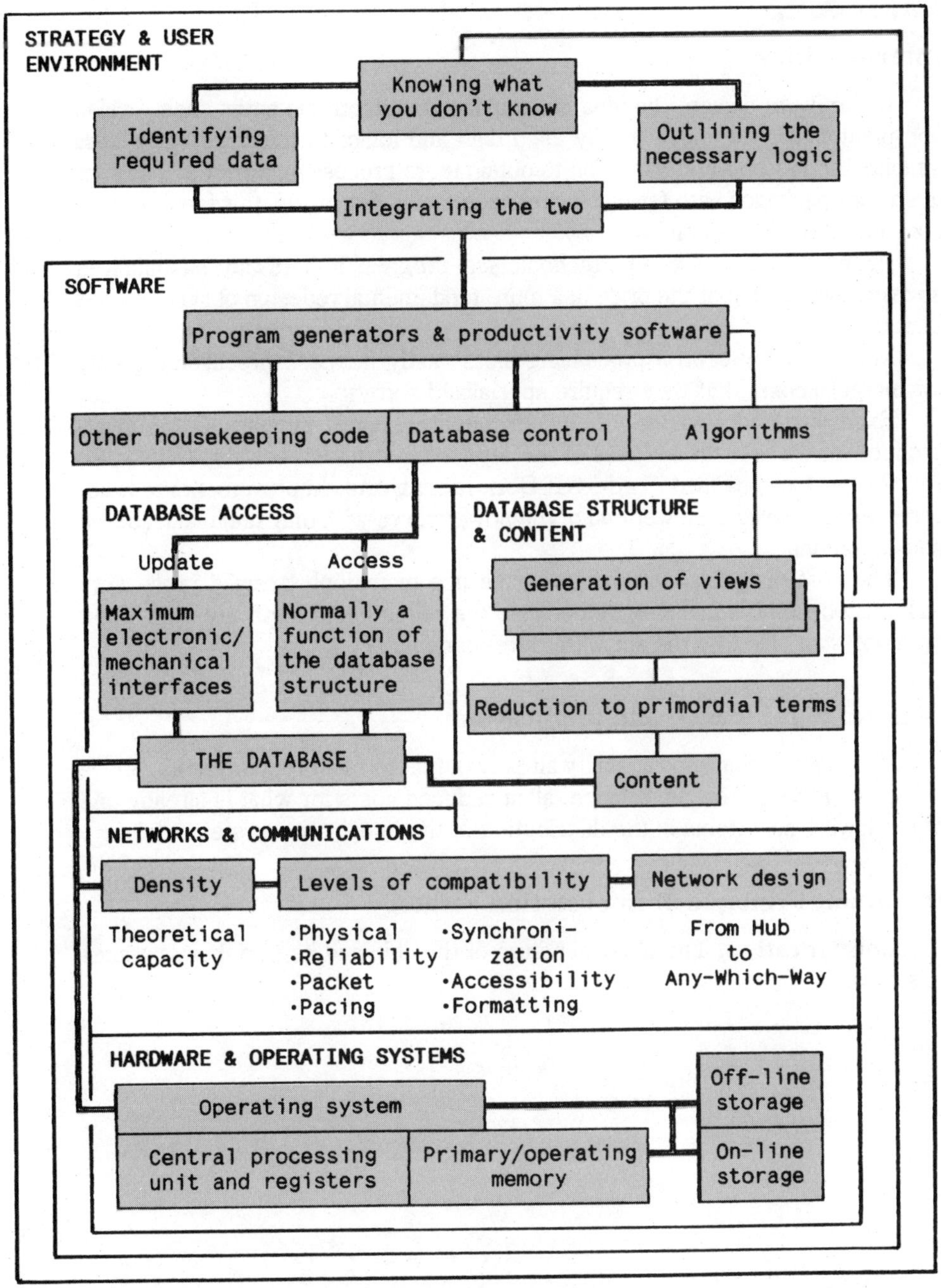


*Fig. C-1. Overview of a system's interior lines. Interior lines are the essence of good systems. These lines exist at all levels; from the architecture of the central processing unit to the managers that use the system for strategic purposes. The maximum effectiveness of interior lines is achieved when all the tiers evince a high degree of integration, which means the capability of comparing and exchanging data and information with the least interference and the fewest delays.*

## HARDWARE

### Interior Lines

In hardware design, the idea is: to make the electronic paths short, wide, and plentiful for the most heavily used data and logic; to minimize or at least simplify the systems software; and to obtain more processing power at less cost in smaller packages with fewer maintenance tasks. Strangely, this ideal is often considered too conservative.

**Problems.** The awesome technological progress in hardware has inspired an overreliance on it at the price of a more fundamental redesign of systems and integrations.

Multiple-array central processing units vastly increase processing power for marginal costs, but they require specialized software.

Excessive hard-wiring of less-frequently used circuits is counter-productive, witness the success of the reduced-instruction-set chip (RISC).

**Power Curves and Trade-Off Considerations.** Improvements to hardware seem to be at the lower end of the power curve with only minimal trade-off considerations.

The cost of special software to make use of multiple-arrayed processors will likely become a major issue because the reduction in hardware cost might be more than offset by the software development.

### General Significance and Implications

Hardware design and capability already outpaces most requirements, and is fast closing the gap on the balance, all at reduced costs for what is already one of the lowest-cost items in the distribution of the information systems dollar.

### Dominant Principle of Information Strategy

**Configuration.** The physical nature of the chip and its peripherals makes this obvious.

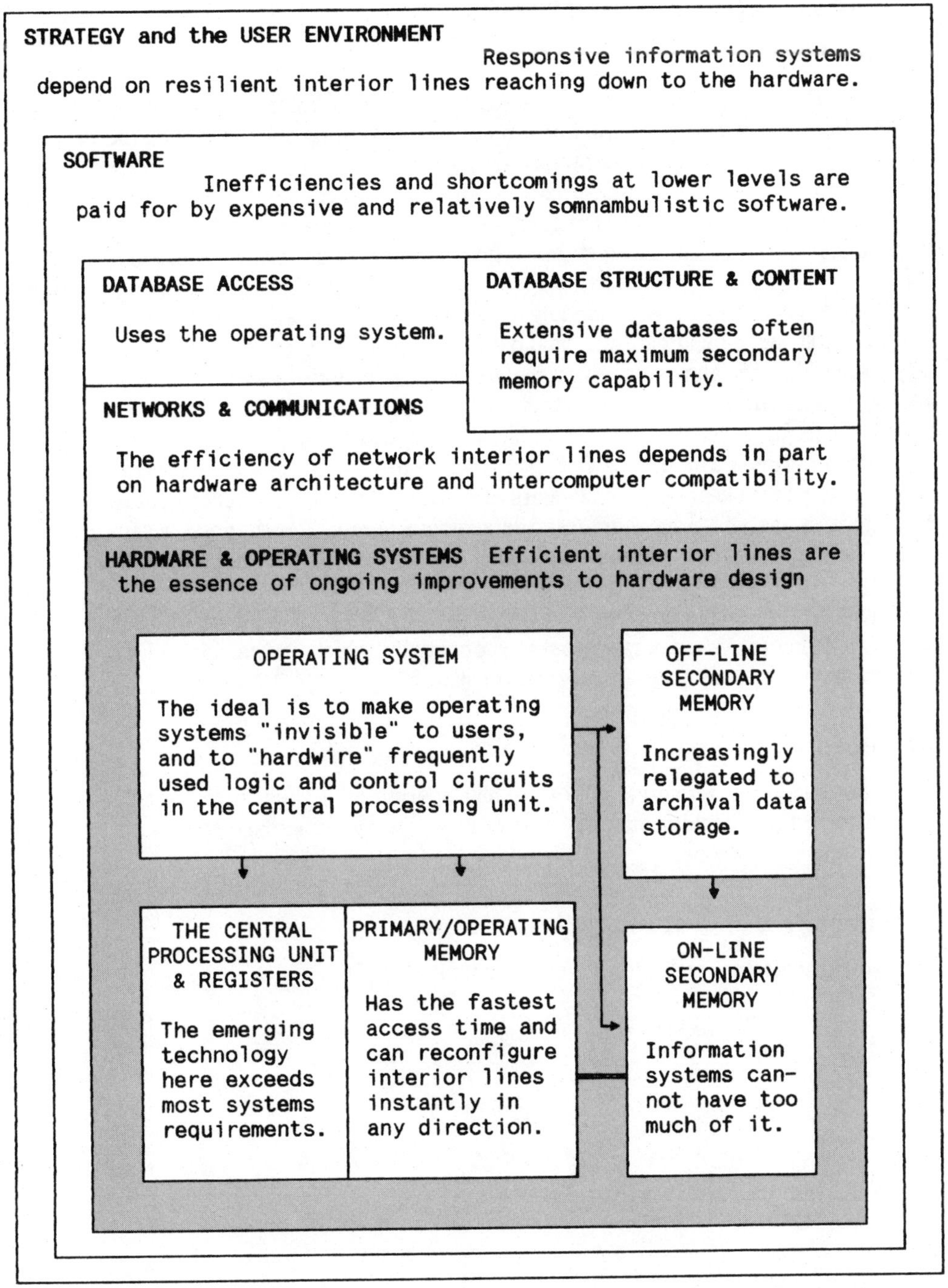


*Fig. C-2. The interior lines of hardware. Hardware and peripherals were the first element of systems to achieve interior lines—exemplified by the integrated circuit. Progress continues to evince radical improvements with no hint of levelling off in the foreseeable future, although too much effort on one aspect can lower overall efficiency.*

## COMMUNICATIONS AND NETWORKS

### Interior Lines

Networks are a Brobdingnagian counterpart to the Lilliputian environment of hardware. The goal remains that of simplifying the routing and increasing the capacity of the paths most frequently used, but the often large number of nodes greatly increases the options, alternatives, and trade-off considerations.

**Problems.** The ease of communications is often used as a substitute for a more fundamental restructuring or redesign of a system, database, or integration.

Communications—notwithstanding the dramatic progress over the past century—still lags behind hardware and database structure in terms of theoretically attainable efficiency, but emerging technology and the Open Standards Interface Agreement is changing this picture so rapidly that compromise designs might be severely outdated within a few years.

**Power Curves and Trade-Off Considerations.** In theory, a centralized database with hub-like spokes to all users offers the maximum efficiency. But to the extent the satellites have different data requirements, the theoretical efficiency can be more than offset by excessive and unnecessary communications traffic.

High-speed, reliable communications, especially when off the beaten track of established networks, can raise costs exponentially, which can quickly reduce the return on investment for an information system.

### Significance and Implications

As an endpoint, networks will eventually operate as if they were a single unit. In turn, this should reduce the use of interfaces and increase the use of merger-type integrations.

### Dominant Principle of Information Strategy

**Configuration.** Again, for obvious reasons.

**STRATEGY and the USER ENVIRONMENT**

Knowledge/data-hungary information systems demand either efficient networks or centralized data.

**SOFTWARE**

Good interior lines in communications indirectly improve those in software by reducing the number required.

**DATABASE ACCESS**

Access begs good networks.

**DATABASE STRUCTURE & CONTENT**

Logical structure and content is usually more independent of network structure than assumed.

**NETWORKS & COMMUNICATIONS**

Network interior lines are not the same thing as capacity.

1. DENSITY is the theoretical capacity to transmit data

2. But the many LEVELS OF INCOMPATIBILITY operate to denigrate the capacity to transmit data and software:

- Physical
- Reliability

- Packet Length
- Pacing
- Synchronization

- Accessibility
- Formatting

3. All which is further weakened by the difficulty of designing an optimal NETWORK. The hub-model is the most efficient in terms of interior lines, but it may not coincide with the distribution of data and processing.

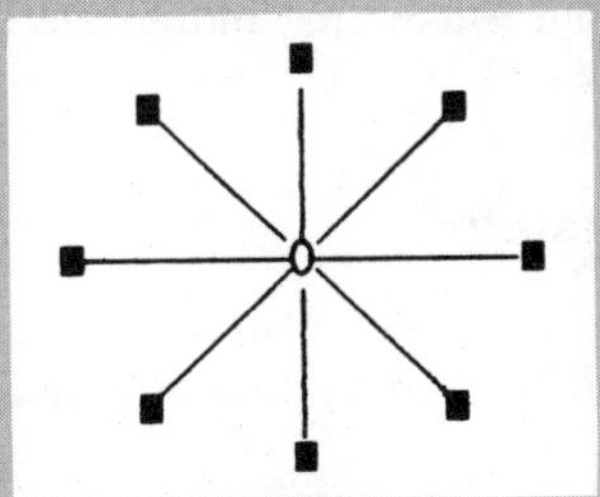

HUB MODEL

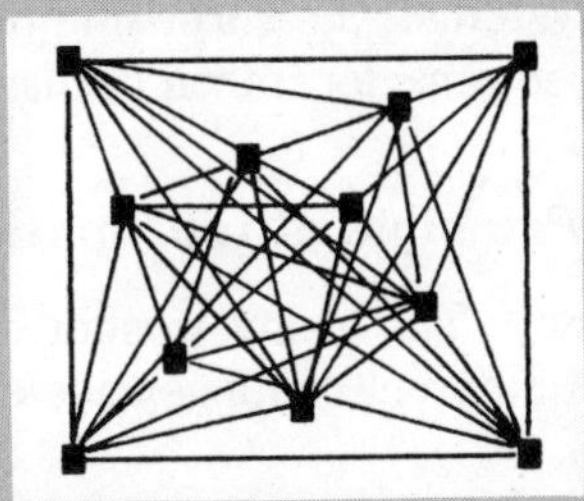

ANY-WHICH-WAY MODEL

**HARDWARE & OPERATING SYSTEMS**

High-capacity hardware is nearly meaningless if a supporting network is inefficient.

*Fig. C-3. Communications and networks. Although networks by definition exemplify the concept of interior lines, in practice they are slow compared to computers. Further, they are usually inundated with incompatibilities. Finally they are often used in lieu of a better design for distributing and accessing data. This is especially true for merger-type integration superimposed over a network of interfaces.*

## DATABASE STRUCTURE AND CONTENT

### Interior Lines

The intent is to reduce ambiguity and linkage among records in a database, and to push that task on software. In that way, every user can develop unique interior lines to reach into a common pool of data without coordinating the work with other users. If the database is expanded, most existing programs will continue to run without revision.

**Problems.** Relating data among separate systems or building a replacement system often runs into logical incompatibilities among the data elements. Standardizing data element definitions and ranges of values is often the single most difficult task in developing information systems, which requires cumbersome utility software to effect linkage.

Many systems still operate in the batch-processing mode, and lend themselves neither to database processing nor to an excerpt-type integration of different databases.

**Power Curves and Trade-Off Considerations.** Increases to the content of the database often yield remarkable improvements up to a point, after which the returns are marginal and the security problems vast.

The relational database model lends extraordinary resiliency to informational databases, but the ideal of the maximum normalization criterion might be too troublesome to use in some applications.

### General Significance and Implications

Integrations increasingly favor the database and excerpt models for use in information systems. The surprising thing about this is that more data is often available in electronic form than perhaps realized.

### Dominant Principle of Information Strategy

**Resiliency.** The ability to shift data into different relationships and patterns to meet different contingencies exemplifies the definition of resiliency.

**STRATEGY and the USER ENVIRONMENT**

If sufficient data is available, any informational requirement can be met. From that point forward, development is a matter of logical and electronic efficiency.

**SOFTWARE**

While the relational database structure makes initial programming harder, the trade-off is resilient interior lines.

**DATABASE ACCESS**

The logic of access programming is often simplified by ironclad adherence to the relational database structure.

**DATABASE STRUCTURE & CONTENT**

1. Once the content issues of the database are resolved, the ideal is to record data only in its most primordial form.

2. This, in turn, permits the generation of an infinite number of views, including views generated from other views, to meet any information requirement.

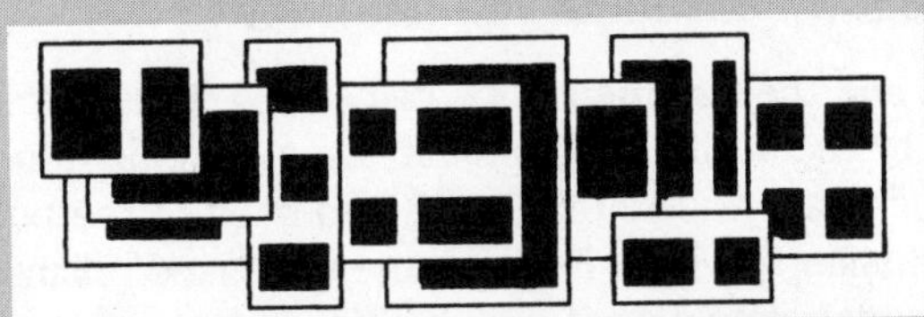

3. And ideally, this will eliminate duplicate data, and permit maximum compatibility checking of inputs and updates to improve the quality of the database.

**NETWORKS & COMMUNICATIONS**

The distribution of the database is the most critical interior-lines issue, assuming the content is adequate.

**HARDWARE & OPERATING SYSTEMS**

For the most part, hardware is available at reasonable cost to meet any database need.

*Fig. C-4. Lining up the database ducks. The majority opinion is that extensive data and knowledge, rather than elegant algorithms, comprise the primary basis for good information systems. But how that data is reduced and organized can make a major difference in the resiliency with which it can be related in different patterns or views to meet different requirements.*

## DATABASE ACCESS

### Interior Lines

The relational database itself facilitates access to data, but in addition the access system can be made more efficient by reducing the amount of human intervention for recording and updating data, and for accessing and creating views of it for applications.

**Problems.** Security is far and away the greatest problem because as databases become more efficient to use, they are even more subject to abuse.

The requirements for audit trails and other quality control measures can increase the paperwork and expenses of maintaining larger databases, at a disproportionate rate.

**Power Curves and Trade-Off Considerations.** Measures to increase the quality of data—validity, correctness, reliability, and so forth—offer worthwhile returns up to a point. Thereafter they offer marginal and perhaps diminishing returns.

The cost of security increases exponentially with increases to the size of the system. If a given amount of data from separate systems is massed into a single system, the efficiency is offset by greater security problems.

### General Significance and Implications

As data and the experience for discerning what is important accumulates, accelerated by the ability to obtain data by electronic rather than manual input, the knowledge base will increase and lend itself to the potential for even more useful information systems. Further, the increased reliance on merger integrations tends to facilitate access and quality control, whereas the older interface model exacerbated the problems.

### Dominant Principle of Information Strategy

**Simplicity.** As data is the foundation of information, a lack of simplicity at the root is often fatal to the branches.

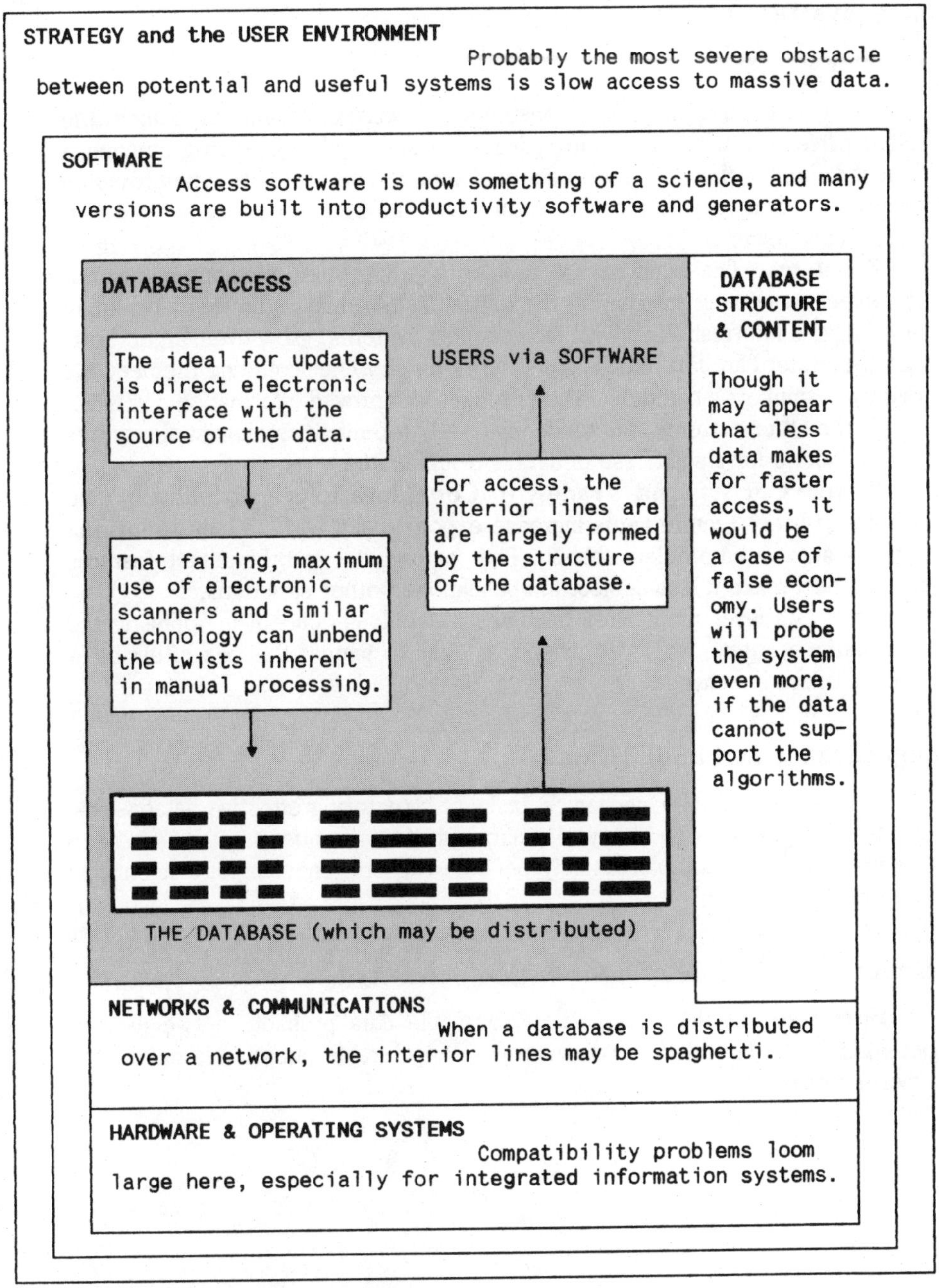


*Fig. C-5. Lines for database updates. Good databases deteriorate rapidly in the absence of timely and correct updates. To improve this process, the ideal system will extend its interior lines directly out to the source of the data, which is difficult in practice. But to the extent that data capture procedures can approach this ideal is the degree to which the interior lines will reach maximum efficiency. As a corollary, the same efficiency is needed for access to data for applications, although separate lines might work best.*

## SOFTWARE

### Interior Lines

The intent is to reduce time-consuming software development to algorithm tasks, preferably with maximum reliance on so-called object programming—closest to human thought processes—and then to use program generators and associated technology to facilitate even that. The benefits are more effective systems and lower costs.

**Problems.** The most severe problem is that when development of the housekeeping code is automated, the logical tasks remain, and for increasingly sophisticated information and decision support systems, grow even larger. Software generators are not reliable substitutes. In short, discounting the need for practical "thinkers" can defeat the purpose of improved information systems.

At the other extreme, the tendency to rely too much on elegant algorithms as a substitute for a solid base of data is troublesome.

**Power Curves and Trade-Off Considerations.** Algorithmic (and knowledge-base) requirements increase exponentially with an increase to the scope of automated problem solving. The costs go up, and the unique features of the model make it less subject to application in other situations.

Return on investment often becomes a nebulous concept in sophisticated information systems, and even when it is easy to gauge, the risk of direct or indirect failure increases.

### Significance and Implications

As the more-or-less mechanical tasks of structuring effective databases—coupled with the growing ability of separate systems to operate as if they were one unit—software will increasingly become the only meaningful challenge in systems development.

### Dominant Principle of Information Strategy

**Initiative.** At the present time, available data probably outweighs the potential for better information systems. Considerable initiative is needed to reverse this process.

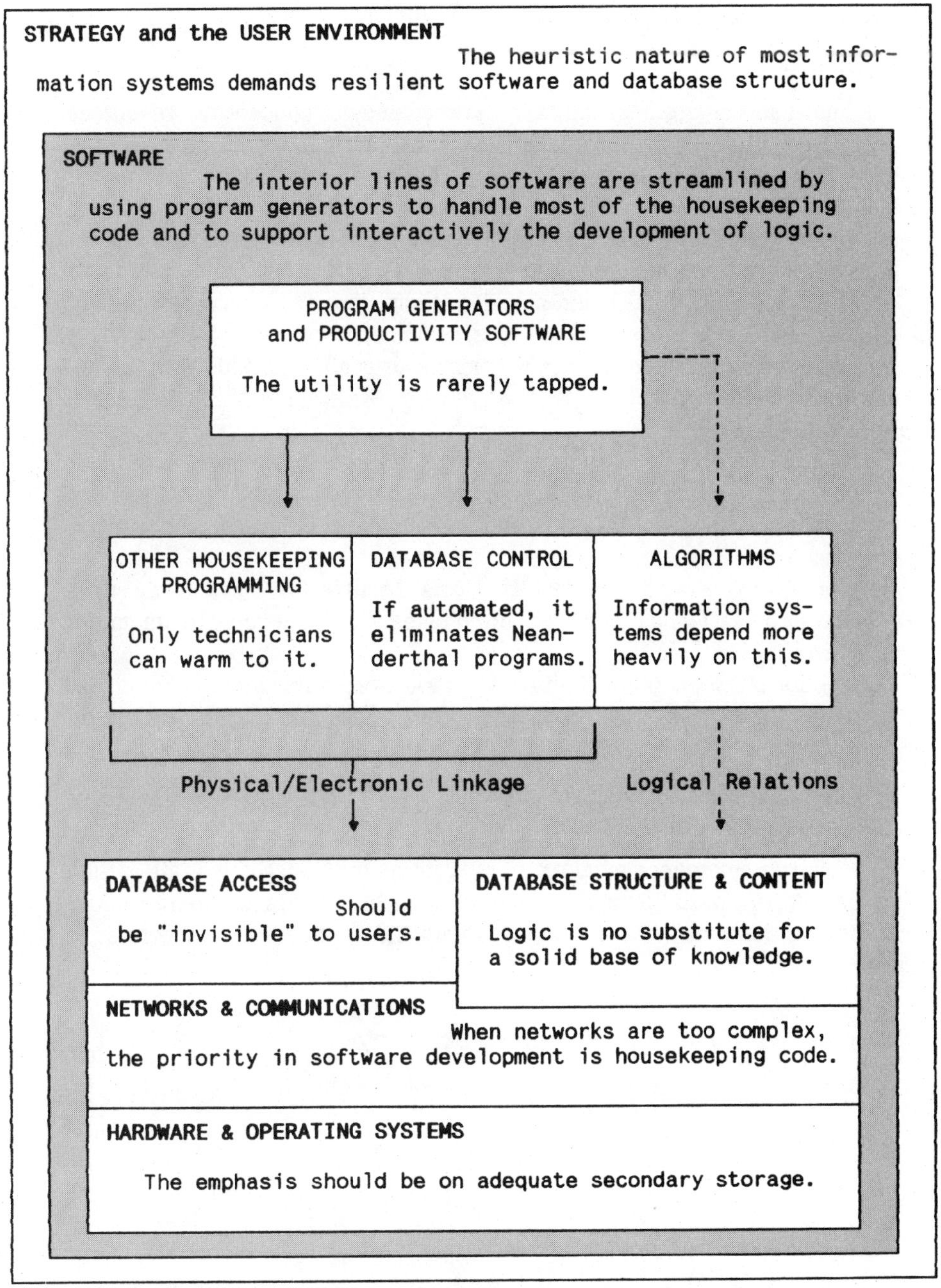


*Fig. C-6. The realm of software. Software serves two purposes in information systems: to execute the logical requirements of management, and to compensate for gaps in the interior lines of any system. Some gaps are inevitable, but the idea is to reduce that usage to a minimum. Further, to the extent a system and its database offers resiliency of access is the degree to which the development of software can concentrate on algorithms and leave the housekeeping code to systems and productivity software.*

## STRATEGY AND THE USER ENVIRONMENT

### Interior Lines

An information system should have the resiliency to concentrate resources to meet strategic requirements, and to reconcentrate them to accommodate the changes that all organizations experience. That is, to the extent the interior lines of a system reach out to the grasp of users, is the degree to which those users will find it easier to mass the data in different configurations to draw inferences appropriate to current requirements.

**Problems.** Unlike transaction-based systems, the return on investment of information systems is more complex to measure and evaluate.

Although strategic effectiveness is laudable, it is often at odds with technical efficiency. Compromise between the two perspectives is difficult to achieve in practice.

Good systems should be simultaneously quick, comprehensive, effective, supportive, and interactively lead the user to a sharper but still heuristic focus on business pursuits, usually with trend lines, what-if analyses, and graphs. That's a tall order.

**Power Curves and Trade-Off Considerations.** Introducing user friendliness into an information system often takes a disproportionate amount of development.

Trade-offs between productivity and market-oriented effort is complex. Productivity is less risky, but marketing often offers the greater return on investment.

### Significance and Implications

Overall, the emergence of information systems have sharpened rather than facilitated competition in the marketplace, but insightful users have better odds. Fewer corporations might be willing to expend the effort to make the most of systems.

### Dominant Principle of Information Strategy

**Objective.** Users are interested primarily in results. Results equal objectives.

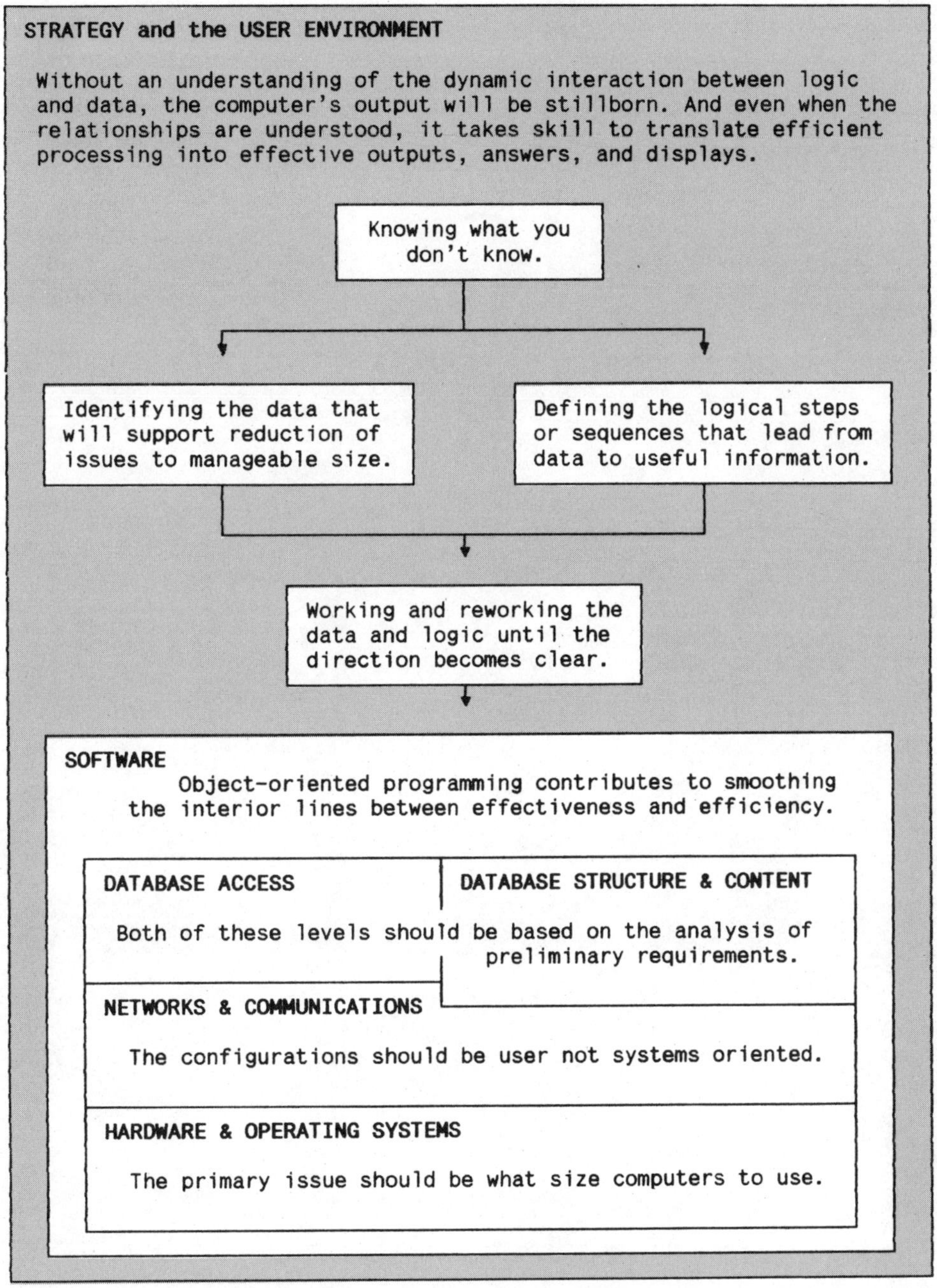


*Fig. C-7. Strategic reach. An information system should contribute to the attainment of strategic goals. The idea is to use these systems to reach as far as possible into the marketplace or alternatively into production lines. Sometimes this can accrue from the collective effect of separate systems; at other times it is accrued by related programs operating off a common database; and in a few cases this is accrued by a genuinely integrated system.*

# References

*Books constitute capital . . .*
*Often in the case of professionals, setting out in life,*
*it is their only capital.*

—Thomas Jefferson

As mentioned in the Preface, approximately one-half million references are available in the field of computer science and information systems. Even if only 2 percent of them would suffice to gain a comprehensive understanding of the field, that would still be 10,000, not counting the difficulty of identifying those select few. Thus to list a mere 32 references here is an insult to the work and scholarship that has gone on over the past 50 years. All that can be said is that the references listed either proved especially helpful or have been noted by many others.


Addis, T. R. *Designing Knowledge-Based Systems*. Englewood Cliffs, N.J.: Prentice-Hall, Inc., 1986. This book matches up expert system technology with the relational database structure, a critical means of improving interior lines of information usage.

Arthur Young Information Technology Group. *The Arthur Young Practical Guide to Information Engineering*. New York: John Wiley & Sons, 1987. The seminal importance of this book is that it shifts, as the title states, the emphasis from software engineering to information engineering, which is the essence of object programming and user orientation.

Beered, Annabel C. *Expert Systems: Strategic Implications and Applications*. New York: Halsted Press, 1987. This is a good survey of a critically important topic, and makes the point clear that interactions between bona fide experts and software engineers are often strained to the point where the automated project is useless.

Bjørn-Andersen, Niels, Daniel Robey, and Ken Eason. *Managing Computer Impact: An International Study of Management and Organizations*. Norwood, N.J.: Ablex Publishing Corp., 1986. A major study in systems effectiveness. The authors make the point that the four keys are flexibility (resiliency), keeping the user foremost in mind, ease of use, and well-developed user support.

Brooks, Frederick P., Jr. "No Silver Bullet: Essence and Accidents of Software Engineering." *Computer*. April 1987, 10–18. Notwithstanding the occasional lapses into academic terminology, this is an article to be "chewed and digested." It strikes at the essence of software as perhaps no other author has ever done. Brooks, incidentally, was the project manager at IBM for the 360-system series of mainframe computers.

Bower, Joseph L. "Managing for Efficiency, Managing for Equity." *Harvard Business Review*. July-August 1983, 83–90. This was the lead article in a self-proclaimed major issue of *Harvard Business Review*. It points out the major and often irreconcilable differences between the political nature of general management and the technical nature of systematic type work. Although it does not focus on information systems, the points it makes are fully applicable.

"Can We Trust Our Software?" *Newsweek*. January 29, 1990, 70–73. This short article summarizes major problems in software development that textbooks fail to describe.

Cash, James I., F. Warren McFarlan, James L. McKenney, and Michael R. Vitale. *Corporate Information Systems Management: Text and Cases*. Second Edition. Homewood, Illinois: Irwin, 1988. This is the Harvard Graduate School of Business Administration text. Although ponderous in spots, it is comprehensive and nontechnical. The chapter on risk is especially insightful.

Crescenzi, Adam D. "The Dark Side of Strategic IS Implementation." *Information Strategy*, Fall 1988, 14–20. Probably the single most convincing reference with respect to the purpose of this book. The author proves almost beyond doubt that management and not technology is the culprit for most systems failures.

Denbigh, Kenneth George and J.S. Denbigh. *Entropy in Relation to Incomplete Knowledge*. Cambridge, England: Cambridge University Press, 1985. This book is at the core of the interior lines argument.

Dreyfus, Herbert L. and Stuart E. Dreyfus. *Mind over Matter: The Power of Human Intuition and Expertise in the Era of the Computer*. New York: Free Press, 1986. The authors are well-known critics of information systems, and therefore present a different picture. This book was the number one best seller, among computer books, in academic libraries in 1988.

Foehr, Theresa. *The Soft Side of Software: A Management Approach to Computer Documentation*. New York: Wiley-Interscience, 1986. It is hard to find an exiting book on documenting software, and this one doesn't end the search. But it is rich in checklists that can facilitate the task of ensuring that documentation improves.

Gottfried, Ira S. "IS Management Problems: Cause and Effect." *Journal of Information Systems Management*, Fall 1988, 76–80. A survey of how CEOs and CIOs view each other, at least as far as can be printed.

Hertz, David B. *The Expert Executive: Using AI and Expert Systems for Financial Management, Marketing, Production and Strategy*. New York: John Wiley

& Sons, Inc., 1988. An excellent general introduction to the subject, with an emphasis on the simpler but equally effective executive support systems.

"How to Make a Strategic Move with Information Systems." *Information-WEEK*. May 26, 1986, 30 – 32. An insightful comprehensive but brief article on how to obtain the best strategic mileage from information systems.

Izzo, Joseph E. "The Embattled IS Fortress: Dispersing Computer Power." *Information Strategy*. Spring 1988, 10 – 14. One of the best articles ever written on the general vs. technical management conflict, as it applies to the difficult question of data distribution and processing.

Jackson, Ivan F. *Corporate Information Management*. Englewood Cliffs, N.J.: Prentice-Hall, Inc., 1986. The whole nine yards in one book.

Johnson, Deborah G. *Computer Ethics*. Englewood Cliffs, N.J.: Prentice-Hall, Inc., 1985. One of the few books that addresses the ethical issues associated with computer systems, aside from the dozen or so that examine or question the implications of artificial intelligence and expert systems.

Kroenke, David. *Management Information Systems*. Watsonville, Calif.: Mitchell-McGraw Hill, 1989. Kroenke is the author of one of the all-time best sellers (*Business Computer Systems*). This new book addresses a higher level of thinking that might interest senior executives.

Leonard-Barton, Dorothy and John J. Sviokla. "Putting Expert Systems to Work." *Harvard Business Review*, March-April 1988, 91 – 98. This article makes the point that the number of parameters operating in an expert system is the limiting factor. The more parameters, the less likely it will be useful, barring a major programming investment.

Massey, David. "Liability for Failed Software." *Journal of Information Systems Management*. Fall 1988, 47 – 52. Perhaps the most clear-headed article ever written on the subject.

Nolan, Richard L. "Managing the Crises in Data Processing." *Harvard Business Review*. March-April 1979, 115 – 126. Although now dated, it still presents a good look at the model (of which the author was one of the originators) of the stages of development in information systems departments. See also Nolan's book *Managing the Data Resource Function*, 2nd Edition, St. Paul, Minn.: West Publishing Company, 1982.

Perrolle, Judith A. "Intellectual Assembly Lines: the Rationalization of Managerial, Professional, and Technical Work." *Computer Social Sciences*. July-September 1986, 111 – 121. This is a fairly objective analysis of the implications using expert system technology to various fields, especially in law and medicine.

Porter, Michael E. and Victor E. Millar. "How Information Gives You Competitive Advantage." *Harvard Business Review*. July-August 1985, 151 – 160. A good picture of the interplay between business, management, and information systems.

Risch, Tore, et al. "A Functional Approach to Integrating Databases and Expert Systems." *Communciations*. December 1988, 1424 – 1437. An important article on the equally important subject of improving the interior lines between users and databases.

Rockart, J.F. and D.W. De Long. *Executive Support Systems: The Emergence of Top Management Computer Use*. Homewood, Ill.: Dow-Jones Irwin, 1988. The book lives up to its title.

Tanenbaum, Andrew S. *Computer Networks*. 2nd Edition. Englewood Cliffs, N.J.: Prentice-Hall, Inc., 1988. A technical book on a technical subject, yet it shows the many options that are available and the advantages and disadvantages of each.

*The DPMA Model Curriculum for Undergraduate Computer Information Systems*, 2nd Edition. Park Ridge, Ill.: Data Processing Management Association, 1986. This 31-page booklet is a gold mine of an index into the whole of information systems.

Toigo, Jon W. *Disaster Recovery Planning: Managing Risk and Catastrophe in Information Systems*. Englewood Cliffs, N.J.: Prentice-Hall, Inc., 1988. A comprehensive approach to a topic that is gaining in importance.

Umbaugh, Robert E., editor. *Handbook of MIS Management*, Second Edition. New York: Auerbach Publishers, 1988. This is about as comprehensive as one handbook can get, although it is more technically oriented than most general managers would care for.

Wolpert, Samuel. *Economics of Information*. New York: Van Nostrand Reinhold, 1988. With a deceptively simple title, this book addresses return on investment in all its ramifications.

Zaleznik, Abraham. "Managers and Leaders: Are They Different?" *Harvard Business Review*. May-June 1977, 67 – 78. A classic article that answers the question in the title. Although a generalized picture, it applies to the differences between management of MIS departments and leadership of projects.

# Index

# C



# D

# E



# F

# T



# U



# V



# W



# Y



# Z